P9-EET-802

AMERICA'S RESPONSE TO CHINA

AMERICA'S RESPONSE TO CHINA

A History of Sino-American Relations

FIFTH EDITION

Warren I. Cohen

Columbia University Press   New York

Columbia University Press

Publishers Since 1893

New York   Chichester, West Sussex

First Edition Copyright © 1971 John Wiley and Sons, Inc.
Second Edition Copyright © 1980 John Wiley and Sons, Inc.
Third Edition Copyright © 1990 Columbia University Press
Fourth Edition Copyright © 2000 Columbia University Press
Fifth Edition Copyright © 2010 Columbia University Press

All rights reserved

Library of Congress Cataloging-in-Publication Data

Cohen, Warren I.
    America's response to China : a history of
Sino-American relations / Warren I.
Cohen. — 5th Ed.
        p. cm.
    Includes bibliographical references and index.
    ISBN 978-0-231-15076-7 (cloth : acid-free paper) —
ISBN 978-0-231-15077-4 (pbk. : acid-free paper) —
ISBN 978-0-231-52172-7 (ebook)
    1. United States—Foreign relations—China.
2. China—Foreign relations—United States.
I. Title.
    E183.8.C5C62   2010
    327.73051—dc22   2009030760

Columbia University Press books are printed on
permanent and durable acid-free paper.
Printed in the United States of America
c 10 9 8 7 6 5 4 3 2 1
p 10 9 8 7 6 5 4 3 2 1

For Nancy forever
(and for the Sixth Edition)

Contents

Preface to the Fifth Edition   ix
Preface to the Fourth Edition   xi
Preface to the Third Edition   xiii
Preface to the Second Edition   xv
Preface to the First Edition   xvii
Acknowledgments to the Fifth Edition   xix
Romanization Table   xxi

Prologue: The Barbarians and the Tribute System   1

1. The Development of the Treaty System   8

2. The United States as a Power in East Asia   29

3. In the Light of the Rising Sun   60

4. The Response to Chinese Nationalism   89

5. China as an Abstraction—The Conflict with Japan   115

6. Communism in China   148

7. The Great Aberration   195

8. Rapprochement—At Last   215

9. In the Shadow of Tiananmen   232

10. America in the Age of Chinese Power   263

Notes *293*
Bibliographical Essay *299*
Index *311*

Preface to the Fifth Edition

I wrote the first edition of *America's Response to China* on the eve of Henry Kissinger's pathbreaking 1971 flight to Beijing—at a time when I was indifferent to the betrayal of the repressive Taiwan regime that I had lived under from 1964 to 1966. I wrote the second edition in 1979 after attending Deng Xiaoping's performance at the National Art Gallery in Washington, amid the euphoria that accompanied the end of Mao's brutal rein and the promise of Deng's reforms. It was soon translated into Chinese by a member of the Fudan University faculty. In 1989 the Tiananmen massacre was perpetrated while I was in Moscow en route to Beijing. The shadow of that tragedy hung heavily over me as I prepared the third edition later that year. Quite rightly, the Chinese authorities ceased to perceive me as a friend of the People's Republic. No one on the mainland dared translate that edition. When the Chinese translated other books of mine, they deleted all references to the events of June 1989—contrary to prior agreement.

In 1999, as Bill Clinton and Jiang Zemin exchanged visits and human rights issues were subordinated to trade ("It's the economy, stupid"), I wrote the fourth edition. By then the release of a wealth of Chinese documents— carefully selected by the regime, of course—proved useful to me and to the authors of the many monographs upon which I relied.

It is now 2009, and the rise of Chinese power over the last decade has been phenomenal. However disastrous the foreign policies of the George W. Bush administration may have been overall, Bush and his aides are generally credited with sensible management of the relationship with China. He stumbled early but recovered quickly. In this fifth edition, the story of China's rise and the American response to it is the principal focus of the new material. My new chapter 10 is based in part on recently published Chinese documents and conversations with several of the American participants in the policy process. Living in the Washington area, I have been privileged to know many of these men and women—and those whom I don't know are acquainted with my wife, Nancy Bernkopf Tucker, who tries, with occasional success, to rein in my fantasies.

Preface to the Fourth Edition

In the closing months of the twentieth century, Chinese-American relations are dangerously close to degenerating into a new cold war. Images of the Tiananmen massacres of 1989 sear the memories of older Americans and their leaders are troubled by evidence of Chinese spying and illegal campaign contributions in the United States. Across the Pacific, young Chinese, their nationalism inflamed by the accidental bombing of the Chinese Embassy in Belgrade by American-led NATO forces, attack the American Embassy in Beijing and set fire to the home of the American consul-general in Chengdu. A decade that began with the United States breaking off high-level contacts to punish China for the brutal suppression of pro-democracy demonstrations ends with the Chinese canceling military and political dialogues to punish the United States for killing Chinese in Belgrade. I can only pray that the next edition of *America's Response to China* does not tell a sad tale of how two nations with no vital interests in conflict stumbled into war.

In this edition I have replaced the epilogue I wrote in the summer of 1989 after having been devastated by the events of June 3 and 4, after I saw the hopes and dreams of my Chinese friends crushed when the People's Liberation Army turned its weapons on the Chinese people. A new chapter 9 carries the story from 1989 to 1999, covering the twists and turns of the Bush and Clinton administrations as they groped for an adequate response to China after the collapse of the Soviet empire. None of the Americans responsible for policy toward China in those years left a record to which we can turn with pride, but it's a record that must not be forgotten. I have also revised parts of chapter 8 to reflect new information available about events in the 1970s and 1980s.

I am grateful to my friends, the *Los Angeles Times* columnist Jim Mann and Ambassador Jim Lilley for reading and commenting on chapter 9—much of which was influenced by Mann's own book, *About Face.* I am especially grateful to my wife, Nancy Bernkopf Tucker, for all she has taught me about Chinese-American relations, particularly as affected by the Taiwan issue. She also read and commented on chapter 9. Harry Harding never got around to reading the new material, but he, too, has taught me a great deal in recent years through his writings, his public lectures, and his critiques of my public lectures. If my judgments strike the reader as misguided, these are the people to hold responsible.

Preface to the Third Edition

Nearly ten years have passed since I prepared the second edition of *America's Response to China*. In that period I have traveled to the mainland nine times and to Taiwan once more. I have worked with Chinese, as well as with British, Japanese, Soviet, and other American scholars in conferences in Beijing, Bellagio (Italy), Chicago, Honolulu, Taipei, and Washington. I have interviewed Chinese leaders whom I never dreamt of meeting and talked with Chinese scholars who had privileged access to documentation on the innermost workings of the Chinese policy process. On the American side, a wealth of new documentation has become available on the Eisenhower years, providing new insights into the thoughts and policies of the president and his secretary of state. I was fortunate to marry the leading student of post–World War II Chinese-American relations and to be granted access to her notes and unpublished papers. My continuing education is reflected in changes in the text.

Obviously more important than my experiences is the fact that the Chinese-American relationship, so painfully wrought by the Nixon, Ford, and Carter administrations, survived eight years of Ronald Reagan. There could be no greater testimony to the importance and durability of that relationship. Details of the twists and turns of the Reagan era will be found in chapter 8 (originally the epilogue).

In addition, I have revised portions of my discussions of earlier issues to reflect my own work on East Asian art and American culture, some superb work on missionary activity in China by Jessie Lutz and others, and the strong currents of social and cultural history which have swirled through the profession in recent years. I am grateful to Kate Wittenberg and the Columbia University Press for allowing me to make these costly changes.

Finally, I have resolved the romanization issue on an expedient rather than intellectually satisfying basis. The first and second editions of the book were prepared when the Wade-Giles system prevailed. Most of us now use pinyin. I have chosen to leave the first seven chapters in Wade-Giles and to introduce pinyin in chapter 8, where most of the characters, like Deng Xiaoping, are easily recognizable to Western readers.

Preface to the Second Edition

I was delighted, of course, by the generous praise the first edition of this book received from reviewers, senators, government officials, teachers, and students. Even my children eventually had kind words for it. Nonetheless, in the very summer that it appeared, in 1971, the need for revision was evident. Henry Kissinger went to Peking, and China and the United States were ready for a new, less hostile relationship. On the eve of Richard Nixon's historic trip to China, I was invited to explain the past to members of the Senate Foreign Relations Committee assembled by Senator J. William Fulbright. My publisher, however, was unimpressed: my book ended in 1970—the breakthrough had come in 1971. I promised to prepare a revised version as soon as diplomatic relations were established. Hoping for a year's reprieve, I found that Watergate, the Gang of Four, and Ronald Reagan had won me seven years—in which I happily wrote two other books.

On January 30, 1979, as my wife and I arrived in Washington for a reception for Teng Hsiao-p'ing, we saw the flags of the People's Republic of China and the United States flying side by side at the White House. I knew my time was up. Recognition was at hand. America's new response to China required a new edition of *America's Response to China*. Here it is.

I have rewritten the last part of chapter 6 in light of extensive new documentation available for the Truman era. The original epilogue has been rewritten and expanded as chapter 7. Much of this material derives from research for my book on Dean Rusk. Events since 1971 are covered in the new epilogue.

I am grateful to James Reardon-Anderson, James Fetzer, John L. Gaddis, Steven Goldstein, Waldo Heinrichs, Michael H. Hunt, Akira Iriye, Walter La Feber, Steven I. Levine, Ernest R. May, Robert Messer, Michel Oksenberg, Thomas G. Paterson, Martin J. Sherwin, Ronald Steel, Nancy Bernkopf Tucker, and Allen S. Whiting for the many insights they have provided through their work and the stimulating conferences and informal discussions in which we have participated over the last decade. The debt we all owe Dorothy Borg is well known. None of these friends has seen the revised edition—though I hold them collectively responsible for its contents.

Preface to the First Edition

Some years ago John K. Fairbank wrote a book entitled *The United States and China*, with which I do not presume to compete. That book remains the best one-volume introduction to China. I have focused my attention on the American response to China, particularly the response of American statesmen who sought to devise an East Asian policy consistent with the ideals and interests of their people. As I wrote, I became increasingly aware of the need to explain American policy toward China in a broad international setting. I have not accomplished this to my satisfaction, partly because of ignorance and partly because I wanted to minimize the overlap with other volumes in this series. However, I have made a continuous effort to remind the reader of the presence of other players and of the larger world arena in which the action I describe occurred.

I have discussed much of what I have written here in a number of articles published earlier. Where the present text conflicts with points I have argued elsewhere, this is my most recent judgment. Where the language seems familiar, this is because I have not attempted to say things differently when I could not be sure of saying them better.

Translations from Chinese sources are my own unless otherwise indicated. Citations have been limited to direct quotations. I would enjoy discussing sources for other statements with interested students.

Acknowledgments to the Fifth Edition

Before the first edition of this book was published, I imposed on several friends and asked them to read it. Tadashi Aruga, Michael Gasster, the late Dorothy Borg, Stull Holt, and James C. Thomson Jr. responded with countless suggestions—which I valued even when I did not follow them. Robert A. Divine read it in his capacity as series editor and Janice Prichard Cohen read it in an earlier incarnation as my wife. My readers saved me from considerable embarrassment and, if I were not so vain about my writing, they might have been able to help more.

Like every historian working in the field of American–East Asian relations, I was indebted to Dorothy Borg and John K. Fairbank for many of my ideas. In the years that followed, countless friends contributed further to my education and to the revisions and additions that appeared in subsequent editions. I am especially grateful to James Reardon-Anderson, Paul A. Cohen (who *pretends* to be my elder and wiser brother), Waldo Heinrichs, Michael H. Hunt, Akira Iriye, Walter LaFeber, Nancy Bernkopf Tucker (long before she was foolish enough to marry me), Allen S. Whiting, and the late Ernest R. May and Michel Oksenberg for the many insights they provided through their work and the stimulating conferences and informal discussions in which we have participated over the years. More recently, I have depended on Jim Mann and Harry Harding to supplement the teachings of Nancy Bernkopf Tucker, who has promised to help me with the next edition. I was also fortunate to have assistance from many Chinese scholars—Wang Xi, Zi Zhongyun, and the late Li Shenzhi and Luo Rongqu, who may be named safely—and others, whom I dare not put at risk. Similarly, I had valuable conversations with many Chinese officials, of whom I assume Huang Hua and Xue Mouhong are safe from retribution.

Romanization Table

The romanization of Chinese characters—long dominated by the Wade-Giles system—used in the first four editions of this book and still used on Taiwan has been displaced largely by pinyin, a system devised in the People's Republic of China. To minimize confusion, I provide below a list of names mentioned in order of appearance in the text in both systems. Names followed by an asterisk are neither Wade-Giles nor pinyin but are common usage.

WADE-GILES	PINYIN
Ch'i-ying	Qiying
Ch'ing	Qing
Tao-guang	Daoguang
Hsuan-tsüng	Xuanzong
Hsien-feng	Xianfeng
Wen-tsung	Wenzong
Hung Hsiu-ch'üan	Hong Xiuquan
Yeh Ming-ch'en	Ye Mingchen
Li Hung-chang	Li Hongzhang

Prince Kung	Prince Gong
Tseng Kuo-fan	Zeng Guofan
Tz'u-hsi	Cixi
Chang Chih-tung	Zhang Zhidong
K'ang Yu-wei	Kang Youwei
Wu T'ing-fang	Wu Tingfang
Yüan Shih-k'ai	Yuan Shikai
T'ang Shao-i	Tang Shaoyi
Hsi-liang	Xiliang
Prince Ch'un	Prince Chun
Sun Yat-sen*	Sun Zhongshan
Sung Chiao-jen	Song Jiaoren
Ma Soo	Ma Su
Chang Tso-lin	Zhang Zuolin
Wu P'ei-fu	Wu Peifu
Sun Ch'uan-fang	Sun Chuanfang
Hu Han-min	Hu Hanmin
Wang Ching-wei	Wang Jingwei
Chiang Kai-shek*	Jiang Jieshi
T. V. Soong*	T. V. Song
Mao Tse-tung	Mao Zedong
Chu Teh	Zhu De
H. H. K'ung	H. H. Kong
Chang Hsueh-liang	Zhang Xueliang
Tai Li	Dai Li
Chou En-lai	Zhou Enlai
Huang Hua	Huang Hua
Ch'en I	Chen Yi
Lin Piao	Lin Biao
Chiang Ch'ing	Jiang Qing
Teng Hsiao-p'ing	Deng Xiaoping
Chiang Ching-kuo	Jiang Jingguo
Hua Kuo-feng	Hua Guofeng
Chao Tse-yang	Zhao Ziyang
Hu Yao-bang	Hu Yaobang
Li P'eng	Li Peng
Fang Li-chih	Fang Lizhi
Chiang Tse-min	Jiang Zemin
Ch'ien Ch'i-ch'en	Qian Qichen

Wei Ching-sheng	Wei Jingsheng
Lee Teng-hui	Li Denghui
Wang Tan	Wang Dan
Chu Jung-chi	Zhu Rongji
Hu Chin-t'ao	Hu Jintao
Wen Chia-pao	Wen Jiabao

AMERICA'S RESPONSE TO CHINA

Prologue

The Barbarians and the Tribute System

Boarding the hydrofoil at Hong Kong in 1965, I crossed the mouth of the Pearl River, which leads to Canton and, an hour and a quarter later, disembarked at Macao where the hills of mainland China (as stylized in reality as they appear in traditional Chinese landscapes) press toward you. Here, despite the imposing Basilica of Sao Paulo and an occasional Portuguese policeman, the awareness of China looming around me was inescapable. The fact that my presence on that dot of land was possible only at the pleasure of the People's Republic intruded on my consciousness far more than it had in Hong Kong, even in the New Territories.

There in Macao, an important source of exchange for the government at Peking, there where red flags and pictures of Mao abounded, I took a leisurely ride to the eastern side of the peninsula, to the Temple of Kun Yam, the Cantonese name for the Buddhist goddess of mercy. A beggar demanding "cumshaw" raced along the carved gate. Within, there was nothing to distinguish the temple from myriads of others. Stepping out into the courtyard, I was afforded one of the least impressive views available in the colony: rows of nondescript, apparently middle-class housing stretching to the horizon. But before me, in the courtyard, stood a stone table, near a small pavilion, bereft of the customary orange peelings—and a nearby plaque declared that at this table, on July 3, 1844, Ch'i-ying, imperial commissioner, and Caleb Cushing, commissioner for the American president, signed the first treaty between China and the United States.

In 1844, in the wake of China's defeat by Great Britain in the "Opium War," the United States obtained a treaty of "peace, amity and commerce" from China. By the very act of negotiating, China conceded to the United States a degree of stature that would have been inconceivable to the Manchu court five years earlier. For the first time in sixty years of contact between Chinese and Americans, a representative of the government of China allowed a representative of the government of the United States to treat with him as an equal—without, of course, surrendering his conviction of absolute Chinese superiority over the American barbarians.

Before they had direct contact, before American independence, the inhabitants of Britain's North American colonies had been well aware of China and its products. The desire for chinoiserie, a romanticized European imitation of Chinese art, eventually replicated by the Chinese, swept Europe in the mid-eighteenth century. The colonists, too, bought enormous quantities of "Chinese Chippendale" furniture, Chinese wallpapers, silks, and porcelains. There was even an occasional touch of Chinese influence on colonial architecture. Less expensive crafts, especially export chinaware, had spread among the less affluent sectors of American society. Shards from cups, dishes, and pots have been excavated from eighteenth-century American homes, taverns, and forts, from Philadelphia to the Mackinac Straits of Michigan. And above all there was tea, the drink of choice for most colonists—when stronger stuff was not available. It was Chinese tea, from Amoy, that the patriots had dumped in Boston harbor that famous night in December 1773.

The Americans wasted little time in reaching China after winning their independence from Great Britain. Almost as soon as word of the peace settlement concluded at Paris reached the victors, the *Empress of China* was outfitted and dispatched to partake of the China trade. No longer blocked from participation in this trade by the British East Indian Company's monopoly within the empire, commercial interests on the eastern seaboard anticipated great profits and conjured up a vast vision of fortunes to be made through trade with Cathay. Here indeed was a promise of compensation for the once profitable but now forbidden trade with the British West Indies. For the next fifty years, American interests in China were wholly commercial.

In these first years of American involvement in China, the government of the United States played a minimal role, consistent with the

fundamental American policy of seeking to extend trade with as few political complications as possible. The merchants were very much on their
own, although they were encouraged by favorable tariff policies and were
allowed to appoint one of their number as consul—without pay. As private businessmen in quest of wealth, they made their own way to the Orient, took their risks, and operated within whatever latitude the Chinese
authorities permitted them. Between the governments of China and of
the United States there was no contact. There were no treaties, no diplomatic missions, no diplomatic relations.

The conditions imposed by the Chinese on the Western merchants
were less than pleasant. Probably the most ethnocentric people in the
world, the Chinese considered their realm the center of the universe, the
Middle Kingdom, and regarded all cultural differences as signs of inferi-
ority. All who were not Chinese were, obviously, barbarians. Europeans
and Americans were distinguished from Inner Asian tribesmen only by
the fact that they approached from the east and by sea rather than from
the northern steppes. The fact that barbarians should come to China in
quest of the benefits of civilization did not surprise the Chinese, who
were prepared to be generous—provided that the outsiders behaved with
appropriate submissiveness.

Since ancient times, relations with the barbarians had been regulated
under the tribute system. Theoretically, all peoples in contact with China
were tributaries. The procedures for this form of contact had become
highly ritualized: entertainment of the tribute mission, audience with
the emperor, performance of the kowtow by the visiting envoys, and the
bestowal of gifts by the emperor. Most of all, the kowtow bothered Westerners. As performed in court, it involved a series of kneelings and pros-
trations, "head-bangings," performed at commands, leaving little doubt
as to who was paying homage to whom.

By the time the Americans arrived on the scene, the tribute system
had long been a vehicle for trade and the Manchus had worked out a
variation for dealing with the barbarians who came by sea. Satisfied with
the Western merchants' acceptance of the inferior role necessitated by
tributary status, the Chinese government did not require the tribute mission to the capital. Whereas the court had traditionally sought the prestige derived from the ritual, by the eighteenth century both Peking and
the local officials found sufficient advantage in the revenue derived from
the trade. Nonetheless, the barbarians could certainly not be allowed free
rein within the empire. They were contemptible not only as foreigners

but also as businessmen—a class of low standing in the Confucian hierarchy, however well its members actually lived.

If the barbarian traders persisted in coming to peddle their wares, to purchase some of the products of the superior Chinese civilization, they had to be restricted to one small area in Canton. Here the possibility of contamination was limited, the disease quarantined, the Chinese people protected. Here Chinese officials would not be bothered by the barbarians but could leave the management of the foreign merchant in the hands of the Chinese merchant.

Hemmed in by restrictions, left without recourse to settle disputes, unprotected by his government, the American businessman, like his European colleagues, remained in China. Obviously, the profits were worth the bother. And at times the bother was considerable, as in the notorious Terranova case of 1821, in which a seaman on an American ship was seized and executed by Chinese authorities in retaliation for a death for which he may have had no responsibility whatever. When Chinese officials demanded that Terranova be turned over to them in connection with the death of a woman allegedly struck by debris discarded from the American vessel, the merchants at first refused. Advised that refusal would mean exclusion of Americans from trade with China, the American business community decided to allow Terranova to be seized after a show of protest. Terranova was tried secretly, with no American present, and sentenced to death by strangulation. After the sentence was carried out, the American government did not protest and the Americans in Canton were commended by the local viceroy for their properly submissive behavior. Such was the state of Sino-American relations under the tribute system, during the years when the Chinese dictated the terms of contact.

The Canton variation of the tribute system had been established at the peak of the Manchu (or Ch'ing) dynasty's strength and prior to the modernization of Europe. The United States entered into the system within a year after the Americans had won their independence, at a time when the United States could hardly have been weaker. In other words, the Canton system had developed at a time when Chinese power relative to the maritime nations of the West was great enough for the Chinese to control the nature of Sino-Western relations. So long as the Chinese retained this position of relative strength, they treated Westerners arbitrarily and with contempt. That the West responded in kind when the power balance shifted was regrettable, but not difficult to understand.

The initial American attempt to place relations with China on a treaty basis came in the 1830s, during the administration of Andrew Jackson. The Jacksonians, like the Washingtonians and Jeffersonians before them, sought the expansion of American trade, and the president sent Edmund Roberts on a mission to find new commercial opportunities in the Orient. He sailed for Canton, not for the specific purpose of alleviating the abuses of the tribute system but rather as part of his general effort to accumulate treaties. Roberts reached Canton in November 1832 but failed to establish communications with the local Chinese authorities, except to receive an order to set sail immediately. His departure apparently relieved the anxieties that his arrival had stimulated within the American community. Some American merchants feared that the attempt to obtain a commercial treaty would antagonize the Chinese, seem less than properly submissive, ultimately hurting existing trade rather than expanding it.

In the 1830s, Canton was also visited by the first American missionaries—courageous men who braved a Chinese promise of death by strangulation to anyone caught propagating Christianity. The missionary effort was at first small, but nonetheless it gave a new and increasingly important dimension to the interests of the United States in China. To the existing commercial involvement was added a religious involvement, a basically humanitarian desire to find a place for the Chinese in the Kingdom of God.

But while the missionaries posed as merchants to avoid the distasteful end that the Chinese offered them, the genuine American businessman faced the problem of finding some article to sell. Furs, sandalwood, and even ginseng (which aging Chinese gentlemen sought in their never-ending search for a means to restore fading potency) had but limited markets, and all together failed to match the value of the items that the West in general sought to purchase. Like the Englishman, the American merchant was increasingly forced to fall back on the sale of opium—though some Americans, to be sure, would neither touch nor condone the drug traffic.

As the decade of the 1830s neared its end, the opium trade became a critical problem for the Chinese government. Obviously, some Chinese officials were deeply concerned about the moral and physical effects of drug addiction. In addition, the very reason for the opium traffic—the fact that the drug provided the West with a marketable commodity the sales of which exceeded the value of Western imports from China—created a financial problem for the Chinese government. In short, commerce with the West, which had traditionally left China with a favorable balance of payments, was now draining China of its hard currency.

The Chinese had no alternative but to put an end to the importation of opium. The English merchants who were largely responsible for the opium trade seemed convinced that there was no alternative to the continuation of this profitable enterprise, and the lines of conflict were drawn. Lacking diplomatic relations with the Chinese government and unable to persuade Chinese officials to receive a diplomatic mission, the traders had no channel through which to arrange a peaceful settlement of the dispute. With the Chinese determined to use force if necessary to put an end to a trade proscribed since 1800, the English merchants petitioned successfully for military support from their government. Thus the two countries, China and Great Britain, were drawn into conflict, into the Opium War.

Given the perspective time grants to the historian, it is readily apparent that conflict between China and the West was inevitable. It is equally apparent that opium provided the occasion rather than the cause of that conflict. So long as the Chinese remained too arrogant to study these barbarians carefully, too arrogant to realize that England in particular had become powerful enough to make good the demand for diplomatic equality—for that long the point of Sino-Western contact could be but a powder keg awaiting a spark. Industrialization and the growth of nationalism had made the West more powerful and more assertive at a time when the Chinese had passed the peak of their power. The phenomenon of dynastic decline, so much a part of China's historical record, had not bypassed the Manchus.

The locus of power had shifted, but China's mandarins had not perceived this. The "foreign devils," the "big noses"—those who the Chinese thought of as savages and treated hardly better—were no longer willing to respond to the arbitrary exercise of authority obediently or submissively. Had the Chinese been able to conceive of diplomatic equality among nations, they might have been spared the Opium War and the century of humiliation that followed.

By the time the war broke out in 1839, the Chinese "barbarian experts," specialists on the West, had at least solved the problem of telling Westerners apart. Though they all looked alike, the Chinese had learned that Americans were not Englishmen and that in fact there existed a heritage of ill will between the United States and Great Britain. Having learned a little about the American Revolution and the War of 1812, Chinese officials concluded that their traditional policy of playing barbarians off against each other (*i-i-chih-i*) might well work here—and called upon loyal and obedient Americans to bring in English heads. Unhappily for the Chinese, the American community in Canton remained out of the action, preferring to take over the local trade, including opium, while the British were otherwise occupied.

The Treaty of Nanking, which restored peace after the British victory, signaled a new phase in the history of China: the end of the tribute system and the beginning of the treaty system. Unfortunately, the new system, though based in theory on the Western concept of diplomatic equality, proved as unequal as the old. For the next hundred years, the barbarian dictated the terms of Sino-Western contact. China's pretensions to universal hegemony vanished in an age in which the Chinese were widely scorned—a once-proud empire reduced to semicolonial status.

1   The Development of the Treaty System

In the tribute system, Chinese disdain for "foreign devils" was readily apparent. Unquestionably, the Chinese in their xenophobia, in their contemptuous treatment of strangers who came to their land, were reprehensible. In this category of evils, there is perhaps only one worse: it occurs when the stranger comes and drives the native up against the wall. Ultimately, this was the tendency of the new order that the West imposed on the Chinese in the years that followed the Opium War. The Americans did not initiate this system, though they offered no alternatives and were quick to demand the privileged status that became possible within the "treaty ports." The special contribution of the Americans came toward the close of the nineteenth century when the *lumpenproletariat* in the United States singled out the Chinese for special favor.

But in the beginning, the British sought to be treated as equals and to place relations between China and Great Britain on a rational, ordered basis—such as was understood in the Western world. In the Treaty of Nanking, the victor's exactions were onerous, but none too severe. Chinese policy had forced the case to be tried on the battlefield and China, having lost the case, paid the costs. Having won, the British indulged themselves in a few desiderata, extending trade to five other ports, as well as regularizing procedures at Canton. The necessity of using force, buttressed by imperial experience in India, led the British to demand the cession of Hong Kong—a base for military as well as entrepreneurial activities in East Asia. For the future, British power would be present to remind the mandarins that Great Britain lacked neither the will nor the ability to insist on equal treatment.

In 1843, the British and Chinese negotiated a supplementary treaty that altered the Canton system and assured the British of most-favored-nation treatment in the future. Whereas duties had heretofore been imposed on Western exports in an arbitrary and capricious fashion, the Chinese tariff was now embodied in a treaty, to be modified only by the mutual consent of the contracting parties. Also with an eye to justice for foreigners, the concept of extraterritoriality was introduced, allowing Westerners accused of crimes to be tried by their own consular officials, according to the legal concepts of the Judaeo-Christian, Graeco-Roman heritage. None of this troubled the Chinese—other than the obvious indignity of having to deal with presumptuous barbarians on a level of equality. China was primarily a cultural rather than a national entity. As such, Chinese officials concerned themselves more with very real problems of ceremony and ritual, leaving abstract conceptions of sovereignty to the West. The fact that consular jurisdiction infringed on Chinese sovereignty and was not a practice incorporated in relations among equals in the West did not bother the mandarins in mid-century. On the contrary, extraterritoriality served them well; it fitted with the traditional attempt to segregate alien elements. That England, with all its rhetoric about the need for equality, was demanding of China a privilege it would never grant to China—or to any other power—would not have pained the Chinese, who never intended to send diplomatic missions abroad and cared little for the fate of migrant Chinese who had forsaken the land of their ancestors.

Similarly, the treaty tariff, harmless enough on the surface, had striking deficiencies of which the Chinese were unaware. First, unlike other commercial agreements in which a nation bound its tariffs, in this treaty, the other party offered no comparable concessions. But, of course, the Chinese assumed that the West needed China's tea and rhubarb and could not conceive of needing any privileges that the English might grant. Having come late to the study of the West, they were blind to the industrialization that served as fount to the power they had been forced to respect—and were ignorant of the protective tariffs that had cradled fragile industries.

Additionally, there was the problem of the most-favored-nation clause that the English and all other treaty seekers demanded. On all other counts the English might have been guilty of exceeding their demands for equal treatment, but this clause was not uncommon in treaties of commerce between equals. Without such provision, commercial treaties might soon become worthless. But in this instance, the catch was found again in the fact that England was offering no concessions to China. The flow of concessions initially—and so long as China remained weak—was one way. Each nation entered into treaty relations with China, received concessions peculiar to its needs, and through the most-favored-nation clause also received whatever concessions any other nation might exact from the Chinese. Because China was weaker relative to each of the nations with whom she dealt, the flow of concessions could not be reversed. Similarly, the fact that each of the powers had the most-favored-nation clause gave each a vested interest in the success of the demands that every other might make. For the United States in particular, the most-favored-nation clause became a means of fulfilling American desires while allowing the British to bear most of the responsibility and onus for having created the treaty system.

As early as May 1839, American merchants in Canton had opted to play by petitioning Congress for a commissioner to negotiate a commercial treaty—and for warships to keep the natives friendly. After receiving advice from others familiar with conditions in China, Congress took no action, but Commodore Lawrence Kearny and the East India Squadron were ordered to the vicinity of Canton. Finding the American merchants in no danger, Kearny refrained from interfering in the Anglo-Chinese war. He fully appreciated, however, the benefits the British would derive from the peace treaty and subsequent commercial arrangements. Dutifully, he pressed the local Chinese officials to extend comparable privileges to his countrymen—and was assured that they would not be "left with a dry stick" (that is, they would not be left empty-handed).

All during the war, Chinese officials, trying to find some way in which the United States could be used to their advantage, sought a policy that would separate Americans from the "obstinate English barbarians." One thoughtful expert noted how well behaved the Americans were in contrast to Englishmen and suggested abolishing duties on American goods and giving the trade of the English to the Americans. "Then," he postulated, "the American barbarians are sure to be grateful for this Heavenly Favor and will energetically oppose the English barbarians."[1] The proposal was never carried out, though the idea of using the United States to fight China's battles never disappeared entirely. Kearny's request, however, suited this general approach to the management of barbarian affairs. I-li-pu and Ch'i-ying, the principal Manchu military and diplomatic figures on the scene, both recommended most-favored-nation treatment for the Americans. Otherwise there would be constant complaints and complications, possible embarrassments to the throne. Then, too, there was always the possibility that the English would welcome the Americans and others from the West into the new trade. Not only would it then be difficult for China to prevent such practices, but the nations sharing the privileges would be grateful to England and resentful of China. Surely it would be better for the privilege to appear to come gratuitously from the emperor. To the emperor this approach made perfect sense: men from afar had traditionally been viewed with equal compassion. If these Western countries were so serious about trade, then obviously "the art of controlling and curbing them" required absolute fairness. And so, in November 1843, the Tao-guang emperor, Hsüan-tsung, declared: "Now that the English barbarians have been allowed to trade, whatever other countries there are, the United States and others, should naturally be permitted to trade without discrimination, in order to show Our tranquilizing purpose."[2] Here, of course, was the origin of the Open Door, or equal opportunity for all traders: a Chinese policy designed to elicit gratitude from the United States "and others," in the hope of banking good will that might later be turned to China's advantage.

And so the Americans, without firing a shot and without issuing a threat, were able to expand their commercial operations along the coast of China. The American flag followed the British to the treaty ports, and, as junior partners, the Americans followed the British for the rest of the century. There was, however, one problem in 1843: the English had their privileges solemnized in treaties and the Americans took theirs by grace of the emperor. If the merchants were willing to settle, there were those in Washington who were not. Having fought at least once for independence from Great Britain, the bumptious American republic had to have a treaty of its own.

Conflicting advice from merchants concerned with the China trade left the administration of President John Tyler without a clear mandate; and, as is usual, with pressures countervailing on a peripheral issue, inaction continued. Dr. Peter Parker, a medical missionary to China, related by marriage to Secretary of State Daniel Webster, had been in Washington urging a diplomatic mission. Shortly thereafter, Webster found himself under pressure from fellow Whigs to resign from the cabinet of

President Tyler. Allegedly desirous of removing himself to the Court of St. James, he decided to create a grandiose mission to China with which he may have hoped to tempt his old friend, Edward Everett, to leave England, providing the necessary vacancy. When Everett failed to rise to the bait, the well-financed mission was entrusted to Caleb Cushing, a former Whig Congressman whose political career had ended prematurely. Thus the able Cushing became Commissioner to China and set off to negotiate with the Chinese—who had so recently received a lesson on Western power and on the seriousness with which the West regarded its concept of relations between states.

Ch'i-ying, the imperial commissioner to whom the emperor had entrusted diplomatic negotiations, learned of Cushing's impending arrival from the American consul at Canton and suggested that Cushing would be wasting his time: if the United States wanted the trade privileges won by England, China was perfectly willing to bestow these on Americans. There was no need for an American envoy to make the long trip across the Pacific. Then Ch'i-ying reflected upon the American mission and the British request for most-favored-nation treatment in the supplementary treaty and deduced that the British expected the Americans to demand the right to go to Peking. In his correspondence with the emperor, it was clear that neither of them was particularly concerned over Cushing's mission, but they were determined not to allow him to go to Peking. The emperor felt that since the American barbarians had never paid tribute, a request to go to Peking could not even be received. As for a treaty between China and the United States, this was a less significant matter, but again the Chinese preferred that treaty relations be avoided in order to preclude complications such as American demands that went beyond those of the British.

When Cushing arrived at Macao, Ch'i-ying was not in residence. The American commissioner promptly allowed it to be known that soon after his ship was provisioned, he intended to proceed north to the mouth of the Pei-ho. In fact, Cushing's instructions directed him to use the threat of going on to Peking as a means of pressuring the Chinese into granting to the Americans the same opportunities for trade as the English had obtained in the Treaty of Nanking. This much the Chinese had already granted to the Americans, making Cushing's threats and indeed his mission superfluous. But despite the misgivings of the American merchants in Canton, Cushing persisted, and after four months of sparring, Ch'i-ying returned to Macao.

1½ 1800s Qing not learning from post experiences
Qing do not see urgency to make changes

Once Ch'i-ying arrived for the negotiations, Cushing could have h
his treaty immediately. The Chinese had concluded that the matter was
one of prestige among the Western countries and had decided to give
"face" to the Americans. They had decided that Cushing's purpose was
"after all, a desire to outshine the English barbarians and, like them, to
set up a treaty in order to show preferential treatment by the Heavenly
Court."[3] Despite the defeat China had suffered at England's hands, it
was possible for a Chinese official to inform the emperor that England,
France, and the United States "look particularly to the character of their
treatment by the Heavenly Court as a measure of national status."[4] But
Cushing continued to bluff about his trip north, delaying the conclusion
of the agreement for about a month. As soon as he agreed to deliver his
credentials and sign at Macao, Ch'i-ying gave him his treaty.

Peter Parker's role in the negotiation was especially important. Not
only did he and two other American missionaries serve as Cushing's interpreters, but he enjoyed and exploited a valuable personal relationship
with Ch'i-ying. He had treated Ch'i-ying's parents in his clinic, winning
the gratitude of the Chinese commissioner. He had befriended two of
Ch'i-ying's aides. At critical moments in the talks, he was able to bridge
the cultural and political gaps and facilitate a successful outcome—
although he had been wrong to urge Cushing to persist in the threat to
travel to Peking. Parker's performance foreshadowed the enormous importance of American missionaries as transmitters and interpreters of
Chinese culture to Americans and American culture to Chinese. For better or worse, they were a major influence, probably *the* major influence,
on American attitudes and policy toward China for more than a hundred
years. Role of NGO, but has monopoly on China + language

The Treaty of Wang-hsia, named after the suburban village in which it
was signed (now part of the city of Macao), was basically a summary, with
significant refinements, of the two treaties that the Chinese had signed
with the British. Again, to the Chinese of the mid-nineteenth century,
these concessions were not of particular importance. Lacking a sense of
nation, they also lacked cause for concern over theoretical abridgments of
national rights.

Cushing's treaty, like those signed by the English, did not lessen the
Chinese conviction of their own superiority—nor their determination to
avoid treating the Westerners as equals. Ch'i-ying's comments on the
West in general and the United States in particular are not merely amusing;
they also indicate how he and the emperor conceived of China's relations.

To Cushing he gushed enthusiastically over the beauty of Tyler's letter to the emperor, but his actual estimate of the level of American culture and understanding can be found in his advice to the emperor on how to reply to Tyler. He warned that of all countries, the United States was the most remote and the least civilized, "an isolated place outside the pale, solitary and ignorant." Obviously such a people would not be trained in the appropriate forms of laws and edicts. Moreover, if the emperor allowed his meaning to "be rather deep," the Americans "would probably not even be able to comprehend." In writing to Tyler, the emperor should, therefore, use a "simple and direct" style and make his meaning "clear and obvious."[5]

These were the days of the clipper ships and if the Americans appeared to the Chinese as a little short on culture, they were without peers in their ability to build those fleet and beautiful sailing craft. The British and their subjects continued to dominate trade, but the Americans offered increasing competition, particularly in the carrying trade. In China, during the early 1850s, with only about 25 of the approximately 200 Western business firms, Americans carried about one third of China's trade with the West. And of the burgeoning trade of Shanghai, rapidly becoming the major treaty port, American ships carried fully half. With the European powers increasingly occupied with the issues that led to the Crimean War, expectations for the market in China gained substance.

Having acquired a treaty of its own, the government of the United States did little to implement it. After July 1844, Americans had access to five Chinese ports and in accordance with the treaty's provisions for extraterritoriality, the American consuls in these ports had sole jurisdiction over Americans accused of crimes in China. But neither of the administrations that followed Tyler's troubled to set up a consular service in China. Not until the entire American consular service was reorganized in the mid-1850s did the American government appoint paid consular officials, responsible to the Department of State. In the interim, American merchants in the treaty ports carried on business as usual, providing consuls out of their own ranks, occasionally from the very firms involved in the opium trade. British consular officials, backed by the power of their government, were willing and able to restrain some of the baser instincts of their countrymen, giving some semblance of justice to the practice of consular jurisdiction. The American consul, if not involved in illegal activities himself, was rarely disposed to call American miscreants to account.

In the absence of jails maintained by his government, he would have been virtually powerless if he had desired to dispense justice. As a result, the behavior of American sailors, particularly in Shanghai, became notorious and set a standard for sailors of all nations in all of the treaty ports. Years later, the first American minister wrote that he considered the "exaction" of extraterritoriality, "so long as the United States refuse or neglect to provide the punishment, an opprobrium of the worst kind . . . as bad as the coolie or opium trade."[6] The American flag became a cover for "every vagabond Englishman, Irishman, or Scotchman." Indeed, the female of the species required little other cover—and consular reports suggested that every blue-eyed whore in the Orient claimed to be an American.

The indifference of the government to events in China is further evidenced by the fact that the American commissioners received no specific instructions from Washington in the decade following the signing of the treaty. The commissioners themselves were a most forgettable lot, with one exception making no impression on the Chinese, who found them all "inscrutable." The one exception, Dr. Peter Parker, held several interim appointments before being named commissioner in 1856. By that time, Chinese officials had, with cause, taken an intense dislike to him, classing him with the more arrogant and intractable British officials of their experience. His years in China had convinced the former medical missionary that the British had developed the proper technique for dealing with the Chinese: firmness was essential and force had to be used where necessary. Parker also developed a plan for an American role in China larger than that contemplated by the majority of his colleagues in Washington. He suggested that the United States establish a foothold in the area, equivalent to the British possession of Hong Kong, and he urged that Formosa be occupied for that purpose. He also suggested that the United States build coaling stations in the area and expand naval operations off the China coast. Parker saw no future in the United States playing the role of petty imperialist when the grander British example lay before it. If his government would follow his recommendations and join with the Europeans in a united front, then the Chinese would show the proper respect for Americans, and American interests in China would be firmly established and protected. Earlier, Commodore Matthew Perry had outlined similar plans and had even begun to implement them, but both Parker and Perry were denied by the politicians back home. Repudiating their pretensions to empire, the government of the United States remained

Treaty ports on the China coast, c. 1850

uninterested in territorial acquisitions in the Far East and until the American Civil War preferred to adhere to its traditional policy of unilateral action rather than cooperating formally with any of the other powers.

Parker's frustrations were due in large part to the fact that Ch'i-ying's successors in the management of barbarian affairs, the men who held what the West called the position of viceroy at Canton, reversed the policy of appeasing the West. Ch'i-ying had never allowed his contempt for the "stupid ignorance" of the West to blind him to the realities of Western power. He had, therefore, counseled a policy of conciliation and adjustment, and his lifelong friendship with the emperor had carried his advice against the militancy possible from the safety of the capitol. But in 1850, the Tao-guang emperor died, and before the year was over Ch'i-ying and Mu-chang-a, the powerful grand councillor who had supported his policies, were both degraded. The Hsien-feng emperor, Wen-tsung, determined on a course that could only lead to new confrontations with the West, refusing to acknowledge diplomatic equality, refusing to honor some of the provisions of China's treaties with the Western powers, and refusing to cooperate in the solution of problems that arose between China and the West. The era of appeasement had ended. *at death of gauguang*

Given the relative power of the West, there is no reason to believe that a provocative policy would have been successful under the best of circumstances. Unfortunately for China, 1850 proved to be an inauspicious time for bravado on the international scene. In that year one of the greatest and most destructive wars in all history, the Taiping Rebellion, began in South China. Here was internal strife on a scale that dwarfed the American Civil War. The Taiping Rebellion lasted fifteen years, ranged over almost all of China, and resulted in the loss of at least 20, and possibly 40 million lives, and in the bankruptcy of the central government. The fact that the emperor persisted in antagonizing the West, in the midst of this great catastrophe, is perhaps the best evidence that the Chinese interpreted their defeat at England's hands as an accident of no lasting significance. Barbarians had inflicted defeats on China on a number of occasions in the previous thousand years or so and China had always prevailed. Contemptuous of Western pretensions to civilization, neither the emperor nor his court would consider the possibility that Western strength might come from a superior technology.

By 1853, the strength of the Taiping movement was readily apparent to the West, as the Taipings occupied the ancient capital of Nanking and their influence spread through the lower Yangtze valley. Of particular interest

[handwritten margin note: Taiping rebellion led by man claiming to be Jesus' lil' bro, religious, even though no religion in China]

to Westerners was the fact that the rebels appeared to be an indigenous Christian sect. In fact, the rebel leader, Hung Hsiu-ch'üan, had studied briefly with an American missionary and had concluded that he was the younger brother of Jesus. Perhaps unfortunately, Catholic missionaries decided that the movement smacked of Protestantism, and none of the Protestant sects could identify with Hung's sexual practices or accept his divine pretensions. Even Issachar Roberts, Hung's former teacher, ultimately felt constrained to repudiate him.

Difficulties with the Peking government allowed most Westerners to harbor hopes for the success of the rebellion. But gradually, responsible American, British, and French officials came to believe that the interests of their respective countries would not be served by the victory of Hung's forces. The more they learned of the ideology and governmental practices of the Taiping movement, the less attractive it seemed. Most of the information available to the American government came from missionary sources, and American policy reflected the rise and fall of missionary hopes for the Taipings. In addition, the rebellion was hurting trade, the principal purpose of the Western presence in China. Some of the merchants transcended this problem by going into the munitions business and kept the rebels well supplied, but the representatives of their governments were ill disposed toward this trade. Humphrey Marshall, the American Commissioner from 1852 to 1854, gradually came to believe that the British were working for the collapse of the Chinese government in order to further their imperial designs. He concluded that the Taipings had to be defeated and that the American government had to act in support of the emperor or risk the division of China between England and Russia, followed by the exclusion of the interests of the United States. Although the Pierce administration, which had inherited Marshall, was not disposed to take action of any sort, the remoteness of events in China from the focus of the Department of State's attention allowed American representatives to do almost anything—provided they did not require support from the United States.

[handwritten margin note: US needed to support the emperor for trade during + after the rebellion]

Marshall really need not have worried, for the British government had no interest in adding China to its empire. On the contrary, the Foreign Office had decided that British commercial interests would never warrant an extensive military or political commitment in China. Indeed, as the Taiping Rebellion progressed and chaos swept the Yangtze valley, the British government feared a collapse of authority in China, which might require a costly British effort to establish order. It was, therefore, the policy of Great Britain to support the Manchu regime in Peking as the least costly means of serving the limited interests of Englishmen in the area. Very likely Marshall's suspicions prevented more active Anglo-American cooperation toward the end he sought.

Two circumstances combined to drive the Americans and the British together in 1853–1854. First, having decided against supporting the rebels as a means of overcoming the refusal of the Chinese government to comply with the treaties of 1842–1844, the United States and Great Britain sought to have these treaties revised in a manner that would preclude further Chinese deceit. To justify revision in 1854 required the two nations to cooperate to meet Chinese obstinacy with some complex Anglo-American chicanery. The American treaty had contained a provision for review at the end of twelve years, but that treaty had been signed in 1844, suggesting to the unsophisticated that the Chinese would not be expected to review the provisions before 1856. The British, however, in their treaty of 1843, had obtained a most-favored-nation provision, by means of which they claimed that they, too, were entitled to have their treaty reviewed after twelve years—the Treaty of Nanking, signed twelve years before. And the Americans, of course, insisted that if the British could have the provisions of their treaties revised in 1854, then the most-favored-nation treatment, to which they were also entitled, gave them the right to have their treaties revised in 1854. Naturally, the Chinese suspected a swindle and were outraged. But the new American commissioner, Robert McLane, under instructions to cooperate with the other Western powers, took advantage of China's distress and accompanied the British to the mouth of the Pei-ho, near Tientsin, to demand revision of the treaties. Despite the internal crisis, the Chinese held firm, not only refusing to negotiate but also treating the two diplomats discourteously. Until the powers were ready to use force, treaty revision would have to wait.

The second condition that drove the United States and Great Britain together was the anxiety in the foreign concessions in Shanghai as rebel forces approached the city. When imperial authority in Shanghai evaporated, the American commissioner and British consul took over responsibility for customs collection. After McLane replaced Marshall, cooperat with British authorities proved relatively easy and the representativ the two governments gradually worked out a system for a foreign torate of customs. Ultimately this evolved into the Imperial

Customs Service, which became the most reliable source of revenue the Chinese government enjoyed in the last third of the nineteenth century—and perhaps in the first half of the twentieth century as well.

By the mid-1850s, the powers were as one in their determination to have the treaties revised. To English and American merchants, the fact that China was rent by civil war, that the imperial government was struggling desperately to survive, seemed irrelevant. Trade was being hampered by the existence of the rebellion and by the willful obstruction of Chinese authorities. In Canton, Yeh Ming-ch'en became a great favorite of the court for his skill at deflecting Western demands and circumventing China's obligations under her treaties with the powers. When the Canton populace rose against the foreigners, it was not the Taipings, but Yeh who planned the movement. To all Westerners who tried to deal with Yeh, there came the conviction that the Chinese would respond only to cannon and shot.

Under these circumstances, the American diplomats in China might have been powerless, given the utter refusal of the government of the United States to take warlike measures against China. Some Americans, merchants and officials both, deprived of recourse to arms, learned to compromise and conciliate—useful techniques for minor powers. But in these years before the United States had the might necessary to neglect diplomacy, it had the option of achieving its objectives in the wake of British power. The lion roared and made the kill; the jackal smiled and picked the bones.

Together, the British and American representatives wandered along the coast of China, seeking to open negotiations for the revision of the treaties. Always their requests were denied, sometimes more rudely than others. The lesser power could tolerate these indignities, but the prestige of the British empire was in jeopardy. In 1856, the Chinese, engaged in the suppression of piracy in the vicinity of Canton, stopped a vessel flying the British flag and removed a number of Chinese alleged to be pirates. A generation removed from the days when they practiced impressment off the coast of the United States, the British were outraged by the offense to their flag. There ensued a contest characterized by the hauteur of Yeh Ming-ch'en and the imperious manner of the British consul. With the Crimean War behind them, the British did not hesitate to use force to resolve the issue. In October, after the British bombarded Chinese forts and the walls of the city of Canton, Yeh declared the existence of a state of war. The British took the city, but then withdrew, followed by the people of Canton, who burned all the foreign property in the area. Great Britain was not quite ready for a showdown.

Toward the end of 1857, the treasury having recovered from the Crimean War, and turbulence in India being stilled for the moment, the British determined to resolve the problem permanently. This time, France also proved willing to fight, in retaliation for the execution of a French priest caught proselytizing in the interior in violation of the law. The Anglo-French forces stormed Canton, took the city, and in January 1858 captured the abrasive Yeh—whom they sent off to India where he remained until his death. But the lesson was lost on the emperor who, unaware of the seriousness of the situation, merely assumed that Yeh had blundered, and remained contemptuous of the West. He was convinced that as soon as the rebellion could be suppressed, China would have the strength to put an end to the Western nuisance.

There are many ways to characterize the American role in China in the 1850s, in the quest for treaty revision. The Chinese differed among themselves, but those most experienced with barbarian affairs saw little to choose from among the various foreign powers. The official in charge of the port of Shanghai, in a discussion of policy toward England and France, suggested that there was no need to work out a special policy for the United States: "they do no more than follow in England's wake and utilize her strength."[7] Another official advised against serious consideration of American offers of cooperation against the Taiping rebels on the grounds that no faith could be placed in American promises. In 1855, the governor of Kiangsu informed the emperor that the Americans were openly giving help to the rebels. Yeh Ming-ch'en had been consistently suspicious of Anglo-American collusion and believed Peter Parker to be one of the craftiest troublemakers ever to come to China. The emperor, however, clung to the idea of isolating the British and using the Americans toward this end. So enamored was he of this idea that when, in November 1856, American ships under Commodore James Armstrong leveled five Chinese forts on the Pearl River near Canton, the emperor did not believe the reports and assumed they came from British propagandists.

Whatever the preferred view of the American role in China, Armstrong's action made it difficult for the Chinese to regard the American presence as more beneficent than that of the other Westerners who were followed by gunboats. To be sure, Armstrong's little war was not unprovoked. The forts had, without apparent reason, fired on an American vessel that passed under them en route to Canton. The proud response of the United

Sum: Brits + US collaborated to get their treaties revised and approved by Chinese empire. This was during Taiping rebellion + they were getting nowhere. Peter Parker was replaced by William Reed.

States Navy was the systematic bombardment of the forts for four days until they were silenced, captured, and the 167 cannon they contained dismantled. Parker was delighted by the action and could point to Yeh's belated apology as evidence that the Chinese responded only to superior force. But the moral was rejected by President Pierce and Secretary of State Marcy, who regretted Armstrong's harsh response. To the Chinese, who received the shot, but not the regrets, American behavior may not have been distinguishable from that of the British imperialists.

The Buchanan administration replaced Parker with William Reed, the first American representative in China with the title of minister. Secretary of State Lewis Cass advised him that the United States sought no territory in China, entertained no political ambitions, but nonetheless insisted on treaty revision. He was instructed to inform the Chinese government that the United States deemed the demands of Britain and France to be just, but he was not to take hostile action. The United States was willing to mediate between China and the Anglo-French allies, hoping to serve its interests most efficaciously in the role of a strong neutral rather than as a junior partner in the alliance against China.

In the spring of 1858, the British envoy sailed again to the Pei-ho. This time he was accompanied by French, Russian, and American diplomats— and British and French fleets. All four countries went to insist on revision of their treaties. Although only the British and French came with guns, the Russians and Americans were no less demanding. As Yeh had charged in his last memorial, their greed was insatiable and they aided each other like a pack of wolves. But the emperor continued to dream of American gratitude, fidelity, and submissiveness. Now he wrote of separating the Russians and the Americans from the English and French in the hope of isolating the latter two. The Chinese officials who met the Western diplomats suffered from none of his illusions. They realized immediately that all four powers were in collusion and insisted that the Americans and Russians were simply trying to get something for nothing: to get their treaties revised by playing the broker's role or claiming most-favored-nation treatment if the Chinese yielded to the Anglo-French threat. After a month in which the Chinese conceded nothing, the British and French fleets attacked and battered the Chinese defenses, while the American and Russian envoys stood aside. Once the way was cleared, the four ministers regrouped and proceeded to Tientsin for negotiations in which the neutrals claimed no less than the victors.

For the Sino-Western discussions that followed the destruction of the Taku forts, the aging Ch'i-ying was brought out of limbo, but his day had passed. When the allies captured Canton, they had found the files containing all of China's correspondence on barbarian affairs, including the many memorials in which Ch'i-ying had commented derogatorily on Westerners and their practices and in which he described the methods he had employed to control them. With these documents they confronted and ridiculed the old man, driving him from Tientsin in shame, to a death sentence from his merciless and ungrateful emperor.

In the days that followed, the Chinese, in desperation, sought American mediation, but the allies were no longer in any mood for diplomacy. The Treaties of Tientsin were dictated, not negotiated. The Chinese were forced to open eleven new treaty ports and to allow the West to navigate up the Yangtze, into the heart of China. Foreigners were granted the right to travel in the interior; missionaries and their converts had to be tolerated anywhere and everywhere. The Chinese tariff was fixed at a meager 5 percent and the opium trade was legalized by placing the drug on the tariff schedule. And finally, the Chinese were forced to permit foreign diplomats to reside in Peking.

The Treaties of Tientsin stripped the Chinese of all protection against foreign exploitation. In particular, the Chinese government was left without control of its economy. The opening of the Yangtze and of treaty ports in the interior meant that foreign goods could be distributed widely subject only to a nominal tariff. Indeed, the tariff was almost always lower than the internal transit charges to which domestic products were subject. Nor did China have any further protection against Western ideas. Foreigners could go wherever they wanted, do as they pleased, independent of Chinese law, with foreign troops and gunboats never far behind. The subjugation of China under the treaty system was almost complete. The guns under which the Chinese signed were British and French, but the Russian and American ministers accepted no fewer rights for their countrymen to exploit.

The emperor, however, had not yet surrendered. Although he was apparently prepared to accept these humiliating treaties, he was determined to see that Peking would not be threatened again. As soon as the Western fleet departed, he ordered the repair and strengthening of the Taku forts and the defenses of Tientsin. When the Western ministers returned in June 1859, to exchange ratifications of the treaties, the Chinese authorities asked them to move a few miles north of the mouth of the Pei-ho, where a delegation awaited them. The British and French, convinced that the Chinese were perpetrating some new deceit and not at all reluctant to teach the Chinese another lesson, responded by firing on the forts. The Chinese defenders returned the fire, with considerably more success than they had enjoyed previously. In fact, the British admiral was wounded in the ensuing battle.

As the fight progressed, Commodore Josiah Tatnall, U.S.N., escorting the American minister, was disturbed by its course. With the approval of the minister, he entered the fray, using a chartered steamship to tow British sailing craft into the line of battle. Solicitous of the British admiral's well-being, he then boarded the British flagship and, as he visited, ordered his crew to assist the English gunners in their chores. "Blood," he allegedly declared, "is thicker than water," and thus was American neutrality compromised and Washington's injunction against hostile action ignored.

To the delight of the emperor and the court, the British and French were repulsed. So heady proved this taste of victory that the emperor assumed that the allies would never return—and a few of his advisers dared to dream of abolishing the Treaties of Tientsin. But the American minister had accepted the alternative place suggested for the exchange of ratifications. The Anglo-French forces left the area, but John Ward, appointed by Buchanan to exchange ratifications, chose to remain behind and make a further effort. After weeks of negotiations, he finally agreed to ride in a tribute cart, and was allowed to travel on to Peking. At the capital, the effort to convert Ward's mission into the traditional tribute mission failed. No acceptable compromise for the kowtow could be reached and Ward, who would bend his knee but slightly, took the bumpy road back to the coast. There he exchanged ratifications with the Chinese and for a year the Americans alone had a revised treaty with the Chinese— although even the bloodied French and English were able to claim their "rights" as most-favored-nations.

But for the Emperor Wen-tsung and for two generations of Chinese yet unborn, it was not the victory of 1859, but the defeat of 1860 that proved decisive. In 1860, British and French forces returned, smashed the Chinese coastal and river defenses, and marched overland to Peking. The emperor surrendered his hopes of using American barbarians to curb English barbarians and he, too, concluded that the United States was in collusion with the more obvious of China's enemies. Into Peking marched the armies of Great Britain and France, on into the emperor's magnificent Summer Palace, which they looted and put to flame, destroying in the process priceless treasures of centuries of Chinese civilization. And the emperor fled to Jehol, where within a year he succeeded in destroying his body—from which the West had driven the spirit.

As a result of the battles of 1859 and 1860, the British and French heaped further humiliations on China. Tientsin was added to the treaty ports. The British took Kowloon on the mainland across the bay from Hong Kong, and the French inserted a clause giving missionaries the right to lease or buy land and to build houses anywhere in China. But once the treaties were ratified, Western support of the Peking government against the Taiping rebels intensified. With these new concessions, the West, more than ever, had a vested interest in the regime from which these privileges had been exacted. This did not prevent British and American merchants from continuing their involvement in arms trade with the Taipings, but at least as significant was the fact that the small mercenary army that had been raised earlier for the defense of Shanghai was incorporated into the Imperial forces under Li Hung-chang. This "Ever Victorious Army," whose first two commanders were Americans, one of whom later defected to the Taipings, and whose last commander was the British officer known as "Chinese" Gordon, helped rid the Yangtze valley of the rebels.

The real hero of the Taiping Rebellion was a Chinese official, Tseng Kuo-fan. It was he who raised the most important of the regional armies that stood against the Taipings when the Manchu banners and all manner of Peking-directed resistance failed. In 1861, as he surveyed the wreckage and reflected on China's humiliation, he discussed the role played by the various barbarians. Despite the American record in China, in which he was not well versed, he singled out the United States as a country whose people were "pure-minded" and of "honest disposition" and who had long been respectful and compliant. He argued that the Americans had always been loyal to China and had never been in alliance with the English and French. With Tseng one of the most influential figures in China for much of the next decade, the prospects for improved Sino-American relations were excellent, but Prince Kung, who took charge of China's foreign relations for most of that ten years, explained what good relations meant to the Chinese. To the emperor he reported Tseng's views and Tseng's feeling that an effort should be made to prevent the Russians from winning over the Americans. In his own comments, he accepted Tseng's brief of American good behavior, adding that "the problem is how to control them and make them exploitable by us."[8] For more than a century after, Chinese officials returned to that conceptualization of the problem of relations with the United States.

As the West intensified its exploitation of China and the Chinese sought ways to exploit the Americans, the missionaries took heart in the new clauses that opened the whole empire to the work of the Christian God. Years later, W. A. P. Martin, an American missionary who had assisted Reed in the negotiations of 1858, looked back on the turbulence of the years 1857 to 1860, looked back at the humiliation of China, and finding it all most gratifying, remarked: ". . . a spectator must be sadly deficient in spiritual insight if he does not perceive the hand of God overruling the strife of nations and the blundering of statesmen."[9] Perhaps Americans of another age may find themselves as deficient as were the Chinese.

In 1861 China acquired the equivalent of a foreign office and its diplomatic practices came gradually to approximate those of the West. In the same year, the United States acquired a secretary of state who sought to work out a program for American action in the Pacific. Surely, here was the beginning of a new era—and here the appropriate place for evaluating American policy in the old.

Although there is no evidence to indicate that the men who formulated American foreign policy had ever consciously developed a policy for the Far East in general or China in particular, by supporting certain actions of Americans in the Orient and rejecting others, the American government had followed a definable pattern that *was* tantamount to a policy position. In other words, while a long-range policy had not been formulated, the ad hoc reactions of the American government to events in China and to the requests of American merchants, missionaries, diplomats, and military men were consistent. American interests were restricted to trade and missionary work. American leaders never seriously entertained territorial ambitions. Prior to 1861, the government of the United States never endorsed the use of force, preferring to extend the rights and privileges of its nationals through diplomacy and the astute use of the most-favored-nation clause. The two occasions on which American warships took hostile action against China were clearly unauthorized and the officer responsible for the more flagrant of the two incidents was advised of his government's displeasure.

When compared with the alternatives offered by Parker or Perry of emulating Great Britain's more aggressive policy, the course chosen was eminently sensible. This was preindustrial America, a nation with vast unoccupied territories, a domestic market yet to be fully exploited, ample investment opportunities for anyone with capital. This was an age in which the locus of power rested in Europe, in which the Orient mattered little in the world balance of power, and in which the state of technology had yet to put forth challenges to the security Americans could enjoy on their side of the great oceans. The United States was a weak and underdeveloped power, which, even had it had the will to exercise political or military authority in East Asia, had not the means. Given its status among the powers, given its limited interests in China or elsewhere in the area, the American practice of trailing British power and utilizing the most-favored-nation clause to further these interests could not easily have been improved on. Although this tactic, which several historians have labeled "jackal diplomacy," permitted no claim of moral superiority over the procedures employed by the Europeans, it was nonetheless a most realistic and satisfactory policy for the United States. The aim of foreign policy is, obviously, the achievement of maximum benefits for the nation in its relations with other countries at minimum cost. And so long as the more powerful predators were willing to tolerate the American presence, jackal diplomacy would work.

But however well suited American practices were to the interests of the United States and its nationals, it cannot be assumed that these practices served the best interests of China or that the Chinese could take a sanguine view of American actions. The treaty system was, after all, imposed on the Chinese by force and if they had little alternative but to tolerate the system, they were not likely to celebrate it. The relatively peaceful manner in which the Americans had acquired the special privileges provided by the "unequal treaties" did not disguise the fact that they enjoyed privileges that the Chinese had not willingly conceded. The United States had been a junior partner, but it was nonetheless a participant in the events that reduced China to a state in which the Chinese had to respond to the demands of not one but all of the powers, while none of them assumed responsibility for the needs of China—a condition with all the disadvantages of colonial status, but without any of the advantages. Although some Chinese officials might perceive the subtle distinction between Americans and other Westerners, it could hardly be expected that the Chinese populace would see a difference in the way in which the various foreigners conducted their affairs in China.

At the time of the Opium War, Chinese officials had hoped that they could count on American support, if not out of American loyalty to China, then because of traditional American hostility toward England. They were disappointed, and in subsequent years correspondence between various Chinese authorities and the emperor indicated a feeling that Americans were a people from whom China could always expect words of sympathy, but never any material support. Increasingly, the mandarins who dealt with foreign affairs came to suspect the complicity of the United States in England's schemes. Although these "barbarian experts" were aware that the Americans were not employing gunboat diplomacy, were not using warships to force concessions, they nonetheless warned the emperor that the Americans always "followed in England's wake"—allowed British gunboats to humble the Chinese and moved in to share whatever new privileges had been exacted.

Clearly, these men were under no illusions as to the role of the United States in China. And yet, the United States could not but benefit from being the least aggressive of the Western powers with which the Chinese had significant contact. If there was little to hope for in dealings with the United States, perhaps there was also less to fear. Chinese hostility toward the West tended to be generalized and the Americans, sharing as they did in the treaty system, could not escape from this hostility. On the other hand, when it served China's purpose to make distinctions among the oppressing powers, when China needed help, the Americans looked relatively friendly and exploitable.

2 The United States as a Power in East Asia

The man who became secretary of state in 1861, William Seward, had quite enough in the way of problems without taking on new ones in Asia. As he awaited the inauguration of the Lincoln administration, one after another of the Southern states seceded, leaving Seward and his president no alternative but to seek the preservation of the United States as the alpha and omega of *all* their policies.

Seward was himself a nationalist after the style of John Quincy Adams—a style which, whatever its virtues, contained some embarrassing connotations. Both men had a vision of America's mission, of Americans as a people chosen to spread the blessings of democracy around the world. And both men seemed on occasion to be impatient with God's schedule and anxious to hasten the process. Like Adams, Seward looked westward and, finding that the continental limits to which Adams had aspired had already been attained, he looked beyond the Pacific to East Asia. Regrettably, he had little patience with Orientals—or anyone else—who failed to appreciate the benefits of the American presence. In this respect, the Chinese fared better than the Japanese, whom Seward considered a semi-barbarous people who might profit from a dose of gunboat-applied civilization—to facilitate the reception of American teachings. For Chinese civilization he had considerably more respect, and then, again, by 1861 the

Chinese had already been given several samples of how the West dealt with nations that rejected progress.

After taking office, Seward's principal task was to muster whatever foreign support he could for the Union and to prevent the rebellious South from receiving any kind of support from abroad. Toward this end, he determined to remove any cause for disaffection in the relations between the United States and the powers, especially Great Britain and France. If, for example, the United States stood shoulder to shoulder with the European powers in the affairs of China and Japan, the Europeans would have less reason to desire the breakup of the Union than they would if the United States posed an obstacle to their plans. A policy of cooperating with Great Britain and France in China proved remarkably easy for the United States and, in Seward's time, of some value to the Chinese.

Despite suspicions of Great Britain in particular and Europeans in general that were never far from the surface among Americans at home, those who went to China had found cooperation with Europeans most natural. Perhaps Tatnall's "blood is thicker than water" provides the easiest explanation: an infinitesimal minority of whites living together in a tiny enclave, backs to the sea, on the edge of a enormous continent peopled by hundreds of millions of hostile Orientals. The differences among the Westerners seemed trivial compared to the differences between Chinese and Westerners. As Chinese xenophobia made no distinctions among foreigners, the foreigners made such distinctions only at their own peril. Similarly, since the Americans and the Europeans were one and all entitled to most-favored-nation treatment, each could hope to benefit from the satisfaction of another's aspirations. In this sense, "thick as thieves" might be an apt substitute for Tatnall's choice of clichés.

Additionally, the revision of the treaties in 1860, the completion of the main props of the treaty system, sated most of the powers for a generation. All were agreed on a policy of sustaining the Manchus and fearful that a further round of concessions might bring about the collapse of the Peking government and with it the structure of the system. To this scene, Seward sent Anson Burlingame, with instructions that made cooperation with the powers the official policy of the United States. And Seward put aside any plans for a larger, perhaps more independent role for his country until he was sure it would survive.

In the 1860s the cooperation of the powers in China benefited the government because the dynasty's hope for survival coincided with the West's conception of its interests there. That such cooperation was fraught with danger for the Chinese was apparent from the way in which the powers worked together in Japan. There, in 1864, the Americans joined the British, French, and Dutch in the bombardment of the capital of the powerful Choshu clan, impressing on the Japanese their distaste for manifestations of antiforeign sentiment. In one instance the foreign gunboats and troops defended, in another they attacked. With no opportunity to play one barbarian power off against another, China was at the mercy of the West.

Unfortunately for China, the death of the emperor in 1861 had left a power vacuum at the court, which the empress dowager Tz'u-hsi gradually filled. In her tenure as the emperor's concubine, she had distinguished herself by her sexual prowess, but after his death she also demonstrated considerable political skill. Initially content with asserting her authority in Peking, she allowed the conduct of foreign affairs to be controlled by the newly formed Tsungli Yamen, generally directed by Prince Kung.

One of the first quests undertaken by the new breed of barbarian experts was for an understanding of this "law of nations" that the West constantly charged them with violating and for which violations they had been rather severely punished. To this end, an American missionary, W. A. P. Martin, translated Wheaton's writings on international law. The process of westernization had begun and as the presence of Western diplomats at Peking heralded China's induction into the family of nations, the Chinese voluntarily began to move away from traditional attitudes and methods. One such step was the decision, in 1867, to send a diplomatic mission, headed by the retiring American minister, to the capitals of the Western powers.

For several years, friendly Westerners, like Martin and Robert Hart of the Imperial Maritime Customs Service, had urged the Chinese to send representatives abroad. In December 1865, Seward had instructed Burlingame to invite the Chinese to send an envoy to Washington. But the stranglehold of Chinese tradition was not easily broken. Some Chinese officials persisted in their conception of China's claim to universal supremacy and insisted that it would be demeaning. In 1866, Hart succeeded in convincing Prince Kung to send a 64-year-old Manchu official on a brief tour of Europe from which he returned prematurely, allegedly horrified by the disgusting manners and practices of Europeans.

When it became known that Burlingame desired to return to the United States, the Chinese government asked him to accompany two of its men on a mission to the Western capitals. Here was striking evidence of China's determination to learn something of the outside world *and* to establish communications with those who controlled the policies of the imperialist nations. Prince Kung realistically did not attempt to roll back the treaty system, but he and his colleagues did hope that by explaining China's actions and intentions to the Western leaders, they could convince the West to ease the pace at which China was being forced to convert from its ancient ways to ways that conformed with practices among the powers. Suspecting that no one of them could be sufficiently persuasive, they invited Burlingame, an apparently well-intentioned barbarian, to assist them.

Wherever the mission went, whether to Washington, London, Paris, or Berlin, Burlingame upstaged his Chinese colleagues, but otherwise gave China no cause to regret his selection. In the United States, he exceeded his instructions and signed a treaty with Seward in which Seward pledged the United States not to interfere in the internal development of China— and included several other provisions with which the Chinese were less well pleased, but about which they never complained. From Clarendon and Bismarck, he also obtained assurances of future moderation. For China, this diplomatic debut proved to be tremendously successful: "The leading Western nations were now committed to a policy of restraint in treaty revision, and this was all the Chinese government wanted at the moment."[1]

Seward, on the other hand, had to settle for a little less than he wanted. He did, however, succeed in moving the American flag considerably closer to the Orient, with the purchase of Alaska and the occupation of Midway Island. His hopes for closer ties with Hawaii and for a transisthmian canal came to naught in his lifetime, but the ideas did not die; nor, for better or worse, did his vision of a greater American role in East Asia pass unfulfilled.

One provision of the treaty Seward signed with Burlingame soon proved exceedingly embarrassing to the United States. This provision, probably the primary reason for the treaty, gave Chinese immigrants the right to enter the United States with the promise of most-favored-nation treatment. In the context of Seward's Far Eastern policy and domestic record, he appears to have attempted to serve three ends with one clause. Most obviously, this was part of the policy he had employed of treating China as an equal among the powers. In addition, Seward may have sought to stimulate and regularize the immigration of Chinese coolies so as to provide a source of cheap labor to facilitate the rapid development of the West. Finally, the man whose opposition to nativism had diminished his chances for the Republican presidential nomination in 1860 was attempting via a treaty to make his own opposition to discrimination against immigrants the law of the land. Once the Chinese were promised most-favored-nation treatment in a treaty, local discriminatory legislation, such as had already appeared in California, became unconstitutional.

But there were over 100,000 Chinese in the United States in 1868, and growing numbers of Americans wanted fewer Chinese rather than more. Interestingly enough, the years that followed the Civil War were marked by great enthusiasm in the United States for the hundreds of thousands of immigrants who came each year from Europe. Indeed, the great majority of the states took official steps to encourage immigration. Nonetheless, as in the past, the American expressed a preference for immigrants most like himself—and the Chinese were the most exotic. Thus, at a time when a desire for increased population was powerful, when the great flow of manpower from Europe was considered essential for rapid geographical, industrial, and agricultural expansion, American ethnocentrism excluded the Chinese. Chinese immigration was in fact considered so distinct from European immigration that it was possible for Irish immigrants to lead anti-Chinese movements without fear of stirring a general nativist reaction. *Chinese immigration= problem for US-China relations*

Agitation for the exclusion of Chinese immigrants and discrimination against Chinese already in the United States left Americans little enough with which to claim the superiority of their own civilization over that of China, but the lumpen element had just begun. In the west generally and particularly in California, violence against the Chinese was all too common. Individual Chinese were subjected to beatings and humiliations, and occasionally they were wantonly murdered. No one captured the discrepancy between the theory and practice of American ideals better than Bret Harte in his famous obituary to Wan Lee: "Dead, my reverend friends, dead. Stoned to death in the streets of San Francisco, in the year of grace 1869 by a mob of half-grown boys and Christian school children." And in the 1870s and 1880s, anti-Chinese agitation grew yet more violent, as lynchings, boycotts, and mass expulsions gave witness to racism in America.

The Chinese in America were, overwhelmingly, "sojourners," men who hoped to earn their fortune and return to China with it. In the "China-towns" that sprang up in San Francisco and other American cities, they congregated and tried to protect themselves and to enjoy some semblance of their culture. They continued to speak Chinese, eat Chinese food, and join lineage and work associations imported from China. On the other hand, far from their ancestral tablets and their women, they developed a subculture in which opium smoking, gambling, and prostitution exceeded Chinese conventions. No people living under conditions so removed from normality were likely to create anything more than a caricature of their homeland. But it was these Chinatowns that gave many Americans their only images of the Chinese and their culture. It was not the kind of interaction that bred mutual respect.

The pressure to exclude Chinese immigrants grew too great for Congress to ignore, and in 1879 a bill was passed that limited to fifteen the number of Chinese that could arrive in the United States on one ship. As the bill violated American obligations under the Burlingame Treaty, President Hayes vetoed it—and was roundly condemned on the Pacific Coast. Given the pressures—and the likelihood that the next such veto would be overridden—the United States sought to revise the Burlingame Treaty. In 1880, after both major political parties opposed further Chinese immigration in their platforms, the United States concluded a new treaty with China in which the Chinese agreed to allow the United States to discriminate against Chinese to the extent of being able to regulate, limit, or suspend—*but not prohibit*—Chinese immigration. Congress responded by suspending Chinese immigration for twenty years, and again the American president vetoed what he considered a violation of the spirit of the new treaty. Congress replied with another bill, this time suspending Chinese immigration for only ten years, extending the suspension to cover skilled as well as unskilled labor. A reluctant president signed this bill into law, but still the racists were not satisfied.

So long as the racist could vote and the Chinese could not, the yellow man knew what it meant not to have "a Chinaman's chance." Congress continued to pass laws violating first the spirit and then the letter of even the treaty of 1880, and there were occasions when the exigencies of domestic politics precluded the presidential veto. And still the racists were not satisfied. In 1885, twenty-eight Chinese miners were brutally murdered in Wyoming and smaller-scale atrocities continued to occur throughout the American West.

In the 1850s, the Chinese government had been indifferent to the fate of Chinese overseas, but the outrages against Chinese in the United States ended this indifference. Nonetheless, China's protests over the treatment of its nationals were to no avail. No matter what the Chinese government felt constrained to accept in treaty revisions, Congress did as it pleased. The issue became a constant irritant in Sino-American relations, with the United States acting unilaterally more and more frequently in violation of its treaty obligations. So unhappy were the circumstances, that diplomatic relations between the United States and China were but nominally maintained from 1892 to 1896. *US + China were not on speaking terms*

American treatment of Chinese in the United States taught China some interesting lessons. Westerners had come to China in violation of the wishes and occasionally the laws of the Chinese people and their government. When these foreigners were treated as barbarians, contemptuously, the Western powers demanded to be treated as equals and, singly or in concert, used gunboats to impose the "superior" values of Western civilization on the unwilling Chinese. The Chinese had been taught, with shot and shell, that violations of treaty obligations were not long tolerated. To America, the Chinese laborer had migrated—to a land that traditionally welcomed, indeed lusted after men with which to swell its population, multiply its produce, and purchase its products. Most Chinese who went to American had been recruited and played an important part in the rapid industrialization of the United States. And in the United States, where Americans controlled the pattern of contact, the Chinese were treated brutally and the Chinese government had no recourse. China had been forced to admit foreigners to its territory and American gunboats patrolled her waters to protect the lives and property of Americans in China, but China had no gunboats to send to America. China had no way to protect its people in the United States, no way to force the American government to admit Chinese to American soil, no way to require the United States to live up to its treaty obligations. The contrast could not be missed by the Chinese, nor would it be forgotten when the people of China could pull themselves together and act as a nation.

In China, as in the United States, the last third of the nineteenth century was marked by efforts to reconstruct a people rent by civil war and to create a modern nation. For the Chinese, the task of modernization was infinitely more difficult than for the Americans. There was, of course, the obvious problem of a relative lack of natural resources. But of greater significance was the fact that China's traditional society was vastly older and more deeply rooted than that of the United States. The Taiping Rebellion had not wrought as significant social changes as had the American Civil War. China's new leaders, Prince Kung, Tseng Kuo-fan, Li Hung-chang, Chang Chih-tung, and others like them were far more enlightened than the preceding generation of officials, less representative of the gentry class, but still committed to the perpetuation of much of the old social order—a major obstacle to the modernization of China. Recognizing the superiority of Western technology, these men sought to adapt it to China's needs, hoping thereby to strengthen China without injury to the Confucian tradition that was the wellspring of their power; they sought the machines of the West, yet hoped to minimize the importation of Western thought. In part, the problems of this new leadership were complicated by the presence of the Western powers in China, by the need to construe modernization first in terms of increasing China's power to withstand the pressures of the imperialists. However great the trials of Americans during the era of reconstruction, they were not aggravated by the presence of predatory powers on American soil.

Needing foreign aid, particularly capital and technical assistance, Li Hung-chang, foremost of the Chinese leaders from the late 1870s to the mid-1890s, hoped to work with Americans, specifically in the development of Chinese railroads and mines. Li was aware that American entrepreneurs did not receive the close support from their government that their European counterparts enjoyed. Problems with American businessmen and engineers were therefore far less likely to involve China in conflict with the American government. Similarly, Li, like Tseng Kuo-fan and so many of the mandarins before him, considered the United States to be the least avaricious and, he hoped, the most useful of the barbarian nations.

Governmental indifference to American investors in China may have been an asset in the eyes of Li Hung-chang, but those Americans who sought concessions found it less salutary. When they sought the services of willing American diplomats in China, the diplomats were ordered by Washington to remain aloof. With no government capital available and no diplomatic support for their ventures, American entrepreneurs had trouble raising the needed funds. In the 1870s and 1880s, there seemed to be ample opportunity for safe and rewarding investments at home and those with capital could not be persuaded to risk their fortunes in China. Li's hope for cooperation with Americans came to naught.

Another serious obstacle to Li's plans, for the self-strengthening movement generally, was the opposition of a powerful faction at the court that opposed foreign investment in the modernization of China. Essentially conservative, this group was suspicious of Li's plans. In addition, the empress dowager, Tz'u Hsi, and others with influence at the court were engaged in more frivolous pursuits, which, however pleasurable they may have been, absorbed precious capital. Funds intended for the building of a modern navy found their way into the construction of a new palace, with disastrous results when the Japanese attacked in 1894. Little of the money squeezed out of the peasants by a rapacious gentry found its way to the central government—and far too little of that which did was used for the development of China's meager resources. The task of modernizing China remained unfinished long after Li Hung-chang and his schemes for American assistance were dead.

While the Chinese, with little success, struggled to come to grips with the challenge posed by the West, the Japanese responded with incredible speed. Only a few years after Perry's visit and the renewal of contact with the West, the Japanese were ready to lay claim to status as a power in East Asia. The moribund Chinese empire provided the grist for the millstones of Japanese imperialism. The island province of Taiwan (Formosa) and the vassal state of Korea both came under Japanese pressures. But initially, the Japanese took control of only the Ryukyu and Bonin Islands. Not until 1894 did a major crisis erupt on the Asian mainland, and it was the anvil of Korea that received the first blow—Korea, where various and sundry Americans played at power politics.

In the late 1870s and 1880s, Li Hung-chang had entertained ideas of drawing the United States into the defense of Chinese tributaries against European and especially Japanese pressures. Aware of the military power Americans had assembled for their civil war and of their growing industrial strength, he was led to believe that the United States was ready for a more active role in East Asia. But his efforts to align the United States with China or even to exploit American good offices achieved little. The United States still lacked the power or, more importantly, the political will to use it across the Pacific. Equally as frustrating to his vision was the tendency of Americans with interests in East Asia to view Japan as an instrument of progress in the region. Li was no more successful in his last-ditch effort to enlist American support for Chinese efforts in Korea.

Initially, the crucial issue was the nature of Korea's relationship to China: was Korea a sovereign nation or was China responsible for that country's foreign and domestic policies? The Western nations never really understood the tributary relationship, but the need to understand the mystery began to disappear after 1876, when the Japanese forced Korea to sign a treaty of commerce in which its independence was stated. Of the Western powers, the United States alone treated the Koreans as a free and independent people. But by the mid-1880s, the Chinese were already attempting to reassert their influence in Seoul.

American recognition of Korean independence indicated that the United States had adhered to its traditional policy of favoring self-determination. Certainly the Chinese could hope for no support from the American government. On the other hand, as admirable as the principle of self-determination was thought to be in Washington, there was no one in a responsible position there who was prepared to guarantee Korean independence. But there were several Americans in East Asia, most notably a missionary doctor, Horace Allen, who worked frenetically to counter Chinese efforts. Hoping to win the support of his government for Korean independence, he was involved in a series of intrigues with the Russians and Japanese for over a decade, at the end of which, although unsuccessful, he was named American minister to Korea!

Despite Allen's role, Korea's place in world politics was determined by Japan's decision in 1894 to tolerate no further extension of Chinese influence. With both nations considering Korea vital to their security, mounting tensions gave way to war. Within six months, the Japanese astonished not only the Chinese but the entire world as they utterly destroyed China's fleet and rolled over its armies in Korea, Manchuria, and China proper almost at will. The decay of the Middle Kingdom had been bared by the people to whom the Chinese referred contemptuously as the "dwarf nation." For Japan, victory brought increased prestige and, more tangibly, Taiwan, the Pescadores, and a sphere of influence in Korea. For China, defeat brought humiliation and the threat of imminent partition. Chinese civilization had been found wanting and East Asia abounded in would-be civilizers.

In Washington, the Sino-Japanese War and its outcome were easily accepted. The United States played its traditional role as disinterested neutral, refusing to become involved in mediation efforts and attempting to retain the goodwill of both nations. To the Cleveland administration, the war did not appear to threaten any American interests. Indeed, sentiment in Washington and among the concerned public generally was pro-Japanese. In part, American sympathies were with Japan because of feelings of paternalism related to the American role in opening that country and because of the great disparity in the size of the combatant countries. But there were also tremendous feelings of contempt for the Chinese and their apparent slothfulness. The American minister to China advised the secretary of state that Japan was only doing for China what the United States had done for Japan: bringing Western civilization. William Rockhill, probably the Department of State's most respected authority on Chinese affairs, insisted that "a good thrashing will not hurt China in the least. . . . It is the only tonic which seems to suit [her]."[2] Similarly, the press and periodic literature, the writings of businessmen and of missionaries reflected the conviction that the Sino-Japanese War was a contest between barbarism and civilization. To all, the Japanese victory provided hope that at last even the Chinese would see the need for reform. And inherent in the desire for the reform and modernization of China was the expectation on the part of government officials, businessmen, and missionaries that their particular interests would be served. The idea that Americans *constantly* believed that the modernization of China was in their interest cannot be overstressed.

China's humiliation provided Americans with only a brief time to gloat. In 1895, only pressure from Russia, Germany, and France prevented Japan from making further inroads into Chinese sovereignty. The European imperialists had not intervened out of sympathy for China, but rather to protect their own interests in East Asia and to be in a position to demand compensation for their efforts. Beginning only a few months after the conclusion of the war, increasing sharply in 1898, the scramble for concessions was underway. To the French, to the Russians, to the Germans, and ultimately to the British as well, went spheres of influence, mining and railroad development privileges—new sorrows for a powerless China—and cause for anxiety among Americans concerned with markets and with the balance of power in East Asia.

Across the Pacific, the American people gradually saw the wounds of civil war healed sufficiently to permit the United States to act again as one nation. With all of their energies under harness once more, they proceeded to industrialize rapidly and emerged in the 1890s as the foremost industrial state in the world. This rapid industrialization caused numerous political, economic, and social problems to which different segments of society reacted differently. One theme that recurred frequently was fear of stagnation, spiritual and economic. Religious leaders and even political figures like Theodore Roosevelt expressed the fear that their countrymen were becoming materialistic, that America was losing its spiritual vitality. But the business community and other political leaders were infected with fear of the more mundane danger of economic stagnation.

In the 1890s a rapidly expanding economy and an accelerated industrial output coincided with the reported closing of the American frontier—an event memorialized in the writings of Frederick Jackson Turner. With the opportunities for developing internal markets apparently no longer without limit, the quest began for foreign markets. In the wake of the Panic of 1893, the worst depression the nation had ever experienced, a sense of impending disaster flowed through the land. To ease the economic crisis, the Populists demanded free silver and the business community was convinced that expansion of overseas markets would provide salvation. Although the greatest effort to find such markets was focused on Latin America and Europe, expectations of vastly increased trade with China were always present. And in the 1890s, trade with China, although never more than an infinitesimal part of total American trade, did grow. The business community became increasingly confident that markets for American exports could be found, increasingly confident that given an equal opportunity, efficient production and marketing procedures would assure the United States of a position of dominance in the realm of international trade. But for those businessmen with interests in China, the chain of events following the Sino-Japanese War allowed no room for complacency.

The government of the United States, during the administrations of Grover Cleveland and William McKinley, was responsive to the fears of economic theorists, merchants, and investors and willing to make efforts to expand trade and to improve the competitive position of Americans in the world market. But the American stake in China was not sufficiently important to warrant much governmental activity there. Nonetheless, in the last months of the Cleveland administration, the American minister to China, Charles Denby, received his long-sought-after instructions to use his influence to extend American commercial interests. For a few months he had the opportunity to demand that the Chinese give consideration to the proposals of American entrepreneurs and speculators, but he was soon reined in by the McKinley administration. Despite the dramatic events of the Sino-Japanese War and the scramble for concessions that followed, few Americans were greatly interested in the Far East, and fewer still were disturbed by governmental inaction. Under these circumstances, businessmen who sought a more active policy toward China were faced with an apparently hopeless situation. In January 1898, they formed an organization, later called the American Asiatic Association, for the express purpose of arousing public opinion—and through it the government—to the threat they believed events in China posed to the interests of the United States. But in the winter of 1898, the American people and their government were far more concerned with a critical situation much closer to home: the Cuban insurrection.

On February 15, 1898, the battleship *Maine* blew up in Havana Harbor. Less than ten weeks later, the United States was at war with Spain—the crusade to liberate Cuba was under way. Incidental to the operations against Spain was an order sent on April 24 to George Dewey, in command of the American Asiatic Fleet: proceed to the Philippines and destroy the Spanish fleet there.

Dewey carried out his assignment, and approximately three months later, Spain was prepared to accept the defeat in battle which it had fully anticipated but which the court had believed preferable to ignoble surrender. The Philippines had fallen to rebel and American arms, and the painful task of determining the future of these islands rested with President McKinley. After several months, the president yielded to the impulse to imperialism. The United States acquired a distant colony. America had an empire.

The roots of American imperialism were varied, and only a fool or an ideologue would insist on one cause for the decision to take the Philippines. But it must be remembered that American businessmen, hitherto opposed to the acquisition of colonies, convinced that superiority in production and marketing techniques would guarantee the commercial hegemony of the United States, now had reason to change their minds. While some worried about economic stagnation at home and others worried about threatened European reprisals against the Dingley tariff, still others warned that European and Japanese imperialists were in the process of closing the door to American commerce in China. Now Dewey's victory at Manila provided an opportunity for the United States to establish a foothold in the Far Fast, to be in a position to compete with the other powers for the treasures and markets of the Orient. As Richard Leopold has written, "the desire for the Philippines and a concern for China became mutually supporting"[3]—and there was no shortage of men to call this to the president's attention. These were not the only voices McKinley

TABLE 2.1   The American Economic Stake in China, 1890–1904[a]

Year	U.S. Exports to China (in $ million)	Percentage of Total U.S. Export Trade	U.S. Investments in China (in $ million)	Percentage of Total U.S. Investments Overseas
1890	3	0.3		
1891	9	1.0		
1892	7	0.7		
1893	4	0.5		
1894	6	0.7		
1895	4	0.5		
1896	7	0.8		
1897	12	1.1		
1898	10	0.8		
1899	14	1.1		
1900	15	1.1		
1901	10	0.7		
1902	25	1.8	19.7	1.2
1903	19	1.3		
1904	13	0.9		

[a]Figures for this and subsequent tables are compiled on the basis of information provided in *Historical Statistics of the United States, 1789–1945*, *Foreign Commerce and Navigation of the United States*, and C. F. Remer, *Foreign Investments in China* (New York: Macmillan, 1933). Statistics on investments comparable to those on trade are not available.

heard urging him on, nor is there any evidence to suggest that he listened to these with particular care. But if, as is generally accepted, the opposition of business interests to war with Spain had reinforced McKinley's own reluctance, then the absence of business opposition to imperialism in the fall of 1898 made McKinley's decision to follow the will of the public that much easier. The United States became an Asiatic power.

The foothold in the Philippines was not, however, enough. Businessmen concerned with trade in China remained uneasy, demanding more vigorous action by their government. McKinley assured Congress that the imperialist powers in China were not discriminating against the United States, but this failed to comfort men who sought markets there. In addition, the acquisition of the Philippines had led to naval interest in a coaling station or base in China and had focused public attention on East Asia in a way that exceeded even the hopes of the lobbyists and publicists of the American Asiatic Association. The pressures on the Department of State mounted in 1899 and before the year was out, Secretary of State John Hay decided to act.

By 1899, the United States had become a world power in the sense that it was not only the greatest industrial nation, but it was also willing to use its new power militarily, after the fashion of the European states American leaders sought to emulate. It had acquired possessions near and far, and the sun shone on the American flag unfurled in East Asia as well as in the eastern Pacific and in the Caribbean. The mood of the American people was assertive and they were prepared to accept, though they did not demand, a more vigorous Far Eastern policy.

President McKinley had remained concerned about events in China even during the war with Spain, but accepted assurances from the powers that they had no intention of disturbing American interests in the spheres of interest they were defining for themselves. Neither British overtures for joint action in China in 1898 nor the lobbying of the American Asiatic Association sufficed to move the administration to action. But there were other currents flowing through the United States, ideas about the importance of China in the world balance of power and about the importance of the United States in the Far Eastern balance. Brooks Adams and Alfred Mahan, generally recognized as the ideologues of American imperialism, both placed great stress on the importance of the power struggle in East Asia, and their views were often reflected in the writings and speeches of Henry Cabot Lodge and Theodore Roosevelt. In 1899, among the men identified with the thought of Adams, Mahan, Lodge, and Roosevelt, the acknowledged expert on China was William Rockhill, and it was to Rockhill that Secretary Hay turned for advice on Far Eastern policy.

Rockhill had perceived what few others yet realized: that the breakup of China would be a disaster. Some of the world's statesmen viewed the disintegration of the Manchu empire with indifference if not outright glee. Rockhill, however, was convinced that a sovereign China, able to preserve order within its own boundaries, was essential to the balance of power in Asia. Consequently, the collapse of China would lead to an intensification of the imperialist rivalry already begun—and possibly to a world war. To prevent catastrophe, he believed the United States should use its new position in Asia and its growing influence in the world for the preservation of China's existence as a nation. If necessary, he was willing to have the United States declare its intention to assist China in maintaining its territorial integrity.

Though Rockhill had a deep interest in and affection for Chinese culture, it was not love of China or the Chinese that led to his advocacy of an American initiative on behalf of Chinese sovereignty. Rather, he viewed stability in East Asia as essential to the development of American economic interests there and to the fulfillment of America's mission as an Asiatic power—and he saw a viable Chinese state as essential to stability. Nonetheless, neither McKinley nor Hay considered the reality of American interests sufficient to justify so drastic a departure from traditional inactivity, nor did they believe the American people prepared for so bold a step. Instead, a chance visit to Washington by Alfred Hippisley, an old friend of Rockhill's, led the United States to undertake a more limited initiative.

Hippisley, an Englishman, was on his way home on leave from his post with the Chinese Imperial Maritime Customs Service. He advised Rockhill of his concern over the scramble for concessions in China and of his fear that the powers with spheres of influence would drive the Customs Service out of their spheres, denying to the Chinese government the proceeds of the tariff. Recognizing the fact that the money collected by the Customs Service was the only assured source of income for Peking, Rockhill well understood the threat to the effectiveness of the Chinese regime. Though not as explicit a danger as the violation of China's territorial integrity, the loss of tariff revenues would gradually but no less certainly bring the end of China's administrative control of its provinces. No government can function without money.

In Washington, and later after reaching London, Hippisley exchanged ideas with Rockhill and drafted a statement that became in its essentials the policy expressed by John Hay in the first of his famed "Open Door" notes. Intended as a note to each of the powers that had acquired spheres of influence in China, Hippisley's draft requested that within their spheres they agree not to discriminate against the trade of other countries nor to interfere with Customs Service collection of tariff duties. If the imperialist powers acquiesced, the goods of all nations would be assured equal treatment in all parts of China. For the United States, which had no sphere of its own, such an agreement was of obvious value. The existence of spheres of influence would cease to be a threat to the growing American trade with China. Markets would be available to those who sought them, pleasing the American Asiatic Association and alleviating concern over economic stagnation. If the Imperial Maritime Customs Service were permitted to continue to function as before, the Chinese government would have revenue necessary for *it* to function—and it would retain a semblance of sovereignty within the spheres of influence. Rockhill would have preferred a stronger statement on behalf of China's sovereignty and territorial integrity, but he realized that his superiors would go no further

China and the imperialists, c. 1900

at this time. He forwarded the draft to Hay, who accepted it and without substantive revisions sent appropriate copies to the various powers, seeking their commitment to the ideas it contained. The notes were the ideal solution to the administration's quest for a new policy toward East Asia that would satisfy the pressures from those who, like Rockhill, were concerned with power politics, from those who sought the expansion of American economic interests, from romantic nationalists eager to see the United States playing a larger role in world affairs—all this without risking an overseas involvement that would disturb a people notoriously skittish about foreign entanglements.

Although the "Open Door" notes served the purposes of the United States, the other powers perceived little benefit for themselves in endorsing a request that they pursue a policy of self-denial in areas under their control. In return for a promise of equal treatment for their commodities, the Americans offered nothing. On the other hand, the United States had not challenged the existence of spheres of influence, nor had it asked for equal opportunity for investment in the various spheres. For the Russians and Japanese, investments in railroad and mining development were crucial, of strategic as well as economic importance. For all of the powers, though there was little to gain from agreeing to the American policy declaration, there was also little to lose. Although no country was eager to bind itself gratuitously to principles it might later find it expedient to violate, no country was willing to offer the United States a gratuitous insult by rejecting the American request. Therefore, most replies were evasive and qualified, as each nation protected the particular interests dearest to it; but all, in effect, endorsed the principles put forth in Hay's notes—and Japan offered no reservations whatever. For the moment, Hay's effort was successful and he and McKinley announced that American interests in China had been safeguarded.

It is worth noting that Hay at no time consulted with the Chinese government, at no time sought any expression of China's needs. To the extent that American policy buttressed Chinese sovereignty, it was of value to China. But the notes were intended to serve the interests of the United States, and their value to China was incidental, a means to American ends. Nonetheless, there is no iron law of interests such as classical economists assumed for wages, and it is clear that in 1899 Chinese and American interests were not incompatible. Both Hay and Rockhill were convinced that the step they had taken had contributed meaningfully to the preservation of the Chinese empire.

The Chinese, however, showed little gratitude. In fact, during the period in which the "Open Door" notes were formulated and delivered, relations between China and the United States were very tense as a result of American discrimination against Chinese immigrants and the extension of discriminatory practices to the new American territories of Hawaii and the Philippines. In September 1899, the month in which the notes were sent to the powers, the Chinese minister to the United States, Wu T'ing-fang, protested against the "utter disregard of the American government for the friendly relations which should exist between the two governments."[4] For several years afterward, instead of the goodwill that Rockhill and Hay had hoped to reap for the United States by their support of China, they harvested the bitter reward due American racists.

In sum, the notes John Hay sent to the powers in 1899 were not intended as an act of benevolence on China's behalf, nor were they so viewed by the Chinese. The notes were expected to serve the interests of the United States in China and East Asia generally as these interests were perceived by the McKinley administration. For over one hundred years Americans had been crossing the Pacific in search of trade and on Christian missions. In the 1890s, the men involved in these activities in China believed that their interests were threatened by the impending disintegration of China, and they hoped for, begged for, and demanded more active support than the American government had ever been willing to give such activities—more active support than the American people had ever been willing to countenance. But the decade of the 1890s found the American people in a different mood. Some historians have referred to a "national neurosis" or a "psychic crisis." Some have referred to social Darwinism or the desire to emulate Europe to explain the change in the United States. But clearly, the American people were prepared to have their government act more vigorously in world affairs. In 1898 they had supported, indeed driven, their government into a crusade to liberate Cuba. Before the year was out, they had indicated their willingness to become an imperial power and had extended American influence to East Asia with the acquisition of the Philippines.

The United States became a power in East Asia immediately after the equilibrium of the area had been shattered by the overwhelming victory of Japan in the Sino-Japanese War and by the race among the European imperialists to grab the choicer shards of the helpless Chinese empire. As Americans in China saw their personal interests threatened, theorists in the United States argued that the nation's interests were at stake in the outcome of the incipient struggle. Rockhill and others believed that these interests could all be served by the preservation and modernization of China. Given the fact that the United States was in no position to guarantee China's territorial integrity, in no position to drive the powers back from the inroads they had already made into Chinese sovereignty, the McKinley administration chose instead to seek the possible: the protection of the material interests of Americans in China by the request for equal treatment of American goods and a modest effort to sustain the prestige and effectiveness of the Chinese government. The response to the notes left much to be desired but brought Hay and McKinley, as well as Hippisley and Rockhill, all they could have hoped to achieve with six pieces of paper. In relation to American interests and strength in East Asia in 1899, Hay's initiative was sound and, for the moment, successful.

Hay and his colleagues had hoped that by exhorting the imperialist nations to ease their pressures, the Chinese government might be able to improve its administration and modernize, thus providing for a stable balance of power and the realization of American ends. But it was already too late to prop up the Manchu dynasty. The tide of dynastic power had long since begun to ebb and Western encroachments, ideological as well as physical, had further complicated the Manchus' efforts to stem the flow. The West had not set the process of dynastic decline in motion—nor could its impact be great enough to reverse that process.

Missionaries had been among the principal purveyors of Western ideology in China and as such contributed to the unrest that existed in China during the 1890s—unrest of which the Boxer uprising was only the most sensational manifestation. Partly because of their ideological role and partly because they were, particularly in the rural missions, the most vulnerable foreign representatives, they became with increasing frequency the targets of Chinese resentment against foreign intrusion. Americans were often among the victims of these antimissionary activities.

The American missionary effort in China, which had begun in the 1830s, had been revitalized in the 1890s, partly as a response to fear of spiritual stagnation. Just as theorists contended that overseas markets would alleviate the danger of economic stagnation, overseas crusades were sought to keep religious fervor at revival level in the United States. One writer contended that Christianity was a religion that would not "keep." If it could not be renewed abroad through missionary activity, Christianity would stagnate at home; the church could not otherwise survive the temptations of materialism.

There is no need to doubt the inherent idealism of the American men and women who served the Christian missions in China. They surrendered the comforts of family and familiar surroundings and went off to face unknown dangers—in answer to the call of their God. Perhaps the greatest danger they faced came from the very people to whom they hoped to bring salvation—from the heathens who were hostile to them and to their teachings. The Chinese had not asked the missionaries to come. So long as the Chinese government had the power to do so, it had forbidden the propagation of Christianity in China. Over the years, the Western powers had forced the Chinese to make one concession after another to permit the missionaries to function where they were not wanted. Despite the idealism of the missionaries, they functioned as a part of the treaty system. Christian missions existed in China because foreign gunboats protected the missionaries, and they were constant reminders of the humiliations China had suffered at the hands of the West.

In China, the Christian missionaries with their belief in the superiority of their faith met their match in the Chinese with their conviction of the superiority of their own culture. Measured in terms of converts, missionary successes were few, but the Christian attack on Chinese customs and the frequency with which local scoundrels obtained church protection inevitably antagonized many Chinese, leading to widespread unrest. As a result, antagonisms grew between the missionaries and the Chinese gentry and the missionaries came to believe that the gentry, the backbone of traditional Chinese society, were the principal obstacle to their success. Having unconsciously worked at destroying traditional society through the introduction of subversive ideas, the missionaries became convinced that the destruction of the old order was essential to the fulfillment of the Christian mission. It was in the hope that the hour of their frustration might be past that American missionaries to China had welcomed the Japanese victory in 1895.

The aftermath of the Sino-Japanese War brought not Christianity triumphant but rather more widespread antimissionary activity in China. Although damage to American missions and injuries to American missionaries were relatively slight, the government of the United States responded with unusual vigor. In 1895, the same year in which he informed the

British that America's wish was law in the Western hemisphere, Secretary of State Richard Olney wrote of the need to "leave no doubt in the mind of the Chinese government or the people in the interior that the United States is an effective factor for securing due rights for Americans resident in China."[5] Fortunately the Chinese yielded on the point at issue before the American minister's desire to have a Chinese town leveled had to be satisfied.

However, Chinese antimissionary riots continued and the pressures of missionaries demanding protection and retribution merged with the assertive mood of the American people generally and led to more vigorous representations by the American government. In this way, the missionaries, like the business community, contributed to the milieu in which a new American policy toward China emerged during the McKinley administration. Just as the churches had supported American imperialism in the quest for more areas in which to spread Protestant Christianity, so they supported a new American initiative in China to further their interest there.

But the months that followed Hay's notes were not marked by reforms leading to the modernization of China's government or society. Indeed, the most promising reform movement of the decade had been smashed in 1898, while the United States fought Spain. Led by K'ang Yu-wei, a Confucian scholar, a group of intellectuals and officials had provided the emperor with a program for sweeping changes in economic, political, military, and educational policy. But even the support of the emperor proved insufficient in face of the opposition of those who considered the reforms too radical. Rallying around Tz'u Hsi, the empress dowager, they succeeded in imprisoning the emperor, halting the reform movement, and executing six of K'ang Yu-wei's closest supporters. At the time of the American initiative in 1899, Tz'u Hsi was firmly in control and the prospects for modernization were poor. Moreover, she and her cohorts channeled unrest spreading through North China into an antiforeign movement. Ultimately led by men known as the Boxers, a loose amalgam of local martial arts and invulnerability ritual societies, the movement was determined to drive the foreigners out of China. The destruction of mission properties and the murder of Chinese Christians increased.

Joining with several European nations, the United States demanded that the Chinese government put an end to the outrages against missionaries and their converts, but to no avail. On occasion the court yielded to pressures and transferred officials offensive to the West, but Tz'u Hsi became determined to take the initiative. The successes of the Boxers in Shantung and Shansi brought confidence that foreign influence could be purged from China forever. China had suffered enough—all foreigners would die and there would be an end once and for all to imperialist encroachments and subversion. To the magic powers allegedly possessed by the Boxers, Tz'u Hsi added the modern arms of the imperial army. She called the Boxers to Peking and ordered the massacre of all foreigners, including the entire diplomatic community. In June 1900, the German minister was killed by a Chinese soldier and the court declared war on all the *war on all foreigners!* powers. Suddenly, the legation quarter became an embattled fortress, subjected to incessant attack, cut off from outside contacts. For almost two months, public attention throughout much of the world focused on the progress of Western and Japanese troops fighting their way in from the coast, seeking to reach Peking in time to save some of the men, women, and children surrounded by the Boxers. In the besieged quarter sat the American minister, E. H. Conger, who months earlier had urged the use of American gunboats, insisting that nothing but a show of strength would move the Chinese. After the Boxer atrocities—the torture and slaughter of hundreds of missionaries and thousands of Chinese Christians—there were many missionaries whose faith did not prevent them from reaching the same conclusion.

The war with Spain had brought American soldiers to East Asia, and the responsibilities of empire, the suppression of the Filipino insurrection, had required the continued presence of these men in Asia. With the lives of American diplomats, businessmen, and missionaries threatened in China, the McKinley administration had both the resources and the will to protect its people and their interests against the Chinese. Among the troops that ultimately defeated the Boxers and lifted the siege of the legations were several thousand Americans. But long before they reached Peking, Hay had sent off another round of notes.

As the war between China and the powers began, Hay realized that American hopes for averting the collapse of China were in jeopardy. The possibility of voluntary restraint by the powers suddenly seemed remote. The Manchus, seeking to preserve the dynasty, had joined with the secret societies, in a desperate effort to channel all dissatisfaction into an antiforeign movement rather than into the customary pattern of antidynastic movements. Given the war and the need for an expedition to relieve the foreigners at Peking, it was likely that the powers generally and the

Russians particularly would find sufficient pretext for further encroachments on Chinese sovereignty. Once the foreign armies marched on Chinese soil, it might well prove difficult to remove them—and it might prove very difficult to protect American interests in China.

In July 1900, after consultations with Rockhill, Hippisley, and Elihu Root, Hay sent off a circular message in which he expressed concern for the importance of preserving Chinese sovereignty, "the territorial and administrative entity" of China. More significantly, he defined the situation in China as a state of "virtual anarchy" in which power and responsibility rested in fact with local authorities. So long as these authorities kept the peace in the areas under their control, they would be regarded as representing the Chinese people. Working from this premise, the McKinley administration proceeded to develop contacts with high-ranking Chinese officials like Li Hung-chang and Chang Chih-tung, who controlled the southern and central provinces, and to provide strong diplomatic support for their efforts to limit the war to North China. Li, Chang, and other powerful Chinese officials suppressed the Boxers and provided protection for foreigners and foreign property. In return the United States successfully deflected proposals from the powers to extend operations against the Boxers to other parts of China. As a result of this Sino-American cooperation, it was possible to preserve the myth that the Boxers were acting spontaneously, rebelling against the Chinese government as well as engaging in hostilities with the powers. Thus the war could be limited in area and intensity and the possible partition of China forestalled. The role the United States sought to play was precisely the role that Rockhill had created for it, that of the manipulator of the Far Eastern balance of power.

In his circular note, Hay had stated American policy for the benefit of the powers. He sought no commitments from them nor did he make any threats. Though American interests in East Asia were sufficient to warrant the kind of force necessary to protect them against Filipinos and Chinese, the United States had no interests in the area great enough to warrant the use of force on the scale necessary to threaten any of the major powers. The United States was opposed to further dismemberment of China and recommended a policy of self-denial to the other powers involved in the international expedition to relieve Peking. And in 1900, as in 1899, the great powers were prepared to accede, at least for the moment, to American wishes—not out of fear of the United States or out of admiration for the principles the Americans professed, but because of the essential wisdom of the course Hay proposed. The satisfaction of further imperialistic ambitions could await a more propitious moment.

The strength of the American position rested in part on the presence of American troops among the forces that had liberated Peking. If the United States was prepared to retain this military posture on the Asian mainland, it might be able to exert considerable influence on the outcome of the negotiations between China and the powers. If American forces were withdrawn from China, the opportunity to shape the peace settlement, to protect and perhaps even further American interests, might be lost.

At home, the McKinley administration found an ambiguous mandate. There had been enormous concern for the safety of Americans trapped in Peking and participation in the relief expedition met, therefore, with general approval. Consistent with the mood of the previous decade, missionaries and businessmen with interests in China continued to press for a vigorous American role in the settlement. But there were also signs pointing in the opposite direction. The anti-imperialist movement was strong and the administration was concerned about military requirements in the Philippines. An involvement in China in hostilities any more strenuous than those of the relief expedition—and with ends less obviously humanitarian—might bring a disastrously negative response from the American people. In addition, the country's resources for military operations would almost certainly be stretched beyond tolerance. Indeed, the military was already anxious to withdraw from China in order to carry out its mission in the Philippines. In sum, the administration recognized that public interest in China was superficial, that it was neither broad enough nor deep enough for the government to be able to muster the support it would need to become involved in power politics on the Asian mainland. In addition, Hay and McKinley realized that though the United States was of necessity concerned with the balance of power in East Asia, though the United States had tangible economic and humanitarian interests there, none of these concerns or interests were worth fighting for.

On the specific question of the nature of the Boxer settlement, American opinion formed a pattern that was to recur. Those with experience in China, the "old China hands," including missionaries, insisted on a policy of firmness, warning that the Chinese would mistake generosity for weakness. Their contacts with Chinese officials had often been abrasive, limiting their sentimental visions. They cherished not China, but the opportunities China gave them—opportunities to reform that "benighted" country, to fulfill their Christian missions, or to make profits. With specific tasks to perform, they refused to indulge in the affectionate kind of pity for the Chinese that was emerging in the United States. Americans free from involvement in Chinese affairs tended to be less vindictive and more wary of becoming entangled in the imperialist intrigues of other powers. Whether private citizens concerned with foreign policy, congressmen, or members of the administration, they were more likely to favor policies framed in terms of traditional American principles of nonintervention, consistent with the newly developing conception of the United States as China's benefactor. The more ignorant that men are of the particulars of a given situation, the more likely they are to respond to it with time-honored universal precepts—though neither side in this debate could claim a monopoly of ignorance.

Lacking a clear mandate, the McKinley administration chose not to withdraw American troops from Peking after the liberation of that city, but withdrew them instead from the allied command under which they had fought their way from the coast. No new troops were committed to East Asia and some were withdrawn from China. Nonetheless, an American military presence remained as evidence of continued American concern. In the negotiations, the United States opposed all proposals that might weaken the Chinese government, as Hay continued to hope for a stable China. If China collapsed and were partitioned, the United States would then face the unhappy task of having to defend its interest in various parts of the empire against adversaries far more formidable than the Chinese. In addition, the unknown outcome of the struggle likely to commence in the vacuum created by the destruction of China was infinitely more threatening than was the existing precarious balance.

The protocol ending the war was signed in September 1901, after a delay occasioned by disputes over the size and distribution of the indemnity to be exacted from China. The powers ultimately agreed on an enormous sum, equivalent to more than $300 million, of which the United States was allotted approximately $25 million. In addition to this tremendous financial burden, China was forced to grant to her conquerors the right to station troops between Peking and the sea—new protection for foreigners in North China and new monuments to China's weakness. China's borders, however, remained intact.

Had American efforts failed to prevent the carving up of China, the McKinley administration was prepared to request a modest portion of the melon for the United States. In particular, naval circles in Washington had been pressing the government to acquire territory in China for a coaling station. Unconvinced of the need for such a base, Hay did nothing until after the Boxer incident, when the pressures on him became particularly intense. A refusal to attempt to obtain the requested territory would have left the administration vulnerable to charges that it was less than vigilant in its efforts to protect Americans overseas—in that it had denied the navy the coaling station the navy needed to fulfill its mission. Therefore, in December 1900, Hay made a perfunctory effort to acquire Samsah Bay in Fukien province, retreating before the first rebuff. Fortunately for America's self-image, China had promised Japan that no territory in Fukien would ever be ceded to a third power. But neither Hay nor McKinley was opposed in principle to acquiring Chinese territory if there were no easier way to serve American interests. Nothing in Hay's notes, either of 1899 or of 1900, committed the United States to a policy of self-denial any more than to a policy of preserving China's sovereignty.

In 1901, following the assassination of McKinley, Theodore Roosevelt became president of the United States, but Far Eastern policy remained the dominion of John Hay until the Russo-Japanese War began in 1904. During these few years, interest in the Far East, never very great in the United States, nearly vanished altogether. Traditional preoccupation with domestic affairs replaced the expansive mood of the 1890s. For Hay and others who continued to be involved with the affairs of China, these years brought little satisfaction. The material interests of the United States fared badly, as American trade declined sharply. The balance of power in the area was threatened by Russian adventurism, and tensions grew between the United States and Russia. But for those more easily satisfied, there were signs that the Chinese government had at last recognized its past follies and that even Tz'u Hsi was prepared to undertake genuine reforms.

Sino-American relations in these few years were really a three-cornered game with Russia playing the third hand and the Chinese attempting to manipulate Russians and Americans to their own advantage. Following the defeat of the Boxers, the Russians left little doubt of their intention of gaining virtually complete control over Manchuria. For American businessmen, particularly those exporting cotton textiles, Manchuria was an important market, absorbing 90 percent of the goods they sold in China. Through the American Asiatic Association and the business press, these men expressed their fears that Russian domination would jeopardize their markets, actual and potential. And they were right; the Russians did not hesitate to discriminate against the nationals of other powers—or to make a mockery of China's claims to sovereignty over her northeastern provinces.

The Russo-American conflict was rooted in American visions of markets in China and in a justifiable concern for the future of existing trade in North China generally and Manchuria in particular. Without this economic interest in the area, it was unlikely that the United States would have continued to oppose Russian encroachments actively. Roosevelt was initially indifferent, suggesting that Russian expansion into China would be good for the Chinese. Consistent with his usual defense of imperialism, he argued that the world benefited when a "civilized power" expanded "at the expense of barbarism." Admitting that he might change his mind if he knew more about American trade needs, he wrote that "exactly as Turkestan has been benefited by Russia's advance, so I think China would be."[6] To be sure, he and others accepted the idea that the United States had a strategic concern in the East Asian power balance, but it was clearly not a vital concern. Russian and Japanese security might be directly affected by events in Manchuria, but in the early years of the twentieth century few Americans could have been led to believe that their own security was at stake.

Given the limits of American interests in Manchuria, Hay and Roosevelt sought merely to obtain from the Russians assurances of fair treatment for American trade. But the Japanese, to whom Russian advances in the area presented a much more tangible threat, were sufficiently concerned to consider the use of force. Early in 1901, they sounded out Hay on the possibility of joint action, but Hay replied unequivocally that the United States was not prepared to use force, singly or in concert with other powers, to achieve its goals in China. American military power in East Asia was reserved for protecting the lives of American nationals and defending the existing territories of the United States.

Determined to stop the Russian advance, the Japanese soon found an ally in Great Britain. Anglo-Japanese cooperation was formalized by treaty in 1902 and the two nations worked intently to prevent Russian domination of Manchuria and to stiffen China's will to resist the demands of the tsar's minions. Soon it became apparent to Hay that the United States could capitalize on Russia's distress, intensifying American pressures while the Russians had to worry about the more dangerous challenge posed by the British and the Japanese. Without joining the alliance, without making any commitments, the United States collaborated with Russia's enemies, attempting to exploit their power for American ends.

As part of his effort to secure American interests in China, Hay began negotiations for a new Sino-American trade treaty in 1902. While the negotiations proceeded, Russian actions in Manchuria convinced him of the need to request the opening of two new treaty ports in those provinces. But, fearful of antagonizing the Russians, the Chinese hesitated. Once the Russians learned of the American demand, they made every effort to force the Chinese to reject it, threatening to retain their troops in Manchuria, perhaps putting them to further use. Although the Russians may have been concerned about the possibility of the new ports endangering the superior competitive position their trade enjoyed while they controlled Manchuria, their principal concern was strategic. If the ports were open to Americans, all the other powers, by means of the most-favored-nation clause in their treaties, would also have access to them. To the Russians, this conjured up visions of hordes of Japanese moving into these cities, creating an immense security problem for Russian forces in the area.

Caught between American demands and Russian threats, the Chinese tried desperately to manipulate the situation to their own advantage. Li Hung-chang was dead, and of the great nineteenth-century mandarins, only Chang Chih-tung remained. With the help of the former minister to the United States, Wu T'ing-fang, Chang succeeded in convincing Yüan Shih-k'ai of the value of opening the Manchurian ports. Yüan had emerged as a powerful figure in North China, with great influence at the court, and his support for the Chang-Wu plan was sufficient for it to be tried. None of these Chinese officials were interested in the trade questions involved, but sought to preserve Chinese sovereignty in Manchuria by bringing in the other powers, especially the United States, Great Britain, and Japan, as a countervailing force against Russia. Once again the Chinese were using the concept of equal treatment of all foreigners in an attempt to use them against each other.

Until the Chinese agreed to open the ports, irritation with the Russians mounted in Washington. Privately, Roosevelt made martial noises, contending that he would be willing to resolve the issue by force were there a likelihood of public support. Hay threatened and cajoled the Russian minister, even warning that the United States might join forces with Great Britain and Japan if the Russians did not stop interfering with the Sino-American negotiations. Roosevelt insisted that the United States did not seek to prevent Russian political control in Manchuria: "All we ask is that our great and growing trade shall not be interrupted and that Russia shall keep its solemn promises. . . . We have always recognized the exceptional position of Russia in relation to Manchuria."[7]

In July 1903, he informed Hay that he had no objection to the Russians' knowing that he was thoroughly aroused and irritated and that he did not intend to yield. Later in the month he wrote again, reminding Hay that "I wish, in Manchuria, to go to the very limit I think our people will stand. If only we were sure neither France nor Germany would join in, I should not in the least mind going to 'extremes' with Russia!"[8]

Russian-American tensions were not eased, however, until the Russians realized that the Americans would not insist on the right of settlement in the new treaty ports. Believing that they could allow the Americans to have their open ports without having to permit Japanese intrusions into what they considered their sphere, the Russians withdrew their opposition to the proposed Sino-American treaty. At this point, the Chinese tried to use the Americans to force a Russian troop withdrawal, by announcing that they would open the ports as soon as Russian forces withdrew from them. But once again, this traditional Chinese tactic failed, as the Americans refused to consider the two issues related. The United States insisted that the ports be opened immediately, regardless of the disposition of Russian troops, and the Chinese were forced to yield.

Although the Russians continued to create problems in Manchuria, discriminating against American trade and encroaching on Chinese sovereignty, the crisis between the United States and Russia had passed. Hay continued to protest against Russian policy, but the Japanese government had decided that the time had come for action. Angered by the Russian refusal to permit settlement in the newly open treaty ports, the Japanese pressed for a showdown. The tsarist government, underestimating Japanese power and determination, misjudging the effect of shifting European coalitions on Asian affairs, perhaps hoping a glorious war would stave off revolution, refused to yield. In February 1904, the Japanese tired of Russian stalling and suddenly attacked the Russian fleet at Port Arthur, to the delight of Roosevelt and every other American who saw his interests in China threatened by Russian imperialism. For them all, as Roosevelt wrote, Japan was playing "our game."

Toward the close of the nineteenth century, after the United States had harnessed its vast energies and become a great industrial power, some of its leaders and many of its people sought to see the nation act as a world power. In 1898, annoyed by Spanish policies in Cuba, the United States trounced Spain, liberated Cuba, and annexed several Spanish colonies, most notably the Philippine Islands. In this way, the United States became an <u>Asiatic power</u>, and now that it had arrived on the scene a statement of American policy was appropriate. But there was nothing new about American interests in East Asia generally or in China specifically. Hay's statement, known as the "Open Door" notes, came as the natural culmination of over one hundred years of American involvement in China. After all these years, the United States had concluded that its interests, economic, cultural, and strategic, were best served by the preservation of the Chinese empire—a view that most of the powers had shared, at least until 1895. Where Chinese sovereignty had been or would be impaired, within the spheres of influence controlled by outside powers, the United States sought equal treatment of the goods of all nations, presuming such practice to be advantageous to American exports. When, as in the first few years of the twentieth century, one of the great powers was determined both to encroach upon Chinese sovereignty and to discriminate against American goods, the United States would express its disapproval, but neither Hay nor either of the presidents he served had any illusions about the extent of American interests in China or in East Asia generally. These interests had long existed. They might become much greater. But they were not vital interests. They were worth diplomatic support, but they were not worth the risk of war with a major power.

The United States entered the twentieth century as an Asiatic power. But despite the importance that businessmen and missionaries attached to their activities in China, neither the people nor the government of the United States could long focus on Asian affairs. There were much more important problems to be dealt with at home. And for those less provincial, the problems of Europe were obviously of greater significance.

3   In the Light of the Rising Sun

Roosevelt's delight over Japanese military success in 1904 was limited by his awareness that Japan might prove to be an even more formidable opponent of American interests in East Asia than Russia. He warned that while the other great powers with interests in the area would have "divided interests, divided cares, double burdens," Japan would have "but one care, one interest, one burden."[1] He was aware that a Japanese victory might someday mean war between the United States and Japan, but he remained confident that if the Japanese were treated with respect, a Japanese-American conflict could be averted. He rejoiced in Japan's assault on Russian hegemony in Manchuria because he was convinced that damage to American interests could be no greater after a Japanese victory. As the war progressed, however, he expressed the desire to see Russia at least survive as an Asiatic power to serve as a check on Japan, keeping Japan's attention focused on the mainland. If Russian power remained sufficiently intact to maintain a semblance of a balance of power in Manchuria, Japan would be less likely to look covetously toward the Philippines and more likely to offer the other powers favorable opportunities for their commerce in the area. Similarly, a less than complete Japanese triumph allowed greater hope for the preservation of Chinese sovereignty over Manchuria and North China. For the remainder of Roosevelt's life, and for years afterward, the problem of how to coexist with Japan's power troubled those responsible for determining American policy in East Asia.

Despite Roosevelt's preoccupation with domestic affairs, his great interest in world politics resulted in close attention to European affairs. He was concerned with the affairs of Asia only during times of crisis, and the most serious of these were between Japan and the United States, the harvest of American racism. While Roosevelt was president, China did not become a serious issue in Japanese-American relations. Indeed, despite the rhetoric of his friends, Brooks Adams and Alfred Mahan, and despite some of his own earlier thoughts, Roosevelt as president found no vital American interests in China and devoted little time or attention to that country.

Indifference to China derived not only from the relatively greater pressures of more urgent affairs, but also from the decline in American economic interests there. In North China and Manchuria, where American cotton textile exports had prospered in the 1890s, trade fell off sharply in the first decade of the twentieth century. In part, political pressure by Russia and then Japan was responsible, but of far greater significance was the decline in American interest in China as a market. There would always be publicists trying to evoke the promise of that market and there would always be a few entrepreneurs, diplomats, and adventurers who would return to the dream; but in general American exporters made no effort to hold or expand their share, and American investors consistently preferred the surer profits to be found elsewhere. Though a few writers might offer eloquent testimony of the potential of China as a source of wealth, the American businessmen who had operated there knew better. They were increasingly aware that the Chinese populace neither had nor was for some time likely to have meaningful purchasing power. They became aware of the absence of an internal system of communications, of the lack of transportation facilities in China. Perhaps of greater significance, the economic panic of the 1890s had passed and in a time of renewed faith in the American economic system, the quest for overseas markets became less frantic and, though never abandoned, was pursued more rationally in less exotic places. Those merchants who continued the quest in China tended to be those least receptive to the advice of American consular officials. They sent goods for which the Chinese had little or no use. They packaged their goods badly. Unlike their British and Japanese competitors, few American firms kept agents in China. They provided no credit facilities or sales organizations. In short, as a result of apathy and ineptitude, the American share of the market in China dwindled.

With Russian expansion having been checked by the Japanese, the years immediately following the defeat of the Boxers witnessed no threat of the partition of China. To the extent that Roosevelt remained interested in the Far Eastern balance of power and its relation to American security, China ceased to be of importance. On the contrary, as Roosevelt easily perceived, the existence of the Anglo-Japanese Alliance and the later Japanese rapprochement with Russia upset the balance in favor of Japan— and good relations with Japan had to be central to his Asian policy. No interest that the United States had in China, tangible or theoretical, was worth the risk of antagonizing Japan. The seriousness of Japanese-American tensions resulting from the treatment of Japanese in California left Roosevelt little leeway to press Japan on the Asian mainland. In short, China might have been forgotten had not the Chinese themselves begun to stir and scratch at the American consciousness.

Roosevelt's contempt for China and the Chinese people derived from their failure to defend themselves against imperialism. Unlike the Japanese, whom he admired, the Chinese seemed to enjoy their archaic society. He doubted that they could ever become "civilized"—that they could ever create a modern nation. He was appalled by their apparent lack of patriotism. The Chinese were contemptible in Roosevelt's eyes not because they were Orientals, but because he assumed that they would never develop a national spirit and that they would forever be content with the glories of the past.

Unknown to Roosevelt, however, changes were taking place in China. On the one hand, the Manchus had undertaken a series of important reforms that, particularly in the realm of education, allowed hope for gradual modernization. In addition, there were manifestations of a rising sense of nationalism among the Chinese, especially in the treaty ports. Resentment against foreign domination of China took more sophisticated forms than the enraged xenophobia of the Boxers. The local gentry, students, journalists, and businessmen began to focus their attention on specific abuses of Chinese sovereignty and to demand an end to the special privileges the powers had wrested from China. They became increasingly sensitive about the subhuman treatment Chinese received in the United States and were angered by the congressional debate and action that led to the permanent exclusion of Chinese immigrants in 1904. As they watched the Japanese hammer away at the Russians in Manchuria, their hopes soared. An Asian nation had defeated a major European power. A country that less than half a century before had been as backward as China had modernized rapidly and become a great power. Perhaps China's condition was not so desperate after all.

Those Chinese who were developing this sense of national awareness constituted but a tiny fraction of that vast nation. Nonetheless, in the first decade of the twentieth century, they came to constitute what passed for an organized public opinion and they were capable of exerting pressure on government officials, local and national, and of stirring mass movements. In 1905 they had their first major success, organizing a sustained nationalist movement that took the form of an anti-American boycott.

The organizers of the boycott were not precisely anti-American. They attempted to indicate their awareness that the immigration policy of the United States reflected the wishes of American labor and not of Americans generally and they hoped to gain the support of other Americans for their efforts. Moreover, the boycotters were concerned with larger issues than American racism, which, however hateful, merely provided a convenient target at which to direct their resentment. They were seeking to strike a blow for Chinese prestige. Unable to match Japan's performance at Port Arthur, they sought a more modest victory. Lacking the military power necessary to strike at the imperialists, they sought to harness the energies that were available to them, to use an organized public opinion against that power least likely to respond with force.

The boycott never received the official support of the Chinese government, which feared the possibility that it might lead to foreign intervention and a new round of humiliations. Nonetheless, many Chinese, especially Wu T'ing-fang and others in the Foreign Ministry, recognized the value of such a popular movement as a diplomatic weapon. Reasonably certain that the United States would not retaliate, the Chinese government acquiesced in and unofficially supported the early efforts of the organizers of the boycott. Had it not, there was always the risk that public indignation might be directed against Manchu rule. Similarly, as agitation for the cancellation of the concession of an American railroad development company mounted, the Chinese government correctly estimated that it could yield to the popular demand without serious risk.

Roosevelt responded to the boycott by demanding that the Chinese government suppress it and by attempting to reduce the cause of Chinese irritation with the United States. He perceived that American prestige was at stake in China and was unwilling to allow the Chinese to treat American businessmen as they would not dare treat the Japanese, British, or Russians. In direct relations between the United States and China over the boycott and other economic concerns that the Chinese government could influence by itself, there were fewer restraints on the use of American power. Roosevelt had not dared to risk conflict with the Russians earlier and he was wary of the Japanese, but against China, gunboat diplomacy was always available. During the anti-American agitation of 1905, the Asiatic Fleet lay at anchor off Shanghai, offering formidable support for the American minister's protests. Other than this obvious evidence of American retaliatory potential, Roosevelt's methods were routine. Rockhill, in Peking, protested frequently, demanded the punishment of the leaders of the boycott, and warned that the Chinese government would be held accountable for losses sustained by Americans. Although the Chinese government refused to accept responsibility for the boycott and rejected demands that it be suppressed, the United States refrained from using or threatening to use the force available.

At home as well, Roosevelt had little success. He could coerce neither Congress nor the individual states, which, like California, legalized discrimination against Asians. His own attitude toward Chinese immigration was clear and creditable. He accepted the exclusion of coolie labor which he lacked the power to prevent and he made every effort to obtain fair treatment for Chinese businessmen and students. The Chinese exclusion acts were a disgrace—a mockery of American ideals, but they expressed the will of the American people and were not Roosevelt's work. Publicly as well as privately, he contended that Chinese complaints were just, that "undoubtedly one of the chief causes of the boycott has been the shortcomings of the United States Government and people in the matter of the treatment of Chinese here."[2] When West Coast businessmen complained of suffering from the boycott, he demanded their support for his efforts "to do justice as well as to exact justice." On the administrative level, Roosevelt was able to do more and he ordered that new instructions be sent to immigration officials that would warn them that discourtesy to Chinese would be grounds for immediate dismissal from government service.

In the fall of 1905, after the boycott movement had been sustained for about five months, it lost its vitality. The Chinese government began to fear that anti-American agitation would lead to violence and, confronted with American protests, ultimately ordered the suppression of the movement.

Probably of greater importance was the fact that Chinese businessmen, who made the greatest sacrifices during the peak of the boycott, began to lose interest. Chinese conditions rather than American policy, at home or abroad, accounted for the change.

Another aspect of the Chinese attempt to reduce foreign influence in their country was their desire to regain control over the construction and operation of railroads. In general, the companies that had succeeded in getting the railroad development concessions had exacted, as part of the price for arranging the financing of the railroads, terms that gave them effective control over the actual construction and subsequent operation of the roads. The leaders of the emerging Chinese nationalist movement were aware of the need for foreign capital, but were eager to be rid of or at least to minimize foreign control. Beginning in 1904 and culminating during the boycott movement of 1905 was an effort directed by Chang Chih-tung to cancel the railroad concession held by the American China Development Company.

The American China Development Company had been granted its concession in 1898 to build a railroad connecting Canton with Hankow. For the next six years, most of the company's movements involved stock manipulations, culminating in the sale of a majority of the shares to a Belgian syndicate—in direct violation of the terms of the contract, which precluded such a transfer. Learning of this, Chang Chih-tung determined to have the contract cancelled. In American hands, the railroad, if it were ever built, would be valuable for the communications network he envisaged as part of his plans for the modernization of China. In the hands of a European syndicate with uncertain political connections, a new danger to China's sovereignty might be in the offing. Aware that the local gentry had consistently opposed the railroad concession on economic grounds, Chang easily stirred up a demand from within Hunan province that the concession be cancelled.

In January 1905, J. P. Morgan and his associates bought the shares held by the Belgian syndicate and the source of Chang's original concern was removed. But by this time, agitation against the American concession had merged with the boycott movement directed against American immigration policy. The year 1905 was a poor time for anyone to be defending American interests in China. Instead, Chang shifted to an attempt to have the contract bought back from the American company. A great popular movement, centered in Hunan, supported this tack—with letters, posters, and demonstrations, if not with money.

To this movement, as to the boycott, the Chinese government proved responsive. Having initially contracted for the railroad with a private company, the Chinese entered into direct negotiation with Morgan for the repurchase of the concession. Once having assured himself and his colleagues of a handsome profit, Morgan agreed to sell. Before the deal was consummated, however, Roosevelt learned of it and sought to intervene. Though he assured Morgan that his interest was "simply the interest of seeing American commercial interests prosper in the Orient,"[3] Roosevelt feared the general effects of the likely loss of American prestige. He was sure that the Chinese "despise weakness even more than they prize justice"—and he might have added that he assumed all nations reacted the same way. Roosevelt exhorted Morgan to hold on to the concession, promising him the support of the American government. He had Rockhill protest to the authorities in Peking. But toward the end of August, after Morgan and Roosevelt conferred, they agreed to allow the concession to be cancelled. Morgan insisted that he could not reject the Chinese offer without disregarding the interests of his stockholders. Reluctantly, Roosevelt acquiesced.

Before the year ended, a number of American missionaries were murdered in China. Though the boycott was fading and the boycott's leaders disassociated themselves from acts of violence, physical attacks on Americans increased. Fearing another Boxer uprising, Roosevelt ordered the reinforcement of the Asiatic Fleet and had the War Department draw up plans for possible operations against China. Fortunately, no military expedition to China was needed. And in December, in his annual message to Congress, the president placed responsibility for the difficulties with China on the American people. He insisted that "grave injustice and wrong have been done by this nation to the people of China." He reminded Americans that they had insisted on just treatment by the Chinese, but warned that "we cannot receive equity unless we are willing to do equity."[4] In direct reference to the boycott, he attributed it to Chinese resentment against the harshness of American immigration policy.

After 1905, the dominant concern of the Roosevelt administration in Asia was the avoidance of war with Japan, and the relatively minor friction with China was all but forgotten. Roosevelt, however, did not forget the surprising signs of spirit that the Chinese had exhibited. His most characteristic expression of approval of Chinese nationalism came in 1907 when the reappointment of Wu T'ing-fang as minister to the United

States was announced. In his previous tour, Wu had persistently and mercilessly bested the Department of State in exchanges over the treatment of Chinese in America and in the new American empire in the Pacific. A strident nationalist, he had been deeply involved in the anti-American activities of 1905. In 1907, Secretary of State Elihu Root asked whether the United States should accept such a man as minister. And Roosevelt replied:

> My feeling would be strongly that we ought not to object to Wu. He is a bad old Chink and if he had his way he would put us all to the heavy death or do something equally as unpleasant with us; . . . [but] I do not object to any Chinaman showing a feeling that he would like to retaliate now and then for our insolence to the Chinese[5]

There were other indications that Roosevelt was aware of Chinese efforts to modernize—and he offered both sympathy and assistance. In 1907 he asked Congress for authority to refund part of the Boxer indemnity in order to help prepare the people of China to adapt to new conditions. A few months before he left the White House, Roosevelt published "The Awakening of China," an article in praise of the new spirit there. He called on Americans to note the changes, the new attitudes toward Western education, the modernization of communications, increasing industry and trade. With perhaps excessive enthusiasm, he portrayed a new China, freed from the shackles of ancient superstitions. At last the impetus had come for "the growth of a real and intelligent spirit of patriotism in all parts of China."[6]

A few days after Roosevelt's article appeared, T'ang Shao-yi, a prominent modernizer, met with Roosevelt to discuss Chinese plans for enlisting American assistance in the development of Manchuria. To T'ang also Roosevelt expressed the hope that the United States could help in the modernization of China. He explained his desire for a strong China in terms of the need for a stable balance of power in East Asia and in the world. So long as China was weak, East Asia would be the scene for a great struggle for power—a struggle that provided a far greater danger of instability than did the emergence of a strong Chinese nation. But T'ang had hoped for more than words; he had hoped for American support against Japanese imperialism in Manchuria. Such support was not forthcoming, for Chinese hopes foundered on the realities of power in 1908.

Roosevelt admired the new spirit of nationalism emerging in China, but he was not prepared to challenge Japan in the interest of China's national aspirations. As he wrote in 1910, an alliance with China, given China's weakness, would provide the United States with nothing but an additional burden. He believed that a strong China was in the interest of the entire world, but in his time it did not exist and he chose not to strain the limits of American power by attempting to take on that burden. For all his rhetoric about America's mission, he suffered no illusions of a Pax Americana; no messianic impulse drove him to risk the security and interests of the United States on behalf of China. While T'ang waited in Washington, Root and the Japanese ambassador, Takahira Kogoro, exchanged letters symbolic of the Roosevelt administration's basic approach to East Asia.

For centuries, the Chinese had successfully employed their tactic of using barbarians to control barbarians, and an unbroken string of failures in the nineteenth century did not suffice to undermine their confidence or bring about a reconsideration. In the early years of the twentieth century, they may have had few alternatives, but there is no indication that they tried these few. There had been little reason for the Chinese to expect that their interests in Manchuria would fare any better under Japanese control than under Russian, but until the Russo-Japanese accord of 1907, the Chinese remained inactive diplomatically, hoping that somehow they might benefit from old hatreds between the Russians and Japanese. When that wistful hope vanished, China, encouraged and even prodded by Germany, returned to the earlier hope of using the United States for Chinese ends in Manchuria. The Germans, increasingly worried by Britain's successful maneuvers to isolate them, developed a grandiose conception of a German-American-Chinese entente in East Asia. But the combination of Chinese weakness and German ambition had no appeal whatever to Roosevelt. Throughout the months of Japanese-American tensions caused by anti-Japanese agitation in California, Roosevelt remained determined not to allow East Asian questions to aggravate the crisis. Indeed, had it been necessary, he would have been willing to sacrifice the trivial economic stake that Americans still held in China in order to appease Japan. With or without the cooperation of Germany, he was unwilling to consider an involvement in Manchuria that could be construed only as intervention on China's behalf in an area of tremendous strategic importance to Japan.

In their efforts, the Chinese were not without American friends. The American community in Shanghai worried about potential Japanese and Russian efforts to undermine its particular interests in China and Manchuria. On a visit to Shanghai in 1907, the secretary of war, William Howard Taft, was convinced of the need for the United States to take a stand against the Japanese threat to the economic interests of Americans in China. In Manchuria, Willard Straight, American consul general at Mukden, conspired with Chinese officials who sought to use American capital against Japan. Within the Department of State, an assistant secretary, Huntington Wilson, shared Straight's hostility toward Japan, and others indicated concern over Japanese infringements of Chinese sovereignty in Manchuria and over reports that Japan was giving preferential treatment there to the goods of its own nationals.

Roosevelt, however, did not consider the sum of the interests of Americans in Manchuria or China proper equivalent to a vital national interest. Japan's interests in East Asia were vital; those of the United States were not. Where there was clear evidence of discrimination against American goods, the government of the United States would continue to protest to the offending power whether it be Japan or any other nation. Given the limited importance of this trade, such protests would never be pushed to the point of precipitating a crisis. As for railroad development in Manchuria, unlike Straight and others, Roosevelt was convinced that if the United States succumbed to Chinese temptations, it would be impinging on an important Japanese strategic concern, a vital interest. For the United States, given the limited nature of its interests in the area, given the limits of its power, its vulnerability in the Western Pacific, such an action would be a needless step toward disaster.

While the Germans, Chinese, and Willard Straight schemed, Roosevelt and Root prepared to bring an end to the Japanese-American crisis, the one essential goal of American policy in East Asia. While T'ang Shao-yi waited in the wings, Root and the Japanese ambassador exchanged notes indicating that the United States, in its Asian policy, sought friendly relations with Japan, and continued to insist on equal treatment for American commerce in China and Manchuria. More than this the United States had never demanded. Japanese imperialism in Manchuria, the encroachments on Chinese sovereignty, were regretted, just as the United States regretted similar encroachments by other powers. But however much the United States valued the territorial integrity and administrative sanctity of China, it had never been willing to interpose its forces between China and those who oppressed her. The Root-Takahira agreement of 1908 contained no statement of new policy on this or any other issue.

In 1909, William Howard Taft became president of the United States. As he was Roosevelt's hand-picked successor, the Japanese and most Americans assumed Taft would follow the course that Roosevelt had set for him. But within a few months after his inauguration, Taft left no doubt that he was determined to be his own man. His Asian policy constituted a sharp departure from past American practices, aggressively promoting the economic interests of the United States to an extent never before attempted and not matched until the late 1990s. This was part of a massive effort to expand American trade and investments throughout the world—an effort most striking in Asia because of the contrast it offered to the policy of the Roosevelt administration, particularly in terms of Taft's willingness to press American interests in the face of Japanese power.

Responsibility for the new tack in American policy toward China and Japan was basically Taft's. As governor of the Philippines and during his Asian tour while secretary of war, he had become apprehensive about Japanese intentions in East Asia without developing any accompanying apprehension about Japanese military strength. As a result, he had concluded that Roosevelt's appeasement of Japan, his willingness to subordinate American interests in China to the quest for Japan's goodwill, was misguided. His views coincided with those of Straight, who had become chief of the Division of Far Eastern Affairs, and of Huntington Wilson, who had been promoted to first assistant secretary of state.

American presidents, like the leaders of all nations, are invariably concerned with the need to further the economic development of their countries, often through the expansion of trade. Taft personally believed in the potential for expanded markets in China proper and in Manchuria. Together with Philander Knox, his secretary of state, Willard Straight, and Huntington Wilson, he also believed that the political ends of the United States in East Asia, a stable balance of power resting on a sovereign China, could be attained by economic means, by "dollar diplomacy." In addition, all of these men believed that in the pursuit of American interests, they were helping China. They assumed the congruity of American and Chinese interests.

Central to the Taft administration's policy toward East Asia was the recognition of the extent to which trade success in China was related to the volume of investments. By forcing American capital into China, Taft and his advisers believed they could break the Japanese hold and simultaneously facilitate the expansion of American trade. Earlier, Elihu Root had attempted briefly to include equal opportunity for investments within the concept of the "Open Door," but as generally understood by the powers, the "Open Door" related exclusively to trade. Nonetheless, the Taft administration, stressing its adherence to the "traditional" and "historic" policy of the United States, insisted that the "Open Door" assured Americans equal opportunity for investment throughout China, without consideration of spheres of interest. Although financial circles in the United States were generally unenthusiastic about investment opportunities in China, preferring surer profits elsewhere, Taft soon found banking support for his policy.

In China, the internal political situation had changed in the early months of 1909, as the result of a coup against Yüan Shih-k'ai. Yüan and his protege, T'ang Shao-yi, were unable to continue their efforts to acquire American support in Manchuria, but the Peking regime continued to seek ways to employ the United States and perhaps Great Britain against the Japanese and Russians. The entire leadership of the Foreign Ministry favored "active American intervention in Manchuria."[7] To the extent that the Chinese controlled their own affairs, the time was ripe for precisely the kind of diplomatic offensive the Taft administration contemplated. Regrettably for both the United States and China, the extent of that control was negligible.

In the summer of 1909, the American effort to penetrate the investment market in China began. After his initial attempts to gain for American bankers a share of a loan China was floating for the construction of a railroad between Hunan and Kwang-tung failed, Taft *personally* cabled Prince Ch'un, urging him to grant American capitalists an equal share of the loan, indicating his "intense personal interest in making the use of American capital in the development of China an instrument for the promotion of the welfare of China."[8] But the prince, regent of China during his nephew's infancy, dared not offend the European powers that had exacted the railroad concession from him. Eager as his advisers were for American assistance, they could not yield to the American request until the United States gained the acquiescence of the British, French, and German banking groups, each supported by its government. The Taft administration's pressures on Peking were misdirected and almost a year passed before the Europeans reluctantly agreed to admit the American group—only to have a new crisis in China nullify the agreement.

In June 1909, Straight left the Department of State to become the representative of the banking group that was to serve as the instrument of American policy. First he went to London, where he met with the European bankers and presented the American request. Then he went to Mukden, scene of his earlier dealings with T'ang Shao-yi. There he found T'ang's successor, the conservative Hsi-liang, no less interested in American-financed railroad development. Just as T'ang and the Chinese modernizers had hoped to use Straight and the American railroad magnate, E. H. Harriman, to counter Japanese and Russian influence in Manchuria, Hsi-liang devised a plan to have the American banking group finance a trans-Manchurian railroad, running from Chinchow to Aigun. If the British could be brought into the arrangement, the Chinese reasoned that their position would be even better. Unable to reassert sovereignty in Manchuria, fearful that the Japanese and Russians would annex rich provinces, the Chinese sought to give other powers a stake in the area, in the hope of using the strength of the other powers to prevent what they were too weak to prevent alone. In October, Chinese officials in Manchuria signed an agreement with Straight to have the American banking group finance the Chinchow–Aigun railroad.

For Prince Ch'un and other Chinese leaders in Peking, this new agreement provided a familiar dilemma. The ends to which the agreement was directed were desirable, but the Japanese and Russians would be angered. Until the United States was willing to counter this pressure, the Chinese government could not act. Despite efforts by the officials in Manchuria to press for ratification of the agreement, the Peking government chose to await the response of the American government.

Instead of exerting diplomatic pressure in Peking, Tokyo, and St. Petersburg on behalf of the Chinchow–Aigun railroad agreement, the Taft administration attempted a broader Manchurian offensive, the Knox "neutralization" plan. Knox proposed the neutralization or internationalization of all railroads in Manchuria. He apparently believed that the Russians might be willing to have other nations underwrite some of their losses with the Chinese Eastern Railroad and he hoped to get British, French, and German support with which to isolate Japan. If the plan worked, if the Japanese could be pressured into surrendering their control of the South Manchuria Railroad, Japan's domination of southern Manchuria could be ended and the threat to Chinese sovereignty in Manchuria greatly reduced. The infusion of American capital into the area would enhance the opportunities for trade, increasing profits for investors and merchants alike. In addition, a great blow would have been struck against imperialism, a great service provided for the people of China. It was a grand dream, but like so many dreams, it failed to survive the rising sun. Japan's position in Manchuria was too strong, her place in the world balance of power too secure, and her determination to resist the American gambit was unfailing. Rather than separating the Russians from the Japanese, Knox's diplomacy drove them closer together and they both rejected his plan in markedly similar terms. The British support for which Knox had hoped was never forthcoming, as Great Britain treasured its alliance with Japan far more than the advantages it might obtain from the neutralization of Manchuria—or the good will of the Taft administration. Similarly, the French stood by their Russian allies, and the Germans, sufficiently worried about encirclement in Europe, were not prepared to challenge the world on behalf of Chinese sovereignty or American investment opportunities—especially after their failure of the previous year. The Chinchow–Aigun railroad, which Knox had proposed as an alternative to neutralization, also failed to materialize.

The Taft administration's diplomatic offensive disturbed not only the other powers with interests in China, but Theodore Roosevelt as well. To his son, Roosevelt bemoaned the inability of "poor Taft" to understand the ingredients of a successful policy toward Japan. By December he was writing and visiting Taft, warning him that Japan could be a serious threat to the security of the United States and to American possessions in the Pacific. He reminded Taft that Japan's interests on the Asian continent were vital, whereas American interests there, *especially* in Manchuria, were "really unimportant, and not such that the American people would be content to run the slightest risk of collision about them."[9] He considered the administration's assumption of an identity of interests with China to be tantamount to madness, contending that to challenge Japan in Manchuria required tremendous military power, equivalent to the combined strength of the British navy and the German army.

Roosevelt carried his argument a step further, offending the moral sensibilities of Secretary Knox. Roosevelt contended that the "Open Door" policy was useless when a powerful nation chose to disregard it and was willing to use force to achieve its ends. So long as other nations had been willing to allow Americans to pursue their limited interests in China, notes requesting equal treatment had sufficed. Now, if Japan chose to deny to Americans their traditional opportunities, words were worthless and the United States lacked the power to challenge Japan to any contest more rigorous than a debate. Given the insignificance of the interests involved, Roosevelt insisted that it was wrong to force the issue. Both the interests and the requests for equal treatment were better abandoned.

In drafting a reply for Taft, Knox asked "why the Japanese need Manchuria any more than does China who owns it now."[10] To Knox and to Taft, to Willard Straight, and perhaps to men of goodwill everywhere, China had the right to control its own territory and its own resources. The Taft administration worked from the assumption that China's aspirations were worthy of American support, that opposition to Japan in support of these aspirations was consistent not only with the ideals but also with the interests of the American people. Knox was offended not only by Roosevelt's apparent willingness to tolerate Japanese imperialism, but also by his willingness to renounce "our historic policy in China." To the measurable interests of the United States in China, to the theoretical importance of the East Asian balance of power, Knox had added a new ingredient with which Americans were to be concerned: the preservation of "our historic policy." For Knox, who was unimpressed by the argument that this policy no longer worked, that the ends for which this policy had been designed were unimportant, the preservation of this policy became an end in itself. Rather than renounce the "Open Door" or prepare to fight for it, Knox and others who followed continued to search for another alternative.

One possibility that the Taft administration had not seriously considered was cooperation with Japan in order to wean the Japanese away from imperialism, improve economic opportunities for Americans, and modernize China. But the fact of Japanese power and of European recognition of that power left the United States no choice. If Americans hoped to increase their economic stake in China, if they hoped to assist in the modernization of China, if they hoped in any way to check Japanese exploitation of China, it would have to be through cooperation with Japan. American participation in the economic development of China was possible only if the United States forced its way into the consortium, cooperating with the European imperialists. But this cooperation, which began in May 1911, could not be focused against Japan. Approximately a year after the United States was admitted to the consortium, the Japanese and Russians were admitted as well. Whatever hope Americans had for ameliorating the effects of Japanese—and European—imperialism in China would have to be realized by working in tandem with the imperialists. There remained, however, the danger that instead of reforming the

TABLE 3.1   The American Economic Stake in China, 1905–1919

Year	U.S. Exports to China (in $ million)	Percentage of Total U.S. Export Trade	U.S. Investments in China (in $ million)	Percentage of Total U.S. Investments Overseas
1905[a]	53	3.5		
1906[a]	44	2.5		
1907	26	1.4		
1908	22	1.2		
1909	19	1.1		
1910	16	0.9		
1911	19	0.9		
1912	24	1.0		
1913	21	0.8		
1914	25	1.0	49.3	1.4
1915	16	0.6		
1916	32	0.6		
1917	40	0.6		
1918	53	0.9		
1919	106	1.3		

[a]Statistics for 1905 and 1906 apparently reflect American gains during the Russo-Japanese war.

imperialists, the Americans would be more effectively co-opted into the league of predators. For Chinese struggling to free their nation from foreign control, the powers now seemed to present a united front. When in 1911 and 1912 the Chinese people rose to rid themselves of both the Manchu dynasty and foreign domination, they found the Taft administration committed to withholding recognition from the nascent republic until its consortium partners were ready to act. For the moment, the American offensive was over.

Despite the Taft administration's more aggressive diplomacy in East Asia, it would be a mistake to assume that Taft and his aides considered American interests in China any more vital than had the previous administration. The new tack in American policy was based less on a revised estimate of the importance of American interests than on a failure to comprehend the limits of American power: a failure to comprehend the need to establish priorities among the nation's overseas desiderata. Taft demanded the exercise of American "rights" in China not because these rights were important but because they existed. Similarly, Knox could insist that the powers recognize China's sovereign rights, less because of any value to be derived for the United States than because these rights existed. Placing altogether too much faith in the power of the dollar combined with a presumably superior moral position, the Taft administration was slow to understand the need to tread carefully when another major power, rightly or wrongly, trampled on the theoretical rights and insignificant interests of the United States in pursuit of its own *vital* interests. An awareness of the realities of power, which Roosevelt had failed to instill in his successor, was gained via experience. Unfortunately, the lessons could not be transmitted to the Democrats who followed Taft. A means of coexisting with Japanese power agreeable to most Americans had yet to be found.

The awakening of China that had impressed itself on Roosevelt's mind continued after 1905 at a quickening rate. The new force in China coursed simultaneously along several channels, each leading toward a modern nation-state, exercising sovereignty within its borders. The Manchu court ran before the tide, moving inexorably toward constitutional government as its only hope of retaining the Mandate of Heaven. But the court could not move quickly enough, even to satisfy those like K'ang Yu-wei, the exiled Confucian reformer, who sought no more radical change than the creation of a constitutional monarchy. K'ang and his followers, however, were no longer among the vanguard. Led by Sun Yat-sen, a revolutionary movement had risen, determined to drive out the Manchus, to establish a republican form of government, and to carry out a land reform program. These forces of unrest, together with the "rights recovery" movement, further undermined the already shaky Manchu regime.

Sun and his friends made a series of abortive attempts at triggering a revolution, including a spectacular failure at Canton in April 1911. At approximately the same time, the rights recovery movement received a jolt when the consortium powers, including the United States, pressured the Chinese government into accepting a loan for the construction of the Hu-kuang railroad. For reasons both nationalist and pecuniary, widespread disorders began in Szechuan province, the center of Chinese financial interest in the railroad. In October, as efforts were underway to pacify Szechuan, a military revolt began in Wuchang. The revolt spread through south China and within a few months, the era of Manchu rule had ended.

During the initial stages of the revolution, the court recalled Yüan Shih-k'ai to command loyalist forces. After almost three years of involuntary retirement, Yüan chose to use this new opportunity to rebuild and solidify his own power. Utilizing the modern Peiyang Army which he had created himself, he defeated rebel forces around Wuhan, then paused, allowing the rebels to destroy the Manchu garrisons in south China.

Having established himself as the principal power in North China, he sent T'ang Shao-yi south to negotiate with the rebel leaders, represented by Wu T'ing-fang. An agreement was reached quickly for the establishment of a republican government; the Manchus were persuaded to abdicate and Sun Yat-sen, returning hurriedly from the United States, was elected provisional president of China.

Though the revolution had apparently been successful and its acknowledged leader had been elected president, the fact remained that real power rested with Yüan Shih-k'ai. Without his support, the future of the Republic of China was bleak. With full appreciation of the realities of power, Sun retired three days after the formal Manchu abdication, to allow for Yüan's accession to the presidency. T'ang Shao-yi became premier and several of Sun's leading followers accepted positions in his cabinet, though the crucial ministries of War and the Interior were held by two of Yüan's most trusted aides. Another ominous sign was Yüan's failure to fulfill the agreement that he would move the seat of government to Nanking, closer to the center of the strength of the revolutionary leaders. Within weeks of Yüan's inauguration, the first constitutional crisis came as Yüan and his long-time friend and colleague, T'ang Shao-yi, clashed over T'ang's handling of financial affairs. Casually disregarding the premier's efforts, Yüan made conflicting arrangements with the consortium. As Yüan continued to override the decisions of the premier and his cabinet, all resigned in June 1912. China's initial experiment with democratic government was on the verge of failure. In the autumn of 1912, as Yüan continued his negotiations with the consortium, Sun Yat-sen's revolutionary party was reorganized as a parliamentary party, the Kuomintang. Though Sun remained the party's nominal leader, he had indicated little interest in parliamentary politics and had accepted Yüan's appointment to a post responsible for railroad development. The actual leader of the Kuomintang was Sung Chiao-jen, and he led the party to an overwhelming victory in the national elections of the winter of 1912–1913. Sung's leadership and the obvious power of the Kuomintang could not be tolerated by Yüan, and in March 1913 he arranged for Sung to be assassinated. Also in March 1913, Woodrow Wilson became president of the United States.

In his first year as president, Wilson's handling of American policy toward China indicated less concern for power politics than Roosevelt had shown and less concern for Wall Street than Taft had shown. From missionary sources, he had learned of China's surge toward modernization and he was determined to offer the Chinese the disinterested assistance of the United States. He was aware of the role played by European and Japanese imperialism in China, and if he could not reform those imperialists, he could disassociate the United States from their policies.

The first question posed for the Wilson administration came from the American participants in the six-power consortium: did the new administration desire the continued involvement of the American group? The bankers were prepared to continue their operations if the government so desired *and* if they could be assured of the support of the government. If not, more rewarding investment opportunities loomed elsewhere. In making his decision, Wilson consulted neither the State Department bureaucracy nor the other countries represented in the consortium. He and Secretary of State William Jennings Bryan mistrusted the bureaucratic remnants of Roosevelt's militarism and Taft's dollar diplomacy. They were hostile to the imperialists and unwilling to accept advice from those steeped in the old politics of the Old World. Progress toward a better world could not be based on the wisdom of imperialism and avarice. Even innocence or ignorance provided a better hope—and Wilson and Bryan went forth, cloaking their policies in these latter attributes. Not even the Chinese were consulted.

Bryan needed advice from no one to know that bankers involved in monopolistic practices would be bad for China. In a lifetime devoted to tilting against the "interests" he had learned that much. Others in Wilson's cabinet contended that China's new course required new policies, arguing against aid to China that was conditional on the Chinese being obligated to the bankers of the great powers. The secretary of commerce indicated the fear that withdrawal from the consortium might jeopardize American trade in China, but no one else seemed concerned with economic considerations; nor did Wilson's cabinet consider the effect withdrawal might have on American relations with the other consortium powers or on the American position in East Asia. Wilson was reported as being "clear in his conviction that we could not request the trust group of bankers to effect the loan, and that we ought to help China in some better way."[11] Without prior notice to the other powers or even to the State Department officials concerned with the consortium, Wilson proceeded to inform the press that the American group in the consortium would no longer have the support of the government.

Wilson later explained that he felt "so keenly the desire to help China that I prefer to err in the line of helping that country than otherwise." If the United States had continued to participate in the consortium, "we would have gotten nothing but mere influence in China and lost the proud position which America secured when Secretary Hay stood for the Open Door in China after the Boxer Uprising."[12] Though Wilson had misread Hay's purpose in 1900, his own administration had, by purging itself of ties with Wall Street, demonstrated its altruistic intentions. Now the United States, standing on higher moral ground, could call the imperialists to account. For China, the new order was about to begin.

The assistant secretary of state, Huntington Wilson, resigned in angry protest, both against Wilson's decision and his cavalier method of reaching and announcing it. The Japanese government protested for similar reasons. But Wilson did not doubt the essential wisdom and righteousness of his course. From Yüan Shih-k'ai, Wilson received an expression of appreciation. But if Yüan expected that Wilson's decision would lead to American loans on a more generous basis, he did not live to see them. On the other hand, if he would be satisfied by American recognition of his regime, this was soon forthcoming. *Wilson recognized Republic of China*

A week after his consortium decision, Wilson advised his cabinet that he had decided to recognize the Republic of China. There was a suggestion that the United States act in concert with the other powers, as it had under the Taft administration, but Wilson chose to go ahead with recognition on a unilateral basis. He informed the ambassadors of the other powers of American intentions, offered to allow them the opportunity to cooperate with the United States, but refused to be bound by the decisions of other governments. Wilson's cabinet was exhilarated by his high moral purpose, but the other powers, especially the Japanese, were not. The Japanese government tried to call Wilson's attention to the fact that the Chinese republic was on the verge of civil war, that Yüan had usurped power, that Sun and the Kuomintang were disputing Yüan's claims to the presidency and preparing to fight—and that recognition at this time "would practically amount to interference in favor of Mr. Yüan."[13] As the cabinet discussed the decision, it was noted that a "prominent Chinaman," Sung Chiao-jen, had just been assassinated and that President Yüan was implicated in the murder. But Wilson did not give these discordant notes serious consideration. The parliament of the new republic was to meet for the first time and the United States extended its blessing to the Chinese experiment in the form of recognition—a striking contrast with the tactic of "watchful waiting" that Wilson employed against the Huerta regime in Mexico. A month later, a civil war broke out in China, as the

Kuomintang, unable to check Yüan by parliamentary means, was forced to the battlefield.

Despite Wilson's policy based on friendship and goodwill toward China, the Chinese made little progress in the direction of modernization. The problem derived not from American policy, which, despite the pretensions of some Americans, could have little effect on the course of China's development, but from China's internal political turmoil. Despite the revolution, traditional Chinese society had not changed radically. The creation of a republic had not inspired the Chinese masses with a sense of nationalism. Worst of all, most of the men gifted with the qualities of leadership were more interested in fulfilling their own political ambitions than in leading China into the modern era. Yüan Shih-k'ai first ignored the parliament, then outlawed the Kuomintang, forcing it out of the parliament. In January 1914, he dissolved the parliament altogether and devoted much of the next two years to preparing the way for the restoration of the monarchy with himself as emperor. With a loan from the consortium, in which the American group was no longer participating, Yüan was able to crush the Kuomintang-led rebellion of 1913, but he was not able to check the political aspirations of his own military men. At every opportunity, his lieutenants enhanced their own power as a price for assisting Yüan in suppressing opposition to his imperial aspirations. During the winter of 1915–1916, a few months before Yüan was to become the Hung Hsien emperor, a succession of provincial military men declared their independence of his regime, Sun Yat-sen intensified his anti-Yüan agitation, and Yüan's men forced him to surrender both his dream and most of his power. In June, Yüan died and with him went the last semblance of national government. The age of the warlords had dawned. Once again in China's long history, regionalism triumphed.

There was, however, another dimension to China's inability to progress more rapidly toward becoming a modern nation state. In addition to enlightened leadership, China needed capital and this would have to come from abroad. Wilson's decision not to support American participation in the consortium, followed in 1914 by the deep involvement of the European powers in the war, left Japan as China's principal source of economic assistance—and the Japanese, unlike the Americans, did not believe that their interests would be served by a strong, modern China. Every Japanese extension of capital to China was made with an eye toward the enlargement and strengthening of Japan's continental empire. However unsympathetic one may have been toward the Wall Street bankers of the American group, their presence in the consortium, particularly after 1914, might have served as a check on the infinitely more predatory intentions of the Japanese. The withdrawal of the American group as a result of Wilson's well-intentioned anti-imperialism worked therefore to the detriment of China by leaving the most dangerous of the imperialist powers unchecked in its control of the financial assistance China so desperately needed. The Japanese were quick to illustrate the point for Wilson's benefit and, to his credit, he learned from the experience.

When the World War began in Europe, the Japanese, in accordance with the terms of their alliance with Great Britain, promptly overran German possessions in East Asia, including the German concession in Shantung. In fact, the Japanese established their control in Shantung to a degree that the Germans had never known. The Chinese had no objection to the German departure, but were not overjoyed by the presence of additional Japanese forces in North China. Nor did these gains satisfy the Japanese. A few months later, in January 1915, the Japanese minister to China presented Yüan Shih-k'ai with the notorious Twenty-One Demands, divided into five groups. The Japanese sought to have the Chinese confirm and legitimatize their gains in Shantung, their existing inroads into Chinese sovereignty in Manchuria, and to acquire new concessions in Manchuria and central China. In addition, the Chinese were to commit themselves not to allow any other power to acquire or lease any harbor, bay, or island along the coast of China. In the fifth group, the Japanese demanded that they be consulted before any foreign capital was allowed into Fukien province, that they be granted additional railroad concessions, that China purchase at least half of her armaments from Japan. Of still greater danger to China's sovereignty, the fifth group also required the Chinese to accept Japanese "advisers" in China's political, military, and economic affairs and to share with the Japanese responsibility for police activities at key points throughout China. Clearly, the Japanese recognized the fact that the European war left them with a free hand in Asia, and they sought to make the most of the opportunity.

Helpless before Japanese pressures, unable to hope for assistance from the European powers, the Chinese again turned to the United States in the hope of using the Americans to check the Japanese. Before the Japanese occupied the German concession in Shantung, the Chinese had tried to get the United States to have the Germans give their leasehold at Kiaochow to the Americans for restoration to China. Again, when the

Japanese, in making their Twenty-One Demands, warned the Chinese to keep them secret, the Chinese leaked the necessary information to the sympathetic American minister, Paul Reinsch. Before the issue was settled, the Chinese enjoyed perhaps for the first time, but certainly not for the last, the assistance of American missionaries willing to work for Chinese ends. The missionaries telegraphed Washington, asking the American government to demand that it be present at negotiations between Japan and China to guarantee justice for the Chinese. The telegram and attendant United Press releases publicizing it were paid for by the Chinese government.

The initial American response to China's plight would have pleased Theodore Roosevelt. When Reinsch forwarded China's inquiry about assistance with the Shantung problem, Robert Lansing, then counselor of the Department of State, asked that the Chinese be assured that "American friendship is sincere" and that the United States would try, by peaceful means, to help China. "But," he continued, "the Department realizes that it would be quixotic in the extreme to allow the question of China's territorial integrity to entangle the United States in international difficulties."[14] Not long afterward, Lansing suggested a Rooseveltian bargain in which the United States would acquiesce in Japanese imperialism in Shantung and Manchuria in exchange for an end to Japanese complaints about land-tenure legislation in the United States and the substitution of Manchuria for the United States as a suitable destination for Japanese emigrants. In Lansing's view, American interests in China were commercial only, and a Japanese guarantee of equal treatment for American goods satisfied the requirements of the "Open Door." But others in the department advanced a broader conception of American interests in East Asia.

The chief of the Division of Far Eastern Affairs, E. T. Williams, was one of the men who believed that with the modernization of China, the myth of the China market would become reality. He argued that despite the fact that existing commercial interests were greater in Japan than in China, a farsighted policy would be based on the assumption that American interests would best be served by a strong and independent China. He wanted the United States to urge Japan to relax its pressure on China and at the same time to extend American assistance for the task of helping the Chinese to create a modern nation, orderly within and able to defend itself from threats without. Like Rockhill, he contended that a strong China was a strong defense for the United States. Williams insisted that both the ideals and the interests of the American people could be served best by an Asian policy that was aggressively pro-Chinese. In 1915, it was Williams rather than Lansing who offered the course that appealed most to Wilson.

When Reinsch notified the American government of the Japanese demands, Wilson was preoccupied with problems arising out of the war in Europe, especially problems created by German submarine warfare. Events in Asia, where American interests were minor, could not compete for his attention with the vital issues of the war across the Atlantic. Pressed by Reinsch, who acted more as China's advocate than as an American minister, Bryan issued the initial statement of the policy of the Wilson administration. Although he restated American concern for China's territorial integrity and the principle of equal opportunity for trade, he appeared to concede the legitimacy of Japanese demands in Shantung, Manchuria, and Mongolia, declaring that contiguity created "special relations" between Japan and those areas. Chinese hopes received a further setback when Bryan indicated that the United States did not intend to take sides in the Sino-Japanese negotiations over the Twenty-One Demands.

Neither the Chinese nor Reinsch surrendered the hope of American intervention. Reinsch advised the Department of State that the Japanese were using American indifference as a club with which to force the Chinese to submit. They were contending that the United States had abandoned China. Gradually Reinsch's cables and additional information about the nature of Japanese demands, especially those of the fifth group, forced Wilson to take the reins of American diplomacy. In mid-April he advised Bryan of his desire to be "as active as the circumstances permit in showing ourselves to be the champions of the sovereign rights of China."[15] With no apparent regard for the concessions Bryan had already made to the Japanese, Wilson warned that the United States did not intend to surrender any of its rights in China or to ask the Chinese to accept infringements on their sovereignty.

Confused by the inconsistency of American diplomacy, the Japanese were nonetheless aware that they now faced American opposition. In addition, as the world became cognizant of the contents of the fifth group of demands, even Japan's ally, Great Britain, protested. But the Japanese realized that the Europeans could still not actively oppose them, and the Americans, given their limited interests, were hardly likely to do more than express their displeasure as the Japanese tightened their grip on China. For the moment, the fifth group of demands was dropped, but the Chinese were given an ultimatum threatening the use of force if the first groups of demands were not met immediately. With no help in sight, Chinese yielded on the next day. For the record, Bryan announced he United States would not recognize any agreement that infringed on American treaty rights, Chinese sovereignty, or the policy known as the "Open Door." Of no help to the Chinese, irritating to the Japanese, for Americans this statement was an important ingredient in the development of the increasingly tenacious myth that they were the "champions of the sovereign rights of China."

During and after the Sino-Japanese negotiations over the Twenty-One Demands, the administration began another practice that was ultimately to become an instrument of Wilson's opposition to Japanese imperialism in China. Having refused to support the American group's participation in the consortium on the assumption that it was involved in monopolistic practices detrimental to Chinese interests, Wilson indicated his willingness to support the aspirations of investors whose activities he presumed would have a more benign effect on China's development. Wilson was still unwilling to have the United States serve as a collector in case the Chinese defaulted on loans, but the potential investor could be assured that his government would support his right against any foreign effort to monopolize loans to China. Initially, Wilson was concerned with no more than extending the economic interests of the United States, a responsibility that he accepted no less readily than any president before or after him. Gradually, he conceived of using economic means, investments by American bankers, as a way of checking Japanese imperialism. By 1916, two American banks had arranged loans to China, supported by Reinsch and Wilson. It had become clear to Wilson that only Japan and the United States could provide the financial support necessary for Chinese development during the World War. In the absence of American competition, Japan had established a virtually unchecked hegemony over China's finances. The Japanese were able to dictate the terms of the loans, exacting concession after concession, constantly gnawing away at Chinese sovereignty.

When the United States intervened in the European war, Reinsch wanted the Chinese to associate themselves with the United States in the fight against Germany so as to enable them to receive direct aid from the American government. Unable to stimulate sufficient interest among private investors, he wanted the government to extend the necessary loans to China. But Wilson was not prepared to have the government play a role he believed to be reserved for private capital. Nonetheless, Reinsch had convinced him of the need to use economic means to preserve China's independence. Swallowing his pride, he turned to the American bankers of the old consortium and asked for help—agreeing to their condition that he announce publicly that the new consortium would be created and new loans issued, at the suggestion of the administration. He further agreed that the government would help the bankers to collect if China defaulted. Good or evil, as in the eyes of the beholder, it was "dollar diplomacy"—the use of American capital to serve the ends of American diplomacy in East Asia.

Reinsch was not happy about the creation of the new consortium, fearing that it would be dominated by the Japanese, but Wilson saw no alternative. Given the degree of hegemony Japan already enjoyed, a superficial cooperation with Japan was necessary for American participation in the development of China—and American participation was viewed as essential for the preservation of China's sovereignty. The Japanese would accept an influx of American capital into China only within the framework of a cooperative venture which, as Reinsch understood, they expected to dominate. The Japanese hoped to draw the Americans into the order they envisaged for China and Wilson hoped to draw the Japanese into the order *he* envisaged for China. At Versailles, Wilson made a further effort to commit the powers to his view of the future of China, a vision based on the cooperation of the powers engaged in a mutually profitable partnership with China.

The combination of Reinsch's activities in Peking, the apparent economic offensive that followed American displeasure with Japan's Twenty-One Demands, and American intervention in the war, assuring the United States a place at the peace conference, worried the Japanese government. In the summer of 1917, a mission headed by Ishii Kikujiro was sent to the United States to determine Wilson's purpose and to determine the extent to which the United States would accept Japan's contention that it was entitled to a special position in China. The discussions between Ishii and Secretary of State Lansing indicated little agreement between the two nations. Nonetheless, the two diplomats exchanged notes that, couched in the ambiguous language of their profession, papered over the differences between the two nations. In the notes, Lansing acknowledged that Japan's geographic position allowed it to have "special interests" in China, but in his discussions with Ishii he specifically denied that *special* meant "paramount." In a separate protocol kept secret until the 1930s, Japan joined the United States in pledging not to take advantage of the war to seek privileges in China that would infringe on the existing rights of friendly powers. To Wilson, this agreement was a great stroke on behalf of Chinese as well as American interests, but the Chinese were not reassured. On the contrary, the Japanese, in a successful attempt to undermine Chinese morale, convinced many Chinese leaders that the Lansing-Ishii agreement was in fact evidence of American acquiescence in Japanese imperialism in China—that recognition of Japan's "special interests" meant acceptance of Japan's "paramount interests" in China.

Reflecting this mood of despair in Peking, Reinsch, in March 1919, wrote to warn of a "strongly marked vein of cynicism in the higher official view of the United States."[16] He noted popular enthusiasm for things American, a tendency to give the United States excess credit for winning the war, and excitement over Wilson's statements on behalf of self-determination, but at the same time a belief that American actions did not match the high standards of American rhetoric. Reinsch contended that the Chinese did not believe Americans considered China of sufficient importance to "justify a forcible insistence" on the "Open Door" principle. Chinese officials had concluded that "more has been promised than will ever be performed." And Reinsch and his Chinese friends leaned forward in anticipation of Wilson's performance at Versailles.

At the Paris Peace Conference, the American and Chinese delegations worked closely together as Wilson hoped to free China from restrictions on her sovereignty. Though the Chinese dreamed of ridding themselves of all of the symbols of their semicolonial status, they were particularly interested in regaining control of the former German sphere of influence in Shantung. Having allied themselves with the victors for just such purposes, the Chinese put forth the restoration of complete Chinese sovereignty over Shantung as their minimal demand. Japan, however, had signed secret treaties with her European allies that bound them to support Japanese claims to the German concessions she had occupied. In addition, in the treaty by which the Chinese had accepted the Twenty-One Demands of 1915, they had also agreed to abide by any German-Japanese decision as to the disposition of the German concessions. Under the circumstances, China's hope and Wilson's efforts on China's behalf came to nought. When the Japanese threatened to quit the peace conference rather than yield, Wilson accepted the Japanese position.

Wilson's decision to yield to the Japanese on the Shantung issue proved to be one of the most strongly criticized of the decisions he made at Paris. Not only the Chinese, but also important segments of the American delegation, including Secretary of State Lansing, were outraged. In China, students went on an extended rampage, beginning what came to be called the May Fourth Movement. In the United States, opposition to the Shantung decision brought influential liberals to the side of Henry Cabot Lodge in opposition to the Treaty of Versailles. But for Wilson there had been no choice. The League of Nations seemed to provide the only hope for a world living in peace and enjoying orderly progress. Without Japan or any of the other major powers, the League would be but a rump organization. If the treaty contained inequities—and he was aware that it did—the League would rectify them. For China in particular, the only hope for the future was to internationalize her problems, to spare her from direct confrontations with Japan and other predatory powers. Within the framework of the League of Nations, China's conflicts with the powers could be resolved peacefully and justly. In Wilson's mind, China's interests and the interests of the United States in East Asia required that Japan participate in the new world organization that would draw Japan away from imperialism and into more acceptable peaceful forms of competition, advantageous to China as well as to the powers. And so he yielded on the lesser issue to keep Japan from leaving the peace conference. The subsequent failure of the United States to join the League postponed the great-power cooperation in China for which Wilson had worked, but in 1922, the Nine-Power Treaty signed at the Washington conference was to constitute an important step in the direction of this Wilsonian goal.

The first three American presidents called on to adjust American policy to the emergence of Japanese hegemony in East Asia were all sympathetic to the aspirations of Chinese nationalists, but differed in their conceptions of the role the United States should play. Roosevelt had both the most sharply developed sense of the limits of American power and the lowest estimate of the importance of American interests, present and future, in China. Combined with the problems created for him by discrimination against Japanese in the United States, his conception of limited interests and limited power led toward the appeasement of Japan. Although the economic interests of the United States in China were not abandoned, at no time was Roosevelt willing to champion China's cause against Japan.

The Taft administration launched a more aggressive East Asian policy in the hope of expanding the economic interests of the United States in

China and especially in Manchuria. Assuming the identity of Chinese and American interests, Taft believed—and the Chinese tended to agree—that an enlarged American stake in Manchuria would be beneficial to China. But Taft and Knox soon found that Japan was too firmly entrenched in Manchuria, too well protected by the structure of alliances developed in the years immediately preceding World War I. The expansion of American interests proved to be possible only in cooperation with Japan. Consequently, in the last months of the Taft administration, the American investment group that it sponsored found itself one of Japan's partners in the six-power consortium.

The Democratic administration of Woodrow Wilson reacted negatively to American participation in the consortium and to American cooperation with the imperialists in China. No less dedicated than his predecessors to serving the interests of the United States, Wilson nonetheless believed that the American people had a larger mission that required assistance to the Chinese people in their quest for independence and modernization. Gradually coming to recognize that "right" alone would not prevail and that the limits of American interests and American power prevented the United States from single-handedly championing China against Japan, he sought to create an international organization that could do for China and the world what the United States could not do alone. His failure in East Asia was but a part of the larger tragedy of the failure of the United States to join the League of Nations.

4 The Response to Chinese Nationalism

The emergence of the United States as an important force in East Asian affairs coincided with increased intellectual and cultural contacts between Chinese and American elites. Missionaries, frustrated by their inability to find converts, to reach beyond the hunger of "rice Christians" to the upper reaches of Chinese society, found a new lure: the Christian colleges, which offered China's future leaders access to Western science and technology. In the United States, great art from the breakup of some of the leading Ch'ing collections became intensely popular with wealthy collectors and imaginative curators, providing Americans with a taste of Chinese culture startling to the habitués of Chinatown—even to admirers of chinoiserie. A level of respect, grudging to be sure, forced its way into the perceptions that Chinese and Americans formed of each other.

In the early years of the twentieth century, young Chinese seeking to master the sources of Western wealth and power, political institutions as well as technology, found more than a score of American missionary colleges designed to meet their demand. This was true especially after the thousand-year-old examination system emphasizing classical Chinese learning was replaced in 1905. Thereafter, modern education, as found in Western and Japanese schools, provided the surest road to public office.

Christian schools soon had more applicants than they could admit. By the end of the World War more than 2,000 Chinese were enrolled in Christian colleges, as compared with 10 in 1873 and 164 in 1900.

In response to a demand that Chinese institutions could not yet meet, some of the Christian colleges expanded and many raised academic standards. They gave their youthful charges, especially the women, a modern education not readily available to them under non-Christian auspices. Indeed, many missionary teachers were recruited by Chinese schools. The impact on Chinese culture, on Chinese intellectual currents, was enormous, but the flow was not one way. The Christian colleges, as they reached out to Chinese intellectuals, became more secular, stressing educational rather than evangelistic goals. Their faculties often thought more about building "Christian character" than about conversion. As the missionary movement reached the point of highest impact on Chinese culture, providing Western ideas to Chinese university students, the students, generally uninterested in Christianity, subverted the initial missionary purpose by inducing the Christian colleges to emphasize language, history, science, and technology. There are few more fascinating examples of the benefits of cultural interaction.

The first two decades of the twentieth century were also the golden age of Chinese art collecting in the United States. The only important collection of East Asian art in America at the turn of the century was at the Boston Museum of Fine Arts, based primarily on Ernest Fenollosa's purchases of Japanese painting and Edward Morse's Japanese pottery. But it was no longer easy to find treasures in Japan and, after the Japanese passed a law to protect their national treasures, even harder to get them out. The Boston Museum turned to China to expand its holdings, taking advantage of unrest there before and after the revolution of 1911. Some Chinese masterpieces came on the market as Ch'ing dynasty mandarins liquidated their estates—or had them looted. Others were unearthed as railroad builders and well diggers stumbled upon ancient tombs.

Surpassing the Boston Museum in the acquisition of Chinese art was Charles L. Freer, a retired railroad car manufacturer. When Japanese art became too rare and thus too expensive, he, too, turned to China. As his collection and reputation grew, so did his sense of mission; he wanted more Americans to recognize the beauty and importance of Chinese art. To this end, he was exceptionally generous with parts of his collection, with advice and assistance to museums, and ultimately with the gift of his entire collection to his country. President Theodore Roosevelt persuaded the nation to accept the gift, and some years later the Freer Gallery of Art opened in Washington as part of the Smithsonian Institution.

Not to be outdone, the Metropolitan Museum of Art in New York, upon the advice of J. P. Morgan, turned to John C. Ferguson to buy Chinese paintings, pottery, and bronzes. Ferguson was a missionary educator with an extraordinary career in China. He founded a school that became Nanking University and administered another for a Chinese leader that became Chiao t'ung University in Shanghai, two of China's greatest universities. He owned a Chinese-language newspaper in Shanghai. He held a series of impressive posts in the Chinese government and undertook several missions for China to the United States. He advised American diplomats and explained Chinese culture to his countrymen in a host of articles.

In the process of becoming a mediator between the two cultures, Ferguson met many of the leading Chinese art collectors and connoisseurs. He read and wrote art history and reference books still essential to collectors and curators. And he bought and sold art. Not least among his accomplishments was his success in awakening the Metropolitan Museum to the opportunities to buy magnificent Chinese art.

By the early 1920s, Chinese masterpieces could be found in all the major American art museums, in Chicago, Cleveland, Kansas City, and St. Louis, as well as in Boston, New York, and Washington. Americans were taking Chinese art seriously and paying high prices for it. It was a step toward accepting Chinese as real people. If their art was precious, the product of sophistication, skill, and genius, then as a people they must be capable of sophistication, skill, and genius.

During the 1920s, however, both the Christian colleges and the Americans collecting art in China became embroiled with the forces of Chinese nationalism. Traditional Chinese ambivalence toward Western learning was less a problem for the colleges than the mounting demand for Chinese control of all educational institutions. Demand for at least joint control of the Christian colleges usually meant demand for elimination of religious instruction, as well as increased influence and salary for Chinese faculty. Art collectors, most notoriously Langdon Warner representing the Fogg Museum at Harvard, encountered harsh opposition to the removal of Chinese treasures. Both educators and collectors were forced to retreat as the Chinese rose to regain control of their country.

In China during the first few years following the collapse of Yüan Shih-k'ai's power, the main stage was dominated by a succession of military figures, each seeking the coalition necessary to give himself supreme power in China. While one group of warlords struggled for control of the Peking government, another group vied with Sun Yat-sen for control of a rival government established at Canton. Frequently, there was simultaneous fighting between North and South for control of all China. Amidst the resulting chaos, the Japanese consolidated their position, tightening their hold on the recognized government at Peking.

As early as January 1917, Reinsch had reported growing dissatisfaction with the regime's apparent subservience to Japan. He warned Lansing of the possibility of renewed revolution and suggested that there might emerge a united young-China movement aimed at ridding the country of reactionary mandarins and monarchists. In 1918, there was occasional evidence to support Reinsch's prediction, as a student movement, spearheaded by students returning from abroad, began to organize against Japanese pressures on the Chinese government—attempting to rouse public opinion to exert a counterpressure. Chinese intellectuals manifested increasing impatience with internal disorder, with the disunity that prevented the nation from mobilizing its energies against external oppression. As dissatisfaction and frustration mounted, especially in the universities, the Shantung issue took on a great symbolic importance. The effort to regain control over Shantung was viewed as a test of the government's will to resist Japan and of China's determination to reverse the imperialist tide that threatened to flood the land. While Woodrow Wilson and the leaders of the other victorious nations met in Paris to determine the shape of the new world, the Chinese waited restively.

Throughout April 1919, rumors spread in Peking of alleged Japanese interference with China's delegates to the peace conference. Quickly, organizations were created and demonstrations planned in an effort to mobilize the nation—and then the news arrived of the decision reached in Paris to leave Shantung in Japanese hands. Beginning with a demonstration in Peking on May 4, hundreds of thousands of students took to the streets in cities throughout China, committing acts of violence against allegedly pro-Japanese members of the government and organizing an effective boycott of Japanese goods. As the movement gained in intensity, Reinsch reported that "a storm of popular indignation swept over the country which is without parallel since the days of foreign intercourse with China." He described "the mobilization of an active public opinion, definite in its aims," as "a new development in Chinese political life."[1] Chinese students had become the ingredient necessary for the cementing of China's "loose sands" into a powerful nationalist force. Joining in the Chinese protest, Reinsch resigned. And in Hunan, a youthful Mao Tse-tung attacked Wilson's failure in his first recorded criticism of the United States.

The foreign community in China was astonished by the effectiveness of the movement, by the widespread expressions of patriotism, by the aroused state of the public. Many Americans, including businessmen, naval officers, and the visiting philosopher John Dewey, responded with great enthusiasm to the awakening of China. For the first time, Chinese intellectuals expressed the desire for a complete transformation of Chinese civilization. They had come to realize that the modernization of China required the destruction of the traditional society and they were demanding precisely the kinds of social and intellectual changes that Americans had long believed would result in the "civilizing," Westernizing, modernizing of China. Politically, antiforeign activity was centered in the anti-Japanese boycott, reinforcing the American assumption that Chinese nationalism would always be directed against Japan and the European imperialists, but never against the United States. Blind to American involvement in the framework of imperialism in China, assuming that the Chinese saw them as they saw themselves—as "champions of the sovereign rights of China"—Americans could be delighted by manifestations of Chinese nationalism. In addition, the students were working to end the civil strife that had disrupted Chinese affairs since Yüan's death—to restore the law and order that Americans deemed essential to China's progress. If the movement begun by the students succeeded, the world could look forward to a unified, modern China, friendly to the United States and able to protect its own territorial and administrative integrity. In sum, Americans expected a strong, independent China to fulfill the traditional aspirations of American businessmen, missionaries, and diplomats and thus responded enthusiastically to the May Fourth Movement.

Although many Americans were sympathetic to Chinese nationalism, interest in China per se was slight. During 1919 and 1920, the years in which Chinese students were most active, most Americans were being drawn back toward prewar domestic concerns. Those concerned with foreign affairs were deeply involved in the struggle over ratification of the Treaty of Versailles. Within the government of the United States, the battle with the Senate, the desperate effort to preserve the structure of the League of Nations, absorbed all of Woodrow Wilson's fading energies. No other issue of international relations could compete with the tragic drama of Wilson's defeat. And it should be remembered that even the issue of the compromise over Shantung, which contributed to Wilson's defeat, was raised not as a matter of having betrayed China, but rather of having betrayed the principle of self-determination. China thus became a significant issue in American politics for the first time, less out of concern for China than in defense of an abstract principle.

The new Harding administration quickly settled the issue of American ratification of the Treaty of Versailles and participation in the League of Nations, but could not escape from the popular demand that the United States take some great step to lead the world toward perpetual peace. Nor could Harding and his secretary of state, the able Charles Evans Hughes, escape from the dangers inherent in the tense state of Japanese-American relations—a legacy of Wilson's opposition to Japanese imperialism. Faced with strong domestic pressures for disarmament at the same time that Japanese naval building seemed to require the United States to launch a massive shipbuilding program to provide for American security, Hughes realized that the only solution to his dilemma was an agreement with Japan to halt the incipient naval race. Hughes was also sufficiently astute to realize that the arms race could not be isolated from a host of other problems, especially the Anglo-Japanese alliance, Japanese imperialism in China, and the balance of power in East Asia. He was receptive, therefore, to British overtures for an American-initiated conference that would include all nations with interests in the western Pacific, including China—but not the Soviet Union. Thus it was in response to the American quest for security outside the League of Nations, without a costly arms race, rather than in response to the rise of Chinese nationalism, that the Washington Conference of 1921–1922 was convened.

Throughout 1921, civil strife continued in most of China. Sun Yat-sen's fortunes rose and, buoyed by the new swell of nationalism, he resumed plans for the military reunification of the country. In July, the Chinese Communist Party was formally established with the help of Soviet agents, who also had discussions with Sun and other potential powers in both North and South. While the Kuomintang and the Communists plotted and the warlords warred, the rest of the world tried to communicate with China through the Peking regime. This government, buffeted by the winds of rising nationalism, was also committed to shedding the shackles of the so-called unequal treaties—the infringements on Chinese sovereignty constituted by the treaty system. And so, at the close of 1921, when China was invited to the Washington Conference, all factions saw an opportunity to reverse the failure at Versailles.

Among the Chinese people, the initial reaction to the invitation was one of great enthusiasm and optimism. The press reflected burgeoning hopes of ridding China of foreign spheres of influence, of extraterritoriality and of restrictions on tariff autonomy. The interested public assumed that Japan would be on the defensive and that the conference would be used to indict Japanese imperialism before the world. But by the eve of the conference a new mood of pessimism gripped thoughtful Chinese who realized that the nation's disunity, chaotic conditions, and empty treasury would force its delegates to negotiate from weakness. Sun's Canton regime had refused to participate in a joint mission, and when his demand for a separate invitation was rejected, he announced that he would not recognize any decisions made at the conference. Fears of what might occur in Washington led a number of nonpolitical organizations to send their own observers. The auspices were less than promising.

From the American vantage point, the Washington Conference proved to be a tremendous success. The Anglo-Japanese alliance was abrogated and to supersede it the Americans and French joined the British and Japanese in a four-power nonaggression pact that committed these nations to nothing more than consultations in the event of difficulties. Infinitely more satisfying to the American people was the Five-Power Treaty in which Italy joined the other four in an agreement to limit the size of their respective navies, thus checking the arms race.

As a result of the equilibrium achieved via the Four-Power and Five-Power treaties, the conference was then free to turn to the matter of China—of great-power competition in the western Pacific and of Chinese aspirations. Sentiment in the United States favored the Chinese position and the American and Chinese delegations worked together closely. On the eve of the conference, Harding's minister to China, Jacob Gould Schurman, sent a cable to Hughes, reporting enthusiastically on the new sense of patriotism that had developed in China since his last visit in 1899 and arguing that the Chinese were entitled to tariff autonomy and the removal of foreign post offices. Pessimistic about the prospects for political unification, anticipating an intensification of violence, he argued nonetheless that the powers would have to be patient and stand aside: "Only the Chinese can solve China's problems and they will do it in a Chinese way."[2]

The main concern of the Americans, Englishmen, and Japanese who met at Washington was neither the development nor the protection of China, but rather the stabilization of their competition in that country. China, like Turkey, was viewed as a potential source of friction among nations, its weakness a temptation to adventurism. First Great Britain offered a proposal designed to commit the others to its perception of an equitable settlement. For the United States, Elihu Root countered with a statement of principles intended to tie Great Britain and Japan to a broad interpretation of the Open Door, extending beyond equality of economic opportunity to include the preservation of China's territorial integrity. The Japanese delegates, once informed of the Anglo-American discussions, sought the acceptance of their claim to special interests in Manchuria and Inner Mongolia.

American insistence on equal opportunity for trade and investments did not trouble the Japanese. They were confident of their ability to compete successfully against the United States or any other country that challenged their economic position in China. American insistence on China's territorial integrity, however, continued to disturb them. But Root, in private talks with the Japanese delegates, assured them that his principles would not affect existing Japanese holdings, allowing them to conclude that their special interests would not be compromised by the proposed treaty. The British were easily reconciled to the apparent Japanese-American agreement.

Ultimately, in the Nine-Power Treaty, the participants in the conference agreed not to interfere in the internal affairs of China; to allow the Chinese to solve their domestic problems, unify their country and modernize it, in their own way and at their own pace. This was the "internationalization" of the American Open Door policy, the contracting parties agreeing "to respect the sovereignty, the independence, and the territorial and administrative integrity of China." Here, all hoped, was a step toward Wilson's solution to the problem of coexisting with Japanese power in East Asia. Had the Soviet Union been included, all of the powers with interests of significance in the area would have been committed to peaceful competition without prejudice to the interests of China.

However, the Nine-Power Treaty came nowhere near fulfilling the hopes of the Chinese delegates who had come to Washington. If the agreement, which contained no provision for enforcement, were respected, then there would be no *further* encroachments on Chinese sovereignty. Most of those rights of sovereignty that China had been forced to surrender during the previous eighty years remained unretrieved. In answer to China's demand to be allowed to set its own tariff rates, the powers offered a five-percent increase on imports and a promise of subsequent discussion. In answer to the Chinese demand for an end to extraterritoriality, the powers offered only a commission to study the problem. In answer to the Chinese demand for the withdrawal of foreign troops from Chinese soil, nothing was done.

Although Hughes had been unwilling to jeopardize the Pacific settlement by challenging Japan's position in Manchuria, the United States had helped the Chinese obtain British and Japanese promises to evacuate leaseholds— including substantial Japanese concessions on Shantung. In supporting the effort against spheres of influence, the Americans, having no sphere of their own, faced no conflict between ideals and self-interest. Toward those privileges of imperialism in which Americans shared, the United States took a less forthright position. As yet, the United States was not prepared to restore tariff autonomy to the Chinese; nor was the American position on extraterritoriality any less rigid than that of the other powers. Hughes and his principal adviser, J. V. A. MacMurray, preferred to wait for the Chinese to bring order to their own affairs before asking Americans to surrender the privileged status that they enjoyed under the treaty system.

Neither negotiations nor results brought satisfaction to Chinese anywhere. Ma Soo, Sun Yat-sen's watchdog in Washington, denounced the proposals put forth by the Chinese delegates as "platitudes and inane generalities." In the midst of negotiations, the secretary-general of the Chinese delegation resigned in protest against the unwillingness of the other participants to consider China's problems in a manner he deemed appropriate—and several lesser members of the mission followed his example. The decision of China's chief delegates to enter into bilateral discussions of the Shantung question with Japan led to protest marches in China and by Chinese in the United States. In Shanghai, 20,000 demonstrators indicated their displeasure with the course of events in Washington. From the vantage point of China, the conference had served the ends of the imperialist powers but had done little for the Chinese. And this point was underscored in Moscow, where representatives of Sun's Kuomintang and of the Chinese Communist Party attended a Comintern-sponsored "Congress of the Toilers of the Far East."

The Moscow Congress had been convened for the general purpose of asserting Soviet interest in any Pacific settlement—of reminding the powers that the Soviet Union also had interests in East Asia. Specifically, the congress had been called to attack the Washington Conference and allegedly spoke for the exploited Asian masses while their masters divided the spoils in Washington. Significantly, in addition to doctrinaire attacks on the imperialists, three different speakers, including the head of the Comintern, criticized Sun Yat-sen's Kuomintang for alleged pro-American sympathies. After Trotsky had called American capitalism the stronghold of world imperialism, the charge was indeed grave. For most Chinese, however, the struggle against very apparent Japanese and British activities was far too important to justify the diversion of any energy into an anti-American campaign. Nonetheless, the Soviet Union had served notice that it would not accept a settlement to which it was not a partner, and in the years following the Washington Conference a growing number of Chinese nationalists surrendered their hopes of American assistance and turned to Moscow.

In March 1920, while the fervor of the May Fourth Movement was still at high pitch, a document reached China indicating that the Soviet Union had renounced all the privileges that Tsarist Russia had extorted from the Chinese. This was the "Karakhan manifesto" by which the Soviet government presumably announced its intention to return the Chinese Eastern Railroad and all mining and forestry concessions—without compensation. The manifesto created a tremendous sensation in China, and Chinese intellectuals, regardless of political affiliation, tended to see the dawn of a new day—a new world ushered in by a Soviet onslaught against imperialism. Regrettably, key passages of the Karakhan proposal were no longer part of Soviet policy. The statement had been issued in July 1919, before the rise of Soviet fortunes during the civil war. By 1920, the Communists were feeling hardly more generous than the Tsarists before them. But Soviet denials of the authenticity of the Chinese text of the manifesto, especially regarding the Chinese Eastern Railroad, received little publicity in China and did virtually nothing to mitigate public excitement. The Russians were still making voluntary concessions far in excess of any offered by the other powers.

From 1920 to 1922, Soviet agents established contacts with important Chinese intellectuals and political figures. Most significant were developments that led to the formation of the Chinese Communist Party and closer ties with Sun Yat-sen. In the summer of 1922, Ch'en Chiung-ming's betrayal forced Sun to flee to Shanghai where, unsupported by any military power, he was temporarily without influence in Chinese politics. As he reached Shanghai, a Soviet envoy, Adolf Joffe, arrived in Peking. After exchanging a few letters with Sun, Joffe went to Shanghai to negotiate with him.

Earlier, Sun had always looked to Japan, to the West, and especially to the United States for guidance and help, but the response had been minimal. With the American government, Sun's stock had declined sharply in the years following the revolution of 1911. Reinsch, Lansing, and Wilson doubted both his wisdom and his principles. Reports from China indicated that even his own associates were embarrassed by his behavior, by his plots, and by his egotism. The American minister, Schurman, despite great sympathy for Chinese nationalism and despite an initially favorable impression of Sun's Canton regime, reported in the spring of 1922 that thoughtful Chinese and foreigners no longer sympathized with Sun and he personally believed that Sun "would be impossible as a responsible statesman."[3] Schurman estimated that Sun's influence was ebbing and his assessment proved correct, as weeks later Sun was driven out of Canton. In Washington, there seemed little reason why Sun, in rebellion against the recognized government of China, driven out of Canton by his own supporters, suspected of unprincipled behavior, should be taken seriously. Perceiving this lack of support, Sun turned to the Russians for the help he desperately needed.

While Sun and Joffe negotiated at Shanghai in January 1923, a reorganization of Sun's Kuomintang along the general lines of the Soviet Communist Party was announced. The foundation for a Kuomintang-Chinese Communist coalition and for an alliance between Sun's party and the Soviet Union had been prepared. In a joint declaration outlining their agreement, Sun and Joffe indicated that the Soviet Union would provide the Kuomintang with aid while accepting Sun's contention that conditions in China were inappropriate for the development of Communism. Shortly afterward, Sun's fortunes took a turn for the better and he was able to return to Canton where forces loyal to him had regained control.

As part of the cooperation between Sun and the Russians, a mission led by Chiang Kai-shek went to Moscow in August 1923, and the Comintern sent Michael Borodin to Canton. In Moscow, where Lenin was dying, Chiang spent three months talking with other Soviet leaders and studying the organization of the Red Army. After his return, he became superintendent of the newly created Whampoa Military Academy where the officers of the Kuomintang army were to be trained and indoctrinated. Borodin, in Canton, became Sun's adviser and helped Sun move the Kuomintang closer to the model of the Communist Party of the Soviet Union. In addition, Borodin established a school for the training of political cadres, giving Sun's followers badly needed lessons in politicizing and mobilizing the masses. And in 1924, the Soviet Union further ingratiated itself with Chinese nationalists by negotiating a convention with the Peking government to surrender some of the privileges of the "unequal treaties."

Despite all these developments and evidence of the increasing success of the Kuomintang-Communist effort to build a mass base for a new Chinese revolution, despite the obvious preparations for the Northern Expedition—Sun's great dream of marching north from Canton to unite China by force—the United States and the other Washington Conference signatories clung insensitively to the hated symbols of imperialism, the privileges of the treaty system. Moreover, it is clear that the United States failed to perceive that Sun's operations were something other than warlordism. In the fall of 1923, when Sun claimed a share of the customs duty surplus, American warships joined those of the powers in a naval demonstration designed to thwart him. Indeed, the Chinese Communist Party charged the United States with having inspired the demonstration.

Schurman recognized Sun's new strength and warned President Coolidge that Sun would be "a power to reckon with," but he undervalued Sun's connection with the Soviet Union and did not take his alleged Bolshevik tendencies very seriously. Nonetheless, Schurman was extremely critical of Sun, whom he considered to be egocentric and ruthless and whom he described as "a compound of William Jennings Bryan and a red-hot Eastside socialist in New York City."[4] But if Schurman was skeptical of the prospects for Communism in China, the one American diplomat who was studying the Chinese Communist movement was not.

J. C. Huston, vice-consul at Canton, wrote to MacMurray, who had been designated as Schurman's successor, and warned that the Russians had changed their tactics in the Far East—that they were no longer bothering to peddle Marxist nostrums for an industrial society. Instead they had chosen to stimulate anti-foreignism in China, to focus on the comparatively easy task of convincing "the average Chinese nationalist that all of China's troubles are due to the blood-sucking imperialist countries."[5] Still the United States refused to make any concessions to China's quest for treaty revision.

From 1922 to 1925, Schurman in Peking and MacMurray in Washington had essential control over American policy toward China. So long as China remained an area of minor concern to the United States, so long as events there were insufficiently dramatic to draw American attention away from domestic affairs and less remote foreign problems, such as those with Mexico, the minister and an assistant secretary would decide policy. Schurman's years in China brought him closer to the views long held by MacMurray: that concessions to China, especially the abolition of extraterritoriality, would have to await order in China. Although "utterly opposed" to foreign intervention, Schurman wanted the United States to insist on its treaty rights in China. He was aware that the Chinese were increasingly unwilling to recognize these presumed rights, but had not conceived of the situation in which China's refusal to honor its treaty obligations would force the United States to choose between intervention and the surrender of its rights in China. In 1924, he called only for the powers to honor their promise to convene a commission to study the tariff question.

MacMurray's position, as he prepared to leave for China in May 1925, was still less sympathetic. He argued that all the powers except China had observed the principles of the Washington treaties, but none had anticipated the extent to which the settlement would be impaired by the Chinese. Attributing China's new burst of nationalism to Soviet agitation, he described the Chinese as having become "very self-assertive, knowing little of what that assertation [sic] means."[6]

Early in 1925, Sun Yat-sen died, and before the matter of succession was clear, on May 30, an incident arising out of a strike against Japanese-controlled textile mills led to the May 30th Movement—a spontaneous outburst of anti-imperialist, antiforeign sentiment that spread from Shanghai through China's cities and ultimately even to the countryside. Arriving in China shortly after the incident, with the country aflame with the fever of nationalism of which he had so recently spoken, Mac-Murray still opposed concessions to the Chinese; not before China honored its treaty obligations could treaty revision be considered. He warned Washington that to yield would "encourage a spirit of irresponsibility with which even the soberest Chinese have recently been infected through various Bolshevik and juvenile nationalistic influences."[7] Officially, the United States refused to surrender unilaterally any privileges enjoyed by Americans, but expressed a willingness to participate in an international conference to discuss these matters.

To the Chinese Communists and perhaps to other Chinese nationalists as well, the American position seemed an obvious ruse. The Communists contended that the Americans knew that their privileges in China were relatively limited and that Japan and England were not likely to second the American suggestion. The Americans were charged with using insincere methods "to deceive the Chinese people and to pursue their monopolistic commercial lust in China."[8] If Americans were genuinely sympathetic with China's demands, they could follow the Soviet example. But the United States was not yet ready to make the appropriate response.

Given the limited importance of China to the United States and the limited interest of Americans in China, the United States could hardly have given active support to Chinese nationalists during the years immediately following the Washington Conference—even if this had been possible without interference in China's internal affairs, which it was not. Nonetheless, it is apparent that the American response to Sun and to the demands of Chinese nationalism was inadequate. Despite the evidence provided by years of observing how easily the Germans, deprived of their treaty privileges at the end of the World War, functioned in China without these privileges, the United States refused to yield. Responsible officials in the American government, particularly MacMurray, failed to appreciate the significance of the intensity with which the Chinese abhorred the symbolic fetters of the unequal treaties. The United States sought to deal with these highly emotional issues within the same rational and legal framework that characterized its relations with nations traditionally treated as equals and enjoying the luxury of domestic tranquility: it insisted that China observe its treaty obligations. Not merely recognizing China's need to modernize but encouraging the process, the United States nonetheless demanded order, seemingly unaware that the ancient scales of Chinese society could hardly be scraped away without the sword. A combination of sterile legalism and a rigid insistence on order shaped American policy.

But after the Northern Expedition began in 1926, the United States was confronted with a new and serious challenge. With virtually all Chinese demanding treaty revision and the Kuomintang-Communist coalition warning of its intention to abrogate the treaties unilaterally if necessary, would the United States yield? If not, what action was the United States prepared to take to prevent China from unilaterally abandoning its treaty obligations?

In fact, the basic American decision to grant tariff autonomy to the Chinese and to negotiate the surrender of extraterritoriality *preceded* the launching of the Northern Expedition, having been reached in the weeks immediately following the May 30 incident. Although MacMurray insisted that treaty revision would reinforce Chinese unreasonableness, his superiors in Washington persisted in their willingness to relinquish privileges Americans enjoyed under the "unequal treaties." Not even the objections of the British and Japanese governments, whose representatives agreed with MacMurray, deterred Washington.

The reversal of the American attitude on treaty revision came in response to the violence of the May 30th Movement, which forced Chinese affairs on the consciousness of the new secretary of state, Frank Kellogg. The American business community in Shanghai was demanding the dispatch of gunboats and MacMurray was insisting on firmness, but Kellogg was concerned with the response of the American people and Congress. It had become increasingly apparent during the early 1920s that public opinion in the United States would no longer tolerate gunboat diplomacy. Indeed, the continued stationing of American troops in China in accordance with provisions of the Boxer Protocol had come under fire. The American people had become increasingly anti-imperialist, increasingly sensitive to the use of force against underdeveloped countries, whether in Latin America or in Asia. Mounting disillusionment with the aftermath of the World War had greatly stimulated movements in opposition to the use of force in world affairs. By 1925, the domestic pressures that would soon drive Kellogg to sign a pact outlawing war were already evident. In addition, increasing numbers of Americans believed that the United States had intervened in the World War to serve the selfish ends

China under the warlords

of a privileged few. Against this setting, the American government could not but be hesitant about preserving American privileges in China with military action.

Beyond the limits imposed on American policy by public opinion, Kellogg's decision to yield to the Chinese demands for treaty revision was influenced by the views of his principal adviser on Chinese affairs, Nelson T. Johnson. Unlike MacMurray, Johnson had concluded that revolution and its accompanying violence and disorder were necessary before the Chinese could slough off the moribund civilization that thwarted their development. Despite occasional nervousness caused by evidence of Soviet influence on Chinese nationalism, Kellogg accepted Johnson's basic premise. Similarly, as he watched China struggle to modernize, he recognized instinctively that the rationale for the old imperialistic perquisites was disappearing; that the United States and all the powers had to prepare to restore to China complete sovereignty as soon as possible. In the process, Kellogg and Johnson were determined to retain what they believed to be America's image as China's leading friend.

If public opposition to the use of force in China made the Kellogg-Johnson policy a necessity, their instincts and assumptions about China converted necessity into virtue. Concerned about Soviet imperialism, they concluded that the success of the Chinese nationalists would be the best defense against that threat. They brushed aside MacMurray's fear of Bolshevism with the fragile conviction that Communism was too alien a concept, too far removed from Chinese realities to succeed in China. Thus fortified, Americans in Washington could share the frequently expressed view of the Chinese revolution as a worthy imitator of the American revolution—a thoroughly praiseworthy quest by the Chinese for the freedom to determine their own future—a freedom promised to them at the Washington Conference. And if the United States led in the restoration of Chinese sovereignty, remained foremost of China's friends, the proponent of self-determination for the Chinese people, then Chinese nationalists could only reciprocate this friendship. In short, the expedient policy of yielding to Chinese demands for treaty revision and the abrogation of the treaty system, of accepting rather than bemoaning the disorder of the modernization process, was determined to be congruent not only with American ideals but with the interests of the United States as well.

With American opinion virtually united in the view that peaceful solutions to all problems were necessary and possible and the American government prepared to surrender the privileges of imperialism in China, the obvious course was to yield as gracefully as possible, brushing aside MacMurray's protests and the legal considerations on which they were based. Once having decided to yield, the rest should have been easy, but *to whom* should the United States yield? From October 1925 to the close of 1928, China was again torn by civil strife, at times more violent than any of the disorders that had plagued that unfortunate country since the collapse of Yüan Shih-k'ai's power. In 1926, the Kuomintang-Communist coalition, while mobilizing the masses behind demands for abolition of the "unequal treaties," was in fact *opposed* to any treaty revision for the simple reason that such revision would aid their enemies by increasing the revenues and prestige of the warlords who controlled the Peking government. On the other hand, the failure to implement surtaxes promised at the Washington Conference was alleged to be unneutral by the enemies of the Kuomintang. Considerations of this kind, rather than hostility to the aspirations of Chinese nationalists, dictated American policy in the years before the Kuomintang achieved at least nominal control over China.

From the summer of 1925 to the summer of 1926, the Kuomintang's newly formed Nationalist government of China fought to consolidate its position in the south. Military success and diplomacy combined to give the Nationalist government a secure base in the provinces of Kwantung and Kwangsi. Similarly, in the north, a combination of fighting and political maneuvering led to a realignment of the various warlords, with Chang Tso-lin, Wu P'ei-fu, and Sun Ch'uan-fang emerging as the dominant military powers in China. With Chang controlling northern China with his Manchurian stronghold and Japanese support behind him, Sun dominant in the five eastern provinces along the Yangtze Valley, and Wu to the west, the route north was blocked by troops outnumbering those of the Nationalists by a ratio in excess of 5:1.

The Nationalist movement faced not only overwhelming military odds, but internal divisions as well. With Sun Yat-sen's death, the struggle for succession began. The basic split within the Kuomintang resulted from Sun's policy of admitting Communists to the Kuomintang and allying with the Soviet Union. The party's right wing, led by Hu Han-min, feared Soviet influence and sought to end the alliance and expel the Communists. The Left, led by Wang Ching-wei, sought to continue the party's Soviet orientation. After an initial balanced government broke down, the

Kuomintang Left, headed by Wang and Chiang Kai-shek, succeeded in squeezing out the Right, expelling the right-wing leadership from the party in January 1926. The Chinese Communists, allied with the Kuomintang Left, seemed to have the situation well in hand.

Suddenly, in March, Chiang struck at Canton. Contending that the Communists were plotting to gain control of the army, he deprived them of all positions of military authority, and arrested many of them. Wang, the head of the Nationalist government, was not forewarned and inter-preted Chiang's maneuver as an indication that he might best retire from the scene. Chiang had seized effective control of Nationalist military power. When Borodin returned to Canton, he had no recourse but to bar-gain with Chiang. Despite a strong urge within the Chinese Communist party to rise in opposition, and support from Trotsky for this position, the Comintern decided the time was not ripe for a split. Instead, Borodin was instructed to offer approval for the commencement of the Northern Expe-dition, continued Soviet aid, and restraints on Communist agitation in return for Chiang's willingness to contain the Kuomintang Right. In July, his position secure, Chiang launched the Northern Expedition.

As Chiang's armies struggled to unite China, the powers stood by and interfered but little. In fact, in December, the British offered to revise the unequal treaties and a month later, the Americans matched the British overture, as Kellogg sought to regain American leadership among those willing to move toward a restoration of Chinese sovereignty. In the fall and winter of 1926–1927, the Nationalist forces first defeated Wu P'ei-fu's troops and then began to drive Sun Ch'uan-fang's men out of the Yangtze valley. In March, a Communist-led uprising in Shanghai eased Chiang's task in capturing that city and a few days later, Nationalist forces occupied Nanking.

Although Shanghai had been taken without serious incident, on ar-rival at Nanking Nationalist soldiers attacked foreigners and foreign property, including the American, British, and Japanese consulates. Sev-eral foreigners were murdered by Nationalist troops, among them the American vice president of the University of Nanking. The looting of foreign property and threats to the lives of foreigners did not stop until after American and British gunboats began to bombard the attackers. Here indeed was a test for the Kellogg-Johnson effort to befriend Chinese nationalism.

Despite claims that the violence at Nanking was the work of agent provocateurs, designed to embarrass Chiang Kai-shek—claims that became increasingly credible as a great power struggle within the Kuomintang surfaced in April—the powers concluded that the Nationalists should be held responsible. Identical notes were delivered to the Nationalist government, demanding punishment of those responsible for the outrages, a written apology from Chiang plus assurances that the Nationalists would prevent the recurrence of such incidents, and reparations for damages and loss of life. A British effort to place a time limit within which the demands would have to be satisfied and to threaten sanctions was rejected by both the United States and Japan.

On the day after the notes were presented, Chiang ordered the arrest and massacre of several hundred Communists and labor leaders at Shanghai. Thus, at a moment of tension between the Nationalists and the powers, he began a crucial series of political and military maneuvers that ultimately enabled him to best Stalin, squeezing out the Communists before they eliminated him. But in the interim, the pressure of the powers for a settlement of the Nanking incident created a grave dilemma. Too recalcitrant a response might provoke intervention and too conciliatory a response would likely evoke allegations of a sellout to the imperialists, undermining Chiang's position in the internal struggle. The two issues had become intertwined and the safest tactic proved to be delay.

Among the powers, the Japanese had the clearest perception of the meaning of the turmoil within the Kuomintang and sought to reach an understanding with Chiang and the opposition government he formed at Nanking. The Americans were troubled and confused. MacMurray warned his superiors against backing Chiang, for whom he had a very low regard. He suspected that the alleged split was being staged by the Russians to deceive the powers, and argued that even a genuine conflict within the Kuomintang would be meaningless because Chiang was as ruthless, untrustworthy, and antiforeign as his presumably more radical opponents. But Kellogg and Johnson received advice from other sources in China and inclined to the hope that a moderate faction was emerging that would be willing to settle the Nanking incident. The Left-Kuomintang-controlled Nationalist government at Wuhan seemed uncooperative, MacMurray's thoughts of working with the northern warlords incredible—in short, there was no apparent alternative. In May 1927, MacMurray was instructed to enter into negotiations with Chiang's foreign minister, but the time was not yet ripe for a settlement. Developments in the internal conflict overshadowed diplomatic efforts.

During the late spring of 1927, there were rumblings within the Wuhan government as some of its leaders became apprehensive about Chinese Communist and Soviet intentions. A conflict emerged between Communist organizers and Soviet advisers on the one hand and the non-Communist military leaders of the Left on the other. Finally, in July, the Wuhan Nationalists turned on their Communist allies and the White Terror swept China. Wherever either Nanking- or Wuhan-controlled Nationalist forces existed, Communists and "radicals" were pursued and massacred. The Soviet advisers, including Borodin, fled the country, as did several leading Kuomintang leftists. The remaining Chinese Communists literally took to the hills, ultimately regrouping in Kiangsi. The party's Central Committee, however, took refuge in the International Settlement in Shanghai, where its leadership was revamped and scapegoats sought for Stalin's errors.

Even after the purge, factionalism continued to prevent the reunification of the Nationalists. In August, Chiang found it expedient to go into temporary retirement and in September, his principal competitor, Wang Ching-wei, followed suit. By November, Wang, T. V. Soong, and the former Kuomintang Right leader, Hu Han-min, had established another government in Canton. The political leadership of the Kuomintang was proving itself sterile, unable to subordinate individual ambitions to the interests of party and nation. The Comintern chose this moment to order an uprising in Canton, the ill-fated Canton Commune. Amidst the disorder, Chiang returned to the fore and in January 1928, once again held the reins of the Nationalist revolution.

Although the Japanese had already chosen Chiang as the man with whom they could work, the Americans were understandably puzzled and depressed by the course of Chinese politics. They were not even cheered by the expulsion of Soviet influence, which to some American diplomats seemed to provide what little cohesion the nationalist movement had had. MacMurray—and even Nelson Johnson—could see little cause for rejoicing at Chiang's return. Whether in China or in Washington, American observers foresaw a return to militarism, with Chiang as perhaps top warlord. They discerned no meaningful ideology, no indication that the Nationalist leaders would carry out the reforms prerequisite to the promised modernization of China. Nonetheless, the United States remained committed to the idea of relinquishing the treaty system.

Reasonably confident of Japanese support, Chiang's regime sought to play the Americans off against the British by seeking an understanding with the United States. In March, the Nationalists were ready to settle the Nanking incident and accepted the American terms, with MacMurray grudgingly expressing regrets for the naval bombardment in which American vessels had participated. But still the United States withheld recognition, awaiting the outcome of the resumed Northern Expedition against Chang Tso-lin and the warlord regime at Peking.

Suddenly, in May, Nationalist troops clashed with Japanese forces in Shantung. Atavistic militarism was on the rise in Japan. In a few days the Japanese army succeeded in demolishing the edifice of goodwill that Japan's statesmen had so carefully labored to construct since they first conceived of Chiang Kai-shek as a moderate nationalist and potential bulwark against Communism in Asia. When the Japanese government attempted to retrieve the situation by forcing Chang Tso-lin to retreat into Manchuria, leaving all of China south of the Great Wall under Nationalist control, the Japanese army assassinated Chang, hoping to create confusion sufficient to justify an army plan to take virtually complete control of Manchuria. The ensuing confusion in Tokyo, combined with the obvious unwillingness of any segment of the Japanese government to contemplate the exercise of Chinese sovereignty in Manchuria, precluded the possibility of Sino-Japanese understanding. Once again in Chinese history, the Americans, at least by default, seemed the most benign of the imperialists.

Although Kellogg and Johnson had few illusions as to Kuomintang unity and the real as opposed to the nominal authority of the Nationalist government, they chose to interpret the successful conclusion of the Northern Expedition as evidence that the Nationalists had established themselves as the de facto government of China. Accordingly, Kellogg instructed MacMurray to negotiate a new tariff treaty. In July 1928, the United States and China signed such a treaty, granting tariff autonomy to China and containing a mutual guarantee of most-favored-nation treatment. Constituting recognition of Chiang's government, the signing of the treaty symbolized the successful conclusion of Kellogg's quest to establish his country as China's principal friend.

Whatever the deficiencies of the American policy of nonintervention in Chinese politics, of the tardy response to Chinese nationalism, it was clear in 1928 that Americans had reason to be satisfied with their government's policy. The Soviet Union, the nation that had interfered most, aiding the Kuomintang, manipulating the Chinese Communist Party, and giving focus to the nationalist movement, had been rewarded with the

almost total exclusion of Soviet influence from China. Japanese med-
dling won few friends in Nanking. In 1928, if only by the grace of God
and the good instincts of Kellogg and Johnson, American policy had facilitated a rapprochement with Nationalist China. Once again, Americans
could view themselves as champions of the sovereign rights of China.

On October 10,1928, "Double Ten," the seventeenth anniversary of the
beginning of the Chinese Revolution, Chiang and his followers proclaimed the existence of the National government of China, under the
"tutelage" of the Kuomintang. Faithful to the Soviet model that had inspired the party's reorganization, the Kuomintang created a government
that was in fact a one-party dictatorship. In December, Chang Hsueh-liang,
who had inherited his father's forces, reached agreement with Chiang
and raised the flag of the National government over Manchuria. To
Americans convinced of the need for order as a prerequisite to progress,
another moment of optimism had arrived. Even MacMurray ceased for
the moment to be a harbinger of doom and admitted that the "hopeless
minority" of sensible and patriotic Chinese leaders might "in time" be
successful.

Chiang's government, however, faced a truly Herculean task—and in
many respects an analogy with the Augean stables may be particularly
appropriate. In foreign affairs, relations with China's two closest neighbors, the Soviet Union and Japan, were strained. The quest for the restoration of China's sovereign rights moved ahead slowly with tariff autonomy
regained by 1930 and a number of European concessions returned to
Chinese control. On the issue of extraterritoriality, the Chinese had less
success as Great Britain, Japan, and the United States refused to yield—
although significant negotiations were in progress at the time of the Mukden incident.

Internally, the problems facing Chiang were more serious. In 1928,
the Chinese government was virtually bankrupt and lacked adequate
sources of income. The powers still controlled the tariff, limiting that
potential for revenue, and a host of economic, social, political, and military obstacles blocked the collection of internal taxes. China's credit rat-
ing was low and the government's aggressive nationalism did not appear
likely to attract new foreign capital. The regime's economic problems were
aggravated by the political situation that, in reality, approximated Mac-
Murray's vision on one of his gloomier days. The government of China
was a one-party dictatorship and all the generals joined the party but, for

the most part, retained their lust for power. Similarly, the various political leaders who had vied for power in the previous decade continued their machinations within the Kuomintang. Lest Chiang ever grow complacent about his ability to harness the wild horses within his own party, Communist forces led by Mao Tse-tung and Chu Teh were mobilizing peasants in Kiangsi and practicing guerrilla warfare.

The stables were far from spotless when the Japanese struck in 1931, but Chiang's regime had made considerable progress toward the solution of its domestic problems—and friendship with the United States had helped. Improved Sino-American relations facilitated the negotiation of loans from private American banks. From the United States—and from the League of Nations—came technical advisers, secular missionaries to aid in the modernization of China. And American corporations undertook the essential task of developing Chinese transportation and communication facilities—the network through which the central government at Nanking could aspire to exercise actual control over all of China. With this assistance, Chiang's determination, and able performances by Chiang's brothers-in-law, H. H. K'ung and T. V. Soong, major financial reforms were carried out, giving the government funds for its operating expenses. In addition, tariff autonomy brought in its wake increased revenue. Gradually, the credit of the Chinese government rose, making more capital available. There were weaknesses, to be sure, as one would expect in a situation where a coalition of landlords and generals ruled. Sun Yat-sen's promise of land reform was lost and China's peasant masses continued to suffer. Government and semi-independent armies devoured far too much of goods and tax revenues. But there was a semblance of order; there were reforms—and there was hope.

In his political maneuverings Chiang proved that the outwitting of Stalin had not been mere luck. Insurrections by Kuomintang generals and alternate governments established by disaffected Kuomintang politicians were squelched as Chiang and his forces out-fought, out-bargained, and out-compromised all of his rivals. Throughout, he remained convinced that the gravest threat to China came from the Chinese Communists, and during lulls in the struggles against his Kuomintang comrades, especially after the Communist attack on Changsha in 1930, he focused his attention on the extermination of the Red menace. Despite a disastrous beginning, the anti-Communist "bandit-suppression" campaigns appeared on the verge of success in September 1931.

The American reaction to the Chinese political scene was first one of disgust and then of cautious optimism. Nelson Johnson went to China in 1930 to replace MacMurray but found his sympathetic attitude difficult to sustain when experiencing the chaotic conditions firsthand. He judged Chiang and his coterie to be devoid of ideals, leading the pack only because of superior finances and arms. No matter where he looked, he could find no Chinese leader willing to do anything but prey on the peasant. He could not decide whether to take the Chinese Communist movement seriously, describing the Communists on one day as Robin Hoods whose influence with the peasants endangered the government and on another as bandits hiding behind the Red flag. In August 1930, he recommended the suspension of talks on extraterritoriality because of the limited control Nanking seemed to exercise at the moment. And yet in March 1931, he contended that Chiang's regime was the "strongest organization that the Chinese have had since 1911" and he guessed that "given five years of peace and reasonable crops the chances of this government surviving will be pretty good."[9] But what passed for peace in China lasted hardly more than five months.

As the diplomatic negotiations for the abrogation of extraterritoriality were strung out, the main focus of China's international relations became Manchuria once again. In the spring of 1929, despite all the internal complications he faced, Chiang chose to begin the task of squeezing the imperialists out of the rich northeastern provinces over which the Russians and Japanese had fought in 1904–5 and in which the Japanese had labored ever after to establish their "special position."

Apparently believing that the Soviet Union could be singled out and pushed with impunity, the Chinese began to harass Soviet citizens and diplomats. In July, the Chinese seized control of the Chinese Eastern Railroad. The Russians demanded an end to the harassment and a restoration of the *status quo ante*, but the Chinese refused. After three months of unsatisfactory negotiations, Soviet forces attacked and ultimately forced the Chinese to yield. The American secretary of state, Henry Stimson, sought to invoke the Kellogg-Briand Pact in which both China and the Soviet Union had renounced war as an instrument of national policy, but to no avail. For his trouble he received a tart Soviet reply that expressed amazement that the United States, while refusing to recognize the Soviet government, nonetheless assumed the right to offer it advice.

The Chinese had been stung, but the nationalist spirit was not so easily subdued. Chiang turned next to the Japanese and sought by more
subtle means to loosen their grip on Manchuria. From the first, American diplomats were convinced that the Japanese would tolerate no infringements of the treaty rights they had amassed. Although there were
exceptions, these Americans generally were willing to acquiesce in continued Japanese control of Manchuria. William Castle, undersecretary of
state, held views similar to those of Theodore Roosevelt and was determined to leave Japan alone on the Asian mainland. Even Nelson Johnson, while underestimating the intensity of feeling within Japan, wrote
in March 1931: "Manchuria becomes more Chinese every day but if Manchuria is destined to become part of Japan, I do not see why that should
necessarily embroil us."[10]

And Japan's Kwantung army, quartered in Manchuria, watching the
area become "more Chinese every day," despaired of the Japanese government's effort to secure its fief. On the evening of September 18, the army
executed its own response to the rise of Chinese nationalism. After setting
off an explosion on the South Manchuria Railroad (which was owned
and operated by Japan), in order to allege Chinese provocation, thousands
of Japanese troops carried out a well-organized plan, capturing Mukden
within hours and beginning the conquest of Manchuria. The age of Japanese militarism had dawned.

5 China as an Abstraction— The Conflict with Japan

When the Kwantung army commenced its operations in Manchuria, the Nationalist government of China was already confronted with internal upheavals sufficient to strain its limited power. Continued factionalism within the Kuomintang had led to the establishment of still another separatist regime at Canton. A graver threat to the government existed in Kiangsi, where the mistakes of his generals necessitated Chiang Kai-shek's personal supervision of the campaign against Communist forces led by Mao Tse-tung and Chu Teh. Informed of the Japanese attack, Chiang chose to concentrate his efforts against the Communists, convinced that they were a cancer that had to be removed before China had a chance to survive against an external enemy. Ordering Chinese forces in Manchuria not to resist, he apparently hoped to deprive the Japanese of an excuse to expand their operations beyond Mukden. In addition to his own efforts to localize the incident, he counted on appeals to the League of Nations, Great Britain, and the United States to mobilize international pressure for the task of checking Japan. T. V. Soong informed an American diplomat that a "military concentration on the North would leave the South a prey to chaos and Communism" and was therefore considered impossible.[1]

Unfortunately for China, the autumn of 1931 proved to be a poor time to attempt to attract the support of the Western world, already grievously burdened by the weight of the Great Depression. In the United States, the search for an escape from economic stagnation fully occupied the administration of Herbert Hoover, not excepting the secretary of state, Henry Stimson. The great majority of the American people had but one foreign policy interest: the collection of war debts owed to the United States by its erstwhile European allies. A broader conception of world affairs was very nearly the monopoly of the American peace movement which, in September 1931, was focusing its attention on preparations for the World Disarmament Conference scheduled to convene in February 1932.

Beyond the American preoccupation with urgent domestic problems, there were other considerations precluding a favorable response to Chiang's appeal. Japan had long been dominant in Manchuria, and if Americans did not like Japan's special relationship to those Chinese provinces, they had grown accustomed to living with it. Leading American diplomats, including those who, like Nelson Johnson, were clearly sympathetic to China, had concluded that it would be best not to interfere with Japan in East Asia. Even Stanley K. Hornbeck, chief of the Division of Far Eastern Affairs, a man long reputed to be pro-Chinese and anti-Japanese, was prepared to accept Japanese domination of Manchuria. Basically, these men recognized the fact of Japan's vital interest in the area and the absence of any significant American interest. Like Theodore Roosevelt, they combined a strong sympathy for China with a disinclination to challenge Japanese power, particularly in Manchuria.

There was also some hope, perhaps wishful thinking, in Washington and other capitals that the Japanese government would be able to regain control and restrain the army. Throughout the decade of the 1930s, a number of Americans argued that Japanese moderates would be hurt if the United States threatened Japan, and in 1931, given the press of other affairs and the limited nature of American interests in Manchuria, Stimson gladly chose to wait watchfully. Regrettably, the day of the moderates had already passed in Japan.

The assurances of the Japanese government to the contrary, the Japanese army continued to advance through Manchuria during the remainder of September and on into October. The Chinese called on the United States to invoke the Kellogg-Briand Pact that the United States had sponsored and that had resulted in the nearly universal renunciation of war as an instrument of national policy. Having been embarrassed by his unsuccessful resort to the pact during the Sino-Soviet crisis of 1929, Stimson held back, hoping the conflict could be halted by direct negotiations or by the use of the machinery provided by the League Covenant. The Hoover administration had no desire to assume the responsibilities of world leadership and Hoover, in particular, feared an effort by the League Council to pass the problem off onto the United States. Nonetheless, as the Japanese army rolled on, Hoover permitted the American consul-general at Geneva to participate in the discussions of the League Council—the first such participation by an official of the United States. After several European nations called on the Chinese and Japanese to remember their obligations under the Kellogg Pact, Stimson sent similar messages. The American humorist Will Rogers, feared, however, that the nations of the world would run out of stationery before Japan ran out of troops to send to Manchuria.

As it became apparent that the Japanese army did not intend to halt short of the complete conquest of Manchuria, there was despair in China. Chiang's hope of localizing the conflict had not been realized and his refusal to fight the Japanese instead of the Communists incited discontent among patriotic Chinese students. In October, he found it necessary to resign as president. Rumors spread through China of a secret arrangement between the United States and Japan wherein the Americans would allow the Japanese a free hand in Manchuria. The Communists contended that the United States was supporting Japanese aggression in the hope of provoking a war between Japan and the Soviet Union. In the United States, there was suspicion within the peace movement of a bargain between the American and Japanese governments. From peace organizations and especially from Dorothy Detzer, executive secretary of the Women's International League for Peace and Freedom, came demands that the United States take some form of action to stop Japanese aggression.

In fact, the United States, during the Manchurian crisis, was confronted with the dilemma that Roosevelt had posed for Knox in 1910. Americans could abandon their insistence on equality of economic opportunity and their concern for Chinese sovereignty or they could prepare to fight a powerful Japan. Within the Department of State, there was essential agreement that American interests in Manchuria in particular and China in general were insignificant; there was no reason to fight. From Secretary of War Patrick Hurley came the information that the military was unprepared to fight—that the American army and navy were not strong enough to fight even if the will to use force existed. And the president

TABLE 5.1   The American Economic Stake in China, 1920–1931

Year	U.S. Exports to China (in $ million)	Percentage of Total U.S. Export Trade	U.S. Investments in China (in $ million)	Percentage of Total U.S. Investments Overseas
1920	146	1.8		
1921	108	2.4		
1922	100	2.6		
1923	109	2.6		
1924	109	2.4		
1925	94	1.9		
1926	110	2.3		
1927	83	1.7		
1928	138	2.7		
1929	124	2.4		
1930	90	2.3		
1931	98	4.0	196.8	1.2

was resolutely opposed not only to the use of force but also to economic sanctions, to which Japan might respond with force. Given this complex of circumstances and attitudes, a decision to appease Japan seemed obvious.

In one important respect, however, the world had changed since Theodore Roosevelt had conceived of it in Hobbesian terms. There now existed an international organization, a multilateral promise to leave the Chinese free to determine their own future, and a nearly universal agreement among nations not to resort to war as an instrument of national policy—machinery for the peaceful settlement of disputes and treaty obligations barring military solutions. The United States had rejected membership in the League of Nations but had been instrumental in working out the Pacific settlement of 1922 and in the creation of the Kellogg Peace Pact first signed in 1928. Most of the nations of the world had joined to form an international community which, however imperfect the compact and however cumbersome the means of enforcement, had nonetheless aroused great hopes among men that peace and justice would prevail throughout the universe. When Japan, by its actions in Manchuria, violated the compact and threatened the peace system, many thoughtful Americans perceived a threat not only to the peace of the world, but to the interests of the United States as well.

The strongest pressure for action came from the peace movement, from supporters of the League of Nations, of disarmament and of the outlawry of war. Whatever the differences within the movement, all recognized the danger and sought means short of war by which to stop Japan. The decision by Stimson and Hoover to enter into discussions with the League provided some hope for these men and women.

The same basic conception of the significance of Japanese aggression was offered by Hornbeck and Johnson and shared by Stimson. Hornbeck approached the problem not from the standpoint of Japan's threat to China or of specific American interests in the Far East, but as a threat to the peace of the world. To Stimson he argued that the Japanese had violated the Kellogg Pact and that "any American protest should not appear as part of traditional American Far Eastern policy but as cooperation with the international movement for world peace."[2] Johnson remained indifferent to the future of Manchuria but was apprehensive of a second world war if Japan could undermine the peace system by brushing aside the League and the Kellogg Pact. To the extent that Americans, in and out of the government, concerned themselves with the Manchurian crisis, they were concerned not with China but with the peace system. When they contended that American interests were at stake, they did not refer to economic interests that they considered insufficient to justify risking Japan's ire. They did not refer to strategic interests in the traditional sense of American concern for the power balance in East Asia. Japan had long dominated Manchuria and the balance was little affected by her current choice of means. But insofar as Japan's choice of means—military aggression—violated Japan's treaty obligations and mocked the League of Nations, it threatened the peace system that these people had hoped would keep the United States out of war.

For Herbert Hoover, however, so indirect a threat could not compete with the very concrete problems he faced within the United States. Congress indicated no willingness to consider Japan's actions a threat to *any* interests of the United States, and in the Senate, especially, there was strong opposition to an American stand against Japan. Not even Stimson was prepared for the United States to take the principal role in East Asia when the League members appeared to abdicate their responsibilities.

And yet, if the United States would not fight, the administration could not accept the alternative of appeasement. Years before, Roosevelt had conceived of an amoral world order in which power considerations were paramount. But a primary assumption of American policy in 1931 was that there existed a new world order in which moral sanctions, appeals to world public opinion, could keep the peace. To Stimson and Hoover there appeared another alternative, that of moral diplomacy—the nonrecognition of the fruits of Japanese imperialism and, if necessary, the condemnation of Japan. In January 1932, Stimson informed both the Chinese and the Japanese that the United States would recognize no impairment of its treaty rights, including those relating to the sovereignty, independence, or territorial and administrative integrity of China; nor would the United States recognize any situation brought about by means contrary to the obligations of the Kellogg Peace Pact. This statement, ultimately labeled the Hoover-Stimson Doctrine, was based on the precedent of Bryan's unsuccessful policy of 1915 at the time of the Twenty-One Demands. But Bryan's failure had come before the creation of the postwar peace machinery, and Stimson had the presumed advantage of appealing to Japan's treaty obligations, as well as lacking a palatable alternative.

Nonrecognition failed in 1932 as it had failed before. The Japanese army was not so easily deterred and, before the month was over, the Japanese navy had made its bid for glory by attacking Shanghai. In a city with the largest international settlement in all of China, with the largest concentration of Americans, Japanese planes bombed Chinese troops and civilians and Japanese ships in the harbor fired seemingly endless salvos into Chinese positions. But unlike their comrades in the Manchurian campaign, Chinese forces around Shanghai resisted fiercely and the Japanese marines required reinforcements.

If some foreigners had been sympathetic to the Japanese cause in Manchuria, prepared to accept Japanese claims of provocation and of special interests, there were indeed few who could condone the attack on Shanghai. The world of 1932 was not yet insensitized to mass murder, and the bombing of a city shocked and outraged public opinion. In the United States, where the Mukden incident had failed to penetrate the usual American indifference to Asian affairs, the Shanghai bombings evoked strong anti-Japanese sentiment. Not only was the traditional wealth of American sympathy for China tapped, but leaders of the peace movement attempted to organize a nationwide boycott of Japanese products.

As a result of the attack on Shanghai, Hoover authorized Stimson to attempt a more elaborate bluff: to send additional warships to Shanghai and to land additional American marines. An official protest was lodged with the Japanese government, and the possibility of economic sanctions, as demanded by peace organizations, was not denied. But the Japanese, undaunted by Stimson's gestures, recognized the bluff and went on their merry way. From the League, where Great Britain and France were dominant, Stimson could obtain but negligible support. In both France and England, attitudes within the government were essentially pro-Japanese, and where concern for the peace system existed, it was ineffective. And in the United States, anti-Japanese sentiment was not sufficient to gain public support for strong action against Japan. Few indeed thought American interests in China, present or future, worth fighting for and fewer still could have accepted the notion of going to war to keep the peace system. Even within the peace movement, as the uselessness of protests and condemnation became apparent, the inclination to oppose Japan declined.

As a last desperate gesture, Stimson decided to protest Japan's actions as a violation of the Nine-Power Treaty of 1922. There was little reason to hope Japan would be any more responsive to this pressure, for the Japanese government had already indicated pointedly that it considered conditions in China very different from those that had existed at the time of the Washington Conference. But Stimson hoped for British support— and again he hoped in vain. Finally, Stimson, recognizing the inadvisability of another unilateral protest, chose to express the American position in a public letter to the chairman of the Senate Foreign Relations Committee, William Borah. The letter contained an appeal to the world to withhold recognition of acts in violation of the Kellogg Peace Pact and the Nine-Power Treaty—to follow the example Stimson had offered in January. He also reaffirmed the American commitment to the principle of the Nine-Power Treaty, to the idea that the Chinese had the right to modernize in their own way, without foreign interference. Finally, Stimson indicated that a violation of one of the Washington treaties, in that it would undermine the entire treaty structure, would free the United States from its obligations under the Washington treaties. In short, Japan's violation of the Nine-Power Treaty would free the United States from limits on the size of its battle fleet and allow it to fortify its possessions in the Pacific.

The effect of Stimson's letter was uncertain. The Japanese did finally terminate hostilities in the Shanghai area, but the basic decision had been reached before Stimson released the letter. The Assembly of the League passed a resolution adopting the nonrecognition policy, but in Manchuria, the Kwantung army had created an "independence" movement. In March 1932, the puppet state of "Manchukuo" was proclaimed. In May, a League-appointed commission arrived in Manchuria to investigate the events that had begun the previous September, but the Japanese army had already accomplished its purpose there. Months later, when the Assembly met and adopted the commission's report, Japan withdrew from the League of Nations. The effort begun by Wilson to internationalize China's problems had come full cycle.

Throughout these months of unsuccessful efforts to bring Japanese aggression to a halt, Chinese hopes waxed and waned. Just before Stimson's letter to Borah, Johnson cabled from China to warn that the Chinese were losing faith in the American will to resist Japan. He feared that if they had further cause to think the United States would acquiesce in Japan's plans for Shanghai, there might be an antiforeign outburst comparable to the Boxer uprising. But in May, Johnson wrote of conversations with Chiang Kai-shek and H. H. Kung in which the latter was especially enamored of the idea of a war between the United States and Japan. Johnson added that he was convinced that this idea of a war "in which the United States will figure as the champion and savior of China is current among many other Chinese occupying official positions."[3] By December, the editor of the *Ta Kung Pao*, China's leading independent newspaper, indicated a sounder understanding of the prospects for American intervention. He contended that the ideals the United States had expressed in its relations with China from 1899 to 1922 had been full of promise for the Chinese, but were of no value, because of the unwillingness of Americans to "put teeth into them." He realized that Manchuria was too remote to compete for American attention, but warned of the danger of underestimating the importance of Japanese control—of the danger that the absence of American support might lead to Communism in China. To the American diplomat to whom he spoke, he concluded:

> The Chinese people thank Mr. Stimson for his pronouncements but they are only words, words, words, and they amount to nothing at all if there is no force to back them. At present there is no force, because America and the League have made it very plain that they will not support with force the ideals which they themselves assert are just and desirable.[4]

Stimson's concern had extended well beyond China to a fear for the peace of the world, if nations could violate their treaty obligations, resort to force, to aggression, whenever it suited their purposes. He had acted less on behalf of China than on behalf of the peace system. The course he and Hoover had followed was not so much pro-Chinese as anti-Japanese—and it was anti-Japanese because Japan, in violating the sanctity of the League Covenant, of the Nine-Power Treaty, and of the Kellogg Peace Pact, threatened to negate the efforts of men to create a new, moral order for the world. In all this, China became an abstraction—the victim in a test case of the interwar peace system. The system failed the test; the world lost the system—and China lost Manchuria.

In November 1932, the American people chose a new president, Franklin D. Roosevelt, and rumors current in Geneva suggested that the policy of the United States toward the crisis in East Asia would be reversed. Early in January 1933, Stimson visited the president-elect to brief him and to attempt to coordinate policy during the remaining weeks of Hoover's "lame-duck" administration. Although Roosevelt's principal advisers were intensely concerned with the critical domestic situation and anxious to avoid any foreign involvements, he nonetheless endorsed Stimson's East Asian policy, presumably on the basis of a long-standing sympathy for the Chinese people. Several days later, hoping to still the rumors, Stimson called Roosevelt, asking for his authorization to notify Great Britain that there had been no change in American policy and that none was contemplated in the future. According to Stimson's memorandum of the conversation, Roosevelt did not object, declaring "that it was the right thing for me to do and to go ahead and do it."[5]

Regardless of Roosevelt's intentions in January 1933, the course he subsequently followed was radically different from that of Stimson, constituting a return to his cousin Theodore's policy of appeasing Japan. The combination of grave problems at home and the sense of hopelessness that followed the collapse of the interwar peace system allowed no leeway for alternatives. The horrors of the depression provided a greater threat to the ideals and interests of the American people than anything anyone could conjure up in Asia. Even within the peace movement, concern for world peace generally narrowed to concern for keeping the United States out of war, and this required muting opposition to Japan. In and out of the government, a limited conception of national interest prevailed and interests were conceived of in measurable terms, in tangibles like commerce, investments, and occasionally missionary interests. All thought of mutuality of interest between the United States and China vanished for the moment.

Within the Department of State, even the men most sympathetic toward China in the past lost faith in the Chinese government and concluded that modernization under Chinese leadership was probably impossible. Some concluded that Japanese domination of China would be in the best interests of the United States—and of China as well! As the Japanese slowly penetrated the Great Wall into China proper, Hornbeck contended that settlement of the Sino-Japanese dispute might be *detrimental* to American interests—that it might be best to keep the Japanese involved in an indecisive struggle in an area where the United States had no vital interests. Opposing measures that might give offense to Japan, he suggested that the price of appeasement, allowing the "principles of our FE policy and our ideals with regard to peace" to be "further scratched and dented," was sufficiently low.[6] From China, Johnson argued that none of the Japanese transgressions concerned the United States directly. Not only did they cost the United States nothing, but "the development of this area under Japanese enterprise may mean an increased opportunity for American industrial plants to sell the kind of machinery and other manufactured goods that will be needed where so much energy is being displayed."[7] Admiral Wainright, returning from duty on the Yangtze, informed military intelligence and State Department representatives that he thought the Chinese "hopelessly miserable" and that Japanese domination would probably be to their advantage. Despite the desire of naval leaders for a rationale to support a shipbuilding program, the admirals who served with the Asiatic fleet in the early 1930s warned against the United States being used to fight China's battles and were skeptical of the potential for American economic interests there.

From all the sources that fed into the decision-making process came support for what Undersecretary of State William Phillips called "our policy of hands off." He called in J. V. A. MacMurray, for whom he had great respect, and MacMurray prepared a 105-page memorandum that provided a brilliant rationalization for inaction. Wilfred Fleisher, a Japan-based journalist, stopped by and advised "a policy of caution, avoidance of pin-pricks, in other words, a reversal of the Stimson policy, in fact the policy we are now pursuing."[8] Even the prominent Wall Street banker Thomas Lamont, deeply involved in world affairs, an advocate of collective security, a leader in China famine-relief work, could not countenance any other role for the United States in the mid-1930s. To Johnson he expressed regret at seeing China under Japanese control, "but if she lacks the strength to protect herself from aggression and exploitation, she cannot reasonably expect the other nations to do the job for her." He might well have summed up the attitude of the Roosevelt administration when he concluded: "Certainly America is not going to court trouble by any quixotic attempt to checkmate Japan in Asia."[9]

Reinforcing the attitudes of the men in Washington was the constant flow of pessimistic reports about the future of the Chinese government. The Americans stationed in China were disturbed by Chiang's efforts to acquire dictatorial power and by the conservative intellectual and social tendencies of his associates. They were appalled by the continued disunity of China in the face of Japanese intrusions. Some were irritated by anti-American tendencies within the Kuomintang—by what they deemed to be a lack of appreciation on the part of the Chinese for the salutary role the United States had played in China. Apart from the endorsement of an American trade mission in 1935 and Johnson's testimony that Chiang and his wife, "unlike most Chinese," behaved decently, like "Protestant Anglo-Saxons," the Nationalist government received very poor notices in the Department of State. And if leading Chinese, within and without the Kuomintang, insisted that Chiang was more interested in personal power than in the interests of the people of China, insisted that Chiang would never fight the Japanese, warned against loans to his government, the United States could hardly be expected to underwrite or undertake China's cause.

In April 1934, the attitudes of the Roosevelt administration received their first test when the Japanese government announced that Japan's "special responsibilities" in East Asia required it to oppose foreign technical, financial, or military aid to China. The administration considered ignoring the Japanese statement, but a British decision to ask the Japanese for a clarification of their new policy and its relation to the Nine-Power Treaty forced the United States to express its view. The statement was a perfunctory defense of American rights that did not disguise the fact that the United States was determined not to challenge Japan. First delivered to the Japanese as an *aide-mémoire*, its release to the American public was followed by an appeal from Secretary of State Cordell Hull to the press, asking newsmen to avoid write-ups that might antagonize Japan.

Of still greater significance were the recommendations of the Division of Far Eastern Affairs in response to Hull's request for a policy that would preclude further friction with Japan. More interested than Wall Street in the development of American economic interests in China, the officers of the division nonetheless opposed further financial assistance by the government and indicated a preference for loans offered through the long-dormant China Consortium—that is, loans in *cooperation* with Japan. They asked that efforts be made to discourage Americans from serving the Chinese government as military advisers and insisted on rigid control of the export of arms and munitions to China. All new projects for China were to be screened to avoid irritating Japan. China had long demanded treatment as an equal nation—now let it "stand upon its own feet." Whatever action the United States might take toward furthering the modernization process in China, alone or in concert with other nations, would be along "practical" lines, as a "good neighbor," dictated neither by Japan nor by the desire to assist China to the detriment of Japan.

At approximately the same time that the Department of State chose to consider avoidance of conflict with Japan as the standard for American policy toward China, Congress passed legislation further indicating American indifference to the fate of China. For months, the domestic silver lobby, led by Senator Key Pittman of Nevada, had been pressing the administration to take action to raise the price of silver. Some concern had been expressed in and out of Congress for the possible harmful effects of a major silver-buying program on China, and an investigation of this problem had been undertaken. The silver lobby, however, was too strong and too impatient. In June 1934, Congress passed the Silver Purchase Act. As some had feared, the effects on China were disastrous. Worth more abroad than at home, the Chinese silver dollar vanished from circulation and began to flow eastward across the Pacific. The results in China were deflation and credit contraction—a sharp recession.

Warnings from American businessmen in China, as well as from the Chinese government, poured into Washington, predicting the imminent collapse of China's economic structure. Just as Japanese military aggression was weakening Nanking's control over the northern provinces, so American silver policy was undermining China's currency, weakening the Chinese government's ability to govern. To Americans, Japanese militarism was anti-Chinese, obvious and reprehensible—the actions of their own government quite different. To the Chinese, the difference between American and Japanese methods and motives mattered little. In the end, it seemed almost like choosing between executioners. The Chinese government begged the United States for help and the State Department reported mounting anti-American feeling in Nanking. Persistent rumors of a Sino-Japanese detente in response to American indifference permeated China.

The Department of State proved most responsive to this mood in China and sought to have the president end the silver-purchasing program or at the very least modify it to pacify the Chinese. Though unwilling to antagonize the Japanese, Hull and Hornbeck did not want the United States to embark on an essentially anti-Chinese program. But the silver problem also involved the Treasury Department, headed by Secretary Henry Morgenthau, a man with very different ideas. Morgenthau was also sympathetic to China's plight, but rather than stop purchasing silver, he and his staff preferred to give the Chinese government financial aid for the purpose of currency reform. Morgenthau, though unwilling to do combat with the silver lobby, was willing to support an aid program to China that would almost certainly anger the Japanese. The Department of State, unwilling to risk this anger, proposed a course certain to arouse the silver lobby, whose spokesman, Senator Pittman, was chairman of the Senate Foreign Relations Committee. Unable to reconcile the two positions at the lower echelons, the two sides appealed to the president.

Roosevelt's preference, when dealing with two subordinates with presumably irreconcilable viewpoints, was to have them locked in a room until they could reach agreement. If this or comparable methods failed, Roosevelt would himself vacillate between the two viewpoints until the problem solved itself or one of his subordinates outmaneuvered the other. In this instance Roosevelt demanded a policy that would give offense to neither Japan nor the silver bloc. Unfortunately, the only policy that seemed to fit these criteria was the existing policy against which China was protesting. And so the president, despite his frequent expressions of sympathy for China, declared that the problem was "China's business and not ours; that they could stop the outflow of silver if they so desired and that it was not up to us to alter our policy merely because the Chinese were unable to protect themselves."[10]

Before the end of 1935, the Chinese were forced off the silver standard, surviving American indifference only by means of a remarkably successful currency reform program launched by H. H. Kung. As part of the program, the Chinese government nationalized silver and then prevailed on the United States to buy a large quantity to help stabilize the new currency. Thereafter, fluctuations in American silver policy ceased to have such overriding significance for China, and the Chinese could hope to avoid paying the price for American domestic politics.

Throughout 1935 and 1936, Japanese encroachments on China continued, but American policy remained basically one of appeasement of Japan. Johnson reported growing dissatisfaction in China with the United States, but for the most part he responded irritably to Chinese complaints. He and Hornbeck often found it necessary to remind the Chinese that American policy was supposed to serve American ends first. They were quick to counter what they viewed as Chinese suggestions that the United States fight China's battles, quick to tell Chiang and his colleagues that the United States had done its share and more for China. Hornbeck, approving such a reply by Johnson to Chiang's complaints, added only the thought that in relations with China, "we are fortunately situated in that our interests and those of China usually run along parallel lines; at least they do not conflict."[11]

In July 1937, as the fighting in China intensified and developed into a major war, the American response remained unchanged. Hornbeck made essentially the same points to H. H. Kung and to the Chinese ambassador to the United States, declaring that the United States had always favored a "strong, unified China," but that American policy was designed to do more than merely help China. He claimed for the United States the privilege of acting on its own conception of national interest—a privilege that the Chinese sometimes seemed to think was exclusively their own.

In the weeks that followed, Chiang Kai-shek became extremely bitter about the role the United States played, particularly over what he viewed as the American failure to cooperate with Great Britain's effort on China's behalf. Though Chiang took his case to Roosevelt, he received nothing but sympathy at that level and not even that much from Nelson Johnson, who wrote: "Certainly nothing makes me lose patience with my Chinese friends so quickly as when I hear them talk about the responsibility of America for aiding to preserve the independence and integrity of China."[12] But if the summer of 1937 represented the nadir of American concern for China, there were already developments in China, Europe, and the United States that would lead to success in the Chinese effort to use Americans against the Japanese.

Ever since the Japanese assault on Manchuria, Chinese patriots had demanded an end to civil strife and a massive effort to drive out the invaders. From the safety of their mountain stronghold, thousands of miles from the Japanese, the Chinese Communists responded to this sentiment by declaring war on Japan in 1932. For several years they called on the people to "firmly oppose the Kuomintang policy of surrender and betrayal and to abandon any illusions about the League of Nations and the United States."[13] In July 1935, while Mao's forces were escaping northward on their historic long march, the Seventh Congress of the Comintern called for a worldwide united front, not against reactionary domestic forces like the Kuomintang, but against foreign aggression—against Japan and the threat of Nazism in rearmed Germany. By the end of the year, the Chinese Communists were calling for a united front with anyone who would oppose Japanese imperialism. In effect they were asking for an end to the Chinese government's anti-Communist campaign, thus enhancing their chances for survival while serving the patriotic interests that they shared with many other Chinese.

The appeals of the Communists found a sympathetic hearing not only among students and intellectuals, but also among government troops sent out to exterminate the Reds. In particular, Communist propaganda made sense to the Manchurian troops of Chang Hsueh-liang, fighting Communists in northwest China when they longed to drive the Japanese out of their homes. Throughout 1936, reports reached American officials of fraternization between Chang's forces and those of Mao—and of Chang's acceptance of the basic Communist premise that Chinese should not be fighting Chinese while acquiescing in Japanese aggression. Edgar Snow, a courageous young journalist who had penetrated the government blockade of the Communist-controlled Shen-Kan-Ning border region, confirmed these rumors. Finally, in December 1936, Chiang Kai-shek flew to Chang's headquarters in Sian, to check on the rumors and to rejuvenate the extermination campaign.

Suddenly, on December 12, China and the world received the shocking news that Chiang Kai-shek had been arrested in Sian by generals demanding an immediate end to the civil war and immediate resistance to Japan. Despite some sentiment in Sian for executing him and in Nanking for bombing Sian to smithereens, regardless of Chiang's presence there, other views prevailed and with the help of Moscow and the Chinese Communists, Chiang survived. The Soviet Union sought to strengthen China as a bulwark against Japan, and Stalin realized that as of 1936, no man had a better chance of unifying China than Chiang. In the course of negotiations that resulted in Chiang's freedom, he agreed to rapprochement with the Communists in a united front against Japan.

On New Year's Day, 1937, the *Ta Kung Pao* prophesied the dawn of a new age: "From today China will have only the united front, and never again will there be internal hostility."[14] Throughout China there was a great burst of patriotic enthusiasm, and the much-maligned Chiang Kai-shek became the symbol of national unity. Americans in China were also caught up in the general euphoria, and diplomats and missionaries alike began to portray Chiang more favorably, sometimes in Christlike terms. The bible that he allegedly read while imprisoned was put on display and would undoubtedly have become a great Christian relic had Heaven ordained a different future for China. Even the American government began to be less pessimistic about the ability of the Chinese to unite. American diplomats were not blind to the continued deficiencies of the Nationalist government, but they responded with perhaps excessive enthusiasm to the first signs of hope. When full-scale war began in China in July 1937, Hornbeck, for one, was more receptive to the idea of stopping Japan.

However, the initial American response to the coming of war in Asia reflected the deep neutralist and pacifist mood that had captured the country after the disillusioning experience of the world's failure to stop Japan in Manchuria. Pressure from within the peace movement intimidated the administration, especially Cordell Hull, and a shipment of bombers bound for China on a government-owned vessel was stopped en route. Roosevelt vacillated on the question of the extent to which the United States would protect its citizens in China, clearly hoping they would all come home to simplify the matter. Led by Dorothy Detzer of the Women's International League for Peace and Freedom and Frederick Libby of the National Council for Prevention of War, pacifists began a campaign for the evacuation of American nationals from the war zone. In the 1930s many, perhaps most, Americans believed the United States had mistakenly intervened in the World War on behalf of the privileges of a few—and they were determined not to repeat the errors of the past.

If Roosevelt's actions were now motivated less by the desire to appease Japan than to appease the American public, it made little difference to the Chinese, who were infuriated. But if the administration was irritated by Chinese demands, it was embarrassed by Japan's obvious satisfaction with American policy, underscored clumsily by Ambassador Joseph Grew in Tokyo. Johnson, in Nanking, warned again of mounting anti-American feeling among the Chinese, even suggesting that Americans in China were in danger. But Roosevelt found one modest, painless way to give the

Chinese some satisfaction also. Taking advantage of Japan's decision not to declare war, he chose to refrain from invoking the neutrality law. Another product of the "lessons" of the World War, this law precluded the sale of arms and munitions, the extension of loans to belligerent nations, and the use of American vessels in trade with such nations. The law was intended to keep the United States out of war by preventing the kinds of involvements with belligerents that were believed to have drawn the country into war in 1917. By not invoking the law, Roosevelt, in theory, was assisting the Chinese, who had been caught unprepared by the Japanese attack and who, unlike the aggressor, needed to purchase war materials from abroad. In practice, this apparent partiality provided the Chinese with nothing but moral support, as no loans were granted before 1939 and little in the way of war materials reached the Chinese from the United States. On this issue, Roosevelt nervously stood up to the peace movement, surviving its attack on his partiality and proving once again that the American people were willing to help China—provided that they could do this by doing nothing.

But the Japanese attack, coming as hopes for peace in Europe dimmed, forced Roosevelt and men of goodwill the world over to think anew of the dangers to the peace and security of their own countries. The interests of the United States in Manchuria, then North China, then Ethiopia, and now the rest of China might not warrant the use of force or the risk of war. But as violence spread abroad and treaties were violated, men troubled by the nationalism of the mid-1930s spoke again of the need for international cooperation, of collective security. A man like Norman Davis, sometime diplomat, close friend and adviser to Cordell Hull, would readily concede that "our interests in the Far East are not worth risking a fight" and then go on to shock those with narrower conceptions of national interest by arguing that "the maintenance of collective action or the defeat of an aggressor like Japan might be principles that would be well worth waging war for."[15] After talking to such men, groping himself for some answer, on October 5, 1937, Roosevelt delivered his famous "quarantine" speech, implying that in the face of an "epidemic of world lawlessness," a quarantine of those so afflicted might protect the larger world community. Though the president in fact had no plan and became increasingly vague when questioned on the implications of his quarantine idea, the advocates of collective security were heartened by his words, and the possibility of a peaceful means of stopping Japan quickened the pulse of many pacifists.

In November, at a meeting in Brussels initiated by the British to discuss the implications of Japanese action for the other signatories of the Nine-Power Treaty, nothing was accomplished as Roosevelt retreated from the implications of his speech. But Davis, heading the American delegation, indicated that the primary concern of the United States was not China, "that we do not view the problem as merely a Far Eastern one but as a world problem where the forces of order had a direct interest in preventing lawlessness and aggression."[16] For the moment, however, the tide of public and congressional opinion in the United States ran against men with so broad a conception of the problem, and Roosevelt, whatever his personal convictions, remained silent. Throughout 1938, well into 1939, the Japanese pushed on, bombing civilians, brutalizing those who did not flee before them, and the United States held its peace. American property was destroyed, an American warship sunk, American commerce ravaged, American citizens killed—but the "lessons" of the World War prevailed. Not for the advantage of a few investors, a few merchants, a few foolish missionaries who risked their lives in war zones, would the United States again be drawn into war.

The American people were not willing to fight for China, but neither were they willing to leave any doubt as to where their sympathies lay. For those Americans who wanted to help China—for whatever reason— the basic problem was to find a means to exploit pro-Chinese sentiments without arousing fear of war. This task was accomplished largely by the American Committee for Non-Participation in Japanese Aggression, an organization conceived by Americans who had been missionaries in China. Renewed hopes for success in a China led by a Christian family that sought their support brought many American missionaries to Chiang's side. Within China, some became Christian cadres in Chiang's anti-Communist campaigns, and at home many more became potent lobbyists for his cause—not only against Japan from 1937 to 1941, but also later, when the United States sought to extricate itself from renewed civil war in China.

Aided by the advocates of collective security anxious to find some way to punish aggressors, and by the Chinese government, these friends of China helped focus American opinion on a demand for an end to sales of war materials to Japan. Although there was little support in the United States for proposals to aid China through positive action, Americans were disturbed by the charge that they were partners in Japan's aggression, feeding Japan's war machine. In the spring of 1939, a Gallup poll indicated that the overwhelming majority of the Americans questioned favored an embargo on war supplies to Japan. Sanctions were now politically possible, had the administration desired to impose them.

At approximately the same time, as the European situation grew more ominous, Roosevelt sought to have the neutrality legislation revised to facilitate aid to Great Britain. The revision proposed by Senator Pittman, extending the concept of "cash and carry" to arms and munitions, would have allowed any nation that had the money and the means to move the goods to purchase anything it needed from the United States—and as such indicated relative indifference to the war in Asia. For Britain the advantages were obvious, and presumably Hitler, forewarned of Britain's ability to obtain aid, would have second thoughts about provoking war. If applied to the Asian war, however, the provisions of the bill would have been markedly disadvantageous to China. China had neither the cash nor the means to carry goods from the United States. Japan controlled the Western Pacific—at least every conceivable port of entry into China. The Chinese were furious and H. H. Kung cabled a clear statement of the problem as viewed by his government, which realized that the United States was acting for the "best interest of the United States and to help the democratic cause in Europe," but was disturbed to note that the bill did not distinguish between aggressor and victim, "thereby tending to penalize China in face of Japan's aggression."[17]

Although the Department of State's program for revision of the neutrality legislation provided nothing for China, no end to the sale of war materials to Japan, Hornbeck, working with members of the Committee for Non-Participation in Japanese Aggression, prodded Senator Pittman into introducing a separate resolution authorizing the president to place restrictions on trade between the United States and any nation that violated the Nine-Power Treaty. With Roosevelt and Hull unwilling to fight for legislation that would openly discriminate against aggressors, this method of discriminating against Japan could supplement the assistance that the cash-and-carry concept would provide for England and France— and China would be satisfied with nothing less.

Other bills providing for economic sanctions against Japan were introduced in Congress, but despite intensive lobbying by various organizations friendly to China and the cause of collective security, these efforts came to naught. Roosevelt and Hull, though pleased to see pacifist sentiment in the United States neutralized, providing the administration with greater freedom of action, opposed economic sanctions, apparently desiring to retain maximum flexibility with Japan. A massive lobbying effort in Washington in July 1939 failed because, as one lobbyist complained, "everyone seems much more concerned with the Neutrality Bills and Europe than the Embargo on goods to Japan."[18]

Sensing the intensification of pressure for anti-Japanese actions, the American government suddenly notified Japan of its wish to terminate the Treaty of Commerce and Navigation that existed between the two countries. Often cited as an obstacle to economic sanctions, the treaty could no longer be used as an excuse. But the administration had no program for sanctions in mind. Afraid that sharp measures against Japan might lead to a crisis at a time when the European situation was ominous, Hull had chosen to give notice on the treaty as the safest means of encouraging China and ridding the administration of the pressures being generated by pro-Chinese lobbyists. Indeed, the Department of State had been considering terminating the treaty for months because of the pressures of the domestic cotton industry and a threat to the reciprocal trade agreements program, so dear to Hull's heart. When the treaty expired in January 1940, Hull continued to thwart the efforts of those who sought economic sanctions against Japan. The risk was too great, given the war in Europe.

Within the Chinese government hostility to the Roosevelt administration mounted, though the Chinese realized that a Republican administration would be even less likely to offer aid in 1940. In the United States, the friends of China began to oppose government policy, for the most part unable to comprehend Roosevelt's evaluation of the relative importance of the European and Asian wars. But many of those who had sought sanctions against Japan were more concerned with collective security than with China. With the coming of the war in Europe, they shifted their energies toward what they considered a more vital cause: aid to Great Britain. Not until the summer of 1940, when Japan had made gestures against the British and French positions in Southeast Asia and began flirting anew with Nazi Germany, did the United States take significant action to retard the Japanese war effort. Even then, Roosevelt was persuaded not to prevent the sale of all scrap iron and oil. In fact, the following year brought a tremendous increase in the sale of petroleum products to Japan.

As American determination to sustain Great Britain became apparent and as the Roosevelt administration's policy of all aid short of war developed, the most alert of China's friends, such as Roger Greene, chairman of the Committee for Non-Participation in Japanese Aggression, recognized the need to tie China to the British war effort if there was to be any hope of American assistance to China. Although Greene was also active in the major Europe-oriented collective security organization, the Committee to Defend America by Aiding the Allies (the White Committee), he was unable to interest his colleagues there in his conception of China as one of the Allies. Throughout the United States, whether men supported or opposed Roosevelt's policy of aid short of war to Great Britain, they were preoccupied with Europe and indifferent to Asia. While those who prevailed in the Department of State doubted that the outcome of the war would be of sufficient importance to risk the provocation of anti-Japanese sanctions, that segment of the American people actively seeking to influence American policy, like those of the White Committee or America First, viewed the war in Asia an abstraction: a relatively unimportant war being fought by relatively unimportant people over relatively unimportant issues. There was no shortage of sympathy for China among Americans, simply doubt as to the relevance of Asia at a time when the "real world" was endangered by Hitlerism. For Greene to win support for further sanctions against Japan or for assistance to China, he had to find a way to demonstrate a relationship between the European and Asian wars, to convince men whose attention was focused on Great Britain's battle for survival that Japan, too, threatened Britain; that China, too, was fighting America's battle. And where Greene himself failed, the Japanese made the fulfillment of his task possible when, on September 27, 1940, they signed the Tripartite Pact with Germany and Italy.

Despite tremendous American sympathy for China, nothing the Chinese or their friends in the United States could have done could have convinced Americans of their stake in the outcome of the Sino-Japanese war as effectively as Japan's decision to ally with Nazi Germany. For the leaders of the Committee to Defend America by Aiding the Allies, the Tripartite Alliance made two wars into one: "it would now seem that China is unmistakably an ally," worthy of the Committee's support.[19] Hornbeck, too, now argued that assistance to the allies affected all fronts and could be given by aid to China as well as to Great Britain, and advised the committee to work for aid to *all* powers resisting the Axis and for restrictions on aid, economic or other, to the Axis. Clark Eichelberger, national director of the committee, wrote that "Britain and China in the Pacific, with Britain in the Atlantic, now constitute our first line of defense."[20]

TABLE 5.2   American Exports to China and Japan, 1932–1940

	Value of Exports (in $ millions)		Percentage of Total U.S. Export Trade	
Year	To China	To Japan	To China	To Japan
1932	56	135	3.5	8.4
1933	52	143	3.1	8.5
1934	69	210	3.2	9.9
1935	38	203	1.7	8.9
1936	47	204	1.9	8.3
1937	50	289	1.5	8.6
1938	35	240	1.3	7.8
1939	56	232	1.8	7.3
1940	78	227	1.9	5.6

Thereafter Japan had to face stepped-up American aid to China and, of even greater significance, the impossibility of negotiating a new Pacific settlement without withdrawing from China. The American response made China the principal beneficiary of the new Axis Alliance.

For several years, the only assistance the United States offered China came in the form of Treasury Department purchases of Chinese silver after China went off the silver standard. Even these purchases were made under conditions that had to be absolutely painless to the United States. Morgenthau was not interested in buying silver to facilitate payment by the Chinese of debts to other than American interests. In February 1939, the United States extended a $25 million purchase credit to the Chinese, well secured by Chinese tung oil and restricted to purchases of American agricultural and manufactured goods. In April 1940, a similar credit of $20 million was granted. The Soviet Union, on the other hand, had already given Chiang's government five times as much aid in the form of credits for military supplies. In the six months following the Tripartite Pact, however, the United States extended credits totaling $95 million. On May 6, 1941, China became eligible for lend-lease. But the flow of oil to Japan still continued as the Roosevelt administration followed its own estimate of the steps appropriate for a policy of encouraging China, checking Japan—and keeping the United States out of war in the Pacific.

In late July 1941, the Japanese appeared in Camranh Bay, on the coast of South Indochina. Appeasement had not stopped the Japanese advance and Roosevelt called the Japanese ambassador's attention to the bitter criticism leveled against the administration for continuing to allow oil to be shipped to Japan. And the criticism mounted among the friends of China and the advocates of collective security. Within the administration, Morgenthau, Stimson, now secretary of war, Harold Ickes, petroleum administrator for national defense, and Hornbeck pressed for a freezing of Japanese assets and for a complete embargo on oil. A last-minute effort by Undersecretary of State Sumner Welles, representing Department of State and military leaders desperately anxious to avoid a showdown with Japan, succeeded in getting Roosevelt to authorize the licensing of some oil purchases. The pressure on Japan was severe and it had the overwhelming approval of the American people, but it was not complete—and high-level Japanese-American talks in Washington throughout the fall of 1941 worried the Chinese and their advocates in the United States.

In China, Mao Tse-tung was warning the party faithful of the possibility of a Far East Munich, and Chiang Kai-shek, with direct access to the American government and to the White House, made no secret of his own fears. From Americans in China came warnings of declining morale in Chiang's regime—of a growing defeatist attitude that would be irresistible if the United States reached a new accommodation with Japan. At a time when American military leaders were urging the president to agree to a modus vivendi with Japan to play for time they desperately needed to build up American defenses, to concentrate their energies on the vital concerns across the Atlantic, Chiang flooded Washington with appeals for the United States to forgo the temptation to appease Japan once more at China's expense. And then a cable from Winston Churchill: "What about Chiang Kai-shek? Is he not having a very thin diet? Our anxiety is about China. If they collapse our joint dangers would enormously increase."[21] That afternoon Hull gave the Japanese a reply that he knew would be unacceptable to a proposal that he knew would be their last.

Until the Japanese added to Great Britain's distress by their maneuvers in Southeast Asia and then joined the Axis, appeasement had been an easy policy to pursue. Afterward, even when the Tripartite Pact became virtually expendable to Japan, the American commitment to the British cause and China's status as an ally prevented a modus vivendi between the United States and Japan. To return to appeasement meant the dashing of hopes raised in China and among China's friends in the United States. It meant betrayal of a nation so recently labeled a "democracy" and one of the allies in the war against aggressors. It meant risking the charge that Roosevelt was concerned only with Great Britain's chestnuts. To some it suggested the possibility of China making a separate peace, with ominous consequences for American and British interests in East Asia. But the Chinese and their friends had succeeded in winning their case. The United States, having once ceased to supply Japan with "the sinews of war," could not again accept the role of merchant of death. Once solidarity with China was proclaimed, there could be no return to the role of passive observer of China's sorrows. And the war came.

The war came and China was an honored ally, but, alas, a second-class ally. Despite the Japanese attack on Pearl Harbor, Roosevelt and his advisers continued to focus their attention on the war in Europe, persisted in their belief that Germany was the greatest danger and Britain their most important ally. China was allotted the role of keeping Japan busy until the major task was completed in Europe. If the morass of China had been a good place in which to bemire the Japanese in 1935, it was at least as useful in 1942. Roosevelt, no less than Churchill or Stalin, denied Chiang an equal role in the process of making strategic or logistical decisions, promising to provide whatever supplies were not needed elsewhere—assuming a way could be found to transport these items over Japanese-held territory, or the Himalayas.

Having celebrated the bombing of Pearl Harbor as the moment of deliverance, the Chinese were bitterly disappointed by the American response. By January 1942, the Chinese attitude was considered so hostile that the Department of State warned Roosevelt against a proposed invitation for Madam Chiang Kai-shek to come to the United States. Failing to obtain either the troops or supplies to which he felt entitled, Chiang asked the United States to provide half of a billion-dollar loan he considered essential for sustaining morale in China. Although Morgenthau had serious reservations about the financial soundness of the loan, and the embassy in Chungking was skeptical about the use to which it would be put, political considerations ultimately prevailed and Chiang received the desired credit with no strings attached. But the loan negotiations did little to establish a foundation for mutual trust between the allies.

Early in 1943, the administration and Congress both offered comfort in the absence of aid. The administration signed a treaty surrendering American extraterritorial rights in China and the Senate readily acquiesced. Congress, unable or unwilling to rectify complaints that the

Chinese were not receiving a fair share of lend-lease supplies, voted instead to repeal the acts excluding Chinese immigrants from the United States. Neither gesture interfered with the prosecution of the war across the Atlantic. The Chinese and their friends in the United States were pleased by these new indications of American respect for China—but they were not satisfied.

In addition to American preoccupation with the European theater, there was another important obstacle to Chiang's hopes for substantial aid from the United States: the long-standing conviction that he was less interested in fighting the Japanese than in using any aid to strengthen his own position in·China's internal power struggle. Despite mounting public enthusiasm for the "gallant struggle" of the Chinese, by the summer of 1938 American diplomats and military observers in China believed that Chiang had stopped fighting, that the Nationalist regime was "conserving and later will probably withdraw its best troops and equipment to ensure its transcendency in domestic politics."[22] By 1940, renewed tensions between Chiang and the Chinese Communists were apparent, and in January 1941, a major battle was fought between government troops and the Communist-led New Fourth Army. British and American efforts to urge a reconciliation were in vain, although a nominal truce lasted until after Japan's defeat. But in the summer of 1941, the American embassy warned that hopes for improved relations between the Kuomintang and the Communists were illusory—that future hostilities were inevitable. Similarly, the American military mission that went to China in the fall of 1941, under General John Magruder, reported that Chiang wanted lend-lease equipment not for fighting Japan, but to protect his government against insurrection after other nations drove the Japanese out of China. When Chiang requested an American general to be assigned as his chief of staff and suggested that it would be best if the man selected did *not* have prior experience in China, the American military suspected the worst.

In this atmosphere troubled by conflicting priorities and mistrust, a smooth relationship between the Chinese and American governments was unlikely. Any such possibility vanished with the selection of General Joseph Stilwell to serve as Chiang's chief of staff. Although an outstanding soldier, diplomacy was not his long suit. His previous experience in China had filled him with admiration for the people, the *lao pai hsing*, but also with a contempt for the leaders who exploited them. Chiang did not

Strong suit?

The Pacific War, December 1941

BERING
SEA

Alaska

CANADA

tu

Aleutian   Islands   (U.S.)

Kiska

Seattle

UNITED
STATES

San Francisco

San Diego

OCEAN

Midway (U.S.)

Hawaiian Islands
(U.S.)

Japanese attack Pearl Harbor,
December 7, 1941

Honolulu

hall
ds

bert
ands
(Br.)

.Ellice
.Islands
(Br.)

Samoan
Is.

American
Samoa
(U.S.)

Japanese possessions, 1941

United States possessions, 1941

Islands mandated to Japan

escape Stilwell's displeasure, and their personal relations deteriorated quickly. To Stilwell, Chiang was a contemptible petty dictator and he dubbed him "Peanut," filling his diary with earthy descriptions and bits of doggerel about their encounters—in addition to a delightful account of the joys of eating roast pig sphincter at T. V. Soong's.

While Stilwell and the American ambassador, Clarence Gauss, complained about the unwillingness of Chiang's forces to engage the Japanese, Chiang complained about the minimal amounts of aid he was receiving from the United States. While the Americans refused to contribute more aid until the Chinese stepped up their war effort, the Chinese refused to step up their war effort until they received more aid. At no time during the war was the circle broken. Instead, frustrations and irritations mounted and Americans in China began to search for Chinese leaders who would fight the Japanese. Chiang's wrath focused increasingly on Stilwell, whose abrasive personality left him an easy target—an obvious lightening rod as the gods of Chungking and Washington readied their thunderbolts.

Although the Departments of State, War, and the Treasury became increasingly unsympathetic to Chiang, reflecting the intense hostility that most of their representatives in China harbored toward the Chinese government, Chiang still had friends in powerful places in Washington. In particular, Harry Hopkins, Roosevelt's alter ego, was exceptionally sympathetic to China's cause and indifferent to the combined opinion of bureaucrats who always seemed to stand in the way of his humanitarian causes. Through Hopkins, the Chinese government and its friends established an irregular channel of communications with Roosevelt and from time to time met with success in overcoming the opposition of the experts to various schemes to help China. Most notably, the plans of Claire Chennault (of Flying Tiger fame) to win the war through airpower, plans that had the attraction of allowing Chiang to keep his troops in reserve, were approved by Roosevelt, who overruled the objections of his chief of staff, General George C. Marshall. The results were catastrophic as Chennault's intensified air attacks provoked a Japanese offensive during which his inadequately defended airfields were overrun. This disaster was aggravated by Chiang's unwillingness to send supplies or reinforcements to the troops defending the fields because they were troops of a general whose loyalty he considered doubtful.

Among Americans in China, disgust with the Chinese government's war effort mixed with repugnance toward the regime's internal policies.

Conservative at its best, the Kuomintang leadership responded to wartime pressures by becoming increasingly reactionary and, to some of these Americans, seemed to be no better than Nazis. Reports from Chungking filled the Department of State with images of Tai Li's Blue Shirts, the Kuomintang Gestapo, stifling dissent and brutalizing intellectuals. Official Washington was kept well informed of the activities of the Ch'en brothers, heads of the notorious "C. C. Clique" and Chiang's closest advisers, who personified the government's reactionary tendencies and whose followers were guilty of venality shocking even to Chinese long inured to corrupt officials.

In contrast, American diplomats, officers, and war correspondents were impressed by reports of land reform in Communist-controlled areas, by evidence that the Communists *were* fighting the Japanese—and not least by the charm of Chou En-lai, the Communist representative in Chungking. These Americans were appalled by reports that 500,000 of Chiang's best troops were being used to blockade the Communists instead of participating in the common cause against the Japanese. Not only did they want to see these government forces used against Japan; they also hoped to see the united front between the Kuomintang and the Chinese Communists become a reality, to see Mao's forces brought under Allied command. And as the war went on these observers sensed that the people in Kuomintang-controlled areas were turning away from the government, while intelligence reports indicated increasing popular support for the Communists, a progressive and militantly anti-Japanese force. Fears also grew that the government would not wait for Japan's defeat before resuming an active campaign to exterminate the Communists. These fears—and the images of the two contending parties—began to seep out of official correspondence and into public print. Newspapers and popular magazines in the United States began to publish unflattering portraits of Chiang's government. Even old friends of the Chinese people, like Pearl Buck, expressed concern publicly.

The American government was determined to avert civil war in China, at least until the end of the war against Japan. Passive resistance by the Chinese was better than no resistance at all. Ideally, American diplomats dreamed of a reformed Kuomintang, acting in concert with the Communists to fight against Japan and to create a liberal democratic government. Toward these ends they insisted that the internal struggle be settled by peaceful means and exerted constant pressure on the Chinese government in an attempt to stimulate the economic and social reforms they considered essential to the survival of that regime. Additionally, the United States sought more contact with and more information on the Chinese Communist movement.

All the frustrations and anxieties produced in two and a half years of wartime "cooperation" were coming to a head in the spring of 1944, when Roosevelt asked Vice President Henry Wallace to go to China and work things out. Chiang and Roosevelt had met in Cairo in December 1943, but the euphoric aura of those pleasant hours along the Nile vanished in the wake of Chiang's next request for a large loan. Roosevelt's charm had failed to suffice, more aid to China was unlikely with D-day in Europe approaching, and Roosevelt turned instead to another favorite expedient, the personal envoy. Wallace arrived in China in June, during the Japanese offensive, found Chiang despondent, the situation depressing. Chiang agreed to allow the United States to send a military observer mission to Yenan, Mao Tse-tung's headquarters, following a group of war correspondents who had flown there a few weeks before. To Wallace's expressions of concern over the Chinese war effort and the government's loss of public support, Chiang countered with suggestions of American, particularly Stilwell's, responsibility, and suggestions of American susceptibility to Communist propaganda. He left no doubt in Wallace's mind of his desire to be rid of Stilwell or to have some personal representative of Roosevelt's at hand to control Stilwell and to give Chiang regular access to the president, independent of both the Departments of War and State.

Roosevelt sent the personal representative Chiang sought, General Patrick Hurley, but otherwise Chiang's time had run out. The failure of Chennault's plan had strengthened Stilwell's supporters in the War Department and weakened the influence of Chiang's only friends in high places. The attempt to use the "red herring" gambit was ill-timed, as Americans had little reason to fear Communism in the summer of 1944. Indeed, all reports from Communist-controlled areas, from war correspondents, military observers, and foreign service officers, indicated that Mao's policies were closer to the program Americans believed essential for China than anything the Kuomintang might provide. At the urging of the War Department, Roosevelt demanded a Chinese offensive and insisted that Stilwell be placed in command of all Chinese forces. Roosevelt, wavering no more, had come down firmly on Stilwell's side. He had lost patience with the Chinese government and flung down the gauntlet.

Failing to hide his glee, Stilwell personally delivered Roosevelt's message to Chiang. With his characteristic lack of tact he permitted both governments to live with the fiction that the tensions between them were the result of personality differences between Chiang and Stilwell. Chiang could not tolerate the affront and the immediate result was his successful request for Stilwell's recall—the "triumph of a moribund anti-democratic regime."[23] But the more significant result, as most contemporary observers noted, was that Chiang would have his way in China and the United States would find other ways to deliver the final blow against Japan. The last vestige of the American hope of China becoming a major theater disappeared in October 1944. The events of the remaining months prior to Japan's surrender were essentially a stage setting for the postwar struggle for power in China.

When Roosevelt became president there was no dispute over national priorities. Feeding Americans, putting them back to work, pulling the country out of the Depression, ending the gravest crisis since the Civil War— *nothing* could take precedence over that task. China was in trouble and Roosevelt and his people often exhibited a sentimental attachment to the Chinese people, but conditions at home sufficed to absorb their sentiment as well as their energy.

Similarly, Americans had helped to create the peace system and the sense of world community that had existed during the 1920s, but that system had collapsed and the sense of community had vanished. Americans bore a share of the guilt for the post-1931 return to international anarchy, but the guilt was by no means exclusively—or even largely— theirs. They had no obligation to restore order unilaterally. They had neither the will nor the means to establish a Pax Americana in East Asia. China in the abstract, as a victim of aggression, did concern men who were advocates of collective security, but they were a tiny and ineffective minority before 1937 and they too turned away when Hitler provided them with more important victims.

Throughout the 1930s, events in Asia concerned Roosevelt little more than they did the American people. Despite his frequently voiced affection for China, he was largely indifferent to her fate, deeming American interests there to be slight, unwilling to concede that Japanese hegemony over China would threaten the United States. In Washington there arose a conviction that the land mass of China would do to the Japanese what the Russian land mass had done to Napoleon. So long as the Japanese were drawn deeper and deeper into China, they would trouble no one else. This conviction continued on into the phase of the war that followed the attack on Pearl Harbor. In the defense of the interests of the United States, it was important to give the Chinese enough aid to keep them fighting, but it was not necessary to give them enough to win. And if they would not fight, Asian affairs could await the settlement of vital issues across the Atlantic. The fight to liberate China was merely a sideshow in the war against the Axis, not an important American priority.

For the first three years of the Sino-Japanese war, the United States allowed itself to be the most important supplier of the Japanese war machine. During the eighteen months preceding the Japanese attack on Pearl Harbor, the United States gradually tightened the screws on Japan—not out of sudden concern for China, but because of the threat posed by Japan's southward thrusts and ultimately by her adherence to the Rome-Berlin Axis. Thus China was transformed into an "ally"—not a real ally, but a symbolic ally, as she was transformed into one of the "democracies," but not a real one. China received all of the praise and some of the loyalty due an ally, but little of the substance. Wartime experiences changed nothing, as the Chinese government did little to change American estimates of its will to fight or of its potential for survival. For their part, the Americans renounced the last of their privileges under the "unequal treaties"—at least in theory, and talked much of China as a great power after the war. Until 1944, Roosevelt was almost Oriental in his attempts to give Chiang "face" when he could not or would not give anything more substantial.

Roosevelt's conception of China as a great power was ultimately incorporated into the United Nations Organization, in part compensation for wartime neglect. But Roosevelt and his advisers also acted on the assumption of a China grateful to the United States, *dependent* on the United States—as Churchill suspected, "a faggot vote" on the side of the United States. Had Roosevelt read Chiang's *China's Destiny* or understood the Chinese Communist movement, he would have understood that neither major force in China excepted the United States from the hostility directed against the imperialists. Had he reviewed his administration's policies toward China, he would have realized how absurd were American pretensions to the role of China's champion. And no matter what the Chinese might themselves have been willing to offer the Soviet Union, the fact that Roosevelt at Yalta, consistent with traditional American indifference as to who controlled Manchuria, undertook to dispose of Chinese territory without China's prior consent was hardly calculated to make the Chinese rejoice. Once again, the Roosevelt years demonstrated that American policy was designed to serve American interests without particular regard for China. The fact that China too benefited was as incidental as it was undeniable. Roosevelt's East Asian policies gave Americans no cause for grievance—and the Chinese no cause for gratitude.

6   Communism in China

The desire to stimulate China's war effort and the necessity for postwar planning intensified American interest in the Chinese Communist movement, but this interest in Communism in China was as old as Mao's, dating back to the days of the May Fourth Movement. As reports of Bolshevik influence in China began to reach Washington, the Department of State had established a new file and had begun routine inquiries into the nature, extent, and significance of this new phenomenon. Although within the United States these were the days of the "Red Scare," of "Palmer's Raids," the initial American response to Bolshevism in China was calm and even sympathetic. Generally, Americans in China, diplomats, army and navy officers, and visiting scholars recognized the intense nationalist fervor of the students who were reading translations of Marxist literature and parroting Marxist phrases. They were aware of the desperate search Chinese intellectuals had been making for some formula that would enable them to "save" China, and were not surprised to find Marx along with a score of other Utopian philosophers on the bookshelves of Chinese students and professors. The American government was sufficiently concerned to ask for information, but events in China were remote enough from American priorities in 1920 and 1921 to preclude panic.

In the mid-1920s, American observers noted the creation of the Chinese Communist Party but were concerned less with Chinese Communists than they were with Soviet agitators and with the imperial anti-imperialism of the Soviet Union. In 1924, the American minister advised the president that the outcome of the turmoil in China might be a non-Western type of government and suggested that the "Soviet feature of the Russian Government might fit into the village communities of China."[1] But he was skeptical, contending that "Communism is wholly alien to Chinese life and sentiment and institutions, and the dictatorship of the proletariat is in complete contradiction with the democracy of the self-governing (or non-governed) patriarchal family communities which cover like clusters of bees the entire country." A year later, J. C. Huston indicated that even the Russians were no longer emphasizing "doctrines of pure communism" but rather were placing new stress on anti-imperialism, on Lenin's concept of the war of national liberation. As unrest in China spread, particularly after the May 30th incident of 1925, Americans like J. V. A. MacMurray worried about Bolshevik influences, but so great was the conviction that Communism could not prosper in China that official Washington remained calm throughout the crises that accompanied the Northern Expedition. The Coolidge administration was convinced that the success of the Nationalist movement would be China's—and the world's—best protection against Soviet imperialism. When the significance of Chiang's split with the Communists became comprehensible to Americans, they were confirmed in their instinctive confidence in China's ultimate progress toward a liberal, democratic, and friendly government.

After the White Terror began in 1927 and the Communists fled and went into hiding, the American government experienced great difficulty in obtaining accurate information about the movement. Reports sent to Washington during the next six years reflected serious confusion and an inability on the part of observers, official and private, to decide whether the Communists were really Communists or just bandits, Moscow-directed or independent, dangerous or insignificant. Until 1930, the Chinese government was similarly bewildered—at least as indicated by the information with which it provided American diplomats. Inevitably some of the analyses received in Washington were excellent, but the policy maker lacked the perspective that time grants the historian and could not easily distinguish between silk purses and sows' ears. In the absence of consensus and in the press of more important matters, ignorance was wedded to indifference.

In 1930 the Communist attack on Changsha forced Chiang to begin to take the Red Army more seriously—although the obvious presence of outright bandits among Mao's forces continued to leave doubt as to the ideological commitment of the rebels. The Communists themselves always insisted they were genuine Marxists, but there was continued suspicion that the Red flag and Communist insignia were being used either to bid for Russian support or to dignify plunder. American diplomats usually referred to the activities of the "so-called 'Communists,'" and whenever the quotation marks were left off by the reporter, they were usually penciled in by those reading the reports in Washington. So long as the Chinese Communists failed to conform to the Russian pattern, so long as they were armed peasants loose in the countryside instead of urban proletarians, everyone seemed confused.

But no matter who the marauders were, in the last five months of 1930 they engaged in intermittent warfare with American gunboats of the Yangtze River Patrol. The American vessels were not opposing Communism but rather fulfilling their mission of protecting the lives of American citizens, usually missionaries, when the Chinese government could not. Nonetheless, Stimson was aroused when the *New York Times* reported that the United States was considering plans to put an end to the "Yangtze Red Raids," and he sent a sharp cable to the legation at Peiping. He indicated concern over the increasing frequency and severity of the fighting and noted that "these attacks are generally attributed to Quote communist or Red Unquote bands."[2] Challenging this characterization as an explanation for all of the incidents, he requested "new and authoritative information with regard to sources and objects of the Chinese firing." Thus prodded by Washington, the American minister gathered new information from a number of sources, including the British navy, but generally only added to the confusion. Wearily, Stimson replied that his main concern was with reducing the number of incidents. An understanding of the Chinese Communist movement would have to wait.

Nonetheless, the legation staff realized that the time had come for a careful analysis of the Communist situation, and this was prepared as part of the minister's political report. Johnson advised the department that there had been an active Moscow-inspired Communist Party in China from 1925 to 1928, but in referring to "Reds" or "Communists" in China after this time, "it must be born in mind that these terms are rarely used in their technical sense, but rather loosely to denote lawless elements which have risen in various parts of the country against constituted authority."[3] Though there were probably indirect connections between Moscow and Chinese revolutionaries, Johnson insisted that it would be a mistake to "ascribe too much importance to these activities and their possible connection with Moscow." He contended that the use of Communist insignia by bandits was intended "ludicrously enough—chiefly as a badge of respectability in the hope of being classed as something above the category of common brigands!" In conclusion, he argued that "so-called Communism" was not the *cause* of chaos in China but rather the *effect* of "certain fundamental conditions."

It should be noted that the basic elements of the pre-1945 American understanding of the Chinese Communist movement had already emerged by 1930. The root of the confusion was not a failure to comprehend the cause of the rise of Communism in China nor a failure to recognize its rural foundation. Nor was it, as later alleged, a failure to understand Marxist-Leninism. Within the Department of State, reports on Communism in China were generally routed first to the Division of Eastern European Affairs, the experts on Communism. What confused Americans in China also confused Washington's experts on Communism—and would-be Marxist-Leninists all over the world. Communists were supposed to be proletarians responding to problems of industrialization under the direction of the Comintern. Could a Communist movement exist beyond Moscow's control, composed of peasants in armed rebellion against conditions of land tenure? In the midst of Stalin's epic struggle with Trotsky, it would have been a foolhardy member of the party faithful who would take a definite stand on this question. For Americans who were most comfortable with their stereotype of a Communist as a city-dwelling Eastern European Jew, it was easier to decide that Mao's bands could not really be Communists and that they would wither away as soon as the Chinese government recognized the need for land reform. And in 1930, once again, the instinctive American response was essentially correct: there was still time for land reform to alleviate the rural misery that played so large a part in rallying China's masses around Mao's standard.

In the next several years, as Chiang's anti-Communist campaigns mounted until the Red Army was forced to flee Kiangsi, the quality of reporting on the Chinese Communist movement improved, though there were still a sufficient number of silly reports to confuse those in Washington and ample evidence to indicate the inability of the Department of

State's experts to separate the wheat from the chaff. There was still un-certainty over Moscow's role, but no question about the growing unrest in rural China or increasing peasant support for the Communists. As the recruits became better disciplined and better indoctrinated, there was increasing evidence of a commitment to Marxist-Leninism, although ap-parently sinicized and absorbed into a pattern of agrarian revolt. Military observers returned from Kiangsi highly impressed by the courage, skill, and discipline of Communist forces.

One Chinese scholar, the secretary-general of the Academia Sinica, provided the legation with an excellent study of the Communist move-ment and of the inherent weakness of Chiang's extermination tactics, arguing that military operations alone would fail. In a passage that the Division of Far Eastern Affairs found especially interesting, he declared that even if Chiang's forces defeated the Communists, the areas recap-tured would not be entirely cleared of Communists, giving them ample opportunity to renew disturbances: "In other words, military success will add sufferings to the people, and it will be impossible to exterminate the Communists by military operations alone. At present, everything in China is at the discretion of people backed with military force. If this state of affairs holds true for long, China will undoubtedly become Commu-nist."[4] Months later, the American minister reached essentially the same conclusion in a confidential report for Stimson: "The shadow of Bolshe-vism will lie over parts of China until a thoroughgoing program of rural economy has improved the lot of the masses and an efficient administra-tion has produced a sense of security in the interior."[5]

Despite this sense of the deep-rooted nature of the appeal of the Chi-nese Communists, Johnson and American officials generally became much less concerned about the movement after Mao's forces began the Long March through Chiang's attempted encirclement. Having decided that Communism in China was "distinctly an agrarian movement among the tenant farming class," Johnson seemed satisfied that the Chinese govern-ment's limited support of rural reconstruction work would ease the dan-ger following the government's apparent military victory. Cordell Hull, briefing the secretary of war prior to the latter's Far Eastern junket in the fall of 1935, explained that "communist-bandit" or "red" was a more ac-curate description than "real communists" and went on to recite John-son's analysis, indicating that the Nationalists no longer resorted to force alone, but now "endeavored to improve the economic condition of the peasants so as to remove the discontent in which 'red' elements thrive."[6]

In the mid-1930s a combination of Japanese and Communist propaganda led to new misunderstandings of the nature of the Chinese Communist movement. Consistently worried about the spread of Russian influence in East Asia, the Japanese began increasingly to rationalize their own imperialism in terms of anti-Communism. The united front appeal of the Chinese Communists, bolstered by the Comintern's call for a united front in 1935, heightened Japanese antagonism to the Communists and would have given greater credibility to Japanese claims—had Americans not been more opposed to Japanese aggression than to Communism. Writing to a leading American newspaper publisher, Roy Howard, Johnson contended that the word "communist" was a new stereotype with which the Japanese would label all opposition: "It is a clever word to use, because all the world now hates the communist, who is associated in the newspaper public's mind with one who is against God, private property and organized Government."[7] Determined not to be taken in by the Japanese, Johnson ceased to take the Communist movement very seriously thereafter.

The Nationalist government, especially after the Sian incident in December 1936, deliberately added to American confusion about the Chinese Communist movement. Fearful that the United States and other Western countries would succumb to Japanese propaganda, the Chinese government sought to play down the extent of Chinese Communist strength and to suggest that Mao and his forces had agreed to stop calling themselves Communists and to give up the class struggle. Although people like Edgar Snow and Owen Lattimore, later harassed for allegedly pro-Communist sympathies, warned that the Chinese Communists were dedicated Communists and Lattimore warned that to suppose they had given up the revolution was as foolish "as to suppose that the Soviet Union is on its way back to capitalism," Americans close to the Nationalists blurred the issue.[8]

When the war came in the summer of 1937, and the Communist Chinese and Nationalist Chinese united in opposition to the upsurge in Japanese aggression, Americans were generally gratified by this evidence of widespread patriotism, of the willingness of the Chinese to submerge their factional disputes to fight the common enemy. Naval intelligence reported that "the Fascist elements of China as represented by Generals Chiang and Pai are working with the Communists in a common cause against the Japanese."[9] Virtually every observer noted that the Communists were being exceptionally moderate in their policies, but only a few, like Lattimore, recognized that the policy shift was tactical rather than permanent. By the end of 1938, Johnson reported that "competent Chinese and foreign observers at Chungking" generally believed that the Communist leaders sincerely desired, "even at the expense of fundamental principles," to cooperate with all who would help expel the Japanese.[10]

A year later, however, the reports of cooperation between government and Communist forces were less sanguine. It was evident that the Communists were using every opportunity to expand their influence and that the government was cracking down. Within the Department of State, the prevailing view was that an open break would be unlikely while both sides were at war with Japan, but that with the end of the war, there would be little reason for further cooperation "and the active struggle for political control in China is likely to be renewed."[11] Almost alone, Nelson Johnson remained optimistic about the prospects for continued cooperation, but the New Fourth Army incident of January 1941 shook even his confidence. By March he was once again deploring the absence of patriotism in China. Tired after eleven consecutive years of representing his country to the Nationalist government, he asked for and received a new assignment. Early in the fall of 1941, the new American ambassador, Clarence Gauss, cabled: "Kuomintang-communist relations remained unchanged; that is, unsatisfactory but not a cause of special or immediate concern."[12] He found Chou En-lai, representing the Communists in Chungking, discouraged. Two months later, the contending parties became America's "Chinese allies" as the Japanese brought the United States into the Pacific War.

During the war, doubts about the relationship of the Chinese Communists to the Soviet Union persisted and some observers remained uncertain as to whether they were really Communists. But there remained no doubt that they would play an important role in the future of China. Their policies within the areas they controlled greatly heightened their popularity with the Chinese masses, at precisely the same time that the people within Kuomintang-controlled areas were becoming increasingly disaffected with the government. As a result of their growing popularity and the success of their military and political tactics, the size of their armies and of the areas under their control multiplied. The Chinese Communists were a force to be reckoned with in postwar China.

Late in 1942, Ambassador Gauss attributed the expansion of Communist influence to the failures of the Kuomintang but believed that the Communists could still be undermined by a program of social reform or destroyed by military force. Though he doubted that the Kuomintang leadership was capable of instituting reforms, he believed they still had the initiative. A few months later, Everett Drumright, one of the foreign service officers more sympathetic to Chiang's regime, noted that its prestige and influence among the Chinese people had continued to decline, referring optimistically to a point of "lowest ebb." Others, less sympathetic, presented vivid portraits of the regime responding to wartime stresses with increasing ineptitude, corruption, and brutality. In contrast there were constant reports of public approval of the efficient, honest, and moderate administration of areas under Chinese Communist control— reports verified when American journalists and officials inspected these areas themselves in 1944. Although the Department of State remained optimistic about Chiang's being able to retrieve the situation through reforms, observers in China became increasingly skeptical, not only about the prospects for reform but also of the ability of the government to suppress the Communists forcibly. It seemed likely that if the trends existing in October 1944 continued, the Communists would become "the dominant force in China within a comparatively few years."[13]

A week after Stilwell's recall, another American observer reported that the Communists were already strong enough to be assured of "postwar control of at least North China," described their phenomenal wartime growth and predicted that it would continue.[14] "Only if he is able to enlist foreign intervention on a scale equal to the Japanese invasion of China" would Chiang be able to crush the Communists. Increasingly, the indicators suggested that China's future belonged to the Communists, not to Chiang Kai-shek. With reports such as these in hand, the American government had to consider its course, now that there was no longer any hope of turning the China theater into an important war zone.

For the immediate future, the United States persisted in its efforts to avert civil war prior to Japan's defeat. Looking beyond that point, the United States continued to seek a strong China as a stabilizing force in East Asia—one of Roosevelt's Four Policemen. This idea had been a consistent theme in American thought since at least 1899. To be strong, China had to be united and that meant seeking not merely to postpone the civil war but to prevent it, to bring about a united and hopefully democratic China. The information available in Washington suggested that the Kuomintang was doomed, but in 1944 and in the immediate postwar years, it would have the advantage in terms of sheer power. The Chinese Communists could not control China now but appeared to have a long-run advantage based on their success in mobilizing mass support. As American policy evolved, the idea of a coalition government between the Kuomintang and the Communists stood out in sharp relief. The Department of State was not ignorant of the history of Kuomintang-Chinese Communist hostility. The foreign service included men who had been studying Chinese affairs almost exclusively for as many as twenty-five years. They were aware that even the Japanese attack had failed to reconcile these bitter foes. As longtime students of China they were not optimistic about the relevance of American political ideals for China, and their contempt for the Kuomintang long antedated wartime frustrations. Their task was to find a way to serve American interest through the creation of a strong China, and they saw only one hope for the immediate future: a coalition government to which the United States would give aid, including military equipment, to the Chinese Communists. Unquestionably this was a long shot, and the odds seem longer now than they did to some men then.

In the autumn of 1944, the prospects for friendly relations between the United States and the Chinese Communists actually appeared to be reasonably good, in marked contrast to the rapidly deteriorating relations between Washington and Chiang Kai-shek's government. To be sure, in its early years, the Chinese Communist Party had parroted a rhetorical anti-Americanism. With occasional prodding from Moscow, the party leadership had consistently disapproved of the United States as a capitalist and imperialist power, and in the early 1930s claimed to see the United States as the power behind Chiang. After Moscow's call for a united front in 1935, Chinese Communist criticism of the United States was muted, but the party leadership remained deeply mistrustful. After December 7, 1941, however, the Communists became extremely friendly toward the United States, not only on the surface, but even in their educational programs. In the quarrels between the United States and the Chinese government, the Communists persistently sided with the Americans. When the Japanese warned China of the dangers of the embrace of American imperialism, the Communists defended the United States against the charges. In 1944, July 4th was celebrated in Yenan with tremendous enthusiasm and fulsome praise for Roosevelt, whose policies were lauded as expressions of the great tradition of freedom and democracy in the United States.

There remained, however, the problem of the relationship between the Chinese Communists and the Soviet Union. The Department of State and military-intelligence observers in China were very much aware of the strength of nationalism within the Chinese Communist movement, of the extent to which Chinese Communist power had developed without dependence on the Soviet Union, and ultimately, of the possibility of Mao's setting his own course, independent of Soviet control. On the other hand, they were also aware that the Chinese Communists, viewing themselves as Marxist-Leninists, were very partial to the Soviet Union and under pressure could be expected to align themselves with and expect support from the Russians rather than from the United States. Civil war would almost certainly heighten their sense of dependence on the Russians—still another reason for working toward a peaceful solution of the Kuomintang-Communist conflict. Indeed, as early as June 1943, John Paton Davies, a foreign service officer attached to Stilwell's staff, warned that an attempt by Chiang to liquidate the Communists might involve the United States in conflict with the Soviet Union. To determine Soviet intentions, Hurley had stopped off in Moscow en route to China in August 1944.

After discussions with Soviet foreign minister V. M. Molotov, Hurley concluded that the Soviet Union was unconvinced by Chinese Communist professions of Marxist faith and did not intend to support Mao against the Chinese government. Consequently, he was optimistic about the possibility of unifying Chinese forces peacefully. Roosevelt gave Hurley his head in China and at Yalta tried to commit the Soviet Union to support of the Chinese government prior to Russian participation in the war against Japan. American policy, as expressed in Hurley's mission and in the Far Eastern Agreement signed at Yalta, was directed toward a peaceful settlement of the internal Chinese struggle, but a settlement that would assure the continued dominance of the Kuomintang.

At Yalta (see text of agreement, below), Roosevelt indicated his continued contempt for China by arranging a postwar settlement in East Asia without Chinese participation or the prior consent of the Chinese government. Primarily concerned with minimizing American casualties in the final battle against Japan, Roosevelt purchased Stalin's commitment to intervene with territory and concessions that belonged in part to China.

In particular, the Russians claimed and Roosevelt granted privileges once wrested from the Chinese by tsarist imperialism and subsequently lost or sold to the Japanese. But he also obtained Stalin's promise to support Chiang Kai-shek's government. For the moment, at least, Stalin was prepared to allow the Chinese Communists to fend for themselves—a painful surprise when revealed to them six months later.

Far Eastern Agreement
(signed at Yalta, February 11, 1945)

The leaders of the Three Great Powers—the Soviet Union, the United States of America and Great Britain—have agreed that in two or three months after Germany has surrendered and the war in Europe has terminated the Soviet Union shall enter the war against Japan on the side of the Allies on condition that:

1. The status quo in Outer-Mongolia (The Mongolian People's Republic) shall be preserved.
2. The former rights of Russia violated by the treacherous attack of Japan in 1904 shall be restored, viz.

   (a) the southern part of Sakhalin as well as all the islands adjacent to it shall be returned to the Soviet Union,
   (b) the commercial port of Dairen shall be internationalized, the preeminent interests of the Soviet Union in this port being safeguarded, and the lease of Port Arthur as a naval base of the USSR restored,
   (c) the Chinese-Eastern Railroad and the South-Manchurian Railroad which provides an outlet to Dairen shall be jointly operated by the establishment of a joint Soviet-Chinese Company, it being understood that the preeminent interests of the Soviet Union shall be safeguarded and that China shall retain full sovereignty in Manchuria.

3. The Kuril islands shall be handed over to the Soviet Union.

It is understood that the agreement concerning Outer-Mongolia and the ports and railroads referred to above will require concurrence of Generalissimo Chiang Kai-shek. The President will take measures in order to obtain this concurrence on advice from Marshal Stalin.

The Heads of the three Great Powers have agreed that these claims of the Soviet Union shall be unquestionably fulfilled after Japan has been defeated.

For its part the Soviet Union expresses its readiness to conclude with the National Government of China a pact of friendship and alliance between the USSR and China in order to render assistance to China with its armed forces for the purpose of liberating China from the Japanese yoke.

While Roosevelt thus tried to strengthen the Nationalist position by depriving the Communists of their most likely source of aid, Hurley went on with his efforts to create a coalition government, to be headed by Chiang Kai-shek. His talks with Chiang and Mao convinced him that both were committed to democracy and that an agreement would be possible if extremists in both parties, British imperialists and American officials hostile to the Kuomintang, could be silenced. Confident that the Communists would get no support from the Russians, Hurley believed it essential to deny them any hope of American support while continuing to aid the Kuomintang government. Thus isolated, the Communists would be forced to come to terms.

Neither Hurley's inherited staff at the embassy nor the foreign service officers serving as political advisers to the military command accepted his estimate of conditions in China or his approach to unifying the country and increasing its contribution to the war. There was agreement on these ends of policy, but the career diplomats were convinced that the intransigence of the Kuomintang was the principal obstacle to Chinese unity; that Hurley underestimated Chinese Communist determination; and that in the absence of aid from the United States, the Communists would seek and obtain aid from the Soviet Union, creating tension between the United States and the Soviet Union over China. The disagreement between the ambassador and his staff was aggravated by the latter's lack of confidence in Hurley—a lack of confidence stemming from Hurley's ignorance of China and from his assumption that his personal estimate of conditions was more accurate than the contrary estimate provided by the unanimous judgment of all observers in the field. When Hurley returned to Washington in February 1945, the embassy staff precipitated a showdown, sending a cable that reached conclusions and recommended tactics contrary to those that Hurley espoused. In particular, they argued that American support was making Chiang unyielding and that a continuation of American policy would probably result in civil war in which the Communists would seek Soviet support. On the assumption that the United States sought to use the Communists against Japan, the cable from Chungking advocated that the United States proceed to do so, supplying them as necessary while giving appropriate assurances to Chiang Kai-shek. The cable was endorsed by all of the embassy's political officers and by the acting commanding officer of American forces in China. With both Hurley and General Albert Wedemeyer, Stilwell's successor, in Washington, Undersecretary of State Joseph Grew sent the cable on to Roosevelt to underline the urgency of the situation and to set the stage for a review of policy.

Hurley reacted angrily, and after discussions at the State and War departments Roosevelt ended the debate by standing with Hurley. American policy in China would be as Hurley defined it: an effort to sustain and reform Chiang Kai-shek's government with no assistance to the Communists except as approved by Chiang. The dissenting foreign service officers were all transferred out of China. The United States would continue to work for a coalition government in China, in the hope of democratizing Chiang's regime, but there could be no question of which side Roosevelt had chosen in the Chinese struggle—and on April 2, 1945, Hurley made an unequivocal announcement to the effect that the American government would support only the Kuomintang regime and would not recognize or supply any other government or forces.

Kuomintang intelligence reports indicate that the Communists had hoped to get direct aid from the United States in the form of lend-lease supplies. Mao and Chou were well aware of American dissatisfaction with the Chinese war effort, with Chiang's refusal to fight, and the Communists had long attempted to exploit this tension. The arrival in Yenan of the American observer group in the summer of 1944 had been viewed as a prelude to broader cooperation between the United States and the Chinese Communists. The Communist leadership was obviously aware of the frictions that had led to Stilwell's recall and to Ambassador Gauss's resignation—and the fact that they were viewed with relative favor by most American officials and journalists in China was public knowledge. In January 1945, Mao and Chou asked for a meeting with Roosevelt to plan the details of military cooperation between American and Chinese Communist forces—and to present their thoughts on China's internal affairs. But this request was refused, and if the Communists nonetheless retained hopes for American support, Hurley's statement and the subsequent purge of the embassy brought an end to the dream.

The anger of the Communists was muffled until after Roosevelt's death, until it was apparent that Truman would not repudiate Hurley. Then, with increasing openness, Mao contended that American policy as announced by Hurley was evidence of the "rampancy of the American reactionaries."[15] Roosevelt had been portrayed as the leader of progressive forces in the United States and his death had been mourned by the Chinese Communist press. Hope had been expressed that Truman would continue Roosevelt's policies, but events of the spring and summer of 1945 were interpreted as evidence that American policy had entered a new anti-Communist phase. For the Chinese Communists, Roosevelt's death gave credence to the fiction that American policy had changed: that Roosevelt's progressive policies toward China had been replaced by Hurley's reactionary policies. Most conveniently, Roosevelt's death facilitated the acceptance of a shift in attitudes toward the United States that had been signaled by Moscow shortly before.

The significance of Stalin's signal for a new Communist position on cooperation with the West cannot be ignored in explaining the sudden, sharp increase in Chinese Communist criticism of the United States. Without the Soviet shift, Mao's anger would likely have remained muted. On the other hand, Mao's anger was caused by American policy and required no prodding from the Russians. Once Roosevelt, presented with the alternatives of cooperating with the Chinese Communists or giving sole support to the Kuomintang government, chose the latter, American policy left Mao no choice but to dance to Stalin's tune and hope for the best. The Soviet Union's anti-Western campaign provided a framework but not the cause for Chinese Communist criticism of the United States.

Once again, en route to China, Hurley went first to Moscow to ascertain Soviet intentions. The Department of State's specialists on China, especially O. Edmund Clubb, were very skeptical about the prospects for good relations between Chiang's China and the Soviet Union, but Hurley was a perennial optimist. Although Soviet-Western frictions were already surfacing in Eastern Europe when Hurley saw Stalin in mid-April, Hurley reported that Stalin endorsed American policy toward China, asking him to report that the United States had "his complete support in immediate action for the unification of the armed forces of China with full recognition of the Nationalist Government under the leadership of Chiang

Kai-shek."[16] Once again, Hurley's confidence was challenged by other American diplomats, this time Averell Harriman and George Kennan of the embassy in Moscow. Both warned that Stalin could not be relied on to support American policy once the Soviet Union entered the war in East Asia. Both believed that when the opportunity presented itself Stalin would work with the Chinese Communists to undermine the Chinese government and to further Soviet ambitions in Mongolia, Manchuria, and North China. Hurley, however, remained unshaken in his conviction. By May, Harriman moved closer to Hurley's view after Stalin stated bluntly that he believed Chiang Kai-shek to be the only Chinese leader competent to unify China and that none of the Chinese Communist leaders were his equal. Harriman concluded that Stalin was satisfied with the price offered at Yalta and that, assuming Roosevelt's arrangements were satisfactory to Chiang, the Soviet Union would cooperate to bring about a unified China under Chiang.

Early in July, T. V. Soong arrived in Moscow to negotiate a treaty whereby China would accept the terms of the Yalta agreement—and the Nationalist government would pay the price necessary for Stalin's support against the Chinese Communists. Before Soong left for Moscow, the Chinese tried to involve the United States in any agreement they reached with the Soviet Union. With regard to Manchuria, Chiang proposed a modified form of the policy the Chinese had attempted to use against the Russians at the beginning of the century: a checking of Soviet influence by bringing the United States and Great Britain into Port Arthur rather than leasing it to the Russians alone. But again, the United States refrained from interposing itself between China and Russian imperialism.

To Soong, Stalin stated categorically that he would support only the Nationalist government and that all military forces in China had to come under the control of that government. But in return for sacrificing the Chinese Communists, he demanded a price higher than he and Roosevelt had agreed on at Yalta. In particular Stalin insisted on virtually complete control of Manchuria. Soong was unprepared to agree to the new Soviet terms and Chiang was still less enthusiastic, but Stalin backed off, willing to settle for control of the Manchurian railroads, Dairen, and Port Arthur. Despite Soviet pressures, Soong held firm, and the Sino-Soviet negotiations were adjourned to allow Stalin to proceed to the Potsdam Conference and Soong to return to Chungking for consultations with his government. Although he hoped to be able to pay a little less, Soong asked

Harriman to inform President Truman that he was satisfied with Stalin's assurances with regard to the Chinese Communists and with the Soviet terms for the proposed treaty of friendship.

At Potsdam Chiang cabled Truman in a further attempt to enlist American support for the Chinese position. Truman would do no more than assure Chiang that he expected him to make no concessions in excess of the Yalta agreements, but within the American delegation at Potsdam concern over Soviet demands mounted. Secretary of War Stimson, Ambassador Harriman, and John Carter Vincent urged the president to support the Chinese. All saw Soviet demands as unreasonable and threatening not only to China, but also to America's "historic" policy. Should the Soviet Union succeed in its efforts to turn Manchuria and North China into its sphere of influence, the balance of power in East Asia would be adversely affected and the prospects for American economic interests in China greatly reduced. Ultimately Harriman succeeded in obtaining instructions authorizing him to protest against Soviet claims in Manchuria and to attempt to obtain Stalin's written promise that the "Open Door" policy would be observed in Manchuria—that equality of opportunity for American commerce there would be guaranteed.

Although strengthened by Harriman's support, Soong's bargaining position was quickly undermined by the Soviet Union's intervention in the war against Japan. On August 10, 1945, Stalin warned Soong that the Japanese would be forced to surrender in a matter of days and that further delay in coming to terms would result in the Chinese Communists moving into Manchuria. To obtain the desired Soviet promise not to interfere in China's internal affairs and to support only the Nationalist government, Soong made concessions beyond those required by the Yalta agreement. When the Treaty of Friendship was signed and the accompanying notes exchanged, Chiang Kai-shek, Madam Chiang, and Soong each gave independent testimony to the satisfaction of the Kuomintang government with the bargain. Unquestionably they would have preferred better terms, but though they were negotiating from a position of weakness, they achieved their essential aim, assurance of Soviet support for their regime, while conceding in Manchuria and Outer Mongolia nothing that this regime had ever controlled.

Meanwhile, in China, the Chinese Communists had refused to come to heel throughout the spring and early summer of 1945. When the Japanese surrendered, the Communists claimed for their forces the right to liberate enemy-held territory, rejecting Chiang's orders that they remain in place, awaiting his instructions. When Chiang invited Mao to Chungking on August 16, Mao refused and the Communists continued to denounce both Chiang and Hurley. But the American response to Communist claims to a right to accept the Japanese surrender was a message calling attention to the fact that General Order No. 1, which required the Japanese in China to surrender to Chiang alone, had been endorsed by Great Britain and the Soviet Union, as well as by the United States. In addition, American forces began to liberate key points in North China to hold them for the Chinese government, and the American government provided transportation to facilitate the movement of government troops into areas they could not otherwise reach before the Communists.

To Mao the American position was clear. What remained in doubt was the degree of support he could expect from his comrades in Moscow. Publication of the terms of the Sino-Soviet Treaty of Friendship provided the initial answer. Despite a brave front offered by the Chinese Communist press, the party leadership was badly shaken by the Soviet betrayal. Party cadres were instructed to tell the people that Soviet policy would work to the party's long-term advantage, but the leadership confessed that "Soviet policy cannot be understood."[17] Without direct aid from the Russians, the Chinese Communists were not ready for civil war. Party strategy had to be revised to avoid confrontations in the larger cities. Uncertain as to Stalin's intentions, Mao would "proceed from hope." On August 28, Mao reversed himself and flew to Chungking for talks with Chiang Kai-shek.

And so the war—and the month of August 1945—ended with Japan's defeat and the remaining contenders for power in China in East Asia all able to find cause for satisfaction—except for the Chinese Communists. The balance of power in East Asia was more favorable to the Russians than at any time in their history. China remained weak and for the moment divided. The only power that could have contested the new Russian position, the United States, had readily accepted it as the price for aid in defeating Japan. For their part, the Americans were as pleased as Stalin. They had eliminated Japanese power and at Yalta had purchased not only Soviet intervention in the war but Soviet support for American efforts to bolster and reform the Chinese Nationalist government as well. The prospects for stability in East Asia were better than those any American could remember, and Hurley, at least, was optimistic about the chances for democratic government in China. There, the government under Chiang Kai-shek had not satisfied all of its desires, but the Japanese invader had been defeated and both American and Soviet support assured Chiang of his ability to deal with the threat of the Chinese Communists. Control of China proper seemed certain, and once the Communists were brought to heel, extending China's rule over Manchuria and the border regions would be relatively easy. Only Mao was left with a "dry stick."

The talks between Chiang Kai-shek and Mao Tse-tung seemed to go well in September, and Hurley's optimism was boundless. Both Chinese leaders behaved less arrogantly and indicated greater willingness to compromise. With the war's end, Chiang had been warned that his possibilities for future American aid were neither unlimited nor unqualified. Mao had no prospects for outside backing and Chiang presumably understood that if he were recalcitrant, American support would evaporate. In mid-September, Hurley returned to the United States, hopeful that by the time he returned, agreement would have been reached. But like Stalin, he had underestimated the determination of Mao and his followers— and perhaps had overestimated the soundness of Chiang's judgment.

Bound by no agreements, Chinese Communist forces continued to spread their influence through North China and on into Manchuria. Blocked first by the Japanese under orders to surrender to Chiang's representatives and then by American marines sent to expedite the disarming of the Japanese, the Communists stayed away from the major cities, but the countryside was theirs—and with it the ability to deny the government use of vital communication links. Chiang nonetheless pressed forward, confident of the ability of his armies to win the trial by battle. Having cooperated with Stalin twice before, he had no doubt of Stalin's willingness to sacrifice the Chinese Communists for his own ends or of his ability to outmaneuver Stalin again, if necessary. Similarly, despite the warnings of the American government, he realized that it could not easily desert him. American actions in support of his forces reinforced his confidence.

But in Washington and in Moscow misgivings arose. The nature of Soviet doubts remains unknown, but Soviet policy vacillated. In late September and October 1945, possibly in response to American moves to exclude Soviet influence from Japan, Russian forces in Manchuria facilitated the movements of the Chinese Communists while hindering the operations of the government. But from November 1945 to the eve of the Soviet withdrawal in March 1946, the Russians appeared to be honoring their commitment to Chiang. In Washington concern mounted over the danger that military operations designed to expedite the surrender and repatriation of Japanese troops would involve the United States in a civil war. General Wedemeyer warned that it was impossible to carry out the mission assigned to him without some incidental aid to the Nationalists in their competition with the Communists. But while some American leaders were troubled by the problem of how the United States was to remain neutral and attempt to mediate while supporting Chiang's forces, the secretaries of war and navy, Robert P. Patterson and James V. Forrestal respectively, pressed for continued aid to Chiang, not at all unhappy about the collateral effect of aiding him against the Communists. Indeed, pressure for an anti-Soviet, anti-Communist policy was mounting in the United States, largely in response to frustrations in Europe.

Amidst these discussions, reports coming to Washington from China indicated that the Nationalists and Communists were in reality farther apart than was indicated by a joint statement issued on October 10—and that there remained little chance for averting civil war. Suddenly, on November 27, Hurley resigned, his optimism shattered. Exhausted by his enormous efforts to bring peace to China, to reconcile what proved to be the irreconcilable, he chose to step aside, showering the blame for failure on all who ever disagreed with him, leaving behind a dung heap of irresponsible charges in which ambitious politicians would soon revel.

Truman wasted little time, calling General Marshall that same afternoon and asking him to go to China as the president's personal representative. As of that moment the administration had decided to keep American marines in China; to continue to move Chiang's troops into North China; to continue efforts to bring about a truce between the Kuomintang and the Communists in the disputed areas still held by the Japanese; and to continue efforts for a political settlement under Chiang Kai-shek. The American government was operating on two basic assumptions, derived from the estimates of military intelligence in China. First, the Joint Chiefs of Staff had reported that the Japanese could not be removed without the help of the marines and that if civil war broke out before they were repatriated, they would be employed by one or both of the Chinese contenders. Disastrous under any circumstances, involvement of the Japanese in the Chinese civil war would almost certainly enable the Russians to extend their control over Manchuria and might bring their intervention in China proper. Secondly, the Joint Chiefs reported that they did not believe that Chiang had the capacity to reunify China by military means. Certainly he lacked the power to control Manchuria. Implicit in both assumptions and policy was the fear that conditions in China would provide for an extension of Soviet influence—to which there was opposition on traditional geopolitical as well as ideological grounds.

Marshall quickly recognized the contradictions inherent in American policy. Ideally, the United States wanted the peaceful unification of China under a liberal democratic government. Given the nature of the two parties contending for control of China, their present and potential military capabilities, American hopes could be realized only by a compromise between the Kuomintang and the Communists in which the right-wing extremists in the former and left-wing extremists in the latter would cancel each other out, precluding both fascist and Communist alternatives to a democratic regime. Marshall's principal effort, therefore, was to be a continuation of Hurley's attempts to mediate between Chiang and Mao. But Marshall wanted to know how he could be expected to mediate while the United States provided military assistance to Chiang, compromising its claim to impartiality. The ensuing discussion again suggested a sense of urgency about unifying China, repatriating the Japanese in North China and Manchuria before the Russians entrenched themselves. On December 9, 1945, Marshall was told that in the event that the Communists were prepared to make concessions, and the Nationalists posed obstacles, he was to warn Chiang that the United States would stop assisting him and deal with the Chinese Communists in North China. In other words, the American government was contemplating bypassing the recognized government of China in order to assure control of North China by Chinese forces—a step it had ultimately rejected in the war against Japan. If the Communists blocked an agreement, the United States would give full support to Chiang and move his armies north.

Two days later, however, Truman and James F. Byrnes, his secretary of state, retreated from the implications of their initial instructions. Marshall was told that even if Chiang proved troublesome, the United States could not abandon him and his government. Given the existing power configuration within China, this would result in a divided China, leaving the Soviet Union supreme in Manchuria. Marshall was authorized to pressure Chiang, but in the end the pressure would be a bluff; no matter how Chiang responded, the United States would have to back him. Nonetheless, Truman wanted Marshall to find a way to give this support with minimal effect on the power balance between Chiang and the Communists. It was a thankless assignment, but it was the only hope of obtaining the kind of government the United States wanted short of an intensive economic and military involvement that the importance of American interests in China had never merited.

After Marshall arrived in China, the Russians fulfilled the letter if not the spirit of their agreement with Chiang Kai-shek's government, withdrawing their forces from Manchuria as soon as they had stripped the area of all equipment of possible industrial value. The stocks of Japanese weapons they left behind proved of great value to the Chinese Communists but hardly mitigated the effect of their pillage in the hearts of their Chinese comrades. Their withdrawal heartened those who had feared they would retain control of Manchuria or hold the territory for Mao's forces. Immediate Russian interests had already been served, and they left behind only fuel to feed the fires of discord, which Stalin apparently expected to produce a divided and weak China.

Although the limited assistance the Chinese Communists received from the Russians allowed Mao to be more optimistic than at the end of the summer of 1945, he still lacked assurance of Soviet support. He found it expedient, therefore, to avoid a showdown that might result in substantial American aid to Chiang. Instead, he sought to avoid fighting and to underscore the nonneutral position the United States followed under Hurley's direction. On December 3, 1945, the Communists agreed to participate in the Political Consultative Conference that Chiang had scheduled to meet in January. Mao advised the party faithful that the concessions Chiang had offered were not merely paper concessions, that American policy since Hurley's resignation was acceptable. In a secret order to party cadres, the Central Committee declared that peace in China was the desire not only of the Chinese people but of the world, and "first among these are the Soviet Union and the democratic faction in the United States. The latter have most recently recognized the seriousness of conditions in China and oppose the Hurley policy which would create civil war in China."[18]

Kuomintang intelligence, however, took a less sanguine view of Mao's new tactics. The moderate policy of the Communists was viewed as a stall—a gamble that, in conjunction with the American Communist Party, the Chinese Communists could disrupt relations between the Kuomintang and the United States and bring about a reversal of American policy. Even before the Political Consultative Conference met, the Kuomintang saw no hope for an accommodation with the Communists. Still confident of retaining Soviet friendship, it charged the Communists with attempting to disrupt Sino-Soviet relations and with making it difficult to carry out the obligations of the Sino-Soviet treaty.

But the Political Consultative Conference seemed to go well, however mistrustful the Kuomintang or elements within it may have been. And Marshall seemed to be having extraordinary luck in his handling of the military situation. He informed Chou En-lai that the United States was committed to transporting government troops to Manchuria, and Chou replied that this would be acceptable to the Communists. Moreover, the movement of these troops into Manchurian cities was actually accomplished without opposition. When Marshall upheld a Communist refusal to permit Kuomintang forces to occupy strongholds within Communist-controlled territory as a precondition to a cease-fire, the government acquiesced. As a result, an effective truce began a few days after the conference opened.

The political and military settlements worked out between the Kuomintang and the Communists in January and February 1946 were received with tremendous enthusiasm by the Chinese people. Throughout this period, the Communist press withheld criticism of American "intervention" in Chinese affairs. Despite considerable military activity that flared for a few days in Manchuria and despite signs that the Kuomintang Right might not accept the settlement, Marshall and the American government were optimistic in the last days of February and early March. Now it was time to show both Chinese factions just how beneficial peaceful compromise could be, and Marshall departed for the United States to arrange for economic aid. With the Treasury determined to balance the budget and mistrust of Kuomintang financial practices widespread, funds were not easily obtained, but Marshall returned to China with a "respectable bundle."

However, after almost a quarter of a century of cooperation, betrayal, and efforts to take advantage of each other, the leaders of the Nationalists and of the Chinese Communist Party knew each other too well, and each waited for an indication of the other side's readiness to overthrow the compromise. Mutual understanding meant only mutual mistrust, and in this atmosphere, both sides soon gave sufficient cause for a breakdown of the cease-fire. The Nationalists persistently attempted to brush aside all restraints on their activities in Manchuria, and it proved impossible to bring about an effective truce in the area. Moreover, to the suspicious Communists, the manner in which the Central Executive Committee of the Kuomintang "ratified" the agreements of the Political Consultative Conference was a warning of intended perfidy. On the other hand, Communist activities in Manchuria offered little comfort to those who hoped for peace. As the Russian troops began to withdraw in early April, the Chinese Communists moved into the vacuum. By mid-April, the civil war was in full swing again, with the Communists capturing Changchun on the very day that Marshall returned to China.

Marshall was able to persuade the Communists to withdraw from Changchun as he attempted to regain the ground lost during his absence. In return for their withdrawal, Marshall obtained Chiang's promise that his forces would halt their advance on the city. But Chiang's word proved without value, and government troops took the city in late May, compromising Marshall's position with the Communists. Desperately— and unsuccessfully—Marshall attempted to get Chiang to understand that American proposals for a truce and a political settlement were designed not to undermine his power but to preserve for him and Kuomintang "liberals" a prominent position in a united China—a position that American military intelligence suggested he could not retain if he insisted on a military solution. But Chiang's forces were in the process of giving the Communists a severe thrashing in Manchuria, and the euphoria of the moment made him still less amenable to American reasoning, or pressure, than usual.

When the successful Nationalist offensive seemed to be losing momentum, Chiang agreed to a fifteen-day truce that went into effect on June 7 and ultimately lasted until June 30. Chiang's conditions for peace required the Communists to withdraw from key points in North China and Manchuria. Again Marshall persuaded the Communists to agree to withdraw from certain areas, contingent on a government agreement to refrain from occupying those areas, and to agree to give the American member of the three-man truce teams the deciding vote. They insisted, however, that Chiang make concessions as to the nature of the civil government to follow the restoration of peace. Clearly the Communists believed a peaceful settlement to be in their interest in mid-1946 and were prepared to offer a tactical retreat. But when Marshall went to Chiang on June 30, the last day of the truce, he found Chiang absolutely unyielding, convinced that he was strong enough to crush the Communists—that the time was ripe for a military solution.

Chiang's decision for all-out war was also based in part on the conviction that regardless of what Marshall told him, he could count on continued and extensive support from the United States. Action taken in Washington throughout June deprived Marshall of what little leverage he had. Bills were introduced in Congress to increase military assistance and "advice" to the Chinese government. While these bills were pending, *Pravda* announced the negotiation of a secret Sino-American lend-lease arrangement. And on June 24, Mao made his first public statement in months, denouncing American policy. He charged that despite all the promises made by Truman and Byrnes, despite international agreements to withdraw its forces from China, the United States continued to maintain a military presence ten months after the Japanese surrender—and that the United States was thus assisting reactionaries within the Kuomintang. He contended that there was no difference between the American practice of organizing, training, and equipping Chiang's armies and the practice of imperialism in colonies of establishing dependent armies. Claiming that the "present imperialist faction" in the United States had reversed Roosevelt's policies, he demanded to know just what these people wanted— bases? Colonies? What? Why were the Americans sending more military aid to the Kuomintang?

On June 27, the House Foreign Affairs Committee reported favorably on the military assistance bill and the next day, Undersecretary of State Dean Acheson announced that the United States *had* reached a new military-aid agreement with the Chinese government to provide it with $51.7 million in "pipeline" equipment until new arrangements could be devised—such new arrangements to include the sale, at bargain rates, of nearly $1 billion in surplus war equipment that American forces had strewn behind them in China and on various nearby Pacific islands. On July 1, 1946, all-out civil war was resumed, and nothing Marshall could say could induce Chiang to agree to a new cease-fire.

When, on July 1, Mao ordered the commencement of an anti-American campaign, he did so because he had come to realize what Marshall had known from the very beginning of his mission: that no matter what happened, the United States would not abandon the Kuomintang government; that even if responsibility for civil war rested with Chiang, the United States would continue to back the Nationalists. It was useless to argue that some of this aid was intended for the Chinese Communists to be expended in the process of integrating Communist forces with those of the government in accord with the February agreements. The Communists had had enough of false promises during the war, promises of equipment that never came, promises of support later repudiated. And there was the further example of the $178 million in goods, most of which came from the United States, which UNRRA was distributing in China in the first half of 1946. Theoretically, UNRRA was working on the principle of relief without regard to politics, yet although the Communists controlled areas containing approximately one-third the population, only three percent of this aid ever reached these areas. And so, in the first week of July, the party faithful received a detailed justification for an anti-American campaign and instructions on how to conduct it.

Throughout July a discouraged Marshall kept trying, pressed on by the Department of State, where hope remained that Chiang could be brought in time to recognize the suicidal nature of the course he had chosen. To help him, Marshall asked to have John Leighton Stuart, a universally respected missionary educator, appointed ambassador. By the end of the month, Marshall concluded that there was no hope for peace so long as the United States continued to aid the Nationalists; that military assistance to Chiang's forces, no matter how well justified earlier, was clearly inconsistent with his efforts to end the civil war. Marshall was no longer very apprehensive about Soviet intentions in Manchuria or toward North China. His remaining objective was to reduce Chinese Communist dependence on Moscow by integrating Mao and his followers in a coalition government. Viewing Chiang's belligerence as the principal obstacle, he asked for and Washington approved an immediate embargo on arms and munitions to China.

Chiang remained convinced that the American government would override Marshall, but Marshall began to withdraw American marines from convoy duty and similar functions, further disengaging the United States from Chiang's military operations. In early October T. V. Soong warned Ambassador Stuart that although Chiang had promised Marshall not to attack the city of Kalgan, the government intended to capture it before agreeing to another truce. The Communists had warned that if Kalgan were attacked they would consider negotiations ended. Marshall was furious at Chiang's apparent duplicity and concluded that Chiang was simply using his efforts as a smoke screen for the continuing military campaign. Marshall warned Chiang that if the fighting did not stop immediately he would request that he be recalled and American mediation efforts terminated. When Truman backed Marshall, Chiang offered a ten-day truce on operations directed at Kalgan, but the Communists rejected his terms. On October 10, Nationalist forces occupied Kalgan and both Marshall and Ambassador Stuart agreed that further mediation was hopeless.

It was November before the American marines were finally withdrawn from China and December before Marshall surrendered completely. In January he returned to Washington to become secretary of state. At this point the matter of American involvement in Chinese affairs ceased to be a question of foreign policy, falling instead into the yet murkier realm of domestic politics.

The American effort to prevent civil war in China by bringing about peaceful unification had failed. The effort had been made because the American government believed in 1945 and 1946, as American officials had concluded long before, that the interests of the United States would be served by the existence of a strong united China that would almost certainly be friendly. In the immediate postwar situation, a strong united China required a peaceful solution to the long-standing Kuomintang-Communist dispute. If civil war came, it would be agony for the long-suffering Chinese people and inimical to China's role as a stabilizing force in East Asia; furthermore, it would both strengthen those elements tending toward fascism in the Kuomintang and increase the dependence of the Chinese Communists on the Soviet Union. A coalition brought about by peaceful means might well have been a liberal democratic regime, achieved by the mixture and ultimate dilution or elimination of the extreme Right and extreme Left. It did not work out that way. It probably *could not* have worked out that way, but even hindsight has yet to produce a convincing alternative.

The absence of a better alternative was evident in the highly significant willingness of the American government to accept failure. When the Truman administration gave up its efforts to mediate at the end of 1946, there was every expectation of an ultimate Communist victory—only the speed of the Kuomintang collapse came as a surprise. But although a Communist victory in China was considered undesirable and although no American government ever took a stronger and more successful stand against Soviet imperialism, a Communist China was considered tolerable. Kennan argued that a Communist China would not threaten the United States; that China was not an industrial power nor likely to become one for some time. He did not believe that China would for a long time be able to exercise military power anywhere beyond the Asian mainland— and the Asian mainland had never been and was not, in 1946, considered an area of great strategic or economic importance to the United States. In August 1946, as the administration prepared to respond to Soviet pressures on Greece and Turkey, General Dwight Eisenhower asked if

Truman understood that war might result. Truman thereupon removed a map of the Middle East from his desk and lectured those assembled on the strategic importance of the Middle East and of the extent to which the United States had to be prepared to go to deny the area to the Soviet Union. No one ever recorded a similar lecture on the importance of the Asian mainland.

Though willing to use its great wealth and power to protect Western Europe and the Middle East from the Soviet threat—a threat unquestionably perceived in terms of American interests—the United States reluctantly acquiesced in the Communist conquest of China. Whatever American ambitions were in East Asia—and they were considerable—the Truman administration, like every administration preceding it, did not consider American interests there to be vital. On the scale of American priorities, unlike the scale of American sympathies, China ranked very low indeed. Despite the universality of the language very shortly to be used in the Truman Doctrine, Truman and his advisers were very much aware of the limits of American power, and they realized that retrieval of the situation in China was well beyond those limits—especially in the face of Soviet pressures across the Atlantic. Had considerations of American interests in East Asia dictated American policy in the ensuing three years, the Truman administration would almost certainly have brought about a total cessation of American involvement in the Chinese civil war. That by 1949 the will to do so existed is unquestionable.

Although Ambassador Stuart remained in China, available if American good offices were sought, and the embassy and State Department staffs continued to search for ways to serve American ends in China, from 1947 to 1949 the administration's main task was to find a way to limit the involvement of the United States without jeopardizing congressional and public support essential to its policies for the protection and reconstruction of Europe. The principal obstacle that had to be overcome was the great sympathy that the American people had for China and their war-born conception of Chiang Kai-shek as the personification of China. So long as the American people persisted in seeing themselves as the champions of China and in seeing Chiang as China, it was difficult to explain why the United States had suddenly chosen to abandon Chiang. This difficulty was greatly compounded by the rise of anti-Communist feeling in the United States, partly stimulated by the administration in its efforts to gain support for the Marshall Plan and NATO, very expensive projects deemed essential to contain Soviet aggression. If China was also suffering from Communist subversion, why should the United States neglect to include Chiang's regime in its aid program? Why was the United States committed to a Europe-first policy? Although these questions were raised on occasion by unscrupulous politicians, there were many Americans as thoughtful and concerned with American interests as were President Truman and General Marshall, who also worried about the course of the administration's policy toward China. In Congress there was broad bipartisan support for resuming aid to Chiang's government—support that transcended geographic and ideological boundaries as well as party lines. The Truman administration never succeeded in convincing Congress or the American public of the wisdom of its policy. Indeed, no real effort to do so was made before August 1949.

Another problem that became increasingly serious after the unexpected reelection of Truman in November 1948 was Republican criticism of his and Roosevelt's policy toward China. Although neither political party ever has a monopoly of extremists within its ranks, the vileness and irresponsibility of some of these attacks suggested that the Republicans had attracted more than their share. In the happier days of 1947, when Republican criticism was circumscribed by the expectation of assuming responsibility for policy in January 1949, it was nonetheless necessary for leading Republican senators like Arthur Vandenberg of Michigan to indicate their independence of the Democratic regime. A staunch supporter of Truman's foreign-aid program, Vandenberg nonetheless took frequent public exception to the omission of China as a beneficiary of American largesse. To retain his support and those of his followers in the Senate, the administration almost as frequently acquiesced in further small involvements on the Kuomintang side of the Chinese civil war. Though these acts would unquestionably antagonize the Communists, the probable victors in that war, the same assumption of the relative unimportance of China that had enabled the administration to tolerate failure there reinforced the conviction that the alienation of Congress was by far the graver danger.

George Kennan's Policy Planning Staff concluded that a Communist victory would result from Nationalist weaknesses "more apt to be indulged and encouraged than corrected by further infusions of American aid."[19] Marshall, however, thought it best to continue small-scale aid to Chiang to try to keep him in power without being trapped into an open-ended commitment. Responsive also to public sympathy for China and to congressional pressures, Marshall agreed to lift the arms embargo in May 1947, enabling the Nationalists to obtain military supplies from the United States once again. Even during the interim when the embargo was theoretically in effect, the marines leaving China found it necessary to "abandon" 6,500 tons of ammunition to Chiang's forces. In the summer of 1947, General Wedemeyer, whose relations with Chiang had been relatively good, was sent to China to investigate the situation there and to determine whether the United States could salvage Chiang's regime.

To Marshall's dismay, Wedemeyer returned with a recommendation for large-scale economic and military aid from the United States, contingent on Chiang's agreement to carry out sweeping reforms. Truman and his advisers did not share Wedemeyer's estimate of the importance of East Asia to American security. They no longer believed that Chiang would carry out reforms that he had been unwilling to effect in the previous twenty years of his rule, and they believed the time had passed when reforms could save his government. Wedemeyer persuaded the Joint Chiefs that an American advisory mission of perhaps 10,000 officers and men would suffice to turn the tide, but Marshall insisted that a major armed intervention, conceivably leading to World War III, would be necessary to retrieve the situation in China. This was a task best left to Chinese boys. He would give Chiang money, but not American military assistance. Finally, it was the conviction of the Truman administration that dollars spent for American security would provide infinitely greater returns when invested in Europe. For reasons never satisfactorily disclosed, this eminently sensible reasoning was denied the American public. Instead, the administration decided to suppress Wedemeyer's report, leaving itself wide open to the charges of deceit that inevitably followed.

Unable to move the Truman administration, Chiang and his friends in the United States concentrated their efforts on Congress and the opposition party. While Mao, the Chinese Communists, and increasing numbers of Chinese intellectuals were contending that American aid to Chiang was delaying peace, aggravating the misery of the Chinese people, Chiang personally informed visiting congressmen that if he were defeated it would be only because the United States had denied him support in China's hour of need. Although intelligence estimates and Wedemeyer's investigation indicated that not lack of equipment but rather corruption, tactical blunders, and defections were loosening Chiang's grasp on the Mandate of Heaven, Republican leaders like Governor Thomas E. Dewey of New York, trying to disassociate themselves and their party from the failure to achieve American ends in China, demanded more aid for the Nationalists. In 1948, in anticipation of the presidential election, the administration attempted to defuse the issue by indicating its willingness to accept an even larger aid program for China than Congress was willing to pass—although after Truman's victory, not all of the $400 million allotted was expended.

Ambassador Stuart, more sympathetic to Chiang's plight than most American officials who had dealt with him over the years, was astonished at Chiang's conviction that the United States would come to his rescue again, at "his almost mystical belief in his power to will into existence American aid to fight against world-wide communism."[20] Stuart attributed Chiang's intransigence, all through 1948, to this conviction and to the confidence that Dewey would be elected and American policy reversed. But Chiang did not greatly overestimate the power of his appeal. In February 1949, 50 senators, 25 of them Democrats, endorsed a proposal to give Chiang a loan of $1.5 billion. Although the administration succeeded, after months of discussion, in getting Congress to settle for $75 million for the "general area of China," it did not dare stop the flow of equipment to China for fear of being charged with responsibility for Chiang's collapse—although it was conceded that the materials would most likely end up in the hands of the Communists.

Years later, Dean Acheson wrote that when he took office as secretary of state, Chiang's regime was on the verge of collapse: "I arrived just in time to have him collapse on me."[21] Chiang had refused to listen to American military advice, including that which had come from Wedemeyer, and persistently overextended his lines reaching for control of Manchuria. As his armies pressed northward, the Communists moved into the countryside behind them, isolating them in their strongholds, cutting them off from retreat. American estimates of Communist strength proved to be low. Nationalist morale deteriorated even faster than anticipated, the process hastened by a debilitating inflation. By the autumn of 1947 Chiang had lost the initiative. The year 1948 was marked by a long string of disasters in which Nationalist forces were destroyed in Manchuria, thousands of Nationalist troops deserted to the Communist side, taking with them their American equipment, and Communist forces began to drive into central China. The bulk of the remaining American supplies were captured by the Communists after a two-month battle that ended in January 1949, costing the Nationalists over half a million men. A few days later, Chiang "retired" once again—after taking the precaution of sending the government's gold supplies and a number of troops to Formosa (Taiwan). Efforts to negotiate a peace short of complete Communist victory failed. On October 1, 1949, Mao proclaimed the establishment of the People's Republic of China, with its capital at Peking. In December, the sometime dictator of China, Chiang Kai-shek, and remnants of the Nationalist government, fled to Formosa to be reunited with the treasures that foresight had already deposited there. The Chinese civil war was coming to a rapid conclusion, ending just as the American government had warned Chiang that it would. American perception of the vitality of the Chinese Communist movement and of the decay of the Kuomintang had been essentially correct, but the rot was deeper than the American government had imagined and the Communist triumph came more rapidly and more decisively than anyone had anticipated. Having become identified with the losers, the American government now had to determine what sort of accommodation was possible with the victorious Communists.

In the first year after the end of World War II, as the Kuomintang and the Chinese Communists vied for control of Manchuria and North China, the Communists were consistently critical of American aid to the Nationalists. To a large extent their criticisms were doctrinaire, reflecting the line emanating from Moscow, couched in what has come to be called "vulgar Marxism." On the whole, however, their principal target was the Kuomintang government, and their complaints over American assistance to that government had a substantial factual basis. Beginning with the anti-American campaign that Mao ordered on July 1, 1946, the attack on the United States became increasingly abusive and increasingly unrelated to the facts. Before the end of the year stories of American atrocities against the civilian population, written in a style that would have made William Randolph Hearst and the *New York Daily News* envious, were distributed widely. Stress was placed on the American "occupation" of China, on the American desire to "colonize" China. Chiang was reduced to playing the role of the "running dog" of American imperialism.

Nonetheless, as victory approached, Mao and Chou were very much aware of the potential value of an accommodation with the United States. In the cold war that had developed between the Soviet Union and the United States, they would unquestionably align themselves with the Russians. But such a posture did not preclude mutually beneficial economic relations with the Americans. Good Communists that they were, Mao and Chou believed that American capitalism needed the market in China to avoid a depression. They were aware that the United States was more able than the Soviet Union to provide the assistance they needed for the reconstruction and modernization of China. And, as Chinese patriots, they were unwilling to become dependent on the Russians. Conceivably, compatible Chinese and American interests could be exploited to China's advantage.

Although their influence was obviously great, Mao and Chou, like Truman and Acheson, operated under domestic restraints. Rank-and-file Chinese Communists and the commanders of the People's Liberation Army (PLA) were intensely hostile to the United States. American support of the Kuomintang, no matter how trivial from an American perspective, had cost many Chinese lives, had caused great suffering in China. Anti-Americanism, opposition to American imperialism, had been an essential element in the revolutionary propaganda with which the masses were mobilized during the civil war. As the PLA moved through China, Mao and Chou were unable to prevent a series of anti-American incidents that were contrary to their policy of distinguishing between the reactionary American government and the democracy-loving American people. An attempt to reach an understanding with the United States would encounter fierce opposition, on both ideological and nationalistic grounds. Obliquely, Mao and Chou indicated that they might be receptive to American overtures, to indications that the United States was prepared to mend its ways and treat China as an equal. They would not beg, waiting instead for the West, which had long oppressed China to risk the first step. They needed a generous gesture from Washington before rapprochement could be explored seriously. But a generous gesture was precisely what the political context in the United States precluded.

As Mao's impending victory became apparent in the winter of 1948–1949, the Truman administration comforted itself with the hope that China could be prevented from becoming an "adjunct of Soviet power." The Russians had not played an important role in the Communist victory. Their absence from Communist-controlled areas, combined with the knowledge of Tito's split with Stalin in 1948, allowed some comfort for American impotence. Acheson, who succeeded Marshall in January 1949, was unperturbed. He was intensely anti-Communist, eager to contain Soviet influence everywhere, but he was an Atlanticist for whom Western Europe was the highest priority. Stopping Communism across the Pacific was desirable, but clearly not as important as European recovery or the creation of NATO. Moreover, Kennan assured him that the collapse of Chiang's regime, however "deplorable," would not be catastrophic. China lacked the resources to become a great power for some time. Kennan also argued that if the Chinese Communists succeeded in taking over China, their dependence on Moscow would diminish. To Acheson, it was clear that the time had come to cut American losses, to stop aid to the Kuomintang.

On February 3, the National Security Council recommended that the United States suspend shipments to China, but congressional leaders urged the president not to take formal action. They did not insist that the Kuomintang continue to receive aid, indicating, on the contrary, their willingness to have aid delayed by informal means. Their ultimate concern was not for Chiang's future, but rather to soothe their colleagues and protect the Congress from its constituents. They feared that public announcement of the cessation of aid would lead to the immediate collapse of the Kuomintang regime—and that they and the president would be held responsible. Truman accepted their advice and restrained Acheson.

In the weeks that followed, Acheson argued that the goal of American policy should be to prevent "Soviet domination of China for strategic ends." Attempts to intimidate the Chinese Communists would force them into complete dependence on the Soviet Union. The most sensible tactic was to develop economic relations with them and concentrate effort on attempts to divide them from the Russians. Reports from the field reinforced hope for an independent Chinese Communist regime. There was evidence of tension between Russian and Chinese leaders and a growing sense that a Sino-Soviet split was inevitable. The question of when might be affected by American actions. In March, Acheson authorized Ambassador Stuart to approach Communist leaders. He told Ernest Bevin, British foreign minister, that Chiang's regime was "washed up," that the United States would cease supporting it after June, and that the United States "henceforth will pursue a more realistic policy respecting China."[22]

The lack of public support for Acheson's approach was evident in his admission to Bevin that it was difficult to withdraw support from Chiang publicly—though he thought Chiang's "extreme supporters" in Congress "were gaining a better appreciation of realities." Stuart was instructed that his reports of talks with Communist leaders were to be sent "eyes only for the Secretary." The American public—and the president—was not quite ready to accept the results of the Chinese civil war.

Mao and Chou were puzzled when Ambassador Stuart remained in Nanjing after the PLA occupied the city. They sent Huang Hua, a former student of Stuart's, who was serving as commissioner of alien affairs, to investigate. Fearful of an American military intervention that might deny their imminent victory, they instructed Huang to listen carefully, talk little, and avoid provocation. When Stuart's secretary suggested that Stuart be invited to Peking, Mao and Chou quickly agreed. They had little hope of reaching an accommodation with the United States at that time but perceived a meeting with Stuart as a temporizing or pacifying step, a means of keeping the Americans relatively docile while the PLA swept Chiang's remaining forces off the mainland.[23] Within the Department of State, however, an extraordinary opportunity to explore the terms of accommodation was perceived. Despite expectations of an adverse public reaction, the department was eager to have Stuart meet the Communist leaders. The president, however, would have none of it. "Under no circumstances" was Stuart to visit Peking. The president did not wish to be held responsible for applying the coup de grace to Chiang. It was only with great difficulty that Acheson was able to dissuade Truman from ordering Stuart to visit Kuomintang headquarters instead of Peking.

At the end of June, Mao contributed to the difficulty of reaching an accommodation with a speech in which he denounced the United States and declared that China would lean to the side of the Soviet Union. Acheson had expected such rhetoric and tried to prepare the Congress and the president for it. He argued that as tensions developed between the Chinese and the Russians, the Chinese would become more insistent on their kinship with the Russians. He would be patient. But if Acheson was unperturbed by Mao's speech, to most Americans it appeared that the Russians had won an enormous victory in Asia. To Americans grimly determined to contain Soviet imperialism in Europe and the Middle East, their attention focused across the Atlantic, it seemed that disaster had struck behind them. The Russians had added vast territory, hundreds of millions of people, and unknown resources to their reservoirs of power. Just as the Tripartite Pact had tied Asian affairs to European affairs in 1940, so awareness of Mao's ties to Moscow linked the two areas in the minds of Americans in 1949. After 1940, the relatively minor concerns of Asia had merged with the vital concerns of Europe, making of

Japan an enemy, to the benefit of Chiang Kai-shek's China. Now, the process was repeated, and after 1949, American opposition to Soviet imperialism, conceived of as anti-Communism, permitted a merger of Asian and European affairs, making of China an enemy, but once again to the benefit of Chiang Kai-shek.

In August 1949, over the objections of the secretary of defense and the Joint Chiefs, the Truman administration made a belated effort to prepare the American people for the conclusion of the Kuomintang debacle with the publication of the famed "China White Paper," a massive volume of explanations and documents, designed to defend the administration against charges that it had "lost" China. Acheson's determination to publish the White Paper despite concern over Mao's "leaning to one side" speech, strong opposition from the Pentagon, reservations among his advisers and in Congress, and while the Kuomintang still held Canton, is best explained as a decision to drive in the last nail. He wanted to end American involvement in the Chinese civil war, to preempt any effort by Chiang's American friends, and to prepare for an accommodation with the Communist regime. But Chiang escaped to Formosa and kept the issue—and his cause—alive.

Few scholars would dispute Acheson's claim that the outcome of the Chinese civil war had been beyond the control of the United States, that Chiang's failure had been largely of his own making, but the effort to persuade the public through the White Paper failed. The Republican Party had a foreign policy issue that it would not let go, and the administration weakened its own case when Acheson also declared that "the Communist leaders have foresworn their Chinese heritage and have publicly announced their subservience to a foreign power, Russia, which . . . has been assiduous in its efforts to extend its control in the Far East."[24] For years afterward, scholars as well as politicians and the public wondered why it was less important to resist Soviet efforts in Asia than in Europe. Acheson had the answer, but, characteristically, he assumed it was too subtle for the American people to understand. He feared that the public would not comprehend the difference between areas of vital concern to the United States and areas of peripheral concern, and he dared not endanger his program for strengthening the NATO countries. So long as he could prevent a major involvement in China, he acquiesced in Truman's unwillingness to alienate further Chiang's supporters, many of whom were genuinely concerned with American interests as well.

In the summer of 1949, as the Communists mopped up Kuomintang stragglers on the mainland of China, the question of what to do about Formosa was debated heatedly in Washington. Earlier in the year, Truman and his National Security Council had concluded that the best way to keep the strategically valuable island out of Communist hands was to foster the Formosan independence movement—a movement of people ethnically Chinese, but long separated from mainland China. The United States did not want to intervene in a manner so obvious as to offend the international community or drive the Chinese Communists closer to the Russians. Acheson explained to Truman that to prevent the Chinese Communists from becoming an adjunct to Soviet power it was necessary to focus on Soviet imperialism in Manchuria and Sinkiang and to "carefully conceal our wish to separate the island from mainland control."[25]

The vision of an independent Formosan regime, free of Kuomintang control, proved to be a fantasy. Within a few months it was clear that the independence movement was weak and that Chiang's supporters dominated the island. Among the new approaches for separating the island from mainland control, the most incredible came from Kennan. He insisted that Formosa was of greater strategic value than the Joint Chiefs would admit and he rejected the thought of reconciling himself to the Communist conquest of the island. The United States had to act. Kennan advocated the use of American forces to throw Chiang's army out of Formosa and the Pescadores and to substitute an American protectorate— a regime independent of mainland control. He wanted to act as "Theodore Roosevelt might have," with "resolution, speed, ruthlessness and self-assurance."[26]

Acheson was unmoved. Prepared to bury the Kuomintang wherever its flag was raised, he preferred to abandon the effort to hold the island. If Chiang's unregenerate followers controlled it, it was doomed to fall to the Communists. They would merely repeat the errors that had brought their defeat in the civil war. An American effort on the island would be wasted and have an adverse effect on the attempt to wean Mao away from Stalin. In August 1949, Acheson persuaded the Joint Chiefs to accept his policy.

In November, however, several prominent Republicans, Senators William Knowland and Robert Taft, joined by former President Herbert Hoover, called on the American government to protect Formosa, eliciting Peking's charges of an imminent American occupation. General Douglas MacArthur and the Joint Chiefs joined in the call for action to deny

Formosa to the Communists, Acheson held the line, forcing the Joint Chiefs to retreat. In the hope of quieting things down, on January 5, 1950, President Truman issued a statement in which he declared that the United States was determined to stay out of the Chinese civil war, had no interest in Formosa, and although it would continue to give economic assistance to Chiang, would offer no military aid or advice. A week later, Acheson made a major contribution to the education of the American public, offering two fundamental points. First, Chinese and Russian aspirations in East Asia were inimical historically, and the United States could best serve its interests in that area not by provoking the Chinese Communists but by counting on Chinese nationalism to turn against Soviet imperialism. Second, the present hostile configuration of forces on the Asian mainland did not seriously threaten the security of the United States, whose "defensive perimeter" included the Aleutians, Japan, and the Philippines, but neither Formosa nor any part of the mainland. Neither the press nor the public evidenced difficulty comprehending his points, and the response seemed favorable. Unhappy as all might be with the Communist triumph in China, the administration and the American people were prepared to accept the inevitable and to learn to live with the People's Republic. Farewell to Formosa.

There remained two obstacles to diplomatic recognition of the Peking government. The first was the strength of those Americans in public office and out who retained an emotional commitment to Chiang Kai-shek's China. So long as Chiang's forces continued to hold out, these people urged, with decreasing success, that he be aided. Some among them were aware that the end was in sight but begged the administration not to deliver the final blow. Rather than risk additional charges of having betrayed Chiang, Truman and his advisers were willing to wait until the Communists conquered Formosa, at which time domestic opposition to recognition could be expected to decline sharply. The second was the fact that Mao, while by no means indifferent to accommodation with the United States, remained hostile and suspicious, unwilling, perhaps unable, to suppress the intense anti-Americanism among rank-and-file Communists. If there was to be a generous gesture, an attempt to appease, it would have to come from the Americans. China had been on her knees too long. New China would not beg the imperialists for recognition.

As Communist forces swept through China in 1949 and consolidated their position in early 1950, they harassed foreigners generally and Americans in particular. An American diplomat in Shanghai was beaten by the police, and several others, including the consul general in Mukden, Angus Ward, were expelled after a year under house arrest. When confronted with outrageous Chinese behavior, Acheson argued that vital American interests had not been affected, that policies likely to drive Mao closer to Stalin were not warranted. He argued that the Ward case was a special situation. In November 1949, as Ward was brought to trial and public anger in the United States verged on explosion, Acheson stressed the fact that no Americans had been killed in Communist-controlled areas. He retained the president's support, but it was apparent that the Chinese Communists and Chiang's friends in America had entered into a symbiotic relationship, feeding off each other's hate, adding to the misery of men of good will throughout the world. Every abuse by Mao's men provided ammunition for those who sought to stiffen American opposition to Mao's government. Every statement by the likes of Senators Knowland, Styles Bridges, and Kenneth Wherry facilitated Mao's anti-American campaign and led to new abuses. The cycle was still very much in existence, recognition of the People's Republic still delayed, as time ran out.

In January 1950, both the United States and the People's Republic mishandled a minor problem to the benefit of opponents of accommodation. Acheson thought he had given the Chinese a clear signal of American intent to establish formal relations as soon as practicable. The Chinese were mistrustful, however, and pressed the United States and other regimes that still withheld recognition. They threatened to requisition their property in Peking, including the consular premises of the governments involved. Acheson devised a compromise, informing the Peking authorities that they could take a large part of the area, but not the building the United States planned to use for its chancellery. Such an arrangement might give the regime face without creating an uproar in the United States. He warned, however, that seizure of the building in question would be unacceptable and result in withdrawal of all American diplomatic personnel in China. Each side apparently thought the other was bluffing. The Chinese seized the building and the Americans went home. The results were unfortunate, but Acheson did not perceive the action as final.

Rather than giving up, Acheson anticipated better opportunities for reaching an accommodation with the People's Republic after Mao returned from protracted negotiations with Stalin early in 1950. He was convinced that Stalin would make exorbitant demands of the Chinese, providing a wedge that the United States could drive home. But in February

1950, Mao and Stalin signed an alliance and, as the months passed, Acheson concluded that there was little chance of an early break between Moscow and Peking, little chance for a more conciliatory Chinese attitude toward the United States for a few years. He was in no hurry. Kuomintang resistance on the mainland would be eliminated quickly. Chiang's escape to Formosa was but a temporary complication; the CIA estimated that the Communists would conquer the island before the end of the year. Perhaps the president would be ready to act after the November elections. In the interim, nonrecognition might please the French, who were troubled by Chinese support for Ho Chi Minh in Indochina. Once Chiang was destroyed there would be no possibility of further American involvement in the Chinese civil war. Acheson—and recognition—could wait. Recognition of the People's Republic was still pending on June 25, 1950, when North Korean forces crossed the thirty-eighth parallel in a massive invasion of South Korea. It was, as they used to say in Brooklyn, a new ball game.

When Truman and his advisers met to determine the American response to North Korean aggression, Acheson's last recommendation was that Truman send the Seventh Fleet to the Formosa Strait to prevent an extension of the fighting to Formosa. Truman agreed and ultimately ordered the fleet to prevent an attack from the mainland *and* to prevent Chiang from attempting any operations against the mainland. Given the fact that the only invasion anticipated was being mounted from the mainland, this "leashing" of Chiang Kai-shek was a pathetic effort to keep from being drawn deeper into the Chinese civil war. Perhaps the principal reason for sending the fleet to the strait was the intense pressure to defend Formosa that the administration both felt and anticipated. Not only had prominent Republicans insisted on the strategic importance of the island, but Acheson's own staff, including Dean Rusk, Truman's secretary of defense, Louis Johnson, and General MacArthur were urging a reconsideration. Once the United States decided to defend South Korea, which had also been placed beyond the "defensive perimeter," it would be increasingly difficult to explain why Formosa should not be defended. If the Chinese Communists attacked the island and simultaneously interfered with the defense of South Korea, the administration would have been terribly vulnerable to attacks from Chiang's supporters in the United States. If, on the other hand, Formosa could be denied to the Chinese Communists without committing the United States to Chiang's cause, the price of fleet operations would be most inexpensive protection. This was the delicate balance that the administration attempted to maintain.

In addition, Truman and his advisers were themselves uncertain of the relationship between the Chinese civil war and the war that had just begun in Korea. They were committing themselves to opposing Communist aggression in Korea, and they spoke of using the Seventh Fleet to prevent the war from spreading. Whereas previously they had seen Mao's planned operations against Formosa as the conclusion of the civil war, these same operations were now placed in the context of the new war in which the United States was opposing Communist expansion in East Asia. No less than their critics, Truman and Acheson seemed unconvinced that a difference existed between the extension of Communist power by civil war and the extension of Communist power by an act of aggression. They were ambivalent as to when the United States should properly and with profit intervene. The decision to send the fleet to the Formosa Strait, made only hours after the North Korean attack, appeared to leave all options open, allowing for the postponement of a more definite decision on China until more information was available. To retain this freedom of action, to keep the desired balance, Acheson persuaded Truman to reject Chiang's offer of troops for use in Korea. And yet, Truman expressly reopened the question of the status of Formosa. No longer would the United States acquiesce in the Communist conquest of the island. Instead, a variety of schemes were resurrected to create an independent Formosa, preferably a liberal, democratic, Chiang-less Formosa.

The administration's new but limited involvement in the Chinese civil war might not have been difficult to reverse, but the chain of events did not stop there. General MacArthur, having spent five years in Japan teaching the Japanese about democracy, adopted a practice of the Japanese militarists and chose to make his own decisions about the importance of Formosa to the United States. Without authorization from the president, he flew to Taipei, where he met with Chiang and promised to coordinate his military efforts with Chiang's. Subsequently, without the knowledge of the Pentagon, he sent three squadrons of jet fighters to Formosa. When the Taipei regime stepped up raids on the mainland of China, Acheson and Truman, who condemned the attacks, were persuaded that MacArthur was responsible. By his words and by his actions, MacArthur gave credence to the fears expressed by Mao and Chou En-lai of impending American attacks on the People's Republic, of an American effort to turn the Korean crisis into an opportunity to return Chiang to the mainland. Certainly the idea was never very far from MacArthur's mind, nor did Chiang's supporters in the United States refrain from voicing it.

Acting as the instrument of the United Nations, American forces came to the aid of the disintegrating South Korean Army, and with the help of units from a dozen other UN members, they held the Pusan perimeter. In September, MacArthur launched a brilliant amphibious operation at Inchon, and by the end of the month, United Nations forces were in virtual control of South Korea. At that point, widespread disagreement emerged as to whether North Korean troops should be pursued across the border. Controversy arose within the United Nations, within the American government, and within the Department of State. With success had come the usual enlargement of war aims, and both the Pentagon and the Far Eastern and United Nations Divisions of the Department of State favored advancing into North Korea in order to create a "unified, independent and democratic government." Toward this end a vague mandate was elicited from the United Nations, although other nations feared that further success might well bring Chinese or Soviet intervention, greatly increasing the dangers and the stakes. The approach of the Truman administration was essentially opportunistic. MacArthur was authorized to cross the line and continue north, provided no large concentrations of Chinese or Soviet forces appeared.

Within the Department of State, George Kennan and Paul Nitze, his successor on the Policy Planning Staff, had opposed crossing the parallel, partly because they considered the move too risky, but largely because they thought it was unnecessary. Kennan in particular thought the opportunity existed to achieve the status quo ante without further fighting, and he was intrigued by the possibility of driving a wedge between China and the Soviet Union, which appeared to have reacted differently to an Indian proposal to trade Peking's admission to the United Nations for an agreement to return to the status quo ante. Kennan and not a few other observers believed that the Russians, hoping to keep the Chinese isolated and dependent, actually did not want Mao's government in the United Nations. The failure of the department to consider seriously the possibility of acquiescing in "the international community's" decision on China's seat in the United Nations Kennan attributed ultimately to "the irresponsible and bigoted interference of the China lobby and its friends in Congress."[27]

Despite Chinese warnings that they would intervene if UN forces crossed the thirty-eighth parallel, MacArthur remained confident that they would not dare—and that if they did, his forces would quickly destroy them. In mid-October, a nervous president flew to Wake Island to confer with his general and was assured that the war would be over by Thanksgiving and the boys home by Christmas. Before the month was over, the Chinese had intervened in force, and two months later, United Nations forces were reeling backwards in the face of the Chinese onslaught. American boys were dying at the hands of the Chinese. The new Yellow Peril had burst forth. China and America were enemies, the road to recognition was impassable, and Chiang Kai-shek's fortunes soared.

His optimism shattered, MacArthur argued that the new war required attacks on Chinese territory, and he was outraged by the limits imposed on him by Washington. Truman and his advisers, including the Joint Chiefs of Staff, were convinced that to defeat the Chinese in North Korea would require a vastly greater effort than limited American resources and power could allow to be used in Asia. The possibility of Soviet participation in a larger war could not be excluded, nor could the possibility of Soviet moves elsewhere in the world, while the United States was preoccupied in Korea. In discussions with Truman, General Marshall (who had become secretary of defense), and General Omar Bradley, chairman of the Joint Chiefs, Acheson suggested that "the Kremlin probably saw advantages to it in the U.S.-Chinese war flowing from the diversion, attrition, and containment of U.S. forces *in an indecisive theater.*"[28] Unable to convince his superiors of his own estimate of how the war should be fought and of the relative importance of Asia, MacArthur began to appeal over the head of his commander in chief, to the American people and in particular to the Republican opposition.

By the time Truman found the courage to relieve the ever-popular MacArthur of his command, incalculable damage had been done to the United States. America was involved in a war with China that MacArthur's verbal and tactical blunders had done much to bring about. The opportunism of the administration, following MacArthur as long as he was successful and tolerating his insubordination, cost the confidence of America's allies. At home, attracted by MacArthur's nostrums for quick victory, loyal to an old hero, the public lost confidence in Truman's leadership. When the confrontation finally came, the abuse from the American Right was intense. From the nether regions of American society flowed a sea of filth, bringing forth a new national hero, Joseph McCarthy, a symbol of the new America.

What MacArthur contended could not be done without massive retaliation against Chinese territory, General Matthew Ridgway accomplished in a matter of months. The Chinese were stopped short of driving UN forces out of Korea, and slowly but surely they were driven back north of the thirty-eighth parallel. There the military situation stabilized, as both Americans and Chinese had achieved the principal goal of their respective interventions. The Americans had successfully contained Communist aggression, and the Chinese had successfully contained an American threat to their security, retaining the North Korean buffer. In July 1951, peace talks began, and after approximately two years of frustrating negotiations and continued small-scale fighting, a truce was concluded. The Chinese withdrew from Korea, but the People's Republic never ceased to be "the enemy."

Chinese intervention in Korea hardened American opposition to the Peking regime and widened the circle of Americans who sought Chiang's return to power—or at very least sought to exploit his aims for American ends. Once again, Chiang became America's ally, and disengagement from Formosa became politically impossible. No matter how much he dragged his heels, Acheson was driven back into Chiang's embrace. Military assistance to the Kuomintang regime was resumed. As sons, husbands, and brothers died at the hands of Mao's legions, criticism of the administration's earlier refusal to aid Chiang against the Communists mounted, and contemptible politicians shouted obscene accusations of moral perversion and treason against those they considered responsible for the "loss" of China. The State Department specialists on China, especially O. Edmund Clubb, John Paton Davies, John Stewart Service, and John Carter Vincent, were abused and persecuted in one of the most shameful and destructive episodes in the history of the United States. When the events of the Korean War convinced most men of the monolithic nature of international Communism, the earlier contentions that Chinese Communism had a strong nationalistic flavor, that Mao would not serve as Stalin's puppet, and that, like it or not, the Chinese Communists would ultimately triumph seemed naive to many—and proof of treason to Joseph McCarthy and all the little joe mccarthys who emerged to pollute America. Later, the essential correctness of the analysis put forth by Clubb and his colleagues was reaffirmed, and they are guaranteed a higher place in the annals of man than that accorded their malefactors, but the damage done to them personally can never be repaired—nor did the United States soon recover from the damage done to the Department of State during the McCarthy era.

On the mainland of China, the visible remnants of cultural interaction between the American and Chinese people were hastily eliminated. The "Resist America, Aid Korea Movement," begun in November 1950, was a clear signal to Chinese at the Christian colleges and at the Rockefeller Foundation–supported Peking Union Medical College and to participants in other Chinese-American cultural programs to separate themselves from their American colleagues. In January 1951, nationalization of the various American-sponsored academic institutions began. Viewed as evidence of cultural imperialism, of bourgeois ideology, these schools could no longer be tolerated. Higher education in China had to be rid of American influence, elitist curricula, and standards that impeded Chinese efforts to foster mass education. American missionaries, foundations, and universities seeking to work in a Chinese cultural context were driven out, to root in Hong Kong and Taiwan. Simultaneously, for a generation of Chinese students, Russian supplanted English as the foreign language of choice.

Thus, among the results of the Korean War were the end of the American presence in China, the reinvolvement of the United States on the losing side of the Chinese civil war, and solidification of the decision not to recognize the Chinese government.

Many years would pass before men in public life dared raise the question again. Similarly, the United States had led the United Nations in the condemnation of China as an aggressor and for years afterward pressured its client states into voting against Peking's representation in the United Nations. Trade restrictions begun as a wartime measure were frozen as none dared reap the whirlwind by suggesting that they be lifted. Indeed, the United States pressed other states into imposing economic sanctions on China as the aim of American policy became, in the 1950s, the isolation and ultimate overthrow of the People's Republic. A nation that the American people traditionally had viewed with contempt, pity, and compassion became one of their most feared enemies.

Long before the United States entered World War II, American officials in China, military and diplomatic, had concluded that Chiang Kai-shek did not want to fight the Japanese and sought to husband his resources to resume his campaign to exterminate the Chinese Communists. They had little confidence in the Kuomintang's ability to govern China or in its potential for survival in the trial by battle that they considered inevitable following, if not preceding, the expulsion of the Japanese. They suspected that in the long run the Communists might prevail and, aware of the strong nationalist tendencies and ideological peculiarities of the Chinese Communist movement, they saw no reason to assume the Chinese Communists were merely an extension of Soviet power.

The much studied wartime experiences of the Americans in China confirmed these earlier estimates and extended the understanding of conditions in China to a wider circle of people in and out of Washington. Within the government of the United States, Roosevelt was apparently one of the last to grasp Chinese realities, one of the last to give up the hope of genuine cooperation with Chiang's regime. Unable to get Chiang to use his forces against the Japanese, he settled for efforts to keep Chinese resistance from complete collapse before the war ended—efforts to avert civil war. To this task he assigned Hurley, ultimately approving Hurley's conviction of the need to support Chiang and the Kuomintang as the center of the unified democratic government they hoped to see emerge in China. Neither Hurley nor Roosevelt would countenance more exuberant schemes to bypass Chiang as a prerequisite to the process of unification.

At Yalta, in February 1945, Roosevelt purchased Soviet support for his policy of seeking a united China, based on the Kuomintang—or so he and Hurley, Chiang, and Mao all thought. When the war ended, the Truman administration left Hurley's orders unchanged. But the postwar situation in China was immediately complicated by the breakdown of Soviet-American cooperation elsewhere in the world. As mutual mistrust increased and conflicting ambitions became apparent, the United States became increasingly determined to check Soviet influence in Asia, denying the Russians a meaningful role in Japan and attempting to minimize the Russian threat to Manchuria and North China. Mirroring the American response, Soviet policy in Manchuria violated the spirit of Stalin's agreement at Yalta and of the subsequent Sino-Soviet treaty. As the Americans sought to aid the Chinese government to regain control of North China and Manchuria, the Russians found the Chinese Communists useful in obstructing these efforts.

In the midst of all this Hurley resigned, briefly focusing American attention on China. The Truman administration, determined to resolve the differences with the Soviet Union that had emerged during the liberation and occupation of Europe, anxious to avoid complications in a peripheral area, sent Marshall to China. Dean Acheson stood as a backup man in Washington. American policy would remain the same; Marshall's mission was merely an extension of Hurley's efforts to unite China peaceably, around Chiang Kai-shek. Where the war with Japan had provided the urgency behind Hurley's attempts, deteriorating relations between the United States and the Soviet Union provided the urgency behind Marshall's. Despite American reservations about Chiang and the Kuomintang, the newly developing international situation seemed to allow the United States little room to maneuver in China.

For the seven years from 1946 through 1952, the dominant influences on American policy toward China were Marshall and Acheson, two of the ablest men ever to serve in public office. Both had been involved in the process of determining American policy in the late 1930s and, like Roosevelt, believed American interests in Asia to be secondary to interests in Europe and events on the Asian mainland to be less relevant to considerations of American security than events across the Atlantic. Both were aware that the locus of power had shifted eastward with the defeat of Germany and the growth of Soviet power, but they realized that it remained nonetheless in Europe. The president they served shared their estimate unhesitatingly.

Both Marshall and Acheson had a deeper understanding of conditions in China than Hurley had acquired, but until the summer of 1946 they continued his approach of attempting to mediate between the two Chinese contenders while their government gave substantial aid to one side. Not until a year after the war had ended did they realize that the peaceful unification of China was virtually impossible; that a liberal, democratic China was inconceivable; that with Chiang Kai-shek determined on a course that would destroy him, it was preferable to disassociate the United States from his government as best as they could. After eight months of studying the problem, Marshall and Acheson concluded that given the limits on American resources, they could be used more profitably elsewhere.

Thus the two men who in 1947 were at the core of the group that launched the United States on its course of opposition to Soviet imperialism, an opposition that they unwittingly allowed to become an anti-Communist crusade, resigned themselves to a Communist victory in China. They realized the hopelessness of attempting to conquer China for Chiang Kai-shek, and they hoped that Chinese Communist nationalism and traditional Sino-Russian antipathies would prevent a Maoist regime from resulting in a significant increment to Soviet power. But more than this, they had to risk disaster in China because of their fear of disaster in Europe—where they knew that vital American interests were at stake.

When the Korean War came, the same patterns of thought and action prevailed within the Truman administration. The conflict in Asia, however, in the absence of fighting in Europe, gave Americans who dissented from the Atlantic orientation of American policy their time of glory. The subsequent loss of public confidence indicated that Marshall, Acheson, and President Truman had failed to convey to the American people not only a sense of the limits of American power but of the priorities to which this limited power had to be applied.

In the end, despite their hopes for Chinese nationalism, Truman and his advisers were forced to conclude that whether Mao was independent or not, he was intensely anti-American. His hostility had to be reciprocated. Publicly, Dean Rusk declared that China had become an instrument of international Communism, a "Slavic Manchukuo," to be opposed no less vigorously than the Soviet Union. As an instrument of American power, Chiang Kai-shek and his rump regime received an eleventh-hour reprieve, continuing the myth that the Republic of China still existed, housed momentarily on Formosa, which all Chinese called Taiwan, a province of China.

7 The Great Aberration

Beginning in the nineteenth century, as the American people gradually freed themselves from concern with continental problems, providing for their security and prosperity through expansion, they became increasingly concerned with external affairs, with the world balance of power, and with the overseas expansion of American power, economic and political. As American interest in the outer world grew, men looked to East Asia as well as to Europe, but Asia was always less important to a nation that faced eastward across the Atlantic. More and more Americans were interested in Asia, concerned with Asian affairs, but those interested in trade found both actual and potential markets more promising in Europe, and those worried about the security of the United States found little reason to focus on Asia. Throughout the history of the United States, until the eve of the twenty-first century, the locus of both economic and political power has rested in Europe. Only missionaries, the men and women concerned with spreading Christianity, found Asia and particularly China more suitable for their efforts.

With the rise of the United States as a world power, the American government pursued essentially the same ends in Asia as it did in Europe, seeking as best it could to create a world in which American interests and ideals could thrive. But, because Asia was less important to the United

States, economically and politically, efforts there were never as intense
and adverse conditions were more readily tolerated. There was a time
when it was part of the conventional wisdom to criticize the United States
for its unwillingness to use force commensurate with its ends in Asia—
particularly in China—but it is more important to understand that
American ends in the area were rarely considered important enough to
warrant the use of force. If they could be acquired with words, well and
good, but the American government and most of the American people
were always ready to settle for much less than they hoped for in China.

There was, however, another thread in the fabric of America's response to China. Though China was unimportant relative to Europe, she
was also relatively weak—and Americans were not slow to perceive this.
From the beginning of the treaty system in the 1840s until World War II,
Americans sought and enjoyed the imperialistic privileges that other nations had wrested from the Chinese. Americans with interests in China
may not have received the degree of support for their efforts to which
they felt entitled, but warships of the United States patrolled Chinese
waters, and American troops were stationed on Chinese soil to protect
the treaty rights of these missionaries and businessmen. If American
interests in China were insufficient to warrant the major involvement
required to block Russian or Japanese imperialism, the prerequisites to
imperialism in China were slight, requiring no more than minor
involvements—from which the government of the United States did not
shrink.

In addition, partly because of its weakness, China provided an opportunity for the inflation of American self-esteem. This could not be accomplished by participation in the imperialist system. That role con-
flicted with American ideals and with America's self-image. Instead, fed
by the lofty rhetoric of statesmen and publicists, the belief developed in
the twentieth century that the role of the United States was different
from that of the other imperialists—that the United States was the
"champion" of China's independence, seeking to protect that hapless
country against European and Japanese imperialists. John Hay and William Rockhill were less than eager to dispel this illusion, which reflected
so well on them and cost so little to sustain. Taft and Wilson actually
contemplated such a role for the United States but abandoned the idea
when confronted with the reality of Japanese power. At the policy level,
such a role never again received serious consideration, but the myth

TABLE 7.1   U.S. Exports to Leading European, American, and Asian
Markets, 1890–1940[a]

Year	Great Britain and France	Canada and Mexico	Japan and China
1890	58	6.2	0.9
1895	53	8.4	1.1
1900	44	9.3	3.1
1905	39	12.3	6.9
1910	36	15.7	2.2
1915	46	12.3	2.1
1920	30	14.3	6.4
1925	27	16.2	6.6
1930	23	20.2	6.6
1935	24	17.0	10.6
1940	31	20.1	7.5

[a]In percentages of total U.S. export trade.

persisted. If no one statesman can be blamed for the illusion, few can escape blame for the failure to dispel it.

In the years before the United States could claim to be the world's greatest power, the national ego was fed by this pretense to a special role in China. Despite the importance of Europe to their security and prosperity, many Americans were wary of involvement in European affairs. Feelings of inadequacy that arose from contacts with presumably shrewd Europeans, such as characterized American attitudes toward their experience in World War I, vanished when Americans worked with allegedly simple Chinese. Unlike Europeans, the Chinese could still be saved. How prevalent these attitudes were cannot be determined; that some Americans still thought this way after World War II is beyond dispute. They were willing to take up the white man's burden in China—and the incredible arrogance of their self-appointed mission was epitomized by a leading advocate of Chiang Kai-shek's cause, Senator Kenneth Wherry, who once told Americans that "with God's help," they could "lift Shanghai up and up, ever up, until it is just like Kansas City."[1]

But though some Americans were more willing to involve the United States in Asian affairs than in the affairs of Europe and though some felt more confident working with Asians than with Europeans, these attitudes were rarely shared by the men responsible for the course of American policy. They, and the politicians, officials, businessmen, and intellectuals to whom they were responsive, retained their essentially Atlantic orientation. Aware of no vital American interests in East Asia, these men assumed that such popular attitudes were insufficiently grounded to sustain a more active policy there. Consequently, all three instances of major American involvement in East Asia occurred incidentally, as by-products of concerns in the Atlantic and in Europe. The power of the United States was first established in the western Pacific by the acquisition of the Philippines, booty from a war with Spain fought over conditions on the island of Cuba. The Pacific war and the subsequent occupation of Japan resulted from American opposition to Nazi aggression in Europe and the decision of Japanese statesmen to tie their country and their cause to Hitler's. Finally, the involvement that is most familiar to young Americans and Asians, the American attempt to contain Communism in Asia, began after the Chinese Communists linked themselves to Stalin and the Soviet imperialism that Americans dreaded and were determined to oppose. On these last two occasions the American government had tolerated conditions in China that it abhorred—until the affairs of China became related to affairs in Europe. Only then, as Asian affairs merged with the vital affairs of Europe, did the United States grudgingly bring its power to bear.

Central to American desires in Asia in the half century that followed Hay's Open Door notes was the existence of a strong, independent China. Most American statesmen believed that if hopes for the expansion of trade and investments in China were ever to be realized, the fetters of imperialism would have to be removed and China would have to modernize. A backward China, dominated by other powers, held no promise for the United States. Congruently, a strong, modern China, able to preserve its own territorial integrity, would provide the best assurance of a stable balance of power in Asia. A weak China had resulted in Russian adventurism in the early twentieth century, Japanese adventurism, particularly in the 1930s—and would continue to draw great powers to disaster near her borders. Moreover, the quest for a strong, independent China was consistent with American ideals and principles, especially traditional anti-imperialism. Thus firmly grounded in American ideals and interests, this aim persisted for fifty years.

The great aberration in American policy began in 1950, as the people and their leaders were blinded by fear of Communism and forgot the sound geopolitical, economic, and ethical basis of their historic desire for China's well-being. Having always assumed that China would be friendly, Americans were further bewildered by the hostility of Mao's

China, leading them to forsake their traditional support of Asian nationalism, not only in China, but wherever Marxist leadership threatened to enlarge the apparent Communist monolith. With the full support of the American people, Truman and his advisers committed the United States to a policy of containing Communism in Asia as well as in Europe. In practice this policy became increasingly anti-Chinese, an unprecedented campaign of opposition to the development of a strong, modern China. There was no longer any question of whether the United States would interpose itself between China and her enemies, for the United States had become China's principal enemy.

The decade that followed Truman's decision to reinvolve the United States in the Chinese civil war witnessed the further development and hardening of anti-Chinese attitudes and policy. The Eisenhower administration tolerated and abetted the McCarthyite emasculation of the Department of State, and Secretary of State John Foster Dulles, a victim of verbal autointoxication, convinced himself of the immorality of Communists, neutralists, and particularly the Chinese Communists. Having promised in the Republican Party platform of 1952 that he would end the neglect of the Far East, he tried to isolate, encircle, and bring about the collapse of the Peking government. There was only one China, the Republic of China, and the United States would recognize no other; nor would it tolerate the seating of Mao's regime in the United Nations. In an era in which many nations received or hoped to receive American aid, Dulles had ample leverage with which to acquire foreign support for his policy. Similarly, he made every effort to isolate China economically, although these efforts were much less successful.

In addition to political and economic efforts directed against China, the Eisenhower administration continued and intensified the military encirclement of China by the rapid development of American bases in East Asia and the signing of mutual defense treaties with those Asian states willing to make anti-Communist professions. To the alliance structure created by the Truman administration's treaties with Japan, the Philippines, Australia, and New Zealand, the Eisenhower administration added commitments to South Korea, Pakistan, and Thailand along with Great Britain, France, Australia, and New Zealand in the Southeast Asia Collective Defense Treaty, and finally, to Chiang Kai-shek's regime on Taiwan. Just as Stalin's unilateral quest for security in Europe had stiffened Western resistance and brought about the very military encirclement he feared, so China's intervention in the Korean War produced a much more threatening military posture by the United States. Of all the bases and alliances, however, the American actions that most gravely concerned Mao's China were those related to Taiwan.

When the United States countered the North Korean invasion of the South by sending troops to Korea and the Seventh Fleet to the Formosa Strait, the Chinese virtually ignored the intervention in Korea while giving vent to their rage at this intensified American involvement in the Chinese civil war. The 300,000 troops preparing to cross the strait were then transferred north to Shantung, facilitating Chinese intervention in Korea when MacArthur's forces advanced to China's border. After China intervened, Taiwan assumed an infinitely greater importance to Americans, especially to the American military who were charged with the responsibility for meeting American commitments to Japan and the Philippines. The defenses of the island were built up, large-scale aid poured in, and American bases developed. One of the first steps taken by the Eisenhower administration was to "unleash" Chiang, to announce that the Seventh Fleet would no longer be used to protect the Peking regime from his efforts to recover the mainland.

However ludicrous the assumption that Chiang's tattered remnants were on the verge of assaulting the mainland, this was the rhetoric that Americans had asked for and to which they became accustomed. But those remnants did not long remain tattered; they were reequipped by the United States and American aid produced another in a series of economic miracles. At last, now that the land belonged not to them but to the leaders of the native Taiwanese, Chiang and his faithful few yielded to American demands for thoroughgoing land reform. Forced off the land, many Taiwanese leaders became industrial entrepreneurs, showing an aptitude that suggested kinship with their earlier Japanese rulers rather than the mainland Chinese liberator-conquerors. Financed by the American government, advised by a host of American specialists in agriculture, business, and public administration, important economic reforms were carried out by the Kuomintang government, providing for a standard of living that, by the early 1960s, was alleged to be second in Asia only to that of the Japanese. This economic prosperity, combined with political repression, stifled the Taiwanese impulse to revolt against the mainlanders. If Chiang's prospects for returning to the mainland remained remote, Taiwan and its lesser island bastions had been converted into formidable obstacles to the unification of China and the conclusion of the Chinese civil war. Moreover, the operations of the Seventh Fleet permitted Chiang's

Taiwan and China

forces to raid the mainland while preventing retaliation by the People's Republic. The CIA facilitated and frequently participated in the planning of these raids. Mao and his comrades did not require ideological reasons for their hostility to the United States.

The American ties to Chiang and the intervention of the United States in the Chinese civil war served to isolate the United States almost as much as it did the People's Republic. Not only leading neutralist countries like India, but several of America's European allies as well, had recognized the Peking government and refused to become involved in what they considered internal Chinese affairs. The prominence of McCarthyism in American affairs and the rigidity of Dulles' anti-Communism further undermined world respect for the leadership of the United States. As the Marshall Plan enabled European countries to recover behind the NATO shield, as it became increasingly apparent that the nature of the Soviet threat had changed after Stalin's death—if not before—Europe became less dependent on American aid and less willing to accept American dictation of policy. Moreover, unable to further their own interests in the face of American competition in Asia, the nations of Europe gradually retreated toward fortress Europe, leaving Asian affairs to the United States. From the wings, many Europeans bemoaned the excessive attachment of the United States to Asia, bemoaned American ignorance of Asia—and generally failed to comprehend the fact that developments in China and Japan were altering the disposition of the world's political, military, and economic power.

As Europe recovered and fears of the Soviet threat receded, the involvement of the United States in Asia deepened rapidly. After the Korean War the United States had vastly more military and economic power at its disposal than in the late 1940s, and with Europe secure, secondary aims could be pursued. Much of America's vast power to do good—or evil—was available for use in Asia. From June 1950 to May 1954, the United States provided the French in Indochina with well over $2 billion in aid. When the French effort to crush Ho Chi Minh finally collapsed at Dien Bien Phu in 1954, the Eisenhower administration saw no need to tolerate defeat for the anti-Communist cause; the United States would fill the breach. When in 1954 and again in 1958, Peking's forces threatened the tiny Nationalist-held islands of Quemoy and Matsu, a few miles off the mainland coast, the United States provided Chiang with the logistical support necessary to hold them and the threat necessary to reinforce Mao's prudence.

And yet, for all Dulles' efforts to harass the People's Republic of China and bring about the restoration of the Republic of China's authority on the mainland, the Eisenhower administration was forced to put Chiang back on his "leash" and to pursue a de facto "two-China" policy. Even before he took office, Dulles warned Chiang's hopeful emissaries that the United States would not fight. In the months that followed, he wondered if Chiang could be managed and feared being drawn into war by the Taipei regime. He probably would have been even more apprehensive if he had known that General MacArthur, from retirement, was urging Chiang to provoke an attack on Taiwan or risk inevitable abandonment during Eisenhower's second term. Ultimately, Dulles exploited Chiang's desire for an alliance to obtain a modicum of control.

⌜Acheson and Truman had refused to ally the United States to the Kuomintang regime on Taiwan. Chiang was confident that Dulles and Eisenhower would be more responsive, but for more than a year he was forced to settle for kind words. There would be no increase in aid because of Eisenhower's budgetary concerns. Dulles was "not unsympathetic," but went on to create a Southeast Asia Treaty Organization (SEATO) from which the Republic of China on Taiwan was excluded. Perhaps it could join later.⌝

In Peking, Mao and Chou watched uneasily as Dulles fashioned SEATO, ostensibly to contain China. They were aware of Chiang's efforts to obtain a mutual defense treaty in Washington. In September 1954 they chose to respond by precipitating a crisis in the strait. Shore-based batteries of the People's Republic bombarded Kuomintang-held islands a few miles off the coast of China. Mao and Chou apparently wanted to prevent consolidation of the Taipei-Washington axis by demonstrating its potential danger to the Americans. If so, the display of Chinese power proved counterproductive. Chiang got his treaty.

In the treaty negotiations the Americans evidenced their determination to rein in their prospective ally. If Chiang insisted on asserting his right to attack the People's Republic, there would be no treaty. Walter Robertson, probably Chiang's strongest supporter in the Department of State, told the Chinese ambassador that "the United States was not in a position to negotiate a defense treaty with any country which might take military actions and put the United States in war."[2] Similarly, the United States refused to commit itself to the defense of various offshore islands still garrisoned by Kuomintang forces. Despite all his wheedling, despite an offer of his word that he would not provoke an attack, Chiang could not get a treaty until he agreed that both the disposition and use of force would be "a matter of joint agreement," presumably precluding the possibility of the Nationalists' involving the United States in hostilities of their choice. Chiang and his negotiators were intensely unhappy, but they took what they could get. In March 1955 Dulles angered Chiang further by advising him to stop telling his people that their return to the mainland was imminent and by refusing Chiang's demand that the United States promise to use its veto if the United Nations voted to seat representatives of the People's Republic.

Perhaps because he was aware of American restraint, perhaps because the Soviet Union refused to support Peking's tactics, in April 1955 Chou En-lai offered to negotiate with the United States. The United States accepted the offer and ambassadorial level talks began in August at Geneva, continuing thereafter in Warsaw. Quickly, agreement was reached on the return of Americans in China and Chinese in the United States, civilians stranded abroad when their countries became enemies in 1950. Sixteen years passed before another major agreement was reached. The divisive issue was Taiwan. The Peking government was prepared to renounce the use of force against the United States in the Taiwan area (assuming a reciprocal renunciation by Washington), but it refused to renounce its right to use force to end the Chinese civil war by conquering Taiwan. The United States insisted that the People's Republic explicitly renounce the use of force against Taiwan as a condition to any larger agreement. Although Chou En-lai and Vice Premier Ch'en I hinted strongly that force would not be used, stressing the increasing likelihood of a peaceful liberation of the island, the impasse remained.

The Chinese soon realized that although the Eisenhower administration would not likely challenge Communist control of the mainland, it sought to bring stability to the region by obtaining Peking's acceptance of Taiwan's independence. Beyond that objective, it seemed clear that Dulles was not interested in accommodation. Dulles refused to meet with Chou to try to hurdle the obstacle. He rejected Peking's overtures for informal contact, blocking a Chinese invitation to American journalists and refusing to discuss trade restrictions. Moreover, the United States continued to strengthen Taiwan's defenses, including the replacement of Matador missiles capable of hitting the mainland with tactical nuclear weapons. In June 1957, Dulles attacked the People's Republic sharply, reaffirmed the most uncompromising American posture toward Mao's regime, and insisted that Communism in China, as everywhere, was only a passing phase. Despite Dulles' words and American actions, the Chinese attempted to continue the dialogue, but the United States ended the ambassadorial talks by transferring the American participant to a distant post.

Evidence that Mao had begun to despair of the success of Chou's initiatives to the Americans appeared in the autumn of 1957 when Mao, exhilarated by Soviet successes in the space race, proclaimed that the East wind was prevailing over the West. It was time for the Soviet Union, China, the enemies of imperialism everywhere, to be assertive. In Moscow, Nikita Khrushchev, for all his flights of rhetoric, was not ready for confrontation—certainly not in Asia. Even during the Middle East crisis of the summer of 1958, the Russians would not seize the day. Mao had earlier warned against following the Soviet Union blindly: "We cannot say that all the Soviet farts smell sweet."[3] In late August 1958 he chose his own course. The People's Republic resumed pressure on the Kuomintang-held offshore islands, harassing shipping and shelling Quemoy. If generous gestures would not move the Americans, would guns?

The answer was ambiguous, but there is some indication that Dulles appreciated Mao's message. The American secretary of state warned that the United States would come to the defense of the offshore islands to prevent an attempt to conquer Taiwan. Chou En-lai reaffirmed China's right to liberate the islands while calling attention to American-aided Kuomintang raids against the mainland. But, he added, the Americans claimed to want a peaceful resolution of the problem and China was willing to talk. For about a month, both sides seemed to be reaching for an accommodation. At the end of September, Dulles was publicly critical of Chiang's policy of maintaining large garrisons on the offshore islands. He expressed doubt about the ability of the Kuomintang to return to the mainland, and he insisted that the United States was not committed to aiding Chiang's forces in recovering the mainland even if there were an uprising against the Communist regime there. Responding to an outcry among Americans at the danger of war on behalf of Chiang's goals, Dulles stressed American flexibility and hinted at American willingness to seek rapprochement with the People's Republic. Privately, he began to explore the possibility of recognition of the Peking regime, without withdrawing recognition of the Republic of China on Taiwan. Meeting with Chiang in October, he forced the Nationalist leader to announce that his mission of ending Communist rule of the mainland would not require the use of force.

From Chiang and his American friends, Eisenhower and Dulles elicited epithets previously reserved for Democrats. The response from Peking

Response from Peking

came on two levels. First, there was a reaffirmation of China's willingness to settle the dispute with the United States in the Taiwan area by peaceful means. A foreign ministry spokesman also inched further in the direction of an implicit assurance that force would not be used against Taiwan: "At any rate problems among the Chinese people can be reasonably solved through negotiation."[4] But Mao's associates became increasingly suspicious of Dulles' intention, increasingly convinced that he was working toward the permanent separation of Taiwan from China, toward a two-China policy. This they would not accept and their position stiffened. Withdrawal of American forces from Taiwan and the strait became a Chinese condition for accommodation with the United States. The crisis over the strait passed, but no new initiative came from either side for the remainder of the Eisenhower administration—nor for a long time after that.

Clearly, in the 1950s, the People's Republic of China indicated an interest in the peaceful resolution of its differences with the United States. Mao, Chou, and other Chinese leaders perceived that some of their goals, especially the conclusion of the Chinese civil war, required coming to terms with the United States. Equally as clear is the fact that the United States would not consider accommodation on terms acceptable to Peking. Dulles wanted the Chinese to consider their civil war as a matter of the past. There would be two Chinas—a big China under Communist control, a small one left to Chiang and his heirs. The two-China solution outraged Taipei as well as Peking and Dulles bequeathed the problem to his successors. It must also be noted, however, that for all the absurd anti-Communist rhetoric of which Dulles was capable, the Eisenhower administration never ignored the People's Republic.

In Washington, government officials concerned with China divided into Taiwan and mainland China specialists, with infinitely greater resources at the disposal of the latter. Similarly, in Hong Kong, the closest observation point available to Americans, the consulate general of the United States quickly developed into an enormous establishment, easily dwarfing embassy facilities on Taiwan. The People's Republic was there, and the United States developed means to observe it that were second to those of no other nation.

In 1961, John F. Kennedy took the reins of the American government, determined to reduce the tensions of the cold war. However, despite considerable success in "building bridges" toward Eastern Europe, the new administration's only initiatives regarding China were further efforts to isolate Mao's regime and an intensification of the American military role on China's southern flank in Indochina. The Kennedy years were marked not by efforts to mitigate Sino-American animosities but rather by dangerous adventurism on the Asian mainland.

Kennedy and his aides faced precisely the situation Acheson had longed to see. A rift had developed between China and the Soviet Union. With Stalin's death, Mao was even less willing to defer to Soviet leadership. Disagreements over a wide range of issues emerged, some ideological, some involving the pace and terms of Soviet assistance to China, and others involving Communist bloc policies toward the West. Rather than support Peking's determination to liberate Taiwan, Khrushchev had advised the Chinese to accept the two-China policy the Americans were obviously prepared to offer. The Chinese were outraged and by 1959 their hostility to the Soviet leader was apparent to Western observers. Angered by Chinese criticism, Khrushchev recalled Soviet aid missions from the People's Republic: let Mao practice the self-reliance he so often preached. Overtures to the United States had gained nothing for the Chinese. Hostile gestures were dangerous in the absence of Soviet support, and by 1961, China could no longer rely on its alliance with the Soviet Union. Could the Sino-Soviet split be exploited to the advantage of the United States? The answer was yes, but not in quite the same way Acheson had envisaged.

The very existence of the split suggested that improved relations with one Communist power might result in the further deterioration of relations with the other. Whereas Acheson was inclined to see the conflict with the Soviet Union as irreconcilable and had sought accommodation with China, Kennedy and most of his advisers thought détente with the Russians both necessary and possible. Overtures toward China would have to wait. Given the fact that the Soviet Union was the one nation in the world with the power to threaten the United States directly and the perception that Khrushchev, unlike Mao, was approachable, the administration had little choice. Aware that a prominent issue between the Russians and the Chinese stemmed from Mao's refusal to accept Khrushchev's estimate of the need for accommodation with the West, Kennedy and his advisers were optimistic about easing Soviet-American tensions and despaired of any effort to improve relations with China.

Kennedy and Secretary of State Dean Rusk concluded that China had become the more dangerous of the two leading Communist states—not to the security of the United States, but to the peace of the world. Presumably insensitive to the horrors of nuclear war, still intensely revolutionary, the Chinese were believed more likely to act aggressively than were the Russians. Overconfident because of the inability of the Eisenhower administration to cope with guerrilla warfare, the Chinese were committed to a course of "indirect aggression," sponsoring, supporting, directing "wars of national liberation." Just as the Russians had been brought to reason through American determination, so the Chinese would have to be taught that their new form of aggression could not succeed. While the administration worked toward a détente with the Soviet Union, it would have to retain its cold war posture in Asia, developing a "flexible" military response with which to meet the Chinese threat to Southeast Asia.

In addition, a firm American response in Indochina would enable Kennedy to retain public confidence in his determination to resist Communist aggression—while he provided for more vital American interests by improving relations with the Russians. The increasingly militant American presence in Asia would undermine the professional anti-Communists enraged by the administration's willingness to coexist with European Communists—and stand as a warning to Khrushchev that Kennedy could not be intimidated. At the very least, the anti-Communist trumpet might be muted, with Chiang's friends remaining blissfully quiet. Kennedy had to pay only the small price of stepping up the American military involvement in Vietnam.

Chester Bowles, Adlai Stevenson, and a number of the administration's young specialists on China questioned Kennedy's approach. They favored ending the rigid opposition to the People's Republic that had characterized American policy since Chinese intervention in the Korean War. They found Rusk responsive, but Kennedy would have none of it. He claimed that Eisenhower had threatened to come out of retirement to oppose any effort to seat the People's Republic in the United Nations. Opposition to recognition was unquestionably intense in the Congress. Mao and his representatives had been abrasive in public and in private. To Kennedy there seemed no point in stirring up the animals—or "primitives" as Acheson had labeled the McCarthyites—in circumstances that held so little promise. He refused to permit the Department of State to reopen the question of policy toward China.

In August 1961 Kennedy secretly promised Chiang Kai-shek that the United States would veto representation for the People's Republic if the

United Nations voted to seat the Peking government. McGeorge Bundy, the president's adviser for national security affairs, tried to dissuade him, but Kennedy believed that domestic pressure would require him to use the veto. He thought it useful to offer the promise in advance of the event and bank some goodwill with Chiang. But he also decided to commit the United States to cooperate with Chiang's forces in covert operations against the mainland—a decision not required by domestic pressure. Overtures from Peking for ministerial level talks were evaded.

Bowles and others tried to persuade the president that Mao's words, the threats that emanated from Peking, were mere rhetoric—that the language was belligerent because China lacked the means to act. They stressed the prudence and defensiveness of Chinese behavior. As Khrushchev precipitated crisis after crisis, the view of a moderate China began to gain. In early 1962 Rusk opposed supporting Chiang's operations against the mainland, contending that the Communist military buildup opposite Taiwan was defensive. The People's Republic seemed remarkably quiescent in the early months of 1962.

Two events in October 1962 undermined the effort to moderate the American view of Mao's China. The first was the Cuban missile crisis. After a week of tottering on the brink of nuclear war, Kennedy and Rusk concluded that Khrushchev had been driven by pressures from his enemies in the Kremlin in collusion with the Chinese. The source for this view appears to have been Anatoly Dobrynin, Soviet ambassador to the United States, in whom Rusk and his advisers had unusual faith. They believed they were gaining insight into the decision-making process in Moscow—and their apprehensions were greater for it. Chinese abuse of Khrushchev for his retreat in the missile crisis underscored this new conception of the meaning of the Sino-Soviet split.

The second event, the Chinese attack on India, occurred in the midst of the missile crisis. The march of Chinese troops undermined the argument that the People's Republic was not aggressive and expansionist. Some analysts, like Rusk, noted that the territory in question had been claimed by Chiang Kai-shek as well. Others argued, as scholars would today, that the Indians had provoked the attack. But to no avail. The willingness of the Chinese to use force and the ease with which they routed the Indians seemed to demonstrate aggressiveness. Moreover, in attacking India, they attacked a nation which had captured the sympathies of American liberals—that segment of American society most receptive to the image of a prudent China. In particular, they stilled the voices of two of the most voluble advocates of a new policy toward China, Bowles and John Kenneth Galbraith, both of whom had a deep attachment to India.

As the Kennedy administration made halting progress toward détente with the Soviet Union, Washington's verbal attack on Peking mounted. Rusk concluded that continued difficulties in Laos reflected a loss of Soviet influence in Indochina. He thought the Russians were attempting to honor the Geneva Agreement of 1962, but that Chinese influence had increased in Hanoi, encouraging greater belligerence on the part of the Vietnamese. Similarly, unrest in Africa was attributed to a Chinese offensive there. Even when the Russians behaved unpleasantly, American analysts suspected that Khrushchev was responding to Chinese taunts. Kennedy worried constantly about a possible Chinese nuclear force, about possible Chinese aggression. In July 1963 he called a special meeting of the National Security Council to discuss his fears. The CIA contended that Chinese policy reflected caution and a marked respect for American power, but Kennedy was not much comforted. He was still troubled by China's announced support for revolutionary movements in Southeast Asia and determined to meet the challenge. In August he voiced his concern publicly, warning Americans that a country of seven hundred million people, soon likely to develop nuclear weapons, with "a government determined on war as a means of bringing about its ultimate success," posed what he considered "a more dangerous situation than any we have faced since the end of the Second World War."[5] The intensity of the president's apprehension was manifested by his decision to explore the possibility of a joint Soviet-American preemptive strike against China's nuclear facilities.

The Kennedy administration, because of the president's attitude toward China, as well as his fears of the so-called China Lobby, had less contact with the People's Republic than John Foster Dulles had countenanced. There were reports that Kennedy would change his policy in his second administration, but he was assassinated before his intentions could be tested. While he lived, he allowed no new initiative. After his death, early in the administration of Lyndon B. Johnson, Roger Hilsman, assistant secretary of state for Far Eastern affairs, created a sensation by outlining a fresh position. In December 1963 Hilsman revealed that American policy was no longer predicated on the assumption that Communist control of the mainland was on the verge of passing. He implied that the United States was prepared to coexist with Mao's China while retaining its commitments to Chiang's "China on Taiwan"—a variation on the theme of two Chinas.

Acceptable to neither Peking nor Taipei, Hilsman's thoughts seemed to disturb few Americans. For the United States they provided an ideal solution. The reality of the existence of the People's Republic could be recognized without abandoning the Republic of China. The fact that Chiang would be furious did not seriously disturb the Johnson administration, within which he had few friends. His main strength had always been the support he could muster among the American people, and the response to Hilsman's speech indicated that the "two China"—or preferably, one China, one Taiwan—concept would be acceptable to them. The real problem was to obtain Peking's acquiesence.

Again, the "lesson" of the taming of the Soviet Union was brought to bear. First the Chinese would have to be convinced of American resolve to contain Chinese expansion and then they would become amenable to the just settlement the United States was prepared to offer. American policy toward China was intended to be two-pronged: simultaneous efforts to scale down tensions and to demonstrate the determination of the United States to stand firm against Chinese aggression, direct or indirect. Slowly China would be brought back into the family of nations, ready to live in peace with her neighbors. The policy came to be known as "containment without isolation."

Regrettably, the Johnson administration perpetuated Kennedy's decision to draw the line in Vietnam. In that tiny country, Rusk insisted on accepting the challenge of the Maoist version of the "war of national liberation," and Hilsman insisted that for geopolitical reasons, because Vietnam straddled one route from China to India, control of it had to be denied to the Chinese. As Hilsman neglected to note that the Chinese had found easier ways of getting to India, so Rusk failed to note that China had far less to do with the struggle in Vietnam than it claimed, that Vietnamese Communism was no more an extension of Chinese power than Chinese Communism was of Russian power. The Chinese had little reason to pay the price the United States could exact for crossing the line in Vietnam, but the Johnson administration greatly underestimated the cost of suppressing Ho Chi Minh's forces—for whom the Chinese, despite massive aid in materiel and support troops, had no intention of fighting. In the mid-1960s more and more of America's vast resources were poured into Vietnam, with disastrous effects on the people of that hapless country and little benefit to anyone. In the mud of Southeast Asia, Johnson established his place in history as the man who greatly escalated the cold war in Asia—and the quest for a normalization of relations with China had to be postponed.

Concern about China, armed with nuclear weapons, was fundamental to the East Asian policy Johnson and his advisers designed after the Chinese exploded their first bomb in October 1964 and Johnson defeated Barry Goldwater in the November election. One observer noted that China's nuclear capability "placed an awesome new weapon in the hands of a government that had shown notorious contempt for human life and for accepted standards of international ethics, even Communist ethics."[6] The idea that the American interest would be served best by an international community living according to accepted rules of behavior was the central element of Rusk's faith. In 1964 and 1965 the People's Republic of China was the one major state that stood outside that order and condemned its norms. Even the Russians at their worst paid lip service to the United Nations Charter. The Chinese championed a different world order and militant behavior that Rusk feared would mean chaos, war, and, in a nuclear world, the destruction of civilization. He saw an analogy between what Mao was doing and what Hitler had done. When the Indonesians left the United Nations, apparently throwing their lot in with the Chinese, Rusk was shaken. It was a success for forces that sought to undermine all that had been accomplished by winning the Second World War. Peking, like a Siren, was luring mankind to catastrophe. It was essential to demonstrate to the world that Mao was wrong, that rejection of civilized behavior did not pay. Rusk understood as well as his critics that Vietnam was a poor place to make a stand, but no better terrain seemed available. If Communist militancy could be defeated in Vietnam, under the best possible circumstances for the Communists, there could be no doubt as to the lesson.

As the United States escalated the war in Vietnam, Chinese leaders grew apprehensive. Once again, as in 1950, they had to calculate American intentions. Would the United States use its vastly increased military power in Indochina to attack the People's Republic? Did American actions against Vietnam threaten the security of China? After a bitter debate which resulted in the purge of the chief of staff, those who discounted the danger prevailed. Clashes between Chinese and American jets in the vicinity of the border heightened the tension, but Mao was troubled much more by what he observed within China, by the erosion of the values that had enabled the revolution to triumph. It was time for reform.

In July 1966, while American planes bombed the north and nearly 400,000 Americans fought in the south of Vietnam, Lyndon Johnson called for Chinese-American reconciliation. The Chinese were not listening. The Great Proletarian Cultural Revolution was under way. It was apparent that the Chinese were turning inward, that Mao was bent on tearing apart his own society and hoping to bring it closer to his Utopian vision. All but one of China's ambassadors were recalled for reeducation. Ch'en I lost control of the foreign ministry. Even Chou seemed unable to protect China's foreign policy apparatus. Peking's influence abroad declined sharply.

With China racked by upheaval, the Johnson administration concluded that American bombers could approach closer and closer to the Chinese border, bombing Vietnam with impunity. But Rusk remained troubled by China's ideological antipathy to the United States and to his values. What would happen after the Cultural Revolution? Among his concerns was one he voiced in October 1967, causing a sensation. What would happen if "a billion Chinese, armed with nuclear weapons," emerged from the Cultural Revolution united, stronger, and determined to implement Mao's rhetoric?

Years later, William P. Bundy, who had served as assistant secretary of state under Rusk, asked himself if perhaps China had been less threatening than it appeared in the mid-1960s. Could a different assessment of China have been made "with a resulting different sense of the importance of seeing the Vietnam struggle through at great cost?"[7] Bundy did not know. For Rusk, the assessment of China's power was less important than what China might become—"a billion Chinese, armed with nuclear weapons." China's strength troubled him less than the expressed intention to destroy the world order to which he was committed. The Chinese had to be converted, had to be tamed, *before* they became a great power. Chinese rhetoric, combined with French President Charles de Gaulle's taunts about the credibility of American commitments in a nuclear world, required staying in Vietnam "for the duration."

By 1968 it was clear to Rusk and Johnson that the Chinese had become at least as hostile to the Soviet Union as they were to the United States. But the American leaders were too involved in, too exhausted by the war in Vietnam to sustain a new initiative toward China. A modest gesture was made in May as the Cultural Revolution seemed to decline in ferocity, but the Chinese announced they would have nothing to do with the Johnson administration. Not even the Soviet invasion of Czechoslovakia in August, much as it shocked and angered Chinese leaders, broke the impasse. And yet, as the Red Guards were brought under control in China and Americans sought to find their way out of Vietnam, a new opportunity for reconciliation was almost at hand.

8   Rapprochement—At Last

The years of the Cultural Revolution marked a period of intense factional strife in China, the details of which may never be known to the rest of the world. Domestic concerns preoccupied China's leaders. A sea of Red Guards swamped the foreign policy apparatus of the state and Peking drifted out of touch with the world. The invasion of Czechoslovakia in August 1968, and the Brezhnev Doctrine with which the Soviet Union justified its action, forced the Chinese to look outward, to face the danger on their borders. While the armed forces of China were involved in a myriad of domestic, essentially civil chores, the Soviet Union had increased its military capability in East and Central Asia. The warning was clear enough: might China be next?

As so often seemed the case in moments of danger from without, Zhou Enlai's voice emerged. In November 1968, after the election of Richard M. Nixon, Zhou called for talks with the new administration, for the resumption of the Warsaw meetings in February, a few weeks after the change of command in Washington. Zhou, his friends, and protégés dominated the foreign ministry, but they could not control national policy. Two days before the talks were scheduled to resume, the Chinese canceled them again. Both Lin Biao, leader of the People's Liberation Army, and Jiang Qing, Mao's wife, were opposed to any effort to moderate policy toward the United States.

[margin annotation: China closed + fearful of USSR]

[bottom annotation: New administration attracts Zhou but Mao's cronies are not bothered to talk.]

American analysts recognized the tension over policy in China. With the possible exception of Lin Biao, Chinese leaders did not seem interested in seeking a reconciliation with the Soviet Union. The issue in Beijing was whether to attempt once more to improve relations with the United States while preparing for conflict with the Soviet Union—or to continue the struggle with both superpowers simultaneously. Zhou and his supporters lost the argument.

In March 1969, Sino-Soviet tensions erupted in two serious border incidents over Chenbao Island in the Ussuri. Clashes between Chinese and Soviet patrols, the first apparently initiated by the Chinese and the second by the Russians, resulted in heavy casualties. Border incidents had delighted the world when they consisted of Chinese guards dropping their pants to wiggle their bare behinds at the Russians and the Russians defending themselves by holding up portraits of Chairman Mao. But there was nothing to laugh at when they started shooting. China had become a nuclear power and the prospect of nuclear war in which fallout respected no one's neutrality was frightening.

Moscow demanded negotiations to settle the disagreements, but the Chinese were unyielding. Their only response was to begin a massive military buildup to prepare for war with the Soviet Union. After several ultimatums were ignored by the Chinese, Soviet forces, supported by helicopters, marched into Xinjiang in August. Fearful of a preemptive strike against their nuclear installations in the region, the Chinese agreed to meet with the Russians. The ensuing talks eased the tension of the moment without alleviating Chinese hostility or determination to resist domination by the Soviet Union. Nonetheless, there were no fresh overtures toward the United States.

In the United States, Richard Nixon, to many the epitome of America's tired and repudiated past leadership, was president. The possibility of easing tensions with the People's Republic seemed as remote as ever. And yet, at times, he seemed to understand the changed mood of the American people and their conciliatory attitude toward China. On Taiwan, Chiang Kai-shek lived on, but in the United States his friends were dying off. A generation of voters existed who had no recollection of Chiang as wartime hero but rather saw him and the Republic of China as obstacles to rapprochement with Beijing—and saw rapprochement with Beijing as essential to the avoidance of future Vietnams. Contributions to organizations identified with the "China Lobby" fell off sharply.

Slowly, cautiously, at no risk to the security of the United States, the Nixon administration signaled its desire to improve relations with China. In July 1969, first travel and then trade restrictions that had existed since the Korean War were eased. The patrols of the Seventh Fleet in the Taiwan Strait ceased. From Beijing came no response. In Warsaw, the American ambassador to Poland spent much of the autumn in discreet pursuit of the Chinese chargé. When the contact was established in December, the American representative proposed a resumption of Sino-American talks. And then, before Christmas, the Chinese said "Yes." Early in 1970, ambassadorial-level conversations began anew. Although the American invasion of Cambodia in May evoked harsh criticism from Mao and led to Chinese withdrawal from the talks, Nixon did not give up. In a press conference near the end of the year he declared that "we must have relations with Communist China."[1] No one of Nixon's acts or statements was of great importance, but because they were made by a Republican president who had long personified the cold warrior—and because the public response indicated that these steps had the support of the American people—the 1970s began on a note of hope for those concerned with the relations between the United States and China—and with peace in Asia. Much would depend on Beijing, for the time had come when neither nation could dictate the terms of contact.

In China, the policy debate continued but there were clear signs that Chinese leaders recognized Washington's new approach. Zhou had been embarrassed politically by his past failure to achieve anything through friendly gestures toward the United States. Struggling to rebuild the foreign ministry, he moved gingerly. Gradually the official imagery of the United States in the Chinese press changed. American power in the Pacific was ebbing—was no longer a threat to China. On the other hand, Soviet adventurism was underscored. Before the end of 1970 Mao was persuaded that the United States might prove a valuable counter to Soviet pressure. In December, Mao sent Nixon an unmistakable signal of his receptivity to American overtures. He told Edgar Snow that he would be happy to talk to Nixon—rightist and representative of monopoly capitalism though he was—because Nixon was the man with whom problems between China and the United States would have to be solved.

The great breakthrough came in 1971, perhaps the brightest spot in the blighted career of Richard Nixon. In his "State of the World" message to Congress in February, the president spoke of the need to establish a dialogue with Beijing. He called for a place for the People's Republic in the United Nations—without sacrificing the position of the Republic of China. There, of course, was the rub—or Catch-22, as another generation might call it. Nixon was offering what appeared to be another variation on the two-China theme that Beijing had consistently rejected. But Zhou and several American analysts had another interesting approach: "one China, but not now." Both Mao and Chiang insisted there could be but one China. Why not agree, commit the United States to the idea of one China, with a tacit understanding that the future of Taiwan would be determined at some later time, by the Chinese themselves, in their own peaceful way. Each side indicated its flexibility on the issue and recognized that of the other. In March the United States eliminated its last restrictions on travel to China. Apparently that was enough to gain Zhou the support he needed. A few weeks later, an American Ping-Pong team playing in Japan suddenly received an invitation to play in China—the first American group of any kind to be invited to the People's Republic. The team went, was received in Beijing by Zhou himself, and its appearance used by Zhou to indicate publicly his understanding that the United States and China were on the eve of a new relationship. He agreed to send a Chinese team to visit the United States. Nixon responded by personally announcing the lifting of a host of remaining trade restrictions and signaling his interest in going to China. Secret cables flew back and forth through a variety of channels, friendly signals flew from every post, and one day in July the world discovered that Henry Kissinger, the president's national security adviser, had just returned from Beijing. On July 15, without warning to friend or foe, Nixon announced that Kissinger had met with Zhou and that he, the president of the United States, had accepted an invitation to visit China within the next year. The days of the great aberration were running out.

In August and September the United States supported the seating of Beijing's representative in the United Nations while giving nominal support to Taipei's effort to retain a seat for itself. An American motion to seat both delegations failed to obtain a majority. An Albanian motion to substitute Beijing's representative for Taipei's won easily. It was one of the least painful diplomatic defeats the United States had ever suffered. Washington had taken a step closer to a one-China policy. In February 1972, President Richard Nixon flew to China, where the old Red-baiter enjoyed a personal audience with the venerable Mao Zedong. An astounded worldwide television audience watched Nixon sit through and then warmly applaud a dreary ballet heavily laden with Communist propaganda. It was indeed a new Nixon and a new relationship between China and the United States.

In the Chinese-American joint communiqué issued at the end of Nixon's week in China, each side stated its position frankly. It was clear that the principal obstacle to regular diplomatic relations, to "normalization" with China, was not the American role in Vietnam but rather Taiwan. The Chinese repeated their opposition to all variations of the idea of two Chinas and insisted that all American forces be withdrawn from Taiwan. The American side conceded that Chinese on both sides of the Taiwan Strait insisted that Taiwan was part of China, that there was but one China. The United States would not challenge that position. While restating American interest in the peaceful settlement of the question, the United States committed itself to the ultimate withdrawal of its forces and installations from Taiwan and promised to "progressively reduce its forces and military installations on Taiwan as the tension in the area diminishes."[2] Privately the Chinese warned that neither trade nor diplomatic relations could advance much farther until the United States withdrew recognition from Chiang's regime. In response, Nixon assured Chinese leaders that the United States would not support independence for Taiwan and he promised to take the steps necessary for normalization after his reelection.

no more 2 China plans.

The United States was bound by the treaty of 1954 to defend Taiwan and its approaches. *Following Korean War, Defense Treaty.* American businesses had developed a multibillion dollar stake on the island. Samplings of public opinion revealed that the American people were unwilling to abandon the people of Taiwan, friends and allies, to the Communists. Nonetheless, the Nixon administration was prepared to abrogate its defense treaty with Taiwan, confident that in the short run the people of the island could defend themselves and that in the long run a peaceful solution could be found. Expecting Nixon to act promptly, the Chinese agreed in 1973 to the opening of "liaison offices" in Beijing and Washington—small-scale embassies in all but name. Normalization was deflected, however, by the Watergate crisis and the domestic political maneuvering that followed. Fighting desperately to stave off impeachment as revelation after revelation linked him to unconstitutional and criminal activities, as tape recordings from the Oval Office left less and less doubt that he had lied, President Nixon became increasingly dependent on the support of conservative Congressmen. Many of these men were longtime supporters of Chiang Kai-shek's regime, "Free

Damn you! Watergate always gets in the war.

China," and bitter enemies of the Communist regime, of "Red China." Unable to risk alienating them, the president postponed further action on the defense treaty. Recognition of the People's Republic was not quite equal in importance to the preservation of Richard Nixon's presidency.

Nixon failed to save himself and was forced to resign from office in August 1974. He was succeeded by Gerald Ford, whom he had named to be vice president less than a year before, following the resignation of the disgraced Spiro Agnew. Ford, even more than Nixon before him, relied heavily on Kissinger to direct the nation's foreign policy—and Kissinger was committed to normalization. But Ford, like Nixon, needed the support of his party's right wing. The need became increasingly great as he developed aspirations to seek election to the presidency in 1976. Challenged for the nomination by Ronald Reagan, long the first choice of Republican conservatives, Ford also hesitated to implement plans for recognition of the People's Republic. Nonetheless, he approved the continued secret exchange of military intelligence on Soviet movements initiated by Kissinger in 1971 and in 1976 approved the sale of computers of potential value for China's development of missiles and nuclear weapons. Restrained politically from abandoning Taiwan, fearful of losing what they perceived as a tacit alliance against the Soviet Union, Ford and Kissinger struggled to find ways to conciliate the Chinese.

In China, the foreign policy consensus Zhou Enlai had constructed so painstakingly began to unravel. The results of his approach to the United States seemed less rewarding than promised. The United States had not renounced its defense treaty with the Republic of China, and recognition seemed no closer than in 1972. Moreover, Kissinger's successful efforts toward détente with the Soviet Union and the erosion of American military power in East Asia were both troublesome to a Chinese government committed to opposing "hegemonism"—the Chinese code word for imperialism. By 1974, the debate in Beijing over issues of foreign policy could no longer be separated from the struggle for succession. Mao was feeble and even his indomitable will would not enable him to defy man's fate. Zhou suffered from terminal cancer. As Zhou sought to maneuver Deng Xiaoping into position to take the reins, a "radical" faction led by Mao's wife, among others, countered with attacks on Zhou's policies, foreign as well as domestic. The radicals did not seek rapprochement with the Soviet Union—there was little interest in that idea among any of China's leaders after Lin Biao's death in 1971—but they did insist that

Zhou was exaggerating the danger of a Soviet attack to justify unnecessary overtures toward the United States.

Succession crises in both the United States and China precluded decisive action in either country from 1973 to 1976. By the end of 1976, the patterns of new leadership in both countries were clear. In China, Zhou died in January 1976 and the radicals, the so-called Gang of Four, succeeded in blocking Deng's accession to power. Instead, Mao chose Hua Guofeng as premier—a man whose proven loyalty to Mao and close cooperation with Deng made him acceptable to the major factions in Beijing. The principal issues of succession were yet to be resolved, however. For months the radicals attempted to mount a purge of Deng and other followers of Zhou Enlai, racing against the ebbing tide of Mao's life. They failed, and with his death in September the radicals lost the one obstacle to their own elimination in Chinese politics. Their leaders were purged in October and the way was cleared for the control of China by moderates pledged to carry out the policies of Zhou Enlai. The regime's anti-Soviet policies continued with minor variations throughout the year, but it was clear that China's government was in the hands of men committed to an improvement of relations with the West in general—and the United States in particular.

In the United States, the election of 1976 brought into office a relatively unknown former governor of Georgia, who insisted upon being called "Jimmy" Carter. Little was known about his views on foreign policy, but his appointments, particularly of Michel Oksenberg to the National Security Council and Richard Holbrooke as assistant secretary of state for Pacific and East Asian affairs, suggested an intention to move forward with normalization.

Reviewing transcripts of Nixon and Kissinger's meetings with Chinese leaders, Carter concluded, however, that the American side had been too conciliatory. He instructed his aides not to "ass-kiss" the Chinese the way Nixon and Kissinger had. When Cyrus Vance, Carter's secretary of state, met with Deng in August 1977, he backed away from his predecessor's willingness to surrender all governmental relations with Taiwan and argued for retaining an American consulate in Taipei after normalization. Angrily rejecting the idea, Deng insisted that once the United States recognized the People's Republic of China, no government-to-government ties with Taiwan could be tolerated. Normalization would have to wait until the Americans were willing to follow the example of the Japanese, who, in 1971, had abandoned all official contact with Taipei as the price for diplomatic relations with Beijing.

One year passed and then another seemed likely to pass without any progress toward a closer relationship between China and the United States. The president's men spoke meaningfully of a SALT (strategic arms limitation) agreement with the Soviet Union as a higher priority. They explained that the treaty to allow Panama to take control of the canal had to come first—for tactical reasons. A Gallup poll in mid-1977 indicated popular resistance to the "abandonment" of Taiwan. It seemed clear that Carter had no sense of urgency, no appreciation of opportunities lost in the past. Soon the White House staff would inform favored journalists, confidentially, of course, that the president would take the necessary action in his second administration. Americans—and the Chinese—had heard it all before.

In the spring of 1978, Carter advisers eager to twit the Soviet Union persuaded the president to press for "normalization." Carter, at the urging of National Security Advisor Zbigniew Brzezinski, discounted Vance's argument that China was not a major strategic power and that the United States would be provoking the Soviets without significant gain. The Chinese greeted the initial American overtures skeptically, but Huang Hua, now foreign minister, and Deng Xiaoping were soon persuaded. Deng had clawed his way back to power, and his sense of urgency was growing. He was not interested in seeing the SALT agreement signed. He was not assured of a four-year term of office, nor could he afford the luxury of postponing a decision until after his reelection. He was in his mid-seventies, threatened at home, and beset abroad by Soviet "hegemonists." A pro-Soviet regime had seized power in Afghanistan. Vietnam threatened a pro-Chinese regime in Cambodia. The Soviet Union extended its influence unchecked in the horn of Africa. Unrest mounted in Iran. Deng was willing to make life a little easier for the American president. Ultimately, he was willing to give implicit assurances that the People's Republic would not resort to force to liberate Taiwan. He would allow the Americans to state that understanding without contradiction. Although he objected strenuously, he would allow them to continue to sell arms to Taiwan. Clearly Taiwan was less important than the danger he perceived from the Soviet Union.

In June 1978, Leonard Woodcock, the labor leader who was heading the liaison office in Beijing, was instructed to present American terms for normalization. By December, Deng was eager for recognition by the

United States as the People's Liberation Army prepared to invade Vietnam. After arduous negotiations, he and Woodcock reached agreement on December 13. The public responded favorably to the president's announcement on December 15 of his intent to recognize the Communist regime at Beijing rather than the Guomindang regime at Taipei as the government of China. To American businessmen worried about inflation, stagnation, and an adverse balance of trade, the lure of the legendary China market took on a new luster.

China market mid 20th century edition

Some Americans were unhappy about the "abandonment" of Taiwan, where Chiang Kai-shek's son Chiang Ching-kuo held sway, but the issue never became as venomous as it had during the second Truman administration. Mainstream Republicans as well as Democrats welcomed the new arrangement and tripped over each other in their eagerness to lead missions to Beijing. Administration assurances that relations with Taiwan would continue much as before, on an unofficial basis, with an American Institute on Taiwan replacing the embassy for purposes of de facto government-to-government relations, eased some concerns. CIA estimates of Taiwan's ability to defend itself and awareness that the People's Republic lacked an amphibious capability adequate to mount an offensive across the strait were also reassuring. Finally, Deng Xiaoping flew to Washington and persuaded a few more doubters that the reunion of Taiwan with the mainland would likely be accomplished by peaceful means. Deng's whirlwind tour of the United States was an enormous public relations success, including magnificent receptions at the White House and the National Gallery of Art and visits to several American cities. In Houston the tiny Chinese leader delighted cameramen and their audiences by posing under a ten-gallon hat. On March 1, 1979, the Great Aberration was officially ended as the United States extended diplomatic recognition to the government of the People's Republic of China—almost thirty years after that government came to power.

The new relationship with China was not all gain for the United States. On Taiwan there was brief, government-inspired anti-American rioting. In Japan there was a well-founded unease derived from fear that in the euphoria over the rediscovery of China, Americans would forget how much more important Japan was to them. And in the Soviet Union there could only be anger as Deng Xiaoping used his American forums to denounce Soviet hegemonism. The afterglow of Deng's visit had hardly faded when, unrestrained by their friends in Washington, Chinese forces attacked the Soviet Union's Vietnamese ally to retaliate against Vietnam's overthrow of the Pol Pot regime in Cambodia, which had cast its lot with China. The conflict ended inconclusively, without Soviet or American intervention, but not without alerting Americans to the problems their new friends could create for them.

Obviously, the Chinese had turned to the United States as a counterweight against the Soviet Union. American efforts to strengthen the foundations of Soviet-American détente through new strategic arms limitation agreements, for example, were opposed by Beijing. In the United States and in Europe, where Hua Guofeng traveled in the fall of 1979, the Chinese sought to stir fear and mistrust of the Russians, to exacerbate tensions between the Soviet Union and the West. As difficulties between Moscow and Washington mounted in 1979, some analysts questioned whether it was possible for the United States to improve relations with *both* China and the Soviet Union. A regression in Soviet-American relations to a pre-détente level of antagonism might well be too high a price to pay for rapprochement with China. At the outset of the 1980s, there remained a vestige of hope that American diplomatists would prove equal to the delicate task of strengthening ties with both Communist giants.

Few of the ostensibly bilateral concerns of American relations with China were without international ramifications. The Chinese were committed to the "four modernizations," to the modernization of their agriculture, industry, military, and science. Despite enormous progress in agricultural development, production figures barely kept pace with population growth. Industry had lost ten or more years during the Cultural Revolution. Obsolescent military technology, an important reason for military support of Deng over the radicals and of Deng's opening to the West, was revealed to the world during Chinese operations against Vietnam. But American assistance to Chinese development, especially the sale of technology with military potential, enraged the Soviets. In addition, even for purchases of material for unquestionably peaceful purposes, China needed foreign exchange, which was not easily obtained while Chinese exports to the United States were denied most-favored-nation treatment, when high tariffs on items originating in China prevented Chinese goods from becoming competitive in the United States. In the spring of 1979, a new Sino-American commercial treaty was negotiated, including provision for most-favored-nation treatment, but this treaty also complicated Soviet-American relations. The Jackson-Vanik Amendment to the Trade Act of 1974, aimed at the Soviet Union, denied most-favored-nation status to any Communist country that denied its people the right to emigrate.

If a special exempon were obtained for China—and the Carter administration promise the Chinese it would not link the issue to its affairs with any other ountry—the anger of Soviet leaders could hardly be faulted.

The most dificult bilateral issue remained Taiwan. Vance had urged Carter to work losely with Congress at the point of shifting recognition from Taipei to Beijing, to obtain a Senate resolution in support of the steps he planed, including arrangements for the continuing relationship with Tawan. Once again, Brzezinski argued to the contrary and prevailed, ths time with unfortunate results. Congressmen determined to protect colgressional power in foreign affairs joined forces with others who suppoed the Taiwan regime. Together they wrested control of the legislation designed to provide a legal basis for relations with Taiwan from the dministration. In addition to generally agreed-upon language to permithe Taiwan regime to enjoy the privileges of a sovereign country, evenhough it was no longer recognized as such, Congress included a clausecommitting the United States to make available "such defense articles and defense services as may be necessary to enable Taiwan to maintin a sufficient self-defense capability." It added yet another clause declaing that military or other coercive action against Taiwan would be considered a threat to the peace and security of the region and a matter of "grave concern" to the United States. Deng and his colleagues were outraged. Embarrassed, Carter could only promise to interpret the Taiwan Relations Act in a manner consistent with the normalization agreement. Arms sales to Taiwan did not become a serious issue in 1979, but trouble began in 1980 when the Carter administration authorized American companies to sell advanced jets to Taiwan. In the hands of an administration less friendly to the People's Republic, less sensitive to its concerns, the arms sales issue could easily destroy the fragile links so painstakingly forged between the United States and China.

In August 1980, Ronald Reagan, recently nominated by the Republican Party as its candidate for president of the United States, announced that he desired to resume official relations with the Taipei government, presumably on the basis of a two-China policy. He refused to endorse the normalization agreement of 1978 or even the Shanghai agreement of 1972 with which Nixon had begun the process. Surrounding himself with advisers known to be sympathetic to Taiwan and hostile to the People's Republic, Reagan aroused grave concern in Beijing—and among

Americans who believed the new relationship with China constituted a major strategic gain for the United States. Reagan's election a few months later and his subsequent behavior forced Deng to reconsider his policies, ending the brief period in which China had "tilted" toward the United States. The relationship entered a very rocky phase.

Reagan's sympathies were clearly with Taipei. His friends, Edwin Meese, for instance, and foreign policy advisers, Richard Allen, Ray Cline, and Richard L. Walker among them, encouraged him to act on those sympathies—as when he invited Taipei to send an official representative to his inauguration. Other advisers, Alexander Haig, his secretary of state, and Michael Pillsbury, for instance, were much more concerned with the strategic advantage of good relations with the People's Republic and tugged him in that direction. Taipei's emissary to the inauguration was forced to become "ill" en route, avoiding affront to Beijing. The formulation of policy toward China, as with most issues confronting the Reagan administration, became a contest between conservative ideologues ("let Reagan be Reagan") and pragmatic advisers struggling for control of the mind of a president who was rarely engaged intellectually. The issue of policy toward China was further complicated by a split between conservatives with links to Taiwan and those whose anti-Soviet goals overcame distaste for the Chinese Communist regime. Months passed before the initial administration posture emerged.

Haig and Vice President George Bush, who had headed the American liaison office in Beijing during the 1970s, convinced the president of China's value as a partner in the confrontation with the Soviet Union. They argued that there might be ways to support Taiwan without alienating the mainland. The administration's determination to sell arms to Taiwan in conformity with the Taiwan Relations Act—as had the Carter administration—was bound to upset Chinese leaders. But if the United States adopted Pillsbury's proposal to sell weapons to the People's Republic, it would simultaneously strengthen a strategic partner and demonstrate its friendship toward the Beijing government—which might then be inclined to overlook sales to Taipei.

Deng, Huang Hua, and other Chinese leaders were indeed prepared to stress Chinese-American unity against Soviet hegemonism, but the machinations of Taiwan's friends, the public statements of Cline and Meese, and Reagan's own remarks left the Chinese in an untenable position. Deng had informed Woodcock in December 1978 that China would never agree to the sale of arms to Taiwan but would set aside the issue to proceed with normalization and with the molding of the anti-Soviet front. In the spring of 1981, the Americans were not only preparing to sell sophisticated weapons to Taiwan, but they were also broadcasting their intent to the world, humiliating Deng. Chinese anger mounted.

In June 1981, Haig flew to Beijing for the first high-level talks between the Reagan administration and Chinese leaders. Like Bush, who had tried to reassure Deng immediately after the election, Haig spoke publicly of Reagan's commitment to the "steady strengthening" of relations between the United States and China. Privately he offered the Chinese access to American military technology. The Chinese were interested, but they would not be distracted: they would not buy arms from the United States if the United States continued to supply Taiwan.

Despite increasing cultural, educational, and scientific exchanges, despite increasing trade between the two countries, despite a $28.4 million Import-Export Bank loan to China in October, tensions over arms sales to Taiwan mounted, exacerbated by Reagan's rhetoric and by articles in the American press, which the Chinese suspected were officially inspired. An editorial in the *New York Times* of November 20, 1981, which referred to Taiwan as an anti-Communist ally and rejected Beijing's right to veto arms sales, infuriated Chinese leaders. Chinese attacks on the Taiwan Relations Act mounted, and then, in December, a new foreign policy line was in evidence in Beijing. No longer was the Soviet Union singled out as the lone hegemonic threat to mankind. The new line lumped the United States with the Soviet Union and attacked both. In one year, the Reagan administration had succeeded in undermining the efforts of Presidents Nixon, Ford, and Carter to create a new strategic alignment with a friendly China at America's side. China chose now to reposition itself equidistant from both of the superpowers.

A year's-end editorial in the *Renmin Ribao*, flagship of China's controlled press, indicated that the arms sale issue would have to be negotiated. In fact, talks had begun in October 1981 when Reagan met Chinese Premier Zhao Ziyang at a conference in Cancun, Mexico, and Huang Hua flew to Washington for talks with Haig. Much of 1982 was spent in search of a mutually acceptable formula, with the American negotiators hampered by Reagan's inability to avoid gratuitous insults to Chinese sensibilities.

In January 1982, the Reagan administration retreated from plans to provide Taiwan with advanced fighter bombers. Caught between pressures from Beijing and from Taiwan's supporters in Congress, the administration declared that Taiwan's defense needs could be met with continued supply of a less sophisticated plane. The compromise satisfied neither Taipei nor Beijing, where John Holdridge, assistant secretary of state for East Asia and the Pacific, had a stormy session with his Chinese counterpart. In February, while Americans celebrated the tenth anniversary of the Shanghai Communiqué, the Chinese ignored it. Deng announced that relations were "not good" and that China could manage without the United States. Scurrilous attacks on the United States began to appear again in the Chinese press. Deliberately, the Chinese chose to generate a crisis atmosphere to increase pressure on the Reagan administration. Neither Holdridge nor Vice President Bush could placate them.

Finally, on August 17, 1982, the United States and China hammered out a new joint communiqué on the issue of arms sales to Taiwan. Although the United States continued to sell arms and refused to commit itself to a date when such sales would cease, it did affirm that its sales would not exceed "in qualitative or quantitative terms" those supplied since the establishment of diplomatic relations in 1979—and that it intended to reduce those sales gradually. Packaged with denials of any intent to resume a two-China or a one China, one Taiwan policy, the agreement proved palatable to Chinese leaders, although Deng did not hesitate to express his reservations.

Reagan had reservations of his own. Immediately after the agreement was announced, he underscored its limits by offering a series of assurances to Taiwan. Among these were promises that the United States would not consult with Beijing in determining what arms it would sell to Taipei; that the United States would not attempt to mediate between China and Taiwan; and that the United States would not put pressure on the government in Taipei to negotiate with Beijing. Secretly, he filed a memorandum with the National Security Council stating that he understood the August 1982 communiqué to mean that the United States would restrict arms sales to Taiwan *only* as long as the balance of power between Taiwan and China was preserved. If the People's Republic upgraded its military capabilities, then the United States would help Taiwan accordingly.

Clearly, Reagan had no intention of abandoning Taiwan. His actions and his unprogrammed remarks about Taiwan continued to undermine the efforts of his diplomatists to alleviate Deng's anger. In October, he created another uproar with public remarks linking the reduction of arms sales to the peaceful resolution of the Taiwan question and to the terms of the Taiwan Relations Act, neither of which was tolerable to Beijing.

In January 1983, the Hong Kong *Ta Kung Pao* contended that relations were at the lowest point since they had been established four years earlier. In addition to Taiwan-related issues, bilateral trade frictions intensified. The United States, protecting its weak textile industry, had imposed restrictions on the import of Chinese textiles, denying to the Chinese the sales necessary to buy the building blocks for their industrial infrastructure. Similarly, the United States government refused to license technology transfers deemed essential to China's modernization. As fears of the Soviet Union receded in both Beijing and Washington, as strategic concerns lessened, these bilateral issues came to the surface.

Over the next two years, however, especially after George Schultz succeeded Haig as secretary of state, the president's rhetoric was brought under control. Shultz did not share Haig's estimate of China's strategic importance to the United States and was unmoved by Beijing's complaints. Nonetheless, he saw no point to having the president give gratuitous offense. Under his guidance the relationship became less dramatic, more businesslike. In 1984 Reagan traveled to China, where he was beneficiary of the extraordinary hospitality for which the Chinese are well known. He learned to say less about Taiwan and related issues, a trade agreement was signed, and more advanced technology was transferred to China. The Chinese were declared eligible for the Foreign Military Sales Program, enabling them to buy weapons directly from the U.S. government with U.S. government financing. The two countries worked closely together to support the mujahadin in Afghanistan against the invading Soviet forces. By the autumn of 1984, Chinese officials startled visiting Americans by indicating their clear preference for the reelection of Ronald Reagan over their old friend, Walter Mondale. The Taiwan issue still rankled, but as trade issues became paramount, Reagan's commitment to free trade seemed more advantageous to Beijing than the neo-protectionism threatened by the Democrats. The pattern held into the presidential election of 1988, when Deng announced publicly his hope that Vice President Bush would prevail over his Democratic opponent.

Ties between the two countries multiplied during the second Reagan administration. Chinese students and scholars flocked to the United States in numbers that led to fears of a "brain drain." University after university in the United States scrambled to establish links with Chinese institutions as the latter struggled to modernize. A wide range of agreements for cultural, scientific and technological, and naval exchanges, nuclear cooperation, and trade were signed by the two countries. Trade grew rapidly in the mid-1980s and the United States quickly emerged as the leading foreign investor in China. The foundation for an enduring, stable relationship was being created.

As the Chinese assessed the world situation in the late 1980s, they were pleased with the results of their opening to the United States. Strategically, they no longer felt threatened by the Soviet Union. They perceived American power to be ascendant once more, the Soviets on the defensive. A new Soviet leader, Mikhail Gorbachev, seemed ready to accede to their demand for withdrawal from Afghanistan, for the reduction of Soviet forces on China's borders, and for assistance in restoring Cambodian independence. They had reservations about their American friends and kept them at a distance with ritual condemnations of American hegemonism. Whenever liberalization faltered in China, attacks on bourgeois democracy and racism in the United States reappeared in the pages of the *Renmin Ribao*. Every weapons sale to Taiwan drew a blast, as did threats to lower the quota on Chinese textile exports to the United States. But Chinese leaders were well satisfied with Ronald Reagan and his legacy, and they studiously refrained from any suggestion of a crisis in the relationship.

Curiously, given the long-standing myth that American lust for the China market was the engine driving the East Asian policy of the United States, China's hope for a growing share of the American market had much to do with the tone of the relationship with the United States. Deng and his heirs rested their hopes for modernizing China on their ability to obtain advanced technology from the West. The two principal options for acquiring the funds necessary were foreign investment in China and Chinese exports. In the 1980s the United States was the leading source of investment capital and one of the leading purchasers of Chinese goods. Investments in China and sales to China were relatively unimportant to the United States, representing about 1 percent of American foreign investment and trade, but that same investment and American purchases were enormously important to China. One Chinese analyst, writing for the Shanghai *Shijie Jingji Dabao* in September 1985, outlined the size of the domestic market in the United States and the spending habits of American consumers and urged Shanghai to seize a share. Economic concerns and the prospect for major American investment and purchases helped assuage various irritations.

When George Bush was inaugurated as president in January 1989, most of the clouds that had darkened the Chinese-American relationship in the early 1980s were gone. This time the Chinese perceived a friend in the White House, the first American president to have served as his country's representative in China. But the Taiwan issue would not go away, and it was becoming much more complicated. Major changes were occurring on "Island China," where the Chiang dynasty had ended and democratic reforms were proceeding far more rapidly than on the mainland. Although the new government in Taipei resisted Beijing's overtures for reunification, it continued to suppress the independence movement and, most strikingly, allowed for vastly increased legal contact between the mainland and the island. Trade, primarily indirect through Hong Kong, and even investment from Taiwan, flourished on the mainland. Visits to the mainland were allowed and a more civil discourse between the Taipei and Beijing governments was evidenced during negotiations over a pair of airplane hijackings. President Bush had every reason to assume that the issue would remain dormant during his tenure in office—and to hope that the two Chinese governments might find a peaceful solution in his lifetime.

9 In the Shadow of Tiananmen

George Bush probably knew more about China and the issues in Chinese-American relations than any president in the history of the United States. In 1971, as ambassador to the United Nations, he had been assigned the hopeless task of leading the fight to keep a seat for Taiwan in the General Assembly. He spent the better part of two years in Beijing as head of the American liaison office in China in 1974 and 1975. When, in the election campaign of 1980, Reagan refused to endorse the Shanghai Communiqué and threatened to reestablish official relations with Taiwan, it was George Bush who flew to Beijing in an attempt to soothe his friend Deng Xiaoping. After he occupied the White House in 1989, he perceived no need for initiatives on China policy from the Department of State or the National Security Council. He intended to be his own desk officer for Chinese affairs.

Bush's vision of the Chinese-American relationship was closer to that of Nixon and Kissinger than to that of Shultz or Reagan. Unlike Shultz, he considered China to be an important strategic partner in the struggle against the Soviet Union. Unlike Reagan, the concerns of the people of Taiwan were not high on his agenda. Certainly he would not jeopardize the relationship with Beijing lightly, either on the grounds that the

Chinese needed the United States more than Americans needed China—or to pacify Taiwan's friends in Washington.

Bush was not unaware of problems that existed between China and the United States. Most troublesome were Chinese arms sales to Middle East countries, especially the sale of antiship Silkworm missiles to Iran, which posed a grave threat to U.S. Navy vessels protecting shipping in the Persian Gulf. There was evidence that the Chinese were supplying missile and nuclear technology to Pakistan and countries less friendly to Americans. Certainly their activities ran counter to American interests in the Middle East. In 1987 the Reagan administration, unable to engage the Chinese in discussions about these activities, announced restrictions on high technology exports to China. The Silkworm deliveries to Iran—for which the Chinese had denied responsibility—stopped and the restrictions were lifted. But the Chinese then surreptitiously sold intermediate range missiles to Saudi Arabia and entered into negotiations for the sale of medium range missiles to Syria, Iran, and Libya. Again they first tested American credulity by denying their operations and then gave vague assurances they would stop. They did not. By their actions and their deceit, the Chinese indicated that there were limits to the Chinese-American partnership.

A number of other issues of lesser salience had emerged in the 1980s. Evidence that Chinese intelligence had penetrated the CIA was troubling, worthy of a protest, but hardly shocking to then Vice President Bush, who had once been director of Central Intelligence under President Ford. Chinese exports, especially of textiles, grew and contributed to the serious trade deficit from which the United States suffered. The Chinese government in a host of ways obstructed the import of American goods into China and frustrated American businessmen who invested in joint Chinese-American ventures. The early euphoria over trade and investment opportunities in China was evaporating and important segments of the American business community were unhappy. These were issues that would have to be addressed, but again, hardly such as to threaten a strategic relationship.

One other issue had consistently been subordinated to national security concerns: China's treatment of its own people, its persistent violation of the Universal Declaration of Human Rights. The government and people of the United States had been highly critical of human rights abuses in the Soviet Union and most communist states. Throughout the cold war, however, comparable offenses by America's allies had been over-looked. American leaders knew China's human rights record could not withstand close scrutiny, but decided to mute their concerns, to treat China as though it were an ally whose internal affairs were not subject to criticism. Such cynicism was consistent with the Realpolitik practiced proudly by Richard Nixon and Henry Kissinger. It was merely hypocrisy when Jimmy Carter, who proclaimed human rights the centerpiece of his foreign policy, chose to ignore Chinese practices. Similarly, the Reagan administration was unsurpassed in its criticism of Soviet abuses, but chose not to focus on such issues in its relations with China.

In addition to the national security rationale for ignoring China's dis-agreeable record on human rights such as the absence of freedom of speech or religion, the suppression of political dissent, and forced abor-tions, there was a widespread view among Americans that China's per-formance was improving. The Cultural Revolution was over and the Gang of Four was in prison. Deng Xiaoping and his successive heirs apparent, Hu Yaobang and Zhao Ziyang, promised relatively benign rule, certainly more humane than anything the Chinese people had enjoyed under Mao Zedong. China was changing. Its economy was opening up and its poli-tics was certain to liberalize over time. Although this view reflected a cer-tain naiveté among Americans, the recurring dream of liberal democracy for China, it should be noted that there were also Chinese who imagined that China was moving toward a more open society, that the Communist Party might tolerate political pluralism as it attempted to modernize the country. Ultimately, it was these Chinese who forced Americans to con-front the realities of Chinese Communist rule.

Signs of trouble had come early, both in China and in Washington. In 1979 and 1980, activists seeking what they called the "fifth moderniza-tion" set up the Democracy Wall in Beijing, a place where wall posters calling for political reform might be read by ordinary Chinese. The move-ment quickly spread to other cities, but was suppressed in 1980 and its most prominent figure, Wei Jingsheng, arrested and imprisoned. The U.S. Department of State criticized the arrest of Wei, but Carter said and did nothing.

Wei's imprisonment did little to contain the intellectual and political ferment in China as Deng and his colleagues attempted to find a safe bal-ance between the freedom necessary to unleash the energies and creativ-ity of their people and the level of repression they deemed necessary to maintain their control. China was unquestionably a more open society than it had been at any time at least since the beginning of the Cultural Revolution—and probably since the days when Mao betrayed his 1957 promise to "let a hundred flowers bloom." But Chinese intellectuals had a long history of interest in Western democracy, illustrated most clearly by their calls for "Mr. Science *and* Mr. Democracy" as their answer to China's ills during the May Fourth Movement following World War I. As China's self-imposed isolation ended in the 1980s and its people renewed their contacts with the West, Western political ideas and social values as well as science and technology proved attractive to many Chinese students.

In October 1986, then Vice Premier Li Peng told a group of visiting American scholars that he did not believe China had to adopt Western values in order to utilize Western technology. Once again, Chinese leaders were hoping to obtain the keys to the wealth and power of the West without sacrificing Chinese values—in this instance without tolerating political dissent or intellectual freedom. The door was open for Mr. Science, but Mr. Democracy was not welcome. Many of China's intellectuals were not content, however, and a wave of student protests swept the country before the end of the year and continued into 1987. Calls for political reforms, for local elections and freedom of expression, sounded initially in Hefei (capital of Anhui province) where the outspoken physicist Fang Lizhi led the chorus, were soon heard on campuses across the nation.

China's rulers were divided as to how to respond to student discontent, but finally chose to attack it as "bourgeois liberalization." Several student leaders were arrested and prominent intellectuals who supported them, including Fang Lizhi, were purged from the Communist Party. Deng's most surprising act was to remove Hu Yaobang from his position as party secretary, allegedly for being too sympathetic to the students.

In Washington it was becoming more difficult to ignore the repressive behavior of the Chinese government. American scholars friendly to China protested against the suppression of student dissent and rejected the apologia offered by Chinese consular officials who carried Beijing's assurances to American university campuses. Congressmen less friendly to China introduced resolutions critical of the campaign against "bourgeois liberalization." Nonetheless, the administration remained persuaded that China was on the right track. Occasionally, to be sure, Deng might have to propitiate the old guard with a step backward for every two steps forward, but economic reforms would continue and, in due course, political reform would follow.

In February 1989, President Bush flew to Tokyo for the funeral of Emperor Hirohito. While he was in the neighborhood, he decided to stop in Beijing to visit Deng. And then something happened. The dissident intellectual Fang Lizhi appeared on the list of prominent Chinese invited to an embassy banquet hosted by the president. Ambassador Winston Lord and his staff thought the invitation would be an unprovocative way for the president to express concern for human rights. They were surprised when the Chinese government objected to the invitation, but with the help of Bush's National Security Advisor Brent Scowcroft, they negotiated an arrangement whereby Fang would be seated at a spot distant from the head table and have no contact with the president. Chinese security officials, however, intercepted Fang as he was en route to the dinner and prevented him from attending. When the Chinese tactics were reported in the United States, rather than criticize China, Bush and Scowcroft blamed Lord for issuing the invitation.

It was increasingly clear that the Chinese government had no intention of carrying out political reforms and that it feared the minuscule movement for democracy that Fang symbolized. It was equally clear that the Bush administration had no intention of intervening in Chinese affairs on behalf of dissidents. That was a tactic American presidents seemed to reserve for opponents of the Soviet regime. Bush and Scowcroft were determined not to threaten Chinese leaders. They would do nothing to undermine the relationship.

Of course, the strategic rationale for the unusual sensitivity of American leaders to the concerns of China's leaders was the desire for Chinese support in the great struggle against the Soviet Union. But by 1989, it was becoming apparent that the cold war was virtually over. In the spring of 1985, Mikhail Gorbachev had emerged as the paramount leader of the Soviet empire. He was determined to build a modern, efficient Soviet economy and he understood that a prerequisite was halting the arms race with the United States. He was determined to end the Western perception of a Soviet threat and to obtain an arms control agreement with the Americans. In 1987 he and Reagan agreed to destroy thousands of intermediate range missiles. In 1988, Soviet forces began to withdraw from Afghanistan and Mongolia. In December 1988, Gorbachev flew to New York and announced to the United Nations that he would reduce Soviet forces *unilaterally* and eliminate units stationed in East Germany, Czechoslovakia, and Hungary. Remaining elements of the Red Army in Eastern Europe would be redeployed in a defensive posture, eliminating the threat to the West. As he explained to President-elect Bush, the Soviets could no longer afford an empire. They were opting out of the cold war. Soviet troops and tanks began to pull back from Poland, Hungary, and East Germany. But if the Soviet Union no longer threatened the United States, was it still necessary for the United States to court China?

Gorbachev, as he attempted to ease his nation's defense burden, sought rapprochement with China as well as with the United States. In May 1989 he traveled to Beijing to affirm his intentions to Chinese leaders. In preparation for his visit, news media from all of the world flooded into China to cover the story. But Gorbachev was upstaged by thousands of Chinese demonstrators who, chanting his name, demanded political reform from their own leaders.

The events that defined Chinese-American relations in the last years of the twentieth century began with the death of Hu Yaobang on April 15, 1989. Mourners by the thousands began to fill the huge Tiananmen Square, the center of Beijing, and in a few days tens of thousands of Chinese assembled there, protesting corruption, inflation, and the arbitrary exercise of state power. Well organized and well led, the student participants were careful to avoid provocation. Very likely, political action had been planned for May 4, to capitalize on the symbolism of the May Fourth Movement. Hu's death provided an arguably more propitious moment with which to begin.

The Chinese government responded with impressive restraint. It allowed the growing mass of demonstrators to control the square through Hu's funeral, through the commemoration of the seventieth anniversary of the May Fourth Movement, and through Gorbachev's visit. The journalists and television cameramen who had come to Beijing to cover Gorbachev's meetings with Chinese leaders were captivated by the revolutionary demand for democracy by Chinese students and the public demonstration of support for the students by workers, doctors, journalists, teachers, scholars—and even policemen, soldiers, and Communist Party cadres. As in 1919, Chinese students abroad demonstrated on college campuses and before Chinese embassies and consular offices around the world. Conscious not only of the precedents in their own history, the student leaders were also aware of the success of "people's power" in overthrowing the dictatorship of Ferdinand Marcos in the Philippines in 1986. Using similar techniques, the students tried to force the Communist Party to allow greater intellectual and political freedom and to become accountable to the people.

Increasingly, evidence of disagreement among party leaders reached foreign observers. Deng and the other veterans of the Long March, of the caves of Yan'an, the "gerontocracy," were angered by student demands that threatened both their power and their vision of a socialist China. They were uneasy about the support industrial workers were giving to the students, fearful of a reprise of the 1980 student-worker uprising in Poland. They wanted Tiananmen cleared, the democracy movement crushed, and its leaders bloodied. Zhao Ziyang, the prominent economic reformer and one-time premier who had replaced Hu as party secretary in 1987, resisted Deng's call for the use of force. Li Peng, now premier, favorite of the old party stalwarts, of those most fearful of economic and political reform, moved to the fore, declaring martial law in parts of Beijing on May 20. But troops sent into the city were obstructed by its citizens, who begged the soldiers not to hurt the demonstrators. Leading military figures of the past circulated a letter urging the government to refrain from the use of force: the People's Liberation Army must never be used against the people. There were rumors that the commander of the forces stationed around Beijing had refused to attack the demonstrators, that his own daughter was among those who had begun a hunger strike.

Toward the end of May, as the numbers of demonstrators occupying Tiananmen Square dwindled, at least some of the original student leaders were prepared to ease the pressure and allow the government some respite, to declare victory and hope for a reasonable response from the government. But suddenly new humiliation was inflicted on Mao's aging comrades. On May 29, a few hundred feet from Mao's tomb on the southwest side of the square, students erected a "Goddess of Democracy and Freedom," a recognizable relative of America's Statue of Liberty. From the corridors of power came the dreaded epithet "counterrevolutionary." Reports of government organized anti-American demonstrations surfaced, indications that elements within the Chinese leadership were attempting to discredit the students by suggesting they were instruments of a foreign power. Deng flew to Wuhan where he rallied military support. Zhao Ziyang had lost the struggle for power and the demonstrators— who were now demanding the retirement of Deng and the ouster of Li Peng—would not be tolerated.

On the night of June 3 and the early morning hours of June 4, the People's Liberation Army launched an assault on the people. Accompanied by tanks, the troops shot their way into Tiananmen Square, crushing all who stood in their way, killing upwards of a thousand men and women, mostly in the western approaches to the square. Thousands more were wounded and thousands more arrested, some of them beaten and summarily executed. Some of this savage repression was caught on film by foreign cameramen and within hours it was shown on television screens all over the world. And much of the world was outraged by what it saw. Demonstrations protesting the Tiananmen massacre broke out in Moscow and Hong Kong as well as across Western Europe and the United States. The popular image of China changed irrevocably. The vision China's friends had for the evolution of its government into a regime that would free its people was shattered. The killing fields of Tiananmen left a stain the Communist Party of China could never erase.

The Bush administration had watched developments in China with great apprehension, expressing sympathy for the goals of the students and the hope that the Chinese government would refrain from the use of force. The president understood Deng and his comrades well enough to know that the friends of democracy would not be well served should the United States appear to be their patron. Mindful of the strategic importance of Chinese-American relations, he was loathe to antagonize Deng. But when the shooting began, Bush, too, was horrified and quick to denounce it, as were many European countries. Rather more gingerly, Japan and the Soviet Union condemned the violence in Beijing.

In the days that followed, the Chinese government brushed aside foreign criticism and began the systematic arrest of demonstration leaders and the purge of scholars, journalists, and officials who had supported the movement for democracy. Continued demonstrations in Shanghai, Wuhan, and Chengdu, as well as the massive demonstrations in Hong Kong, did not deter Deng. Chinese television showed prisoners who had obviously been beaten being sentenced to death amidst denials by the government that its troops had killed demonstrators. According to the Chinese government, all violence had been perpetrated upon the PLA by counterrevolutionary hooligans and few if any demonstrators had been killed—a line difficult to sell abroad when foreign television cameras and other eyewitness accounts captured the reality.

On the morning of June 4, as the troops fired on their own people and security forces began to round up student leaders and their sympathizers, Fang Lizhi and his wife took refuge in the American embassy. In Washington, President Bush suspended the sale of weapons to China and broke off contacts with the PLA. But there were demands in the United States for stronger action to punish the "Butchers of Beijing." The administration canceled a series of high-level visits. Under pressure from Congress, the president ordered arrangements to extend the visas of Chinese students in the United States. He announced that his government would work to postpone Chinese applications for loans from international financial institutions. Congressional declarations from members across the political spectrum denounced the Chinese government and many legislators called for even harsher measures.

In Beijing troops fired into the compounds in which foreign diplomats, journalists, and their families were housed. Deng denounced American criticism as interference in Chinese affairs and hypocrisy. He yielded nothing. There would have to be more attention to the campaigns against "spiritual pollution" and "bourgeois liberalization," Chinese euphemisms for Western values. While insisting China would continue its economic reform program and the opening to foreign investors essential to it, he purged the government of its leading reformers, Zhao Ziyang and his associates, and alienated the intellectuals upon whom much of the program depended. Foreign investors hesitated and some turned elsewhere. Clearly the modernization of China had suffered a setback. Deng's obsession with order and his contempt for democracy had led him to jeopardize all he had accomplished in the dozen years since he had fought his way back to power.

Chinese-American relations were probably the shakiest they had been since Kissinger and Nixon reopened the dialogue with the People's Republic in the early 1970s. But despite mounting public hostility toward China among the American people and Congressional pressures for punitive action, Bush and Scowcroft were determined to keep the lines of communication between Washington and Beijing open, to preserve some of the gains of the 1970s and 1980s. Still fighting the cold war, they feared driving the Chinese back into Soviet arms. Bush insisted that the relationship was enormously important, essential to the nation's security. He rejected demands that he recall the American ambassador from Beijing. And he decided that however unwise it might be in terms of American domestic politics, he had to reach out to his friend Deng, to assure him of his desire to resume strategic cooperation as soon as the public rage against China subsided.

Three weeks after the People's Liberation Army gunned its way into Tiananmen Square, George Bush sent a secret mission to Beijing. It was not, of course, a secret from the men who had ordered the massacre, but rather from the American people. Publicly, to appease popular outrage, the administration had declared that it would have no high-level contact with China. Privately, the president acted as he thought best for the nation. Scowcroft, accompanied by the deputy secretary of state, met with Deng and other Chinese leaders. His assignment was to reopen the lines of communication between Bush and Deng, to indicate to Deng that the public furor over Tiananmen had forced Bush to impose sanctions, but these would be lifted as soon as possible. Deng could help with a few appropriate gestures, such as releasing some demonstrators, allowing Fang Lizhi and his family to leave China—and ending the public executions. Most of all, Scowcroft was to convey to Deng that Bush believed that friendly relations with China were extraordinarily important to the national interest of the United States. In this courtship, Bush was not coy about his desire.

Deng understood Bush perfectly and played his American suitors brilliantly. He blamed China's problems on the United States, which he insisted interfered constantly in China's internal affairs. Among his grievances he even included the suffering China had endured assisting Korea against American aggression from 1950 to 1953! The Americans, by criticizing China's handling of the Tiananmen demonstrators and imposing sanctions, had created the tension in relations. It was up to the Americans to find their way out. China had no need to repent.

Despite Deng's response and the general Chinese attitude that they had done the United States a great favor by agreeing to receive Scowcroft, Bush's emissary saw the trip as a success. He had carried out his assignment: he had talked to Deng and kept the Chinese from isolating themselves. It was a level of self-delusion that came to characterize Bush's management of the relationship with China. Over the next several months the administration battled an unforgiving Congress determined to demonstrate its displeasure with the Chinese government. As the Soviet empire unraveled and one communist state after another collapsed in Europe, few members of Congress shared the president's conviction of the importance of the relationship with China. Few were prepared to resume the level of discourse the two countries had enjoyed at the beginning of 1989. Moreover, public opinion polls showed a sharp drop in favorable attitudes toward China among the American people. In February 1989, several months before Tiananmen, 72 percent of those polled reported favorable perceptions of China. Only 31 percent retained favorable views in the first poll taken after the bloodshed, in July 1989.

Two men who did advocate putting aside differences over the Tiananmen "incident" were Richard Nixon and Henry Kissinger, both of whom traveled to China in late 1989 and returned to urge Bush to send another mission to Beijing. They reported that Deng was ready to deal. He would allow Fang Lizhi to leave if, in exchange, the president would invite a Chinese leader to visit the United States early in 1990, presumably with full honors symbolizing American respect for the post-Tiananmen Chinese regime.

Bush liked the package Deng was offering, but wanted it implemented in two stages. First the Chinese would release Fang and then, pointing to China's generous gesture, Bush would invite Jiang Zemin, Zhao Ziyang's successor as party secretary, to Washington. Scowcroft returned to Beijing to meet publicly with Deng and his associates. It was clear the Chinese were hurting. They wanted sanctions lifted so they could obtain loans from the World Bank. They wanted American technology, especially satellites produced by the Hughes Electronics Corporation. They wanted to resume the high-level meetings that would demonstrate the legitimacy of their government. Pleased by Bush's veto of a bill introduced by Congresswoman Nancy Pelosi (D-CA) that would have extended the visas of Chinese students they wanted him to use all of his power to prevent a potential Congressional override. But once again, they offered little in return.

Scowcroft asked the Chinese to let Fang leave, to lift martial law and give amnesty to Tiananmen demonstrators, to stop jamming the broadcasts of the Voice of America, and to give further assurances that they were not selling missiles to countries in the Middle East. He wanted evidence of Chinese concessions that he could offer Congress. Deng refused to let Fang leave unless the United States lifted sanctions. Instead, he was willing to release a few minor figures detained in the aftermath of Tiananmen. A Voice of America correspondent was accredited. And once again the Chinese denied that they were selling missiles in the Middle East. It wasn't much, but again, Bush was pleased that he had kept the lines of communication open. Unfortunately for his relations with Congress, word of Scowcroft's secret June visit to Beijing leaked out. The deception troubled many Americans and gave the opposition Democrats an issue with which to belabor the administration. Bush never seemed to grasp the intensity of public anger over Tiananmen and could not prevent the radical shift in popular attitudes toward the People's Republic.

Bush succeeded in finding the votes he needed in the Senate to sustain his veto of the Pelosi bill, but only with a commitment to protect the Chinese students by executive order. Many members of Congress were affronted by what they perceived as merely an effort by the president to demonstrate that foreign affairs, especially relations with China, were his private preserve. Seeking a means to punish China for the Tiananmen massacre *and* to assert Congressional influence over policy toward China, Congress focused on the annual renewal of most-favored-nation (MFN) treatment of Chinese exports to the United States. MFN had been granted in 1980, but because China was a communist country, the law required the president to recommend continuance every year—and Congress could reject his recommendation. The struggle between a Congress controlled by Democrats angered by human rights abuses in China and a Republican president determined to subordinate human rights issues to his conception of the nation's strategic interests defined the debate over policy toward China until the closing months of the Bush administration.

Denial of MFN treatment to China's exports would have severe consequences for Chinese-American trade. Tariffs would increase sharply, cutting imports into the United States by an estimated 50 percent, costing China at least $6 billion annually in 1990–1991. The Chinese doubtless would retaliate against American goods. Defenders of MFN argued that a trade war would hurt American workers, as well as Chinese. It would deny poor Americans access to cheap Chinese goods. They claimed it would set back economic and political reform in China. But initially even Bush and Scowcroft considered the possibility that denial of MFN might be necessary to impress upon the Chinese the intensity of American anger.

The debate in Congress and the American media over MFN accomplished what previous sanctions, Bush's letters to Deng, and the two Scowcroft missions failed to do: it awakened China's leaders to the terrible cost of alienating the United States. Although some Chinese leaders, adamantly opposed to political reform and skeptical of economic reforms, were willing to pay the price, arguing that with the collapse of the Soviet Union, China no longer needed American cooperation, shrewder diplomatists prevailed. Recognizing Bush's eagerness for reconciliation, they argued successfully for throwing him a bone or two, giving him an excuse to support the renewal of MFN. In the spring, they announced the release of some dissidents and their intention to buy $2 billion worth of

Boeing airplanes, and they repeated their willingness to allow Fang Lizhi to leave if Bush reciprocated.

Bush lived up to Chinese expectations and recommended renewal of MFN, but the Congress was unmoved by Beijing's gestures. International human rights organizations such as Amnesty International and Asia Watch reported that conditions in China were getting worse rather than better. Some representatives insisted on withholding MFN until China stopped jamming Voice of America broadcasts. Others demanded safeguards for the cultural integrity of Tibet or the rights of the people of Hong Kong, who were scheduled to come under Chinese rule in 1997. Efforts by the administration to persuade Congress that China was still important despite the apparent end of the cold war; that a hostile China could create problems for the United States in Korea and Southeast Asia, as well as in the Security Council of the United Nations, won few votes for MFN. A majority of members of the House voted against renewal, but the vote was close enough to assure the president that a veto could not be overridden. A second vote, on a Pelosi-drafted compromise measure advocates called "conditional extension," passed the House by a veto-proof margin of 384–30. This bill would have renewed MFN for one year with an understanding that conditions stipulated by Congress would have to be met if it was to be renewed again in 1991. Both bills died when the Senate adjourned for the year without voting on them, but the future of MFN was uncertain.

By the end of 1990, China was clawing its way back to international respectability. Its greatest asset was the potential for profit the country's modernization offered to businessmen all over the world. Although the Japanese were arguably the most avaricious, American and European buyers, sellers, and investors also chafed at the prospect of being denied billions of dollars, marks, or francs because their political leaders were troubled by the way the Chinese handled their internal affairs. Issues of human rights did not loom large on many corporate balance sheets. Nonetheless, lobbyists for American firms with interests in China insisted that involvement in international trade and finance would lead inexorably to democracy in China. China's economic reforms would lead to an expanding middle class that would inevitably demand political power. To deny China MFN would hurt middle-class Chinese rather than their leaders—and result in the delay of political reform. In July 1990, the "G-7" meeting of American, Japanese, and European finance ministers accepted a Japanese proposal to relax sanctions. World Bank and Japanese loans began anew, and the Japanese and several European countries resumed high-level diplomatic contacts with China. The Americans could not be far behind.

The Chinese would not do the one thing that would have eased relations with the United States overnight. Had China's leaders expressed regret for the loss of life in the Tiananmen massacre and released the student leaders they had imprisoned, the Bush administration and most Americans might well have been prepared to return to the euphoric days before June 4, 1989. Doubtless some Chinese leaders felt remorse, but Deng and Li Peng did not—and they and not Zhao Ziyang and his aides spoke for China. Fang Lizhi and his family were allowed to leave China in June 1990, and several hundred other less-known prisoners were freed at least temporarily, but official Chinese denials of the tragic circumstances of the previous year were offensive to a world that had seen the truth on television.

Chinese leaders realized they had to find a new basis for a cooperative relationship with the United States, a new means of impressing Americans with the importance of the relationship at a time when, at the end of the cold war, few perceived a need to curry favor with a regime that had treated its own people so brutally. It was essential to demonstrate that a friendly China could be an asset to the United States—and that an unfriendly China had an enormous capacity for mischief. Efforts to suggest that China would be a valuable counterweight to a resurgent Japan may have resonated with American trade officials frustrated by dealings with their Japanese counterparts, but most foreign policy specialists in the United States continued to see the Japanese-American alliance as the key to American security in the Pacific. Chinese cooperation with UN efforts to bring peace to Cambodia was more impressive, as were Beijing's growing ties with Seoul and its increasing willingness to share information about what was going on in North Korea. It was Iraqi leader Saddam Hussein, however, who, by invading Kuwait in August 1990, gave China its best opportunity to demonstrate its continued relevance.

Once American leaders decided to rescue oil-rich Kuwait from Iraqi aggression, they needed broad international support. The extraordinary financial deficit run up by the Reagan administration required Bush to seek funds from other governments to pay for planned American military operations. These operations would have to be cleared with the Soviets, longtime supporters of the Iraqi regime. The administration wanted the UN to impose sanctions on Iraq, requiring the support of the permanent members of the Security Council of the United Nations. Superb diplomacy won Bush Soviet acceptance of his policy and the necessary financial aid. The Chinese voted in favor of economic and political sanctions against Iraq, but threatened to veto the use of force.

Clearly, the Chinese were in a wonderful position to obstruct America's response to the crisis in the Persian Gulf—and the leadership in both Washington and Beijing knew it. After informal meetings between Qian Qichen, the Chinese foreign minister, and James Baker, the American secretary of state, in Cairo and New York, an agreement was reached: if China voted for UN sanctions including the use of force, the Chinese foreign minister would be invited to the White House to meet with President Bush; if China abstained, he would still be invited to Washington, but would meet only with the secretary of state. In either case, an official visit to Washington by a senior Chinese leader would be an important indication that China was no longer being treating as a pariah nation. The Chinese chose to abstain, allowing the American-led forces to attack Iraq, but the foreign minister brushed aside the negotiated agreement and demanded a meeting with the president. Bush, grateful that the Chinese had not used the veto, eager as always to encourage their cooperation, undermined Baker and agreed to the meeting. If the Chinese had any doubts of their ability to manipulate American leaders, this episode should have eliminated them.

On the other hand, Baker persuaded the president to insist upon Chinese acceptance of an American agenda for renewed engagement. Bush obtained Qian's agreement to high-level discussions in Beijing on issues of human rights, trade, and the proliferation of weapons of mass destruction. For the moment, Chinese-American relations were back on track and Bush, the commander-in-chief, basked in the glory of his successful management of the very brief war in the Gulf.

There was, however, little public support for a return to the pre-Tiananmen relationship between China and the United States. A 1990 poll indicated that only 16 percent of the American people perceived China as a friendly nation and in 1991 only 35 percent had a favorable view of it. Congress was unrelenting and the battle over MFN in 1991 was as bitter as it had been the year before.

China continued to do little to justify Bush's approach. Throughout the Gulf War, the state-controlled press kept up a steady flow of anti-American propaganda. The political atmosphere within China did not improve and China's use of unpaid prison labor to compete with the products of

American workers outraged labor unions and their supporters in the United States. The trade imbalance in China's favor accelerated as manufacturers once based in Hong Kong and Taiwan moved their operations to the People's Republic to take advantage of low labor costs there and China continued to obstruct the efforts of American exporters. Internationally, despite frequent denials, China persisted in selling missiles and was reported to be helping Algeria build a nuclear power reactor. Beijing was doing something to alienate almost every sector of American opinion.

In Congress, new bills to condition the renewal of MFN on improved Chinese behavior at home and abroad gained broad support in both houses. The American legislators demanded the release of political prisoners, an end to forced abortions and to the export of goods produced by prison labor, and guarantees that China would stop contributing to the proliferation of missiles and weapons of mass destruction. They demanded that the president certify that China had made significant progress in the protection of human rights, and that it had stopped aiding the murderous Khmer Rouge in Cambodia. They wanted assurances that China would abide by the provisions of the Anglo-Chinese joint declaration on the reversion of Hong Kong. They asked that China stop obstructing Taiwan's admission to GATT, the international trade organization. Were the Chinese to meet all these conditions, China would have emerged as one of the most liberal, responsible states in the international community. It was not going to happen.

Bush was determined to fight the proposed bills and the Chinese were willing to give him a little help. They promised to stop the export of prison-manufactured goods and to stop cheating on their quota for textile exports to the United States. They would give better protection to intellectual property rights—patents and copyrights—held by Americans. They would buy more American goods. They would be responsible about transferring nuclear technology, would consider signing the nonproliferation treaty, and might even adhere to the guidelines of the regime established to control the transfer of missile technology. For the most part, they were promising to stop doing what they previously had insisted they were not doing.

The American Congress was unmoved by the Chinese gestures or the president's charge that the legislators were attempting to isolate China and thus threatening peace, stability, and democracy in Asia. The House again passed its bill for conditional renewal of MFN by a veto-proof margin. The administration had to change tack. It could not fight the Congress. It had to indicate that it shared Congressional concerns, but would find a better way to deal with them than through the proposed legislation. Secretary of State Baker's reading of the domestic political situation and more realistic estimates of Beijing's behavior pointed the way. It was time to look tough if the president was going to win enough votes in the Senate to save MFN.

In the spring of 1991, in the weeks prior to the Senate vote on its bill for conditional renewal of MFN, Bush met with the Dalai Lama to demonstrate his sensitivity to the worries of the friends of Tibet. He cited the Chinese for infringement of intellectual property rights and threatened retaliation. In retaliation for Chinese missile exports, the administration denied licenses for several high technology items the Chinese wanted to purchase. Most strikingly, Bush split with Beijing on the issue of Taiwan's accession to GATT, ending American support for the simultaneous accession of both the Taipei and Beijing regimes and endorsing the prior admission of Taiwan. The Senate passed its bill nonetheless, but Bush's apparent willingness to stiffen his approach to China won enough votes to prevent the override of his veto. The administration had gained additional time to attempt to engage the Chinese on terms acceptable to Congress and the American people.

In November 1991, Baker became the first cabinet officer to travel to China since Tiananmen. He, no less than Bush, was eager to strengthen the bilateral relationship, but there were difficult hurdles to overcome. He found the Chinese extraordinarily intransigent. Li Peng informed him that China's leaders were doing him a favor by agreeing to meet with him. As always, the Chinese negotiating stance was to offer no concessions, insist that American behavior was an affront to the Chinese people, and demand that the United States atone for *its* sins. Baker was less susceptible than most of his predecessors, yielded nothing, but came home with little more. Again, in a pattern familiar to those experienced in negotiating with the Chinese, some progress was made on the eve of his departure: the release of a few more political prisoners was announced and Qian Qichen gave him more promises of China signing the nuclear nonproliferation treaty and adhering to the missile regime—*after* sanctions were lifted.

By the end of 1991, the Chinese government was less fearful of being isolated in the world, victimized by the "American hegemonists." Most of the world's diplomats had come back. Investors were slowly returning.

China's exports to the United States—and favorable balance of trade—continued to grow rapidly. It could not always get the technology it wanted from the United States, but the Europeans and the Japanese usually had a reasonable substitute they were delighted to make available. Tourism had resumed and while Americans remained suspicious of China, they visited in droves and spent millions. And China could find graduate schools to train its young people all over the United States.

There remained two potentially disastrous steps the United States might take in its relations with China. One was the refusal to renew MFN and the other was increased support for Taiwan. Bush had alleviated Chinese concern about MFN, but the annual review was humiliating. It was apparent that every spring human rights activists, anticommunist ideologues, friends of Tibet or Taiwan, and other groups unfriendly to the Beijing government would air their grievances and condemn China. The Congress would respond to these complaints by passing bills to terminate or set conditions for MFN. Presumably the president would veto these bills, but there was always the chance that his veto would be overridden—or that he might choose not to fight Congress.

The other danger to the relationship was posed by the continued de facto independence of Taiwan. Nixon and Kissinger, Ford, and Carter had all accepted the "one China" formula upon which Beijing insisted: Taiwan was part of China. Reagan had unnerved Chinese leaders by his evident affection for Taiwan and his reluctance to endorse the Shanghai Communiqué, but he had been reined in. Nonetheless, the Taiwan Relations Act and continued American arms sales to Taiwan had been persistent irritants, papered over by the August 1982 agreement. And now, in 1991, Bush, who had proved so malleable in the past, had been willing to offend Beijing by withdrawing American opposition to allowing Taiwan to join GATT before the People's Republic.

Both issues, MFN and arms sales to Taiwan, exploded in the American election campaign of 1992. Bush came under intense fire for being soft on China, for "coddling dictators." Every Democratic candidate for the party's presidential nomination denounced Bush for his renewal of MFN without conditions, as did Patrick Buchanan, who challenged Bush for the Republican nomination. The Democratic nominee, Bill Clinton, called the 1992 renewal "unconscionable" and spoke critically of Bush's efforts to work with Chinese leaders who continued to crush efforts for political reform, were irresponsible in their export of missile and nuclear technology, supported the Khmer Rouge in Cambodia, and brutalized the people of Tibet. Continued demonstrations of his sensitivity to Beijing's concerns would not likely help Bush at the polls.

Quite independently of election year politics, several of Bush's national security advisers were arguing that the time had come to sell Taiwan the F-16 fighters Taipei had been begging for since 1981. There were several powerful arguments to be made. First, the Taiwan Relations Act required the United States to provide Taiwan with the weapons it needed to defend itself. In 1992, China had purchased twenty-four Sukhoi-27 all-weather fighter planes from Russia, beginning a modernization of its air force that might challenge Taiwan's long-standing air superiority. Selling Taiwan the F-16s would help it to maintain the margin it needed for its defense. Moreover, Taiwan might turn to France for Mirage fighters at a time when American arms manufacturers were desperately seeking new markets to compensate for restraints on the Pentagon as a result of the end of the cold war. Senior officials in the Department of Defense were not indifferent to the plight of their suppliers.

But there was an even more powerful argument for ignoring Beijing's strictures and increasing military aid to Taiwan. Its most persuasive advocate was James Lilley, former ambassador to China and close associate of the president since they had served together in Beijing in the 1970s. In late 1991, during a brief return to private life, Lilley argued publicly that the Shanghai Communiqué was an anachronism; that in the twenty years since Nixon's historic journey to China, Taiwan had become a democracy governed by Taiwanese who did not share the view that there was only one China and that Taiwan was a part of it. The overwhelming majority of the people on the island preferred to be independent of mainland China. Appointed assistant secretary of defense in 1992, Lilley warned that Taiwan's loss of air superiority would create a dangerous instability in the region and won the secretary of defense over to his side. With allies in the National Security Council, they outmaneuvered the opposition in the State Department and pressed the president.

The president wavered, respectful of Lilley's views, but fearful of the repercussions. Domestic political considerations ultimately overcame his doubts. Trailing Clinton in the polls, Bush traveled in late July to Texas, a state that he could ill afford to lose. General Dynamics, manufacturer of the F-16, announced on the eve of his arrival that it would have to lay off 5,800 workers at its Fort Worth division. Leading Texas Democrats immediately blamed Bush for betraying the interests of Texas workers as well as Taiwan by refusing to sell the planes. On his way to Texas, Bush informed reporters he was taking a new look at the F-16 question. Over the objections of State Department specialists on China and the American ambassador to China, the president announced the sale of 150 F-16s to Taiwan several weeks later.

Quietly, an effort was made to pacify Beijing, but there seems little doubt that Chinese leaders were shaken and outraged by the sale. The assumption that time was on their side with regard to the "return of Taiwan to the motherland," that the Americans would do little to stop mainland forces from growing powerful enough to intimidate Taiwan, was shattered. Those Americans who insisted that with the end of the cold war China should no longer be treated as if it were indispensable to the nation's security had apparently prevailed. Washington would no longer kowtow to Beijing—and that was not good news to Chinese leaders.

And worse news was on the way. In November 1992, the American people discarded Deng Xiaoping's friend, George Bush, and chose as their president Bill Clinton, a man pledged to the idea of conditioning MFN on China's meeting American demands on human rights, non-proliferation, and a host of other issues. Moreover, Clinton immediately named as his assistant secretary of state for East Asia and the Pacific Winston Lord, an outspoken critic of the Chinese government since he had stepped down as ambassador to China on the eve of the Tiananmen massacre. Policy toward China would be controlled by men determined to hold Beijing to account for its transgressions at home and abroad.

Clearly, China and the United States seemed headed for confrontation, the relationship Bush struggled so hard to preserve endangered. Clinton's national security adviser, Anthony Lake, spoke of a foreign policy designed to enlarge the area of democracy, rhetoric that implied increased pressure on nations that denied their people political freedom. The proponents of conditional MFN drafted new bills in both houses of Congress, confident that this time there would be no presidential veto.

Within the White House, however, other voices prevailed. Other advisers, on economic and domestic political affairs, reminded the new president that his promises to revive the economy had been critical to his electoral victory. They warned that precipitating a trade war with China would harm the United States as well as China. They persuaded him to ask the drafters of the conditional MFN legislation to back off and accept instead an executive order that would renew MFN for another year, but set conditions for 1994. The president would be required to certify that

China had made significant progress toward the release of political prisoners and the protection of the heritage of the Tibetan people, and had stopped jamming VOA broadcasts. The linkage to arms sales was dropped. Clinton's conditions were milder than the legislators wanted, but they deferred to their president, leader of their party.

In Beijing, the sighs of relief were palpable: China was assured of MFN for another year. The Clinton administration might be manageable after all. But if the Americans expected the Chinese to take a few steps, however modest, toward meeting the president's conditions, allowing him to certify their "significant progress," they miscalculated. Deng and his associates chose to call Clinton's bluff. The Chinese economy had recovered after its initial post-Tiananmen stumble. It was growing rapidly. There were enormous opportunities to make money in China, to sell and to invest. American businessmen did not intend to be left behind—and Chinese leaders were very much aware of growing pressure on the administration to keep the door open.

In August 1993, only three months after Clinton signed the executive order, the administration prohibited the sale of satellites to China as punishment for its sale of missiles to Pakistan. The Chinese turned to European suppliers. Representatives of the American corporations affected, including major contributors to Clinton's presidential campaign, rushed to the White House and persuaded the president to grant them waivers. Ron Brown, Clinton's secretary of commerce, once a leading critic of Bush's efforts to maintain friendly relations with China, reversed himself and pressed the president to put human rights issues aside and focus on expanding trade. He successfully urged the president to allow the Commerce Department rather than State or Defense to determine what technology might be sold to the Chinese.

Businessmen eager to find their fortune in China were not the only ones pressing Clinton to be gentler in his dealings with the Chinese. Military intelligence officers missed the pre-Tiananmen contacts with PLA officers. They were becoming increasingly concerned about the efforts of the North Koreans to develop nuclear weapons and suspected the Chinese could be helpful in averting a crisis on the Korean peninsula. In general, senior officials of the Defense Department, civilian as well as military, were ready to resume contact with their Chinese counterparts.

It was the Department of State that was left with the thankless task of persuading the Chinese to meet the president's conditions for renewing MFN in 1994. In March of that year, Warren Christopher, Clinton's secretary of state, preceded by John Shattuck, assistant secretary of state for Human Rights, flew to Beijing to argue the case. Their mission failed. Shattuck met with Wei Jingsheng, China's best-known dissident, recently released from prison. Chinese security forces arrested Wei a week later and ultimately returned him to prison. Other dissidents were rounded up to demonstrate China's defiance. When Christopher proceeded to Beijing nonetheless, Li Peng was contemptuous, informing him that the Chinese embassy in Washington had assured him that Clinton would grant MFN in any event—and that Christopher did not speak for the president. Clinton did nothing to disabuse the Chinese of their assumptions, nothing that might suggest support for his secretary of state or the concerns of the human rights community.

In Washington the Department of Commerce, the National Economic Council, and National Security Council staff sympathetic to business interests shouldered aside the Department of State with the acquiescence of the president. The influence of the business community over policy toward China was increasingly evident. Perceiving little if any threat to the security of the United States, the men and women who determined policy toward China stressed the importance of trade and investment, the value of good relations with China for the American economy. They stressed "engagement" with China to a president who was himself disengaged from the process of determining foreign policy.

It came as no surprise when, in the spring of 1994, amidst a corporate public relations campaign suggesting that serving American economic interests in China would bring democracy to that benighted country, Clinton abandoned his expressed concern for human rights and extended MFN without any conditions. With few exceptions, most notably Congresswoman Pelosi, House Majority Leader Richard Gephardt (D-MO), and Senate Majority Leader George Mitchell (D-ME), the Democrats followed suit. The closest Clinton came to imposing sanctions on China was in early 1995 when he rode to the rescue of the American entertainment industry: he threatened to impose penalties if China did not sign an agreement on intellectual property rights that would have forced it to reduce the manufacture of pirated movies, CDs, and computer software. For its inspiration, the Clinton administration seemed to be resurrecting Calvin Coolidge's famous dictum: "the business of America is business."

Human rights violations in China continued to trouble a broad spectrum of Americans who were appalled by the lack of political, intellectual, and religious freedom in China; the suppression of minority cultures, especially Tibetan; the exploitation of prison labor; the marketing of human organs harvested from those executed by the state; and recurring evidence of forced abortions. But as the memory of Tiananmen faded, these issues had little impact on American policy toward China. American officials were prepared to concede that the Chinese government was occasionally brutal, but they stressed the increasing openness in Chinese society and the overall improvement in the quality of life of Chinese citizens in the years of Deng Xiaoping's preeminence. Moreover, they insisted that despite its failings, decent working relations with Beijing were essential to American economic interests and to stability in Asia. Having surrendered the threat of withholding MFN, however flawed a weapon it was, the United States was left with no means of inducing China to abide by the principles of the Universal Declaration of Human Rights. And certainly no other major power was prepared to take the lead.

Trade between the United States and China grew enormously and rapidly in the mid-1990s and China became an increasingly important trading partner of the United States. Even this presumably mutually beneficial relationship generated friction as China exported far more than it imported, creating a serious balance of trade problem for the American government. China's restrictive practices affecting the import of American goods lost it some of its business supporters, but the tensions over trade relations were trivial beside those that exploded over Taiwan in 1995 and 1996.

The democratization of Taiwan had continued in the mid-1990s and created domestic political problems for the Guomindang. The opposition Democratic Progressive Party had appealed to the Taiwanese majority on the island with a call to independence. Its popularity posed a threat to the Guomindang generally and specifically to President Lee Teng-hui as he prepared to run in the first direct election for president that the Chinese people had ever known. Although Lee was a native Taiwanese and his candidacy assured the Guomindang a substantial share of the Taiwanese vote, he and his advisers believed it was important for him to play a more assertive role internationally, to signal that he, too, favored independence if it could be achieved without provoking an attack by the People's Republic.

Specialists on Taiwan affairs in the American government were well aware of the changes that had occurred on the island and of its efforts to gain an international role commensurate with its de facto independence. A desire to adjust to these changes—without angering Beijing—prompted an ineffectual reassessment of Taiwan policy in 1993. The United States could not easily treat Taiwan authorities as leaders of a sovereign state without appearing to violate the commitment every administration beginning with Nixon's had made to the principle of one China.

In 1994, Lee Teng-hui decided to force the issue by requesting a visa to stop over in Hawaii en route to Central America. His request was denied, but as a symbolic gesture, the Department of State offered him a reception in a transit lounge at an air force base. Lee rejected the gesture and began a strikingly successful lobbying effort with the American Congress. Since the end of World War II, only Israel had been more successful than Taiwan at manipulating the American government, but there had been few triumphs for the Taiwan regime since the Taiwan Relations Act of 1979. In 1994, the Senate passed a resolution calling upon the State Department to issue visas to Taiwan officials. In the months that followed, lobbyists for the Taipei government worked assiduously on Capitol Hill, generating enormous pressure on the administration to grant Lee a visa to enable him to attend a reunion at Cornell University, where he had earned his doctorate. The administration refused and assured Beijing Lee would not be allowed to enter the country.

In May 1995, the U.S. House of Representatives demanded that the administration issue a visa to Lee by a vote of 396–0. The vote in the Senate was 97–1. Taiwan's lobbyists had performed ably, but the key to their success was the fact that Taiwan was now a democracy, assuring it support across the political spectrum rather than merely from the declining cadre of right-wing Chiang Kai-shek supporters that had served it so well in the 1940s, 1950s, and 1960s. Delight in the political evolution of Taiwan combined with anger at the "Butchers of Beijing" prompted American political leaders to support Taiwan with full knowledge that their actions were offensive to the People's Republic. Congress was sending a message to the perpetrators of the Tiananmen massacre. Clinton and his advisers concluded that they had no choice: Lee was permitted to visit Cornell in June 1995.

Chinese leaders were enraged by what they perceived as American deceit and American willingness to give a platform to a man they saw as an obstacle to the reunification of China. They reacted strongly. They recalled their ambassador to the United States and refused to accept the credentials of the newly appointed American ambassador to China. They broke off the "cross-strait" dialogue they had been having with Taiwan officials—a promising effort toward peaceful reconciliation and conceivably reunification. And in July, the PLA conducted a week of military exercises in the Taiwan Strait, including the firing of four nuclear-capable missiles into the seas just north of Taiwan. Beijing's intention of intimidating the people of Taiwan was obvious—and it was successful. Support for independence declined on the island, its stock market fell sharply, as did the value of its currency in international markets.

Apprehensive as tensions rose in the Strait, Clinton's advisers succeeded in focusing his attention on the danger Chinese actions posed for the United States. The president wrote to Jiang Zemin, now president of China, inviting him to Washington and assuring him that the United States would oppose Taiwan's independence, support neither two Chinas nor one China, one Taiwan, and oppose Taiwan's admission to the UN. The letter seemed to have the desired effect, the Chinese ambassador returned to Washington, the new American ambassador was received in Beijing, and, for the moment, the sense of crisis passed.

In the hope of avoiding an escalation of Beijing's efforts to intimidate Taiwan, the Clinton administration sent several protests against the PLA exercises to Chinese leaders in the fall of 1995. American diplomatists left no doubt in Beijing that the United States insisted on a peaceful resolution of the issues between China and Taiwan. The Chinese responded by reminding Americans that unlike the 1950s they now had the ability to strike American cities with nuclear missiles, that military intervention by the United States in defense of Taiwan could be very costly. China left no doubt that accommodating the United States was not high on its list of priorities. The Clinton administration responded by sending an aircraft carrier, the U.S.S. Nimitz, and support ships through the Taiwan Strait. A dangerous test of wills had begun.

In February 1996, disregarding American concerns, the PLA began massing troops across the Strait from Taiwan. In March, just before the presidential election in Taiwan, the PLA opened fire with missiles, bracketing the island, splashing in its coastal waters, a compelling demonstration of the ability of the Chinese military to devastate Taiwan without an invasion. Again Taiwan's stock market fell, as did its foreign exchange reserves. Fear wracked the island's people.

In Washington, even those officials most determined to find a basis for friendly relations with China understood that the United States had to respond to the challenge. National Security Adviser Anthony Lake warned a senior Chinese diplomat that military action against Taiwan would have "grave consequences." To back up those words, Clinton ordered two carrier battle groups to the vicinity of the island. It was the first military confrontation between China and the United States since Kissinger and Nixon traveled to Beijing.

On Taiwan, the presidential election was held on schedule and Lee Teng-hui won an impressive victory. If China's intent had been to undermine Lee in favor of a candidate committed to reunification, it had failed. His defiance of Beijing had not harmed his political career. Now he was the first popularly elected president in Chinese history. The troops of the PLA folded their tents, concluded their exercises, and returned to their barracks. The American warships sailed away without firing a shot. The crisis was over. Lee was triumphant but his people had a clear indication of how Beijing might respond to further provocation. Chinese leaders could not have been pleased with his electoral success, but they were well aware of the impact their exercises had had on the islanders. American leaders were reminded that China could easily become a dangerous adversary, that the partnership of the 1970s and 1980s had ended with the Tiananmen massacre, that the efforts by both Bush and Clinton to accommodate China's rising power in the world had not been reciprocated by the Chinese. It was time for a new approach.

Friendly relations with China would not likely be possible in the absence of a shared enemy, such as the Soviet Union had been in the 1970s and 1980s. The events at Tiananmen had demonstrated the enormous gap between the values held dear by the American people and those that motivated the Chinese government. On the other hand, given China's great capacity for jeopardizing American interests around the world, it was essential to develop a good working relationship, for the two governments to be able to accept their differences, cooperate when possible, and avoid confrontation when cooperation proved impossible. To this end the Clinton administration proclaimed a policy of "comprehensive engagement," remarkably similar to the Bush administration policies of which Clinton had once been so contemptuous.

In July, Lake went to Beijing to explicate American policy for China's leaders. He assured them that contrary to the expressed fears of the PLA, the United States did not seek to contain China. On the contrary, he had come in hope of a strategic dialogue, a discussion of each side's perception of the world's trouble spots and how together they might work for a stable and mutually beneficial peace. Lake proposed an exchange of state visits by Clinton and Jiang Zemin following the November presidential election in the United States.

Although hostile noises continued to emanate from Chinese military leaders who were not quite ready to forget Clinton's show of force in March, Jiang Zemin and his advisers concluded that they would work with Clinton. Robert Dole, his opponent in the election campaign of 1996, did not make policy toward China a major issue, but he did call for a stronger commitment to the defense of Taiwan. There was certainly nothing to be gained from his election. The Chinese made a few minor concessions to the United States, such as a temporary crackdown on the manufacturers of pirated CDs. The Chinese government also may have contributed illegally to Clinton's campaign. And Jiang prepared to visit the United States in 1997, where he was to be received with full honors.

The men and women responsible for organizing summit meetings—meetings between national leaders—always try to come up with an agreement between the leaders that will demonstrate the substantive importance of their discussions. For months Chinese and American diplomatists labored in vain to reach such an agreement. The Americans wanted the Chinese to stop helping Iran with its nuclear program, stop selling missiles to Pakistan and to various states in the Middle East, and to release some well-known dissidents from prison. Most of all, the Chinese wanted a public statement from Clinton repeating his private assurances that the United States would not support Taiwan's independence or its admission to the UN and that it adhered to the "one China" policy. They wanted to be sure that Lee Teng-hui and everyone else in Taiwan got the message. The Chinese also wanted the remaining Tiananmen-inspired sanctions lifted.

The American negotiators refused both Chinese demands. The Chinese negotiators refused to discontinue missile sales, suggested they might release the most prominent dissident, Wei Jingsheng, and offered to stop aiding Iran's nuclear program in exchange for access to American nuclear power equipment and technology. At the actual summit meeting in Washington, Jiang and Clinton finally reached agreement on the last point: Clinton would allow sales of restricted nuclear technology to China and Jiang would end China's role in Iran's program.

Americans generally were more impressed by the televised exchange between the two presidents during which Clinton declared China to be on the wrong side of history with regard to human rights and democracy. On that occasion and later, when speaking at Harvard, Jiang played a weak hand well, and never stopped smiling despite unfriendly demonstrations. After he left Washington, a State Department spokesman offered the public assurances regarding Taiwan that Jiang had hoped to get from Clinton, but it was enough to win Wei Jingsheng's release—and exile to the United States.

China and the United States had agreed to disagree on issues of human rights and missile sales and to resume a working relationship. To Beijing that meant preventing the United States from actions that might embolden Taiwan to declare independence and retaining access to the American market and American technology. In return the Chinese offered limited access to their market, sporadic but important assistance in coping with the volatile North Korean regime, and the occasional release of a political prisoner. Although the administration concluded it could do no better, Congress and many interested Americans were not satisfied. Criticism of Clinton's approach mounted in the spring of 1998.

The occasion for anger with Clinton was his intervention to permit the Loral Corporation to sell a satellite to the Chinese government in the midst of a Justice Department investigation of allegations that Loral and Hughes Electronics had given the Chinese assistance that enabled them to improve ballistic missile guidance systems. Both corporations had been important contributors to Clinton political campaigns and it appeared that the president was less focused on national security concerns than on repaying major donors. At best, he was putting corporate interests—and the jobs they claimed were at risk—ahead of what many analysts believed to be the national interest in minimizing assistance to the PLA. His aides defended his policies by noting that every previous administration, beginning with that of Nixon, had used sales of technology of possible use to China's military as a means of strengthening the relationship. What they did not tell the public was that they had evidence that Chinese spy operations in the United States had enabled the PLA to make extraordinary progress in the development of advanced nuclear weapons.

Despite the heightening domestic criticism of the administration's policy toward China, Clinton was committed to go to China in 1998. Once again he needed gestures from the Chinese government that would justify the trip and his efforts to improve Chinese-American relations. He wanted the Chinese to release more dissidents, including Wang Dan, the most appealing of the student leaders of the Tiananmen demonstrations. He wanted them to sign the United Nations Covenant on Civil and Political Rights committing China to international rules on human rights. Neither of these steps would necessarily signify changes in China's de facto human rights policies, but they would play well in the American media. In return, he was prepared to drop the annual American effort to have China condemned by the UN Commission on Human Rights. A deal was struck and Wang Dan, like Wei Jingsheng, was shipped off to the United States in April 1998. In June, Clinton went to China.

The visit began inauspiciously with the Chinese providing their American critics with additional ammunition. On the eve of Clinton's flight they detained more dissidents. They denied visas to journalists employed by Radio Free Asia, a network funded by the U.S. government for the express purpose of promoting democracy in Asia. And they insisted that the welcoming ceremony for the president's party be held in Tiananmen Square. Clinton was not deterred.

Human rights advocates were initially outraged, but although little of substance was accomplished at the summit, the president succeeded in redeeming his policy of engagement. Both sides trumpeted an agreement to retarget their intercontinental ballistic missiles, to point them away from each other. The agreement meant little, since the target settings could be changed back in a few minutes. But Clinton delighted Americans with a forceful condemnation of the Tiananmen massacre in his televised joint press conference with Jiang. In a second public address televised across China, he again criticized China's record on human rights and called for democracy and free speech for the Chinese people. For the first time, an American president, given an opportunity to speak to the Chinese people, challenged the repressiveness of their government and publicly urged their leaders to undertake political reforms.

Clinton's performance in Beijing, his forthright censure of China's human rights record, and his affirmation of values shared by most Americans, assured him of a public relations success at home and muted protests against the summit. Less attention was given to remarks he made in Shanghai a few days later. There, presumably in return for the opportunity to speak directly to the Chinese people, he gave the Chinese leaders the public assurances they had long sought regarding Taiwan: the United States would continue to support the principle of one China; it would not ·support Taiwan's independence or admission to the United Nations or any other international organization that required statehood for membership. Certainly American leaders hoped the issue would fade away and that somehow Beijing and Taipei would find a peaceful solution to the dilemma.

For the remaining months of 1998 and the early months of 1999, the United States was engulfed by a scandal involving sexual improprieties in the White House and the president's unsuccessful efforts to deny them. Partisan opponents of the president, primarily House Republicans, were determined to impeach him and remove him from office. Most other issues, domestic or international, suffered from neglect. In the case of Chinese-American relations, that neglect may have been beneficial. After the Senate chose not to convict the president on the charges brought against him by the House and the Congress returned to more mundane issues, his policies toward China came under renewed attack.

Off-balance as a result of charges that his administration had jeopardized the nation's security by responding inadequately to evidence of Chinese espionage and distracted by an American-led NATO attack on Yugoslavia, Clinton stumbled badly during the April 1999 visit to the United States of Chinese premier Zhu Rongji. Fearful of seeming too friendly toward China, he described as inadequate concessions offered by Zhu in exchange for American acceptance of China's entry into the World Trade Organization. Pressed by outraged corporate lobbyists who had been delighted by the concessions, Clinton reversed field and sent Zhu home with assurances that a deal would be reached before the end of the year. It was an embarrassing performance, largely unnoticed by the media preoccupied with coverage of the plight of the Kosovo refugees.

As the Kosovars fled "ethnic cleansing," the murders and rapes inflicted on them by Serb forces, NATO intervened by bombing Serbia, with a disastrous impact on Chinese-American relations. The Chinese opposed NATO's operations as interference in the internal affairs of Yugoslavia and an illegal sidestepping of the UN Security Council—where they could have blocked military action. On May 7, NATO accidentally bombed the Chinese embassy in Belgrade, killing three Chinese. The Chinese government rejected American explanations and encouraged its people to believe the attack had been deliberate. Outraged demonstrators in China besieged the American embassy in Beijing and set fire to the home of the American consul general in Chengdu. The incident revealed the intensity of nationalist emotions among ordinary Chinese and bred a current of anti-Americanism that seemed to surprise Washington. It was apparent that Chinese leaders unfriendly to the United States had been strengthened by the incident—and that it might be a very long time before the level of civility Jiang and Clinton had attained through summitry could be retrieved.

As the presidential election campaign of 2000 began (in 1999), the American foreign policy elite, especially its Republican component, was divided. On one side stood those who perceived China as a potential threat to the United States, supported by men and women profoundly concerned about human rights abuses within China. They groped for a policy that would force Chinese leaders to be more responsive to their concerns. On the other side could be found those eager to trade with China, backed by analysts, many of whom were no less concerned about security and human rights, who perceived no alternative to continued engagement with a government that frequently behaved reprehensibly.

"Engagement," the pursuit of a working relationship with a disagreeable regime, has rarely been attractive to Americans of any political persuasion. If a government is certifiably nasty, if its leaders are openly hostile to American values and frequently pursue policies contrary to the interests of the United States, Americans are not easily persuaded of the value of befriending it. During World War II, most recognized that the United States allied with Stalin's Soviet Union out of a desperate need to keep it in the war against Nazi Germany. During the cold war, they grudgingly accepted the fact that the American government developed strategic partnerships with a wide range of reprehensible regimes, including that of Mao Zedong, as it struggled to contain the Soviet empire. In the 1990s, with no apparent threat to the security of the United States, it was much more difficult to provide a compelling case for paying court to the "Butchers of Beijing."

And yet thoughtful men and women understood there was no alternative. China was unquestionably a major power with great influence in East Asia. Its power and influence were likely to increase in the foreseeable future. Containment, which appeared to have succeeded with the Soviet Union, was impractical. The United States could not contain China alone, and there was scant prospect of support from other nations when fear of communism had all but vanished with the collapse of the Soviet empire and China posed little direct threat to any state. War was unthinkable: although Chinese and American objectives were hardly identical, the two nations had no vital interests in conflict. Although reasonable analysts would surely argue over when to offer carrots and when to look for sticks, diplomacy, by whatever name, was the only option. Crisis avoidance was the minimum goal.

10 America in the Age of Chinese Power

Contrary to the expectations of many Western analysts, China recovered rapidly from the sanctions imposed on it after the Tiananmen massacre and the brutal repression that followed. As a potential market and as a source of cheap labor and inexpensive imports, China was very important to the international business community, which did not fret long about the human rights abuses of its government. Sanctions were soon lifted, capital flowed into China, and even the Clinton administration put aside its concerns about the "Butchers of Beijing" in order to give priority to expanding the American economy through increased trade with the People's Republic. To justify the reversal of policy, Clinton's spokesmen joined those of corporations like Boeing and AIG to repeat the mantra that economic growth in China would lead to a powerful middle class within the country that would demand democratic reforms. They argued that serving the interests of American business would simultaneously further the prospects for democracy in China. It was nonsense, of course, but persuading themselves it was true allowed them to ignore the reality that they were actually strengthening a repressive regime.

And China's leap into the global economy, as Deng Xiaoping anticipated, brought his country back into the ranks of great powers. After nearly three decades as the world's fastest-growing economy, its GDP increasing at a rate of nearly 10 percent annually, it became, early in the twenty-first century, the world's third largest economy and third largest trading economy. By 2007 it was contributing more to global economic growth than any other country. Its appetite for raw materials and energy grew accordingly, and China became a major worldwide competitor for these resources. To ensure its access to oil, much of which was controlled by major Western companies, it undermined the efforts of the United States and the European Union to stop genocide in Sudan and to rein in Iran's nuclear weapons program. In 2006 China became the world's largest holder of foreign exchange reserves, estimated at more than two trillion dollars in 2009, much of it in U.S. Treasury and mortgage-company bonds—arousing fears that it could disrupt the American economy by dumping its holdings. Not least, China's burgeoning economic power enabled it to spend heavily on the modernization and expansion of its military forces. And China's rapid rise was occurring as the Japanese economy continued to stagnate.

Deng's successors had to determine how Chinese power would be used and what role China would play in the world. Deng had warned against ostentatious displays of power, urging younger leaders to continue to insist that the country was a mere developing nation. China could not hope to match the military strength of the United States for a long time. Without yielding any ground on the issue of Taiwan, it should avoid provoking Washington. The brief crisis in the Taiwan Strait in 1996—when the United States responded to the PLA's missile "tests" bracketing Taiwan by sending two carrier battle groups to the area—forced Chinese leaders to weigh their policy options. They concluded that Deng's advice remained valid. In the early 1990s the prevailing view among Chinese analysts had been that the power of the United States was declining and that the emergence of a multipolar international system was imminent. By the mid-1990s, to the dismay of China's leaders, it was apparent that the United States was in fact growing stronger. China had no choice but to attempt to achieve its goals in an American-dominated unipolar world. Maintaining a good working relationship with Washington was essential in order to continue the economic development necessary for domestic stability. Perhaps someday the Americans would cross a line and force a hostile response from Beijing. That day had not yet come. Jiang Zemin and Bill Clinton exchanged visits in the late 1990s and, without significant advances on any issue, both sides claimed to be engaged in a "strategic partnership."

As China's national security elite became more sophisticated, a number of its analysts recognized what political scientists call the "security dilemma": While the PLA became more powerful and China's ability to defend its interests increased, its offensive potential would be disquieting both to its neighbors and to the United States. An arms race like the one that had contributed to the collapse of the Soviet Union might follow. In the 1990s the Americans were already bolstering their alliances in the region, apparently preparing to contain China. Anxiety abroad had to be minimized as China moved to claim great power status.

To reduce widespread apprehension about the potential impact of China's "rise," Beijing engaged in a wide range of multilateral activities designed to demonstrate that China was a responsible member of the international community. In 1996 it participated in the creation of the Shanghai Five (later the Shanghai Cooperation Organization) along with Russia, Kazakhstan, Kyrgyzstan, and Tajikistan (and in 2000, Uzbekistan), ostensibly to preserve the security of Central Asia. It signed the Comprehensive Nuclear Test Ban Treaty and supported American efforts to cope with the North Korean nuclear threat. In 1997, during the Asian financial crisis, it won friends in Southeast Asia by refraining from devaluing its currency, thus sparing Indonesia and Thailand further grief. The Chinese also began to demonstrate flexibility in managing differences with ASEAN states over the resources of the South China Sea, becoming less confrontational and less bullying in their relations with the Philippines and Vietnam.

In addition, seeking to constrain the United States and hasten the arrival of the longed-for multipolar world, Chinese diplomatists devised a variety of "partnerships" with major powers. With Russia they crafted a "strategic cooperative partnership" that they insisted was not an alliance or directed at any third country. Neither Moscow nor Beijing was ready to antagonize Washington. Chinese leaders sought to develop similar ties to Great Britain, France, and Germany, anticipating a strategic relationship with the European Union. They even worked toward partnerships with Japan and India, two nations with which their relations were prickly. But their highest priority was always achieving a stable relationship with the United States. They needed the American market, American technology, and some sort of modus vivendi regarding Taiwan.

Primarily because of the NATO bombing of the Chinese embassy in Belgrade, Jiang's strategy for managing China's relationship with the United States came under fierce attack in 1999, in "The Great Peace and

Development Debate."[1] But the Belgrade incident was merely the trigger for an explosion of nationalist discontent, an opportunity to vent for those convinced that American policy toward China was in the hands of men and women determined to contain China, to prevent China from becoming a great power.

The Chinese were already concerned about the American use of NATO forces to attack Serbia during the crisis over "ethnic cleansing" in Kosovo and were troubled by the willingness of the United States to bypass the UN Security Council. They were even more troubled by the precedent for interfering in the internal affairs of a sovereign state. Might the Americans consider similar action on behalf of the Tibetans or the Uighers of Xinjiang? In response to the embassy bombing, anti-American demonstrators—abetted by the government— besieged the U.S. embassy in Beijing and set fire to the home of the American consul-general in Chengdu.

For the next several months, Chinese analysts critical of the regime's effort to seek a partnership with the United States gained unprecedented access to the media. Insisting that American policy had become hostile to China, some called for the creation of an anti-hegemony coalition, an alliance of anti-American states. Jiang Zemin was under enormous pressure, especially from the PLA, to end strategic cooperation with Washington. Stubbornly, he held his ground and by late summer the debate faded away, and no policy change was instituted. The PLA proved willing to accept accommodation with the United States provided Jiang continued to provide ample funds for military modernization.

Taiwan provided the first test of Jiang's decision to maintain course. In March 2000 Chen Shui-bian, candidate of the pro-independence Democratic Progressive Party (DPP), was elected president. Beijing offered the obligatory threats but did not unleash the PLA: no crisis in the Strait occurred. The Clinton administration quickly warned Chen against provocative action, and the senior American diplomat in Taipei helped prepare his inaugural address—in which he promised not to declare independence or cross any of the lines Beijing had drawn.

The arrival of George W. Bush in the White House in January 2001 led to the second test. Despite his rhetoric critical of China during the campaign, it was widely assumed both at home and abroad that Bush would continue his father's indulgent policy toward the People's Republic. The new president's advisers, however, argued that the elder Bush and Clinton had been too accommodating to the Chinese, that they were strategic "competitors" rather than partners. They insisted that America's true strategic partners across the Pacific were Japan and South Korea. They were eager to confront China and to demonstrate that the United States would not tolerate any challenge to its preeminence in East Asia—or anywhere else. They intended to leave no doubt in the minds of China's leaders of their goal to strengthen Taiwan. Bush deliberately excluded Jiang from the list of leaders to whom he placed courtesy calls after his inauguration.

Then on April 1, 2001, an American reconnaissance plane (EP-3), on a routine mission off the coast of China, collided with a Chinese interceptor. The Chinese plane crashed into the sea, and the pilot was never found. The American plane made an emergency landing at a Chinese base on Hainan Island. To the surprise of President Bush and his advisers, the Chinese detained the crew, refused to return the plane, and demanded an apology. The White House responded by trying to intimidate China. In Congress and across the nation there was talk of finding some means of forcing the Chinese to release the plane and its crew. Bush's national security team seemed confused when the Chinese did not immediately come to heel. Indeed, at first no senior Chinese official would take calls from Washington or meet with the American ambassador in Beijing. Nationalist and anti-American sentiment in China was inflamed, demonstrations spread, and a crisis loomed.

Led by Deputy Secretary of State Richard Armitage, the Bush administration quickly evinced a more realistic understanding of how to deal with China. Each government was well represented in the other's capital, and after a few days their ambassadors met with officials authorized to negotiate. Shortly afterward Bush offered and the Chinese accepted an expression of regret for the loss of their pilot and the failure of the American crew to obtain clearance before they landed on Chinese territory. The crisis eased.

Although Bush had withheld the apology Beijing had demanded, there was no denying his rapid retreat, if not abject surrender. He had learned a valuable lesson: China was too strong, too important to American business interests to be ignored, and too proud to be dictated to by the American superpower. A little of the humility in foreign relations that he had promised during the election campaign proved necessary. Perhaps more striking was Jiang's willingness to ignore popular anger and to accept something less than the apology his regime had promised to obtain. His strategy of cooperating with the United States was working to China's advantage, and he saw no reason to change it.

Chinese-American relations were back on track and running reasonably smoothly soon after the EP-3 incident, although the plane was not returned until July. Friendly relations seemed beyond reach, given the profound differences that remained between the two countries—what Qian Qichen, principal foreign affairs adviser to Chinese leaders, called "basic contradictions." Some of these were readily apparent in April 2001. The U.S. Department of State reported a worsening of China's performance on human rights, especially with regard to Christians, the ostensibly religious Falun Gong sect, and Tibetans. Noting the arrests of Chinese American scholars by Chinese security forces, it also issued a travel advisory for Chinese Americans who had been critical of the People's Republic or who had ties to Taiwan. Bush, who had earlier said the United States would do "whatever it takes" to defend Taiwan, announced once more that the use of force would be an option should the PLA attack Taiwan—adding, however, that Washington's one China policy had not changed. He authorized arms sales to Taiwan that included destroyers and, provocatively, diesel submarines. The Chinese were relieved that he had not included Aegis-equipped ships, suitable for integration into an American missile defense system, but protested vociferously nonetheless.

In June, however, American and Chinese negotiators reached agreement on the issues that were preventing China from joining the World Trade Organization (WTO). In July, Secretary of State Colin Powell flew to Beijing to assure Chinese leaders and TV audiences of his county's desire for friendship. He succeeded in gaining the release of the EP-3. To further underscore the improved relations, Bush called Jiang Zemin for the first time. The two men discussed their differences amicably, and Jiang threw the Americans a bone by arranging to have three ethnic Chinese scholars, two Americans citizens and one holder of a green (permanent resident) card, all of whom had been arrested for espionage, shipped back to the United States.

For the Chinese, the major event in the summer of 2001 was the announcement that the Olympic Committee had awarded the 2008 summer games to Beijing. Hundreds of thousands flocked to Tiananmen in jubilant celebration: the age of humiliation was over. China's return to greatness had been recognized and not even the United States, which many Chinese blamed for their failure to win the games in 2000, had stood in the way.

For Americans, however, September 11, when Osama bin Laden's minions destroyed the World Trade Center in New York, was the most unforgettable day of that summer. Jiang Zemin was among the first world leaders to offer condolences and his country's support in what would become the "war on terrorism." In October, Jiang and Bush met at an APEC (Asia Pacific Economic Cooperation) meeting where Jiang expressed approval of the American attacks on the Taliban and bin Laden in Afghanistan. He also persuaded Bush that Chinese suppression of Muslim/Uigher separatism in Xinjiang was part of the campaign against terrorism, winning Washington's endorsement of China's dubious contention.

In the years that followed, both countries were pleased with the relationship despite the festering Taiwan issue and China's appalling record on human rights, as well as its obstruction of international efforts to stop genocide in Darfur and Iran's effort to obtain nuclear weapons, and its support of brutal regimes such as those of Robert Mugabe in Zimbabwe and the junta in Burma. China bought Boeing jets, and the United States facilitated China's entry into the WTO in December 2001. Bush also signed a proclamation promising the PRC permanent "normal" (formerly "most-favored-nation") trading status—although the U.S. trade representative warned that he did not expect China to honor all the commitments it made to gain entry into the WTO.

In February 2002, thirty years after Richard Nixon's celebrated trip to China, George W. Bush flew to Beijing where he and Jiang pledged long-term cooperation against terrorism and muted their differences. A few months later, Jiang's heir apparent, Hu Jintao, was invited to meet Bush in the Oval Office and given opportunities to introduce himself to the American people. And in October Jiang was invited to the president's ranch in Crawford, Texas—another indication of the improved tone of the relationship.

But in Taiwan Chen Shui-bian, encouraged by sympathetic figures within the Bush administration, goaded Beijing bit by bit. At the beginning of the year he announced that the name "Taiwan" would be added to the passports of his constituents, heretofore citizens of the Republic of China (ROC). Unsurprisingly, spokesmen for the People's Republic complained that he was moving stealthily toward independence. Chinese leaders were well aware of the "secret" meetings held in Monterey, California, between representatives of Taiwan and the U.S. Department of Defense to discuss Taiwan's defense needs but found a publicized meeting between Taiwan's defense minister and Paul Wolfowitz, the American deputy secretary of defense, intolerable. They canceled planned exchange visits between vessels of the U.S. Navy and the Chinese navy—and denied an American warship an anticipated visit to Hong Kong.

In August 2002 President Chen declared the existence of "one country on each side of the Strait," angering Beijing once more and worrying those Americans eager to avoid tension in the region. Taiwan's premier was invited to the United States, apparently another step toward treating the Taiwan government with more respect but also an opportunity to explain the need to rein in his president. After the Jiang visit to Crawford, Chinese concerns seem to have been alleviated. High-level talks between the Chinese and American military resumed, as did port calls by U.S. ships into Hong Kong and Qingdao. The PRC "White Paper" of 2002 contained a softer tone on Taiwan. Chinese analysts continued to warn Americans about the danger in the Strait, but their American counterparts were persuaded that the People's Republic was too busy on other fronts to be bothered by Taiwan and was showing greater flexibility on the issue.

What Bush did not tell Jiang—or for that matter his own secretary of state—was that he had decided to invade Iraq and overthrow its brutal dictator, Saddam Hussein. Nonetheless, Chinese leaders chose to put the maintenance of good relations with the United States ahead of their discomfort with American belligerence. China supported the UN Security Council demand that Iraq comply with all disarmament requests and, unlike France and Russia, did not play a prominent role in opposing the resolution to authorize the use of force. Whereas the French and Russians declared their intention to veto the resolution should it be brought to a vote, the Chinese did not. American analysts concluded the Chinese were likely to abstain.

The People's Republic was adamantly opposed to the Bush administration's penchant for "regime change," but in the case of Iraq its leaders determined that its interests there were not sufficiently important to jeopardize improved relations with the United States. They had reason to believe the Bush administration would demonstrate its gratitude—and they were right. The Americans invaded Iraq in March 2003, and in April the United States announced that for the first time since 1989 it would not sponsor a resolution in the United Nations Human Rights Commission condemning China for its human rights abuses. During that year, the relationship continued to warm. Occasionally Congress or a mid-level Washington official would go "off message" and criticize China's human rights record or its currency manipulation, but the signs of cooperation were much more pronounced.

In April the United States announced that Chinese assistance in drug enforcement had helped break a heroin-smuggling operation. In August the United States deferred to Chinese leadership in the six-power talks on North Korea's nuclear weapons program. A few months later Bush met with Hu Jintao, Jiang's successor, in Bangkok at an APEC meeting and again in Beijing. Hu's charm offensive stressed his government's focus on economic growth and regional cooperation, and Chinese analysts were notably optimistic about the future of the relationship. China's new defense minister flew to Washington to meet with Secretary of Defense Donald Rumsfeld and National Security Adviser Condoleezza Rice, and shortly afterward the Chinese navy sent ships to visit the American base on Guam. Hu threw the United States another bone, deporting a Chinese American convicted of obtaining state secrets, a man whose congressional friends put him high on the American priority list.

The greatest reward—an almost unthinkable reward—symbolizing the extent to which relations between Beijing and Washington had improved over the past three years came in December when Premier Wen Jiabao visited the United States. Taiwan's president, Chen Shui-bian, had irritated President Bush. In his campaign for reelection he had used language designed to intensify Taiwanese national consciousness. Bush had sent a special envoy with a letter requesting Chen to back off, to stop provoking China with rhetoric and actions that implied he intended to declare independence from China. Chen ignored Bush, outraging a president accustomed to having his way. With Wen Jiabao standing beside him in the Oval Office, Bush publicly rebuked Chen. No Chinese leader could have imagined a better Christmas present. Analysts in Taiwan were badly shaken, fearing abandonment by the United States once more, as Washington chose to strengthen its ties to Beijing.

In March 2004, however, despite a disputed vote count, Chen Shui-bian was reelected president of Taiwan, and the anxieties of Chinese leaders soared. No government on the mainland could risk the internal consequences of inaction in the face of a move toward independence by Chen. With the disappearance of ideological bonds as "socialism with Chinese characteristics" came to look a lot like capitalism, and communism as Mao had imagined it had been all but forgotten, nationalism provided the glue that held the Chinese nation together—and reunification with Taiwan was its indispensable goal.

Bush's remonstrations with Chen notwithstanding, the Chinese, especially the military, blamed American arms sales to Taiwan and talk about defending the island for Chen's continued intransigence and the unwillingness of the Taiwanese to accept unification. Beijing showed its displeasure by criticizing the occupation of Iraq by the Americans and by playing a less helpful role in the efforts to halt North Korea's nuclear program. The Chinese were further irritated by Washington's efforts to have Taiwan granted observer status at the World Health Assembly. In July Condoleezza Rice traveled to Beijing in an unsuccessful effort to assuage Chinese concerns. Her Chinese interlocutors demanded an end to or a substantial diminishing of arms sales and a more effective effort by the United States to contain Chen. She demurred, and neither side was satisfied. Chinese forces in Fujian, across the Strait from Taiwan, were increased.

Friction over Taiwan intensified throughout the autumn. Colin Powell flew to Beijing in October and heard Chinese leaders insist that the Taiwan Relations Act of 1979, guaranteeing Taiwan the assistance it would need to defend itself, violated American commitments to China: as always they claimed that the "three communiqués" of 1972, 1978, and 1982 constituted American promises to gradually reduce arms sales to Taiwan. Powell rejected the Chinese argument, seeking to pacify his hosts by declaring that Taiwan was not an independent country and that eventual unification was the outcome everyone sought. He also might have called attention to the fact that the Taiwan legislature had yet to approve the purchase of the arms offered by the United States in 2001. The Chinese were not mollified, and their military buildup continued. In November Qian Qichen, writing in the English-language China Daily, was harshly critical of the Bush administration's foreign policy. In December— in a further effort to pacify China and warn Chen Shui-bian—Armitage, speaking on PBS, declared categorically that the United States was not required to defend Taiwan. Ingenuously, he reminded his audience that the Constitution gave Congress the right to decide when the country went to war. Once again he pronounced the official mantra: all agree there is only one China and Taiwan is part of it.

Both the Chinese and American governments wanted to focus on economic issues, but Chen's provocative rhetoric and the belligerent posture of the PLA kept the embers burning uncomfortably close to the Taiwan powder keg. *If* the PLA attacked across the Strait, would the United States come to Taiwan's defense? For years American policy had stressed "strategic ambiguity," trying to keep both Beijing and Taipei guessing as to what the American response would be. If it was clear that the United States would defend Taiwan, American leaders feared that Chen or others on the island would behave dangerously—perhaps declare independence— sparking an attack from the mainland. On the other hand, if it seemed certain the United States would not defend Taiwan, then most analysts assumed nothing would restrain the PLA. The most important point, inescapable to the national security elite in both Beijing and Washington, was that the Taiwan Strait was the most dangerous place in the world— the only spot on the globe where two great nuclear powers might stumble into war.

Chen was relatively quiet in the early months of 2005, but distrust of him and his intentions ran deep in China. In January there were indications that the National People's Congress (NPC) was drafting an "anti-secession law" intended to legitimize military action should Taiwan declare independence. The Chinese were not deterred by American complaints, and they were angered by the announcement that a new Japanese-American security cooperation agreement included a region of which Taiwan was a part. Moreover, Tokyo and Washington issued a joint statement calling for the peaceful resolution of the Strait issue, a further annoyance to Beijing. In March the NPC passed the anti-secession law, and the Chinese government warned Japan and the United States not to meddle in its management of the Taiwan issue, insisting as always that it was a domestic matter—since Taiwan was part of China.

Only a year or so earlier, analysts in the United States had argued that Chinese-American relations were the best they had ever been, but none of the persistent issues—Taiwan, human rights, and, increasingly, economic concerns—had been resolved. By 2005 the post 9/11 honeymoon seemed to be over. In April, Rice, now secretary of state, returned to Beijing, went to church, criticized the anti-secession law, and called upon her hosts to show more respect for human rights and especially freedom of religion. She offered none of the conciliatory words with which Powell had tried to comfort Chinese leaders. The possibility of a confrontation over Taiwan seemed to be growing. And in July a PLA general serving as a dean at China's National Defense University warned that China would respond with nuclear weapons if the United States targeted the mainland in the event of a conflict in the Strait.

Nor did other aspects of the relationship provide much with which to balance the stress caused by differences over Taiwan. In 2004 the U.S. Department of State accused China of regressing in the area of human rights, and the Chinese countered with their negative assessment of the state of human rights in America. The two nations repeated the charade in 2005. At the WTO, the United States filed a case against the People's Republic, and the U.S. Department of Commerce retained "nonmarket" status for China, denying the Chinese trade concessions. By 2005 Congress, noting the enormous deficit in American trade with China, was pressing the Bush administration to demand that Beijing revalue its currency, which was widely perceived as undervalued in relation to the dollar. A cheaper yuan facilitated Chinese exports to the United States, and an overvalued dollar hampered American exports to China. The constant struggle over China's violation of intellectual property rights—its pirating of CDs, DVDs, computer software, and a host of other items—intensified, as did the perennial quarrel over Chinese textile exports to the United States. A relatively new concern centered around efforts by Chinese corporations with links to the Chinese government to buy major American corporations. The purchase of IBM's personal computer unit by Lenovo was approved by the United States, but when the state-owned China National Offshore Oil Company attempted to buy UNOCOL, a medium-size American oil company, panic over competition for control of energy resources prevented approval of the deal.

The drift toward confrontation slowed late in 2005. Leaders in Beijing and Washington wanted desperately to find a continued basis for a good working relationship despite their sharp differences. Late in September, Robert Zoellick, then deputy secretary of state, called for China to become a "responsible stakeholder" in the international system. It was a role Chinese analysts believed their country was ready to play. It was indeed time for China to stop reveling in victimhood, to move beyond whining about the "century of humiliation" at the hands of the imperialists, and accept the responsibilities that came with great power status. The earlier arguments of Jiang Zemin and his advisers, insisting that good relations with the United States were essential to China's continued economic growth, still had merit. Oozing reassurances, Bush and Secretary of Defense Donald Rumsfeld visited China in November, and before the month was over an agreement was reached to avoid a textile war.

The perspectives of the national security elites in both capitals remained different, however. The Pentagon's Quadrennial Defense Review

(QDR), while parroting the call for the PRC to become a responsible stakeholder, reasserted the doctrine of preemptive strikes: the United States would not wait to be attacked before taking offensive action against perceived threats. The QDR, combined with the director of national intelligence's annual threat-assessment testimony calling attention to China's rapidly rising power and expanding global reach and labeling China a potential "peer competitor" set off alarms in Beijing.

China's interest in being perceived as having a responsible foreign policy did not extend to assisting Western efforts to contain Iran's nuclear ambitions. In 2005–2006, Iran provided China with an estimated 12 percent of its oil imports. Zoellick flew to Beijing in January 2006 to urge Beijing to support a British, French, and German proposal for sanctions against Tehran. He failed. He fared no better when he pressed the government on economic issues, which were causing increasing trouble in American domestic politics. The administration feared Congress would pass a trade-sanctions bill against China, but Chinese negotiators were unyielding. A revaluation of the yuan was not in China's interest, and Chinese leaders rightly argued that the economic problems the United States was confronting were the result of Washington's policies, not their own. And they counted on their friends in the American business community to come to their aid. On cue, the U.S.-China Business Council insisted, justly, that the ballooning trade deficit with China reflected a narrowing deficit with other countries that were moving their manufacturing operations to China—where labor was cheap and docile.

Predictably, Chen Shui-bian stoked the flames once more by calling for the abolition of the National Unification Council, a Taiwan organization that worked, however perfunctorily, on the issues that would have to be resolved before "Island China" could be unified with the mainland. Equally as predictably, Beijing denounced the proposed action as an unacceptable step toward independence, and Washington offered its ritual reaffirmation of its one-China policy. The Chinese foreign minister urged the United States to restrain Chen, and the Americans were able to limit Chen to an announcement that the National Unification Council would cease to function. Proudly, the Bush administration's senior China analyst noted that Chen had not *abolished* the Council—and claimed credit for the difference. But anger at Chen was close to the boiling point in Washington. Ted Galen Carpenter, a prominent public intellectual with the libertarian Cato Institute, published a book, *America's Coming War with China*, expressing fear that Taiwan would suck the United

States into a war in the Strait. He urged disengagement from Taiwan and elimination of any official policy on the unification issue—although he had no objection to arms sales to the island.[2]

The Taiwan issue continued to fester while Chen remained in office—and his term would not expire until 2008. Analysts in Beijing were convinced he would take some major step toward independence before he left the presidency. Washington was equally apprehensive and trying frantically to prevent any action that would provoke a military response from the mainland—and bring about Carpenter's nightmarish scenario.

In April 2006 Hu Jintao flew to Washington and met with Bush. The talks solved nothing but proved useful in assuring each leader of the other's good intentions. Both men understood the extent to which their countries economies were intertwined and the enormous value, strategically as well as economically, of maintaining good relations. Hu intended to maintain Jiang Zemin's grand strategy, and Bush and his advisers, like the Reagan and Clinton teams before them, had learned the importance of gaining some level of cooperation from China. The United States had too many concerns around the globe that could easily be aggravated if China perceived the Americans as hostile—and many international problems could no longer be resolved without help from Beijing. Differences over Taiwan, China's appalling record on human rights, currency valuations, trade barriers, and the like had to be subordinated to the joint management of threats from terrorism and nuclear proliferation. The "lesser" issues would be raised and contended over, but their resolution would be postponed indefinitely. Both in China and in the United States analysts in think tanks wrote about maturing Chinese-American relations. They wrote of a major change in the Chinese worldview and of a greater emphasis on international accommodation. Certainly the Bush administration had come a long way from where it had started in 2001. In December 2006 Bush declared the relationship the "best ever."

Although Congress remained unhappy about currency manipulation after Hu's visit to Washington, China gave way on other economic issues by allowing greater access to its domestic market and stiffening its effort to stop violations of intellectual property rights. The U.S. military and the PLA increased their contacts, and Beijing was noticeably more cooperative with American efforts to deal with the Iranian and especially the North Korean nuclear problems. The PLA also attempted strenuously to assuage American fears about its military modernization, insisting it would take at least twenty years to catch up with American military power—and more likely one hundred.

Before the year was out the Chinese and American navies held their first joint exercises. The two governments worked together on port security and on the policing of fishing in the North Pacific. Secretary of the Treasury Henry Paulson led a large delegation of cabinet-level economic policy makers to Beijing for what would become a formal twice yearly "strategic dialogue." The United States was making a grand effort to engage China, to edge China closer to the role of responsible stakeholder in the international system.

In the United States celebrities, like the actors Mia Farrow and Richard Gere, and nongovernmental organizations, such as Amnesty International and Human Rights Watch, remained profoundly troubled by China's performance at home and abroad. China's mistreatment of dissenters, the Communist Party's negation of the rule of law promised to the country's citizens, and the repression of Tibetans and Uighers were intolerable sins for men and women of goodwill. And Chinese support for the Sudan government, despite its genocidal policy toward the inhabitants of the Darfur region, aroused further indignation. But for the Bush administration—and the majority of the national security elite—these issues were negligible when weighed against the need for China's help in dealing with North Korea.

In July, Pyongyang caught the world's attention by firing a long-range ballistic missile. The possibility of North Korea's acquiring the capability to launch nuclear-tipped missiles shattered Bush's resolve to reject negotiations with Kim Jong Il's regime. Bush and Hu shared their concerns, and Bush, to the discomfort of Vice President Richard Cheney and Defense Secretary Rumsfeld, set the Department of State to work with the Chinese Foreign Ministry to find a way to restrain Kim. In October the North Koreans removed any remaining doubt about whether they had nuclear weapons by testing a nuclear device. Chinese and American negotiators intensified their consultations. With China taking the lead, six-party talks on dismantling North Korea's nuclear weapons began in December. In February 2007 an agreement was reached to get Pyongyang to dismantle its main reactor in return for fuel aid—an agreement very much like the one the Bush administration had denounced Clinton for accepting in 1994.

At home the Bush administration was in trouble, and the Chinese knew it. In the midterm elections in November 2006, the president's Republican Party, held responsible by the public for the unpopular war in Iraq, suffered major setbacks and lost control of Congress. The president had two years left to serve, but now he would be hamstrung at every turn by his political opponents. Demonstrating their increasingly sophisticated understanding of American politics, the Chinese pronounced Bush a "lame duck."

Assessing the immediate future, Chinese analysts worried about the new Congress. They noted that Congress was always a breeding ground for "China threat" theories, but they feared most the possibility of protectionism, recognizing that Democrats were more responsive to labor concerns about lost jobs and about "outsourcing" than were Republicans. They also perceived the Democrats to be more concerned with human rights issues. The road ahead might be bumpy, but the English-language *China Daily* laid out Beijing's official estimate: a solid foundation had been built for future cooperation between the two countries. China needed an open international system, and good relations with the United States were essential for its peaceful development—which would be in accord with American interests. American misgivings about China's development were unfortunate. It was time for them to act in accordance with their long-expressed desire to see the emergence of a strong, prosperous, and open China.

The schizophrenic nature of the relationship persisted through the remaining years of the Bush administration. One American analyst called the relationship stable and complicated. Parts of each government worked well together, at least on some issues, and other parts seemed determined to roil the waters. No clear, consistent pattern emerged. In January 2007 the Chinese conducted an anti-satellite test, destroying one of their aging devices. The test was seen in Washington as a threat to American satellite communications, an essential element of the capability of the U.S. military. Vice President Cheney criticized the test and warned of China's rapid military buildup. Inquiries to Beijing went unanswered, and the foreign ministry seemed genuinely puzzled and apparently uninformed about the test. Despite increasing contacts and growing cooperation between the Pentagon and the PLA, mutual suspicion lingered.

Similarly, the Bush administration had soured on Chen Shui-bian and indicated publicly its unhappiness with his continuing provocations.

Nonetheless, he was allowed to make stopovers in the United States on his international travels, reinforcing Chinese skepticism about American determination to restrain him. Moreover, in February 2007 the Department of Defense announced a plan to sell Patriot missiles to Taiwan. And when, shortly after returning to Taipei, Chen announced his four "wants," including independence and a change of name from the Republic of China to something more indicative of Taiwan's de facto independence, Beijing was not satisfied with American criticism. The PLA continued to augment its offensive capability across the Taiwan Strait and warned the United States not to interfere.

It was apparent that the United States had minimal influence over the democratically elected president of Taiwan, but Deputy Secretary of State John Negroponte tried to appease China by criticizing Chen's decision to hold a referendum on the island on the question of whether to attempt to join the United Nations as "Taiwan." Although the Chinese ambassador in Washington expressed China's appreciation, the PLA was focused on missile sales and, as retribution, denied several U.S. naval vessels entry to Hong Kong. Once such incident gained considerable press coverage in the United States: on Thanksgiving Day 2007 the *U.S.S. Kitty Hawk* was sent away while the families of the ship's crew waited ashore, preparing to celebrate the holiday. In February 2008 Thomas Fingar, the highly respected deputy director of National Intelligence, a longtime student of Chinese politics, declared the military confrontation in the Strait as one of the most worrisome threats to American interests.

In the spring of 2008, as the people of Taiwan prepared to vote for a new president, both Chinese and American leaders hoped Chen's party would be driven from power, easing the crisis in the Strait. Fearful that a DPP victory might trigger an attack by the PLA, two U.S. carrier battle groups hovered in the area to act as a deterrent. Even as it became evident that Ma Ying-cheou, the Kuomintang candidate who favored improved relations with the mainland, would win the election, the Chinese continued to fret—fearing that the American-educated Ma would gain new support for Taiwan from Washington. Ma's election in May, however, came as a tremendous relief to both the American and Chinese governments— and resulted, at least in the short run, in greatly reduced tension in the Strait. In the months that followed, American military analysts concluded that a fundamental change in PLA tactics, a shift from plans to invade Taiwan to a posture designed to prevent a Taiwanese declaration of independence, had taken place.

The pattern of alternating highs and lows was equally apparent in economic relations between the United States and the People's Republic. Washington accused Beijing of subsidizing exports and threatened to impose tariffs on Chinese goods. A few weeks later the United States filed a complaint with the WTO alleging Chinese violations of intellectual property rights (IPRs). But in May, in another Strategic Economic Dialogue, Chinese representatives agreed to increase market access, open their financial sector to foreign investment, promote energy security, protect the environment, and strengthen the rule of law, especially as applied to IPRs.

Preceding and following the dialogue, the issue of product safety made headlines internationally. The cause of the deaths of many American dogs and cats was traced to toxins in pet food originating in China. Tensions rose as poisons were found in toothpaste and prescription drugs, illegal antibiotics in catfish, eels and shrimp, melanin in milk products, and lead paint on toys imported from China. The Chinese launched a public relations offensive to demonstrate renewed efforts to regulate and monitor the production of all the tainted items, but they also replied by condemning American food and health-supplement exports to China. They declared American sardines, beef, pork, and chicken unsafe. And in September they launched their first case against American trade practices in the WTO. Both American and Chinese officials acknowledged that quarrels over such issues would never disappear, but the two countries had mechanisms for managing them. It seemed unlikely that they would ever disrupt their relationship, however bumpy they might make it.

Chinese diplomatists demonstrated striking sophistication in the early years of the twentieth-first century and worked increasingly well with their American counterparts. Again, some of the differences between the two nations were likely to persist for some long time. China's interest in exploiting the resources of neighboring Burma and its indifference to the brutality of the Burmese military junta, its lack of sympathy for the democracy movement in that benighted country, precluded support for American pressures on the Burmese regime. Similarly, it was unmoved by the atrocious practices and corruption of Robert Mugabe's government, continued to provide it with arms, and obstructed efforts to call Mugabe to account. Its policy toward Iran often frustrated American and European diplomats trying to prevent Iran from obtaining nuclear weapons—although there were occasional indications that the nonproliferation cause had its advocates in Beijing, even if China's thirst for oil trumped their efforts.

However, more hopeful signs of a willingness to cooperate appeared. The Chinese government was embarrassed by the public relations campaign challenging its support of the Sudanese government accused of genocide in Darfur—at a time when China was preparing to take its place in the sun by hosting the 2008 Olympics. Suddenly a special Chinese envoy appeared in Khartoum and, in concert with American efforts, gently nudged Sudan's leaders to cooperate with the UN. Progress was minimal, but the Americans expressed appreciation for the Chinese effort. Most obvious—and most important—was the Chinese diplomatic effort with North Korea.

China was probably the only country in the world with any leverage over Kim Jong Il—and it did not have much. It could hamper the flow of food and energy that North Korea needed desperately, but with a government indifferent to the suffering of its people and unanswerable to anyone, Chinese pressures had limited impact. Moreover, Kim and his court were not unaware that the Chinese feared the collapse of his regime. If the North Korean government crashed, thousands of North Korean refugees could be expected to pour into Manchuria—a flow China anticipated having to staunch forcibly. Moreover, the collapse of the Democratic People's Republic of Korea leading to the reunification of Korea might extend American influence to China's northeast border. It was not a scenario anyone in Beijing welcomed. Carefully weighing its interests and options, China took the lead in pushing the North Koreans *and* the Americans into talks. Chinese leaders considered a nuclear-armed North Korea undesirable. They did not want the Japanese to use Kim's nuclear weapons as a rationale for developing their own; nor did they want to risk an American attack on North Korea. The principal American negotiator, Assistant Secretary of State Christopher Hill, and Secretary of State Rice praised the Chinese efforts and saw them as improving Chinese-American relations.

Many prominent Americans, such as Carla Hill, former USTR, and Admiral Dennis Blair, former CINCPAC, argued that the policy of engaging China had been an enormous success, contending that it had brought great prosperity to both countries and had facilitated the peaceful development of East Asia. They called for greater efforts to integrate China into the international community, a positive approach to China's rise rather than an attempt to contain the People's Republic. Polls commissioned by the Committee of 100, an organization of leading Chinese Americans, indicated public pressure for a tougher policy toward China was lacking. But in addition to differences over economic matters between the United States and China, profound concerns about Beijing in the Pentagon and in the human rights community remained—and these were shared by the American public.

In May 2007 the U.S. Department of Defense issued its 2007 *Report on Chinese Power*, which expressed uneasiness about the opaqueness of China's military spending program and the threat of Chinese military power to American interests. The Chinese reacted angrily, insisting the Pentagon exaggerated the threat. In June Secretary of Defense Robert Gates, successor to the discredited Rumsfeld, met with Chinese defense leaders in Shanghai and succeeded in lowering temperatures on both sides. Ever more military-to-military contacts were arranged, and a few months later a military hotline was established between defense departments. The Chinese media reported that more cooperation than competition now existed between the two sides. Early in 2008 several retired American flag officers launched the "Sanya Initiative," a program through which they met regularly with Chinese counterparts in an effort to counter the warnings of American analysts who trumpeted the China threat. Nevertheless military-to-military relations remained relatively undeveloped and characterized by mutual mistrust and were usually the first to be disrupted whenever the Chinese were irritated by American actions.

The one issue that could not be resolved—and possibly will never be resolved —was human rights. In the cold war era Washington consistently ignored human rights violations in countries friendly to the United States. In the 1970s and 1980s that included China. After the collapse of the Soviet Union, China became less important strategically, and misgivings over Beijing's domestic policies, specifically how it treated its people, were less easily muffled. The June 4, 1989, massacres focused the attention of the American people on China's human rights record, and Americans did not like what they saw. The United States was forced by nongovernmental organizations (NGOs), such as Amnesty International and Human Rights Watch, the Dalai Lama, and exiled Chinese activists to protest Chinese behavior. Congress demanded annual reports on the state of human rights around the world and demonstrated particular interest in China's progress—or lack thereof—toward more humane treatment of its people. In the early years of the twenty-first century Americans constantly complained, and the Chinese constantly rejected those complaints. Occasionally, however, they released a dissident from prison, as when Wei Jingsheng and Wang Dan were shipped to the United States. By the time the Bush administration took hold in Washington, it was apparent that even without the cold war good relations with China were enormously important. Kissinger and his disciples consistently argued that what China did within its borders did not matter nearly as much as achieving Chinese cooperation on a host of global issues, such as nuclear nonproliferation and the war on terror. These so-called realists, supported by much of the business community, rejected the priority the human rights community gave to the Chinese government's treatment of dissidents, its unwillingness to allow its people religious freedom, and its suppression of Tibetan culture. But many members of Congress, conservatives and liberals alike, were appalled by Beijing's abuses, and no administration in Washington could evade the issue.

In March 2007 the Department of State's human rights report referred to the People's Republic as one of the world's most systematic violators of human rights. In June President Bush, visiting Prague, met with Rebiya Kadeer, a Uigher dissident recently released from a Chinese prison. In October he met with the Dalai Lama, who was in Washington to receive the Congressional Gold Medal. Congress, too, issued a report critical of China's human rights record. In February 2008 a senior State Department official met with the Dalai Lama and criticized Chinese policy toward Tibet. On each of these occasions Chinese spokesmen protested, but as the Chinese ambassador to the United States conceded, leaders in Beijing had little hope of persuading Americans to stop interfering in what they, like Kissinger, righteously called their internal affairs.

Anti-Chinese riots in Tibet early in 2008 led to condemnations in the Western media of China's role there. On this occasion it was evident that the Tibetan demonstrators had lost patience with the peaceful efforts of the Dalai Lama to achieve independence for his country, committed acts of violence against Chinese in Lhasa, and provoked a forceful response from the local Chinese authorities. An apparently spontaneous outburst of anti-Western, intensely nationalistic demonstrations ensued across China. Few Chinese questioned their government's contention that Tibetan society was feudal and barbaric and that China was bringing civilization and economic development to the region. Many were outraged by what appeared to be Western bias in favor of Tibet—disregard for Tibetan provocations and gratuitous criticism of China. The Dalai Lama was embarrassed by the violent actions of his erstwhile followers, and the Chinese government blamed him and attacked him with relentlessly crude propaganda.

Tibet's plight was quickly forgotten when a severe earthquake, killing tens of thousands, hit Sichuan province in May. The Chinese people gained the world's sympathy as they grappled with this disaster, and their government won applause for its rapid response to the tragedy, which contrasted favorably with the nearly simultaneous refusal of the Burmese government to help many thousands of its people savaged by storms and flooding.

In the United States the primary focus of the media in mid-2008 was the upcoming presidential election. The travails of the American economy, teetering on a recession with mounting unemployment and a threat of inflation, were uppermost in the minds of the people, and the continuing wars in Iraq and Afghanistan were also troubling. Some Americans worried about North Korea's nuclear weapons and Iran's nuclear program, but policy toward China was not a major issue before the election was over. Only in August when all eyes were focused on the 2008 Beijing Summer Olympics, was China center stage.

For the Chinese government, the opportunity to host the Olympics enabled it to demonstrate to the world the country's new wealth, status, and national pride, which it considered a vindication of its policies over the past quarter century. It spent billions of dollars to prepare Beijing, importing great architects from all over the globe to construct world-class buildings. Pictures of the "Bird's Nest" and the "Water Cube," the principal stadium and the structure for aquatic events, respectively, appeared constantly on television and in magazines and newspapers across the world. It made extraordinary efforts to reduce pollution in the city, moving factories, restricting traffic, and sending away workers whose physical appearance did not meet the standard of modernity party leaders wished to display. The opening of the games— a truly impressive display unmatched by any city that had ever hosted the games before— was spectacular. And Chinese athletes performed magnificently, winning more gold medals than those of any other country.

On the other hand, the Chinese government made only cosmetic efforts to comply with its promise to the Olympic Committee to improve its human rights performance and to allow complete freedom to the foreign press. It spent extraordinary sums of money to enhance security in Beijing, to suppress dissent. Cameras were set up throughout the city. The police and military presence increased enormously, and potential Chinese demonstrators were detained well before the games began. Out-of-town petitioners seeking redress of grievances against officials in their native towns and villages were prevented from entering the city and either returned home quickly or were held by police if they penetrated the first layer of security. When the foreign reporters and photographers arrived, they found their movements restricted and their access to sensitive Internet sites blocked. Responding to criticism the government announced the establishment of zones in three parks where protesters might assemble—but licensed no one to assemble in them and detained most people who applied. The protest zones thus remained empty during all the athletic events. A few foreign protesters, advocates for causes such as freedom of religion or freedom for Tibet, attempted to unfurl banners near the site of the games or in Tiananmen Square but were quickly stopped by the police and deported. Contrary to the hopes of the Olympic Committee and of men and women of goodwill throughout the world, the Chinese government became more rather than less repressive as it hosted athletes and dignitaries from around the world, including the American president, George W. Bush.

In the fall of 2008 the presidential election returned to the forefront of public interest in the United States. The Chinese, generally uneasy about any change of administration in Washington, preferring to deal with the devil they knew, waited patiently for the outcome. Little progress was made on any of the bilateral issues that divided China and the United States. Bush, a remarkably unpopular president, had limited influence and little political capital. The Chinese would wait for the next administration, but, unfortunately, so would the North Koreans. Only the moderation of tensions in the Taiwan Strait moved apace without the Americans. But even the issue of Taiwan's status could easily flare up, as when the Bush administration announced a major arms sale to Taiwan in October, triggering an angry Chinese response including cancellation of high-level military-to-military talks and ship visits to Chinese ports. In all, however, the Chinese—and Americans responsible for policy toward China—were relieved to find both presidential campaigns focused on other issues.

The electoral victory of Barack Obama in November delighted much of the world but not Chinese leaders. Quite apart from the Chinese disdain for blacks, whether African or African American, the government of the People's Republic has persistently favored continuity in Washington.

Given its dependence on export trade to sustain China's economic growth, it is especially suspicious of presumably pro-labor Democrats. The Chinese Communist Party tolerates no free unions at home, no nongovernmental workers organizations. It is fearful that American workers, fighting to keep their jobs, will succeed in using their influence with the new Democratic-controlled government to gain protectionist policies. It anticipates increased pressure to stop manipulating its currency. Beijing also continues to suspect Democrats, not least Hillary Clinton, the new secretary of state, of being too closely allied with human rights activists.

In speeches delivered in Washington in December 2008, both the Chinese ambassador and the Chinese State Council's principal spokesman on foreign affairs spoke warmly of the mutually beneficial relationship that existed between China and the United States and of the importance to China of maintaining course. But they both laid down markers for the incoming administration: stay away from China's "core" interests in Taiwan and Tibet—and avoid protectionism.

The Chinese probably have little to worry about. The new president has never demonstrated much interest in policy toward China and has more pressing foreign as well as domestic issues to confront. Neither he nor Hillary Clinton has ever questioned the value of the policy of engaging China; neither has any ties to Taiwan. Both are certain to criticize China's human rights performance—which regressed in 2008—but both have surrounded themselves with "realist" advisers who can be expected to give priority to strategic and economic issues. Barring extraordinary circumstances, such as a PLA attack on Taiwan, a concerted offensive against American space satellites, or some other major effort to disrupt American strategic communications, the Chinese will find the continuity they crave in Washington's policies.

Many years ago, in the conclusion of his classic study of the Far Eastern policy of the United States, A. Whitney Griswold remarked that the Far East was still as remote, "relatively," from the United States in 1938 as it had been in the era of sail. No one would make that claim at the beginning of the twenty-first century. East Asia has become an inescapable part of the American present—and of the American future. Retreat from the tremendous involvement on the Asian mainland occasioned by the war in Vietnam was inevitable, but a retreat to indifference toward Asia proved impossible. In addition to the rise of the strongest Chinese state in the American experience, the United States had to adjust to the economic power of Japan, the burgeoning economic power of Korea, Taiwan, and the countries comprising ASEAN (Association of Southeast Asian Nations), and, in the late 1990s, the Asian financial crisis. Asian culture, most obviously food and art, permeates the culture of the United States. Asian Americans constitute a new intellectual elite in American society and have become increasingly active politically. Large numbers of recent Asian immigrants strengthen the links that bind the United States to those lands across the Pacific. In an era when businesspeople, scholars, and strategists are focusing on the "Pacific rim," American statesmen can no longer be mere "Atlanticists."

In the early years of the twenty-first century, two major issues continue to divide China and the United States. The first is clearly ideological: Americans will never again trust a communist dictatorship that denies basic freedoms to its own people. The second, Taiwan, became ideological when democracy emerged on the island. American leaders speak in good faith when they declare again and again that they can—and will—accept any solution acceptable to both the people of Taiwan and those of the mainland, any peaceful resolution of their differences. But after Taiwan became a functioning democracy controlled by the majority Taiwanese, it was evident that they were highly unlikely ever to accept Beijing's rule. On the other hand, there was no reason to doubt Beijing's continued determination to prevent Taiwan from being accepted as an independent nation by the international community. Trying to discourage Taipei from acting provocatively, Washington prefers to remain ambiguous as to how it would respond if war broke out between Taiwan and the People's Republic. There appears to be a consensus among American leaders, however, that the United States would be obliged to come to the defense of Taiwan in the event of an unprovoked attack.

Neither of these issues is susceptible to American-imposed solutions. Chinese leaders will carry out political reforms if and when reforms serve their purposes. Optimists point to the village elections of the late 1990s and see movement, however glacial, toward democracy. Others see evidence of genuine interest in the rule of law and developments in China that suggest the possibility of an independent legal system in the near future. Still others have been impressed by Beijing's tolerance of democratic institutions in Hong Kong after the territory's reversion to Chinese rule in 1997. On the other hand, it is absolutely clear that China's communists are determined to control the flow of information to their people and that they will not permit the organization of an opposition party. Frequent arrests of Internet operators and would-be party organizers demonstrate the limits of their tolerance. Americans can and will provide support for elections, for the rule of law, and for the people of Hong Kong, but their influence will be marginal at best.

More frightening is the division over Taiwan. Nothing Americans can say or do is likely to persuade China to surrender its claim to sovereignty over the island. Everything the United States does to support the Taipei regime, including the arms sales required by the Taiwan Relations Act of 1979, serves as an irritant and allows Beijing to justify steps it takes around the world that run counter to American interests. In 1999 it was apparent that China was stationing scores of missiles across the Strait from Taiwan, and American intelligence officers estimated that there likely would be hundreds of missiles aimed at Taiwan from the Chinese side over the next several years. In response, Taipei's friends in the United States lobbied for the island to be included in a theater missile defense (TMD) program the American government was exploring for protection of its forces and friends against possible North Korean missile attacks. Few analysts outside of the Pentagon and the defense industry thought such an antiballistic missile defense was feasible, and fewer still imagined it could prevent Beijing from devastating Taiwan, but the Chinese were infuriated by the possibility of Washington making TMD available to Taipei. American officials were displeased by the evident intent of China to step up its intimidation of the islanders. The impasse continued. Continued high-level talks between American and China leaders reduced the likelihood of a confrontation between their countries, but both Taipei and Beijing are capable of provoking a new crisis at any moment.

Given the realities of China's new role in the world, it is apparent that Americans are going to have to do what they do least well: learn to live with uncertainties and unresolved issues. They will have to keep talking to people they do not like and accept the fact that those people will continue to do things that Americans find intolerable. They will have to recognize that although their country entered the twenty-first century as the most powerful nation in the world, it will not be able to control the actions of other peoples. In due course, they may even understand the need for engagement with China.

As I write in the summer of 2009, it is clear that that the power of the United States relative to China has declined strikingly over the last decade. While the Chinese economy grew at an exceptionally rapid rate, the American economy stalled and, triggering in 2008 the worst financial crisis since the Great Depression, slid into recession. Globalization, the growing interdependence of national economies, guaranteed that much of the rest of the world would also be hurt badly by conditions in the United States. Practicing state capitalism, China was less exposed to the vagaries of the market, but it could not escape the worldwide downturn. American consumers were the principal purchasers of Chinese exports, and a large percentage of China's trillions of dollars in foreign reserves were in U.S. Treasury bonds. The Chinese might take some pleasure in the failures of the American system, but they too would suffer from them. As the Nobel Prize–winning economist Paul Krugman quipped, the United States had achieved a balance of trade with China: the Chinese ship Americans poisoned toys and seafood, and Americans pay them with fraudulent bonds.

Similarly, American influence in the world, having peaked in the "unipolar moment" of the late 1990s, is probably at its lowest level since the 1930s. The administration of George W. Bush succeeded where the propagandists employed by Hitler, Stalin, and Mao failed: it made the United States a pariah, largely as a result of its invasion of Iraq, its approval of torture in violation of the Geneva Convention, the symbolism of the Guantanamo prison complex, and the appalling photographs of the mistreatment of prisoners at Abu Ghraib. International public opinion polls recorded widespread unhappiness with the United States, even among its allies—and a broad consensus that Washington posed a greater threat to the world than did Beijing.

There can be no doubt as to the importance of the United States getting its economy back on track and regaining the moral leadership it won at great cost during World War II and the cold war. As the largest debtor nation, it can no longer use its largesse to aid old friends and gain new ones. Indeed, many of its actions internationally are constrained by the fact that it has to borrow money from China, now the leading creditor nation, and other governments that do not share American values and goals. Regaining respect for the United States will not be easy, and it will not happen quickly—and certainly not without practicing some of the humility that George W. Bush urged in his 2000 presidential campaign.

A long time ago, before the Opium War, China was able to dictate the terms of its contact with the United States and most of the rest of the world. For better or worse, the rise of Chinese power in the early years of the twenty-first century, coincident with America's decline, suggests that

China will, more often than not, be calling the tune for the foreseeable future. Simply stated, Washington has little leverage with the men in Beijing. American leaders' best hope for good relations with China requires focusing on common interests, such as nuclear nonproliferation, suppression of criminal activity, especially the drug trade, environmental problems, the search for alternative sources of energy, and efforts to minimize the dangers from terrorists.

If there is a basis for optimism, it can be found in the fact that the existing international system, largely an American creation, has made China rich and powerful: it now has a stake in preserving it. China needs a benign international environment in which to continue its economic growth—and that growth is essential if the Chinese Communist Party is to preserve its monopoly on power. Chinese leaders have been responsive to American arguments when persuaded they are being asked to conform to international norms rather than to serve American interests. China has been engaged actively in UN peacekeeping operations and has shown restraint in its exercise of veto power in the Security Council. It has won its current standing by behaving responsibly.

With the overwhelming exception of its posture toward Taiwan, which it considers a domestic affair, Chinese foreign policy has been flexible and pragmatic. The People's Republic shows no signs of aggressive intent toward anyone. Its leadership appears "risk-averse" and American military analysts discern no Chinese effort to develop force projection capabilities outside East Asia. The PLA air force and navy are at least a generation behind those of the United States, although they are likely to achieve parity with American forces in the western Pacific by 2015, leaving Taiwan without defense.

Of course, there are no indications that Washington and Beijing can resolve their differences over Taiwan. Nonetheless, if the Chinese remain eager to avoid conflict and willing to tolerate Taiwan's autonomy, and if Taiwan avoids steps toward formal independence, the issue should be manageable. The trend toward eventual integration of the two entities seems inexorable as their economies intermingle, intermarriage grows because hundreds of thousands of Taiwanese businessmen reside on the mainland, and tourism and direct air communications across the Strait increase.

Looking past the Taiwan issue, other reasons can be found for unease about the future of Chinese-American relations. Although the ideological hostility of the Maoist era and the immediate aftermath of the Tiananmen massacres hardly exists today outside the PLA in China and the far Right in the United States, it will continue to flare up. Political reform in China is not progressing. The growing middle class is content with things as they are. It has been co-opted and will not champion political reform, liberal democracy, or a multiparty system. Nor is there much evidence of increased respect for human rights among China's rulers. And whenever China persecutes Tibetans, Christians, or human rights activists, whenever the government suppresses civil society, Americans will respond angrily. American criticism of Chinese behavior will exacerbate already virulent nationalism, provoking rage at the audacity of those who would meddle in China's internal affairs. These incidents are unlikely to lead to conflict, but they are constant reminders of the difference in values between the two societies and reinforce China's determination to replace the United States as the world's dominant power—and to balance the United States in the near term. Similarly, American leaders will see no choice but to resist China's growing military power. The United States will spare no effort to maintain air and naval superiority in the western Pacific and to strengthen its alliances in the region.

It should not be forgotten that China is still a poor country measured in per capita income. Its continued economic growth is challenged by enormous environmental problems. The World Health Organization estimates that air pollution in China causes 400,000 premature deaths annually. The country suffers from a serious shortage of water—and much of what it has is toxic, unsuitable for industry or agriculture. In addition, there are serious demographic problems—the familiar one of a rapidly aging population and the less common one of a grave shortage of women (118 men for every 100 women), caused by widespread abortion of female fetuses by families determined to have their one child be a boy. The distribution of the great wealth accumulated since Deng introduced his economic reforms is extraordinarily unequal, leaving huge numbers of Chinese poor and dissatisfied. The country is plagued by social tensions; thousands of demonstrations occur there every year because the people have little means of obtaining redress peacefully. And all these problems are aggravated by endemic corruption.

In brief, it is conceivable that the greatest danger posed by China is not its rising power but the possibility, however remote, that it will collapse.

Many years ago, Theodore Roosevelt declared that "it is to the advantage, and not to the disadvantage of other nations when any nation becomes stable and prosperous, able to keep the peace within its own borders, and strong enough not to invite aggression from without. We heartily hope for the progress of China, and so far as by peaceable and legitimate means we are able we will do our part toward furthering that progress."[3] Today, much as in the time of Theodore Roosevelt, American leaders want— and American interests require—a peaceful, prosperous, open, responsible, and cooperative China. The chances of China realizing those hopes are reasonably good, given the extent of shared interests and what are likely to be the primarily domestic concerns of both nations in the near term. Americans who study and work on Chinese-American affairs would also like to see a democratic and friendly China. They are not likely to see either in the foreseeable future. And in the early years of the new millennium most Americans are not so sure that a strong China is in their nation's interest.

Notes

1. The Development of the Treaty System

1. Memorial, I-li-pu to the Emperor, February 6, 1841, Earl Swisher, ed., *China's Management of the American Barbarians* (New Haven: Yale University Press, 1953), pp. 57–58.

2. Edict, November 15, 1843, ibid., p. 137.

3. Memorial, Ch'eng Yü-ts'ai to the Emperor, April 22, 1844, ibid., p. 146.

4. Memorial, Ch'eng Yü-ts'ai to the Emperor, April 9, 1844, ibid., pp. 142–143.

5. Memorial, Ch'i-ying to the Emperor, December 14, 1844, ibid., p. 177.

6. William B. Reed to Lewis Cass, June 30, 1858, 36th Cong., 1st sess., *Senate Executive Document No. 30*, p. 355.

7. Memorial, Lin-k'uei to the Emperor, March 15, 1851, in Swisher, *China's Management of the American Barbarians*, pp. 190–191.

8. Memorial, Prince Kung to the Emperor, January 24, 1861, ibid., p. 697.

9. W. A. P. Martin, *The Awakening of China* (New York: Doubleday, Page, 1910), p. 169.

2. The United States as a Power in East Asia

1. Immanuel C. Y. Hsü, *China's Entrance Into the Family of Nations* (Cambridge: Harvard University Press, 1960), p. 170.

2. Rockhill to Alfred Hippisley, October 30, 1894, quoted in Marilyn Blatt Young, *Rhetoric of Empire* (Cambridge: Harvard University Press, 1968), p. 22.

3. Richard W. Leopold, *Growth of American Foreign Policy* (New York: Knopf, 1962), p. 212.

4. Wu T'ing-fang to John Hay, September 12, 1899, U.S. State Department, *Foreign Relations of the United States* (Washington, D.C.: GPO, 1901), p. 214. This series will be cited hereafter as *Foreign Relations*.

5. Olney to Charles Denby, minister to China, September 19, 1895, quoted in Young, *Rhetoric of Empire*, p. 81.

6. Roosevelt to George Ferdinand Becker, July 8, 1901, in Elting E. Morrison, et al., eds., *Letters of Theodore Roosevelt*, 8 vols. (Cambridge: Harvard University Press, 1951–1954), 3:112. Hereafter cited as *Letters*.

7. Roosevelt to Albert Shaw, June 22, 1903, *Letters*, 3:497–498.

8. Roosevelt to Hay, July 29, 1903, *Letters*, 3:532.

3. In the Light of the Rising Sun

1. Roosevelt to Spring Rice, March 19, 1904, in Elting E. Morrison et al., eds., *Letters of Theodore Roosevelt*, 8 vols. (Cambridge: Harvard University Press, 1951–1954), 4:760.

2. Roosevelt to T. C. Friedlander, November 23, 1905, *Letters*, 5:90–91.

3. Roosevelt to J. P. Morgan, July 18, 1905, *Letters*, 4:1278–1279.

4. Theodore Roosevelt, *State Papers as Governor and President, 1899–1909* (New York: Scribner's, 1925), pp. 376–377.

5. Roosevelt to Elihu Root, September 26, 1907, *Letters*, 5:809.

6. "The Awakening of China," *Outlook* (1908), 90:665–667.

7. Robert Irick, "The Chinchow–Aigun Railroad and the Knox Neutralization Plan in Ch'ing Diplomacy," *Harvard Papers on China*, 13:89.

8. Taft to Prince Ch'un, in U.S. State Department, *Foreign Relations of the United States* (Washington, D.C.: GPO, 1909), p. 214.

9. Roosevelt to Taft, December 22, 1910, *Letters*, 4:190.

10. Quoted in Henry F. Pringle, *Life and Times of William Howard Taft*, 2 vols. (Hamden: Archon Books, 1964; reprint), 2:685–686.

11. E. David Cronon, ed., *Cabinet Diaries of Josepheus Daniels, 1913–1921* (Lincoln: University of Nebraska Press, 1963), p. 8.

12. Ibid., p. 17.

13. *Foreign Relations*, 1913, p. 109.

14. *Foreign Relations*, 1914, Supplement, pp. 189–190.

15. Wilson to Bryan, April 14, 1915, quoted in Arthur Link, *Wilson* (Princeton: Princeton University Press, 1960), 3:294.

16. *Foreign Relations*, 1919, p. 282.

4. The Response to Chinese Nationalism

1. Reinsch to Lansing, U.S. Department of State Decimal File, 893.00/3235, National Archives (hereafter referred to by number, NA).

2. Schurman to Hughes, in U.S. State Department, *Foreign Relations of the United States* (Washington, D.C: GPO, 1921), 1:315–320.

3. *Foreign Relations*, 1922, 1:707.

4. Schurman to Coolidge, April 8, 1924, Jacob Gould Schurman Papers, Collection of Regional History, Cornell University.

5. Huston to MacMurray, April 30, 1925, J. V. A. MacMurray Papers, Princeton University.

6. Transcript of lecture given at Foreign Service School, Washington, D.C., May 1925, MacMurray Papers.

7. MacMurray to Kellogg, quoted in Dorothy Borg, *American Policy and the Chinese Revolution, 1925—1928* (New York: Institute of Pacific Relations, 1947), p. 63.

8. "Kao wu-sa yung-tung chung wei min-tzu fen-tou te min-chung" (Proclaim May Thirtieth Movement as Masses Struggle for National Freedom), July 10, 1925, in *Chung-kuo wen-t'i chih-nan* (Guidebook to Questions of China), 2:65, Archives of the Bureau of Investigation, Ministry of Justice, Republic of China.

9. Johnson to William Castle, March 25, 1931, Papers of Nelson T. Johnson, Library of Congress. A copy of this letter, passed on to Stanley Hornbeck, chief, Division of Far Eastern Affairs, is filed as 893.00/11642, NA.

10. Ibid.

5. China as an Abstraction—The Conflict with Japan

1. Willys Peck, Consul General, Nanking, reporting interview with Soong, December 8, 1931, U.S. Department of State Decimal file, 893.00/11656, National Archives.

2. Memorandum, September 24, 1931, 793.94/1889, NA.

3. Memorandum of conversations, May 24, 1932, Papers of Nelson T. Johnson, Library of Congress.

4. Quoted by Peck, January 7, 1933, 893.00/12284, NA.

5. Memorandum of telephone conversation, January 13, 1933, 793.94/6064, NA.

6. Quoted in Dorothy Borg, *The United States and the Far Eastern Crisis of 1933–1938* (Cambridge: Harvard University Press, 1964), pp. 569–101.

7. Johnson to Hornbeck, June 1, 1933, Papers of Nelson T. Johnson, Library of Congress.

8. Diary of William Phillips, June 24, 1935, Harvard University.

9. Lamont to Nelson Johnson, May 19, 1936, Papers of Nelson T. Johnson, Library of Congress.

10. As reported in the diary of William Phillips, December 12, 1934, Harvard University.

11. Hornbeck to Johnson, March 13, 1937, 711.93/350, NA.

12. Quoted in Borg, *The United States and the Far Eastern Crisis*, p. 315.

13. Quoted in Wang Chien-min, *Chung-Kuo Kung Ch'an Tang Shih-Kao* (Taipei, 1965), 3:33.

14. Quoted in Jerome Ch'en, *Mao and the Chinese Revolution* (New York: Oxford University Press, 1967), p. 230.

15. As reported in the diary of J. P. Moffat, September 29, 1937, Harvard University.

16. Davis to Anthony Eden, as reported in the diary of J. P. Moffat, November 2, 1937, Harvard University.

17. Forwarded by Ambassador Hu Shih to Pittman, April 10, 1939, SEN 76A–F9 CFR Neutrality China–Japan, Papers of the Senate Foreign Relations Committee, NA.

18. Undated memorandum [July 1939], Papers of Harriet Welling, University of Chicago.

19. Clark Eichelberger to William Allen White, October 1, 1940, with enclosure. Papers of William Allen White, Library of Congress.

20. Eichelberger to Mrs. Lewis Mumford, October 22, 1940, with enclosure. Papers of the Committee to Defend America by Aiding the Allies, Princeton University.

21. Quoted in Herbert Feis, *Road to Pearl Harbor* (New York: Atheneum, 1962), p. 318.

22. Consul General, Hankow, to Secretary of State, August 16, 1938, 793.94/13695, NA.

23. *New York Times*, October 31, 1944, p. 1.

6. Communism in China

1. Jacob Gould Schurman to President Calvin Coolidge, April 8, 1924, Schurman Papers, Cornell University.

2. Stimson to Legation, September 30, 1930, U.S. Department of State Decimal File, 893.00/11224A, National Archives.

3. Johnson to Stimson, October 12, 1930, 893.00B/771, NA.

4. Yang Chien remarks, forwarded by Willys Peck to Secretary of State, August 11, 1932, 893.00/12140, NA.

5. Johnson to Stimson, February 13, 1933, 893.00/12291, NA.

6. Forwarded by Hull to George H. Dern, September 19, 1935, 033.1190 Dern, George H./46, NA.

7. Johnson to Howard, December 31, 1935, Papers of Nelson T. Johnson, Library of Congress.

8. Counselor, American Embassy, to Secretary of State, enclosing Lattimore analysis and articles, August 2, 1937, 893.00/14179, NA.

9. Office of Naval Intelligence Report, 761.93/1623, NA.

10. Johnson to Hull, November 29, 1938, 893.00/14288, NA.

11. Everett Drumwright, abstract of dispatch prepared by Willys Peck, October 31, 1939, 893.00/14480, NA.

12. Gauss to Hull, October 3, 1941, 893.00/14800, NA.

13. John S. Service, October 9, 1944, Department of State, *United States Relations with China, with Special Reference to the Period 1944–1949* (Washington, D.C., 1949), p. 573. Hereafter cited as *The China White Paper.*

14. John Paton Davies Jr., November 7, 1944, Ibid, pp. 566–567.

15. Mao Tse-tung, "How Yu Kung Removed the Mountains," *Selected Works* (London: Lawrence and Wishart, 1956), 4:317–318. See also Kuomintang Bureau of Investigation Report No. 184, April 28, 1945, Archives of the Bureau of Investigation, Republic of China; and *Chieh-fang Jih-pao*, May 2 and 8, 1945.

16. Patrick J. Hurley, April 17, 1945, *The China White Paper*, p. 96.

17. Hu Hsi-kuei, *Shih-chü pien-hua ho wo-te fang-chen*, mimeographed transcript of lecture to cadres, August 30, 1945. Archives of the Bureau of Investigation, Republic of China.

18. Kuomintang Bureau of Investigation Report No. 229, March 11, 1946, reprinting undated document of January 1946. Archives of the Bureau of Investigation, Republic of China.

19. George F. Kennan, *Memoirs (1925–1950)* (New York: Bantam, 1969), p. 394.

20. J. Leighton Stuart, *Fifty Years in China* (New York: Random House, 1954), p. 202.

21. Dean Acheson, *Present at the Creation* (New York: Norton, 1969), p. 157.

22. Memorandum of Acheson-Bevin conversation, April 4, 1949, U.S. State Department, *Foreign Relations of the United States: Far East and Australasia* (Washington, D.C.: GPO, 1949), 7:1138–1141.

23. Interview with Huang Hua, October 1986. See my "Conversations with Chinese Friends: Zhou Enlai's Associates Reflect on Chinese-American Relations in the 1940s and the Korean War," *Diplomatic History* (1987), 9:283–9.

24. Letter of Transmittal, Acheson to Truman, July 30, 1949, *The China White Paper*, p. xvi.

25. Acheson to Truman, March 3, 1949, PSF/Box 205, Papers of Harry S. Truman, Harry S. Truman Library.

26. Kennan memorandum PPS 53 (enclosure dated June 23, 1949), July 6, 1949; *FRUS*, 1949, vol 9: *Far East, China*, pp. 356–64.

27. Kennan, *Memoirs*, p. 520.

28. Acheson, *Present at the Creation*, p. 474. Italics added.

7. The Great Aberration

1. Quoted in Eric Goldman, *The Crucial Decade—and After* (New York: Vintage, 1961), p. 116.

2. Record of Koo–Robertson discussions, November 12, 1954, Papers of V. K. Wellington Koo, Columbia University.

3. Quoted in John Gittings, *The World and China, 1922–1972* (New York: Harper & Row, 1974), p. 236.

4. Quoted in Roderick MacFarquhar, ed., *Sino-American Relations, 1949–1971* (Newton Abbot: David and Charles, 1972), p. 168.

5. Quoted in MacFarquhar, *Sino-American Relations*, p. 200.

6. Richard P. Stebbins, *The United States in World Affairs, 1965* (New York: Harper and Row, 1966), p. 148.

7. William P. Bundy, unpublished manuscript, chapter 32.

8. Rapprochement—At Last

1. Presidential press conference, December 10, 1970.

2. *Sino-U.S. Joint Communiqué*, February 28, 1972 (Peking: Foreign Languages Press, 1972), p. 6.

10. America in the Age of Chinese Power

1. David Finkelstein, *China Reconsiders Its National Security: "The Great Peace and Development Debate of 1999"* (Alexandria, Va.: The CNA Corporation, 2000).

2. New York: Palgrave Macmillan, 2006.

3. In Elting Morrison et al., eds., *Letters of Theodore Roosevelt*, 8 vols. (Cambridge: Harvard University Press, 1951–1954), 6:1405–1407.

Bibliographical Essay

The primary sources that have proved most useful to me are reflected in the endnotes. Although I have read in Chinese sources and interviewed Chinese and American participants, my interpretation rests largely on American archival and manuscript materials—and the work of other scholars. As a guide to the latter, I offer the following observations.

Two useful historiographic references are Warren I. Cohen, ed., *New Frontiers in American–East Asian Relations* (1983) and Warren I. Cohen, ed., *Pacific Passage* (1996). Of particular value in the latter volume is Chen Jian's comprehensive survey of the Chinese literature on Chinese-American relations.

For an understanding of the tribute system and the development of the treaty system, John K. Fairbank's *Trade and Diplomacy on the China Coast* (1953) remains the best point of departure. James L. Hevia's *Cherishing Men from Afar* (1995) offers a more generous analysis of the Chinese perspective in the late eighteenth century. The student who wishes to explore the American role in China from the American Revolution through the nineteenth century will find new works in relatively short supply, but would be well advised to start with Eileen P. Scully's essay in *Pacific Passage*. Kenneth S. Latourette's *The History of Early Relations Between the United States and China, 1784–1844* (1917) and Tyler Dennett's

Americans in East Asia (1922) continue to be useful. The most important survey of this period, however, is Michael H. Hunt's brilliant *The Making of a Special Relationship* (1983). Hunt's book is especially strong on the Chinese side and contains excellent bibliographic references. Edward V. Gulick's *Peter Parker and the Opening of China* (1973) is beautifully written as well as informative. A more recent essay by Macabe Keliher, "Anglo-American Rivalry and the Origin of U.S. China Policy," *Diplomatic History,* 31 (2007), gives more weight to the role of Caleb Cushing than Gulick or I have. Another work of considerable value, despite its narrow focus, is Jonathan Goldstein's *Philadelphia and the China Trade* (1978). Goldstein's argument raises important questions about Stuart Creighton Miller's *The Unwelcome Immigrant* (1969)—a bitter and sometimes overstated indictment of American attitudes toward the Chinese between 1785 and 1882. For attitudes toward the Chinese and their art in this period, see Janice P. Cohen and Warren I. Cohen, "Art and American Understanding of East Asian Culture, 1784–1900," in Akira Iriye, ed., *American–East Asian Cultural Relations* (1987).

Frederick Wakeman Jr.'s "High Ch'ing: 1638–1839," in James B. Crowley ed., *Modern East Asia* (1970) provides a wonderfully succinct introduction to China as the first American visitors found it. Mary Backus Rankin describes "Social and Political Change in Nineteenth-Century China" in Merle Goldman and Andrew Gordon, eds., *Historical Perspectives on Contemporary East Asia* (1999). Chinese attitudes and policies are examined in Wakeman's *Strangers at the Gate* (1966) and in the documents translated and edited by Earl Swisher in his *China's Management of the American Barbarians* (1953).

David L. Anderson's *Imperialism and Idealism* (1985) is a useful analysis of the thought of individual American policy makers, which also touches on the immigration issue. Valuable insights into the relevant aspects of American society in the last part of the nineteenth century are provided in John Higham's *Strangers in the Land* (1963), a study of attitudes toward immigrants, and in Walter LaFeber's classic *The New Empire* (1963) and his more recent *American Search for Opportunity, 1865–1913* (1993), both explanations of expansionist tendencies. Marilyn Blatt Young's "American Expansion, 1870–1900: The Far East," in Barton Bernstein's *Toward a New Past* (1968), is particularly thoughtful.

Missionary activities in this era and later can be followed in John K. Fairbank, ed., *The Missionary Enterprise in China and America* (1974), Fairbank and Suzanne W. Barnett, *Christianity in China* (1985), and Daniel

H. Bays, ed., *Christianity in China* (1996). Among a number of superb monographs, I found Jessie Lutz's *China and the Christian Colleges, 1850–1950* (1971) most useful. Irwin T. Hyatt's *Our Ordered Lives Confess* (1978), Philip West's *Yenching University and Sino-Western Relations, 1916–1952* (1976), and Jane Hunter's *The Gospel of Gentility* (1984) are also of exceptional interest.

A sampling of works on China after the Taiping Rebellion would still have to begin with Mary C. Wright's *The Last Stand of Chinese Conservatism* (1957). More specialized but also important are Immanuel C. Y. Hsu's *China's Entrance Into the Family of Nations* (1960) and Paul A. Cohen's *China and Christianity, 1860–1870* (1963). Cohen's essay, "Ch'ing China: Confrontation with the West, 1850–1900," in Crowley's *Modern East Asia,* is very useful. Knight Biggerstaff's "The Official Chinese Attitude Toward the Burlingame Mission," *American Historical Review,* 41 (1936) remains of interest. Albert Feuerwerker's *China's Early Industrialization* (1958) and Hao Yen-p'ing's *The Commercial Revolution in Nineteenth-Century China* (1986) provide valuable insights into the transformation of China's economy. Sherman Cochran's *Big Business in China* (1980) is a model study of how multinationals functioned there from 1890 to 1930. See also William Rowe's two-volume study of *Hankow* (1984, 1989) and R. Bin Wong, *China Transformed* (1997), a provocative and persuasive approach to China's economic development.

For the Boxer War and events preceding and following it, Michael Gasster's *China's Struggle to Modernize* (1972) is a tour de force. Li Chien-nung's *Political History of China, 1840–1928* (1956) remains a useful survey, of particular value for its coverage of the late nineteenth and early twentieth centuries. Luke Kwang's book on the reform movement of 1898, *A Mosaic of the Hundred Days* (1984) is now the standard work on the subject. On the Boxers, see Joseph Esherick, *The Origins of the Boxer Uprising* (1987) and Paul Cohen's magisterial *History in Three Keys: The Boxers as Event, Experience, and Myth* (1997). Michael Hunt's essay, "The Forgotten Occupation: Peking, 1900–1901" *Pacific Historical Review,* 48 (1979) is instructive on the American role.

There is an abundant literature on American policy toward China at the turn of the century—on the origins and meaning of the Open Door notes—but the reader must proceed with caution. A. Whitney Griswold's *The Far Eastern Policy of the United States* (1938) is seductively written but narrowly researched. Its persistent theme of British manipulation of the United States reflects what passed for wisdom and realism in the 1930s.

Paul A. Varg provides additional information of importance in his *Open Door Diplomat* (1952), which should be supplemented by Harvey Pressman's "Hay, Rockhill, and China's Integrity: A Reappraisal," *Papers on China* (Harvard University), 13 (1959). Charles S. Campbell's *Special Business Interests and the Open Door* (1951) and Marilyn Young's *Rhetoric of Empire* (1968) are essential to an understanding of the limited role played by American businessmen in the shaping of American policy. Thomas J. McCormick's *China Market* overstates the relationship between the search for economic opportunity and policy toward China. More convincing analyses can be found in several of the essays by economic historians, particularly that by Peter Schran, in Ernest R. May and John Fairbank, eds., *America's China Trade in Historical Perspective* (1986). Perhaps the most sensible place to start is with Akira Iriye's essay "Imperialism in East Asia," also in Crowley's *Modern East Asia.*

East Asian policies are sadly misunderstood in Howard K. Beale's *Theodore Roosevelt and the Rise of America to World Power* (1956). Because China was of so little importance to the United States in the early years of the twentieth century, the principal corrective studies have focused on Roosevelt and Japan. However, Raymond Esthus's "Changing Concepts of the Open Door, 1899–1910," *Mississippi Valley Historical Review*, 46 (1959) and Paul Varg's *The Making of a Myth* (1968) contain insights and information for both the Roosevelt and Taft years. Jerry Israel's *Progressivism and the Open Door* (1971) is provocative and thoughtful. In *The Foreign Policies of the Taft Administration* (1970) Walter Scholes and Mary Scholes cover China thoroughly. A particularly valuable explanation of Chinese policy in these years is Akira Iriye's "Public Opinion and Foreign Policy: The Case of Late Ch'ing China," in A. Feuerwerker et al., *Approaches to Modern Chinese History* (1967). Michael Hunt's prizewinning *Frontier Defense and the Open Door* (1973) supersedes all previous work on the subject, specifically for the years 1895 to 1911. Hunt does much to devalue Willard Straight's currency. See also Wang Guanhua, *In Search of Justice* (2001) for a superb study of the boycott of 1905.

Especially useful for examining Wilson's approach to East Asia are Roy Curry's *Woodrow Wilson and Far Eastern Policy* (1957), Li T'ien-yi's *Woodrow Wilson's China Policy, 1913–1917* (1952), and Arthur Link's *Wilson: The Struggle for Neutrality, 1914–1915* (1960). Noel Pugach's "Making the Open Door Work: Paul S. Reinsch in China, 1913–1919," *Pacific Historical Review*, 38 (1969) is thoughtful and balanced. For a more detailed account, see his *Paul S. Reinsch* (1979). Another view of Wilson's approach to China can be found in my "America's New Order for East Asia: The Four Power Financial Consortium and China, 1919–1946," in W. I. Cohen and K. W. So, *Essays in the History of China and Chinese-American Relations* (1982). For a superb historiographic article on Wilson as diplomatist, see David Steigerwald, "The Reclamation of Woodrow Wilson," *Diplomatic History,* 23 (1999). The most thorough examination of China's role in World War I is Xu Guoqi's *China and the Great War* (2005).

The standard study of the rise of Chinese nationalism after World War I is Chou Tse-tung's *The May Fourth Movement* (1960), but see also Bryna Goodman, *Native Place, City, and Nation* (1995), which focuses on developments over a broader period in the vicinity of Shanghai. Prasenjit Duara refers to everything of value on the subject in *Rescuing History from the Nation* (1995). My "America and the May Fourth Movement: The Response to Chinese Nationalism, 1917–1921," *Pacific Historical Review,* 35 (1966) is at best a useful backdrop to the major work on the response to Chinese nationalism, Dorothy Borg's *America and the Chinese Revolution, 1925–1928* (1947). Russell Buhite's "Nelson Johnson and American Policy Toward China, 1925–1928," *Pacific Historical Review,* 35 (1966) casts light on an important figure. My *Chinese Connection* (1978) also has material of value for this era, especially on the role of the mercenary journalist George E. Sokolsky. The single best book on the Guomindang regime in its first decade is Lloyd Eastman's *The Abortive Revolution* (1974).

For the postwar relations of the Pacific powers, Akira Iriye's classic *After Imperialism* is excellent, though excessively critical of American policy and too sanguine about Japanese policy. Iriye's book and Sadao Asada's "Japan's Special Interests and the Washington Conference, 1921–1922," *American Historical Review* 67 (1961) must be read to correct American misapprehensions about Japanese promises and practices. Roger Dingman's *Power in the Pacific* (1976) is also of value. J. Chalmers Vinson's *Parchment Peace* (1956) and Thomas H. Buckley's *The United States and the Washington Conference, 1921–1922* (1970) are useful studies of the American side. Vinson's book focuses on the Senate and public opinion, and Buckley analyzes diplomatic negotiations. Robert T. Pollard's *China's Foreign Relations, 1917–1931* (1933) remains of value, and Allen S. Whiting provides the Russian perspective in his *Soviet Policies in China, 1917–1921* (1954).

Robert H. Ferrell's *American Diplomacy in the Great Depression* (1957) places the response to the Manchurian "incident" in its proper setting. The best insights into the thought of Henry Stimson are found in Elting

E. Morison's *Turmoil and Tradition* (1960). Christopher Thorne's *The Limits of Foreign Policy* (1973) is a magnificent synthesis, highly critical of American policy. For a more sympathetic view of Stimson, see my "American Leaders and East Asia, 1931–1938," in Akira Iriye and Warren Cohen, eds., *American, Chinese, and Japanese Perspectives on Wartime Asia, 1939–1949* (1990). Discussions of the diplomacy of the Manchurian crisis by Luo Rongqu and Hosoya Chihiro in the Iriye and Cohen volume are strikingly—if not surprisingly—different.

Dorothy Borg begins her extraordinary *The United States and the Far Eastern Crisis of 1933–1938* (1964) with a summary analysis of the Manchurian incident and goes on to describe the astonishing passivity of the American government in the face of Japanese expansion in China. For a sense of the insignificance of American investments in China through 1937, C. F. Remer's *Foreign Investments in China* (1933) and Hou Chiming's *Foreign Investment and Economic Development in China, 1840–1937* (1965) are indispensable. James C. Thomson Jr.'s *While China Faced West* (1969) is an important study of the role of Americans as reformers in Chiang Kai-shek's China.

Unquestionably, the book with which to begin the study of American–East Asian relations in the 1930s is the prizewinning *Pearl Harbor as History* (1973), the results of a pathbreaking conference of Japanese and American scholars, edited by Dorothy Borg and Shumpei Okamoto. Herbert Feis's *Road to Pearl Harbor* (1950) remains useful for the years immediately preceding the conflict between the United States and Japan, but it must be supplemented by Waldo Heinrichs's brilliant *Threshhold of War* (1988). Paul W. Schroeder's *The Axis Alliance and Japanese-American Relations, 1941* (1958) raises important questions about the wisdom of American policy, especially in relation to Japanese activities in China.

For wartime diplomacy, Feis's *The China Tangle* is excellent on the American side. Xiaoyuan Liu has written a superb account, including wonderful material from the Chinese archives, in *A Partnership for Disorder* (1996), a book that covers the years 1941 to 1945. Three fine volumes of military history, *Stilwell's Mission to China* (1953), *Stilwell's Command Problems* (1956), and *Time Runs Out in CBI* (1959) were produced by Riley Sunderland and Charles Romanus. For a critical view of both Chiang and Stilwell, see F. F. Liu's *A Military History of Modern China, 1924–1949* (1956). Barbara Tuchman's *Stilwell and the American Experience in China, 1911–1945* (1971) is good on Stilwell. Russell D. Buhite's *Patrick J. Hurley and American Foreign Policy* (1973) is a balanced portrait. The attractiveness of the Chinese Communist Party to American observers is demonstrated in Kenneth E. Shewmaker's *Americans and Chinese Communists, 1927–1945* (1973). Michael Schaller's *The U.S. Crusade in China, 1938–1945* (1979) offers an explanation for Chinese Communist suspicion of the United States. John W. Carver's *Chinese-Soviet Relations 1937–1945* (1988) is a major contribution to our understanding of the maneuvers of Stalin, Chiang, and Mao. Lloyd Eastman offers a splendid obituary for the Guomindang in his *Seeds of Destruction* (1984) covering the years 1937 to 1949. Read skeptically, Jonathan Fenby's *Chiang Kai-shek* (2004) is a useful biography. Jay Taylor's *The Generalissimo* (2009) is more insightful.

Amid the vast literature on Chinese Communism, Benjamin Schwartz's *Chinese Communism and the Rise of Mao* (1958) is still a good place to start. Lyman Van Slyke's *Enemies and Friends* (1967) is an excellent analysis of the united front in thought and action, especially valuable for its insights into the Xi'an incident. Edgar Snow's classic *Red Star Over China* (1938) is essential reading, and Chalmers Johnson's *Peasant Nationalism and Communist Power* (1962) contains provocative ideas, as does everything Johnson writes. Stuart Schram's *Mao and Communist Power* (1962) and Jerome Ch'en's *Mao and the Chinese Revolution* (1967) are useful. Frederick Wakeman's *History and Will* (1973) is a brilliant examination of the roots of Mao's thought. Fascinating insight into the American intelligence community's perceptions of Mao's China can be found in *Tracking the Dragon* (2004), a declassified collection of over seventy National Intelligence Estimates on China for the years 1948 to 1976.

My articles analyzing "The Development of Chinese Communist Policy Toward the United States," *Orbis*, 12 (Spring and Summer 1967) cover the years 1922 through 1945. A highly sophisticated analysis of some of the same material—and much additional material—can be found in James Reardon-Anderson's *Yenan and the Great Powers, 1944 to 1946* (1980). Odd Arne Westad complicates the story magnificently in his *Cold War and Revolution* (1993), which focuses on Soviet-American relations and the origins of the Chinese civil war, 1944–1946. A great wealth of fresh work on the late 1940s has appeared in more recent years. Robert J. McMahon's essay, "The Cold War in Asia: Toward a New Synthesis?" *Diplomatic History* 12 (1988) is a superb overview of writings to that date. Marc S. Gallicchio has written a major new interpretation of the events of 1945, *The Cold War Begins in Asia* (1988). Steven I. Levine's *Anvil of Victory* (1987) includes valuable insights into the Marshall Mission, especially with regard to events in Manchuria. For Chinese images of the United States in this critical period, see Zhang Hong, *America Perceived* (2002).

The two most important books on the United States, China, and the cold war are the conference volume edited by Dorothy Borg and Waldo Heinrichs, *Uncertain Years* (1980) and Nancy Bernkopf Tucker's *Patterns in the Dust* (1983). For arguments at variance with what McMahon calls the "Cohen-Tucker thesis," see Robert M. Blum, *Drawing the Line* (1982) and William W. Stueck Jr., *The Road to Confrontation* (1981). Answers to "Was There a 'Lost Chance' in China?" can be found in a series of brief essays by Chen Jian, Michael Sheng, Arne Westad, and John Garver in a symposium I edited for *Diplomatic History* 21 (1997). Sheng spells out his argument in *Battling Western Imperialism* (1997). See also Thomas J. Christensen, *Useful Adversaries* (1996). For a Chinese perception of American policy toward China from 1945 to 1950, see Zi Zhongyun's *No Exit* (English ed., 2003). A useful documentary record is Zhang Shuguang and Chen Jian, eds., *Chinese Communist Foreign Policy and the Cold War in Asia* (1996).

The leading authority on the Korean War is Bruce Cumings, and his two-volume *Origins of the Korean War* (1981, 1990) is the place to start. William Stueck's *The Korean War* (1995) is valuable for his discussion of tensions within the Western alliance and of the international ramifications of the war. On the American side see James I. Matray, *The Reluctant Crusade* (1985) and Rosemary Foot, *The Wrong War* (1985). Allen Whiting's classic *China Crosses the Yalu* (1960) must be supplemented by three fascinating volumes based on Chinese and Soviet sources: Sergei Goncharov, John W. Lewis, and Xue Litai, *Uncertain Partners* (1993), Chen Jian, *China's Road to the Korean War* (1994), and Zhang Shuguang, *Mao's Military Romanticism* (1995). The *Bulletins* of the Cold War International History Project of the Woodrow Wilson International Center for Scholars provide a fount of valuable information. See Kathryn Weathersby's essay, "New Findings on the Korean War," 3 (1993) for evidence of Soviet involvement in the North Korean invasion and volume 6 (1995) for an extraordinary range of Soviet documents on the war, largely cables to and from Stalin.

The grim story of the McCarthyite purge of the China service and the tactics of the "China Lobby" can be followed in Gary May's *China Scapegoat* (1979). John Paton Davies Jr. tells his story in *Dragon by the Tail* (1972). John S. Service reflects on his tribulations in *The Amerasia Papers* (1971). See also Robert P. Newman, *Owen Lattimore and the "Loss of China"*

(1992). Ross Y. Koen's once suppressed *The China Lobby in American Politics* was reissued in 1974. Stanley D. Bachrack carries the story to 1971 in *The Committee of One Million* (1976). My essay, "The China Lobby" in Alexander DeConde, et al., eds., *Encyclopedia of American Foreign Policy* (2d ed., 2002) will save a busy reader much time.

The literature on the United States and China after the Korean War now includes many excellent works, much of which is surveyed by Nancy Bernkopf Tucker in her essay in *Pacific Passage*. Gordon H. Chang's *Friends and Enemies* (1990) is especially good on the Eisenhower and Kennedy years. Older studies such as the essays and documents in Roderick Mac-Farquhar, ed., *Sino-American Relations, 1949–1971* (1972), Robert G. Sutter's *China Watch* (1978), and David Allan Mayer's *Cracking the Monolith* (1986) remain useful. Three important conference volumes covering the 1950s are Harry Harding and Yuan Ming, eds., *Sino-American Relations, 1945–1955* (1989), Richard H. Immerman, ed., *John Foster Dulles and the Diplomacy of the Cold War* (1990), and Warren I. Cohen and Akira Iriye, eds., *The Great Powers in East Asia, 1953–1960* (1990). In all three, begin with the essays by Nancy Bernkopf Tucker. See also those by Chen Xiaolu and Wang Jisi in the Harding and Yuan volume and by Marc Gallicchio, He Di, and Qing Simei in the Cohen and Iriye volume. An article central to the debate over the crises in the Taiwan Strait in the 1950s is He Di and Gordon Chang, "The Absence of War in the U.S.-China Confrontation over Quemoy-Matsu in 1954–1955: Contingency, Luck, Deterrence?," *American Historical Review* 98 (1993). Earlier works by J. H. Kalicki, *The Pattern of Sino-American Crises* (1975) and Thomas E. Stolper, *China, Taiwan, and the Offshore Islands* (1984) are still essential. A more recent book, Robert Accinelli's *Crisis and Commitment* (1996), is excellent on U.S. policy toward Taiwan, 1950–1955. Two excellent books providing insight into Chinese policy making are Chen Jian's *Mao's China and the Cold War* (2001) and Zhang Shuguang's *Economic Cold War* (2001). Nancy Bernkopf Tucker, ed., *China Confidential* (2001) provides firsthand narratives by American diplomatists who worked with Chinese affairs from 1945 to 1996.

The focus on the Cuban Missile Crisis and the war in Vietnam has obscured much of American policy toward China during the Kennedy and Johnson years. Three books helpful for understanding Chinese behavior in this period are Peter Van Ness, *Revolution and Chinese Foreign Policy* (1970), Bruce Larkin, *China and Africa, 1949–1970* (1971), and John Garver, *Foreign Relations of the People's Republic of China* (1993). Useful material on the American side include Roger Hilsman, *To Move a Nation* (1967), Arthur Schlesinger Jr., *A Thousand Days* (1965), and Lyndon B. Johnson, *The Vantage Point* (1971). Missing pieces of the puzzle will be found in my *Dean Rusk* (1980), Nancy Bernkopf Tucker's "Threats, Opportunities, and Frustrations in East Asia," in Warren I. Cohen and Nancy B. Tucker, eds., *Lyndon Johnson Confronts the World* (1994), and Noam Kochavi, *A Conflict Perpetuated* (2002). See also Tucker's *China Confidential*. For this period and beyond, Leonard A. Kusnitz's China-focused *Public Opinion and Foreign Policy* (1984) is essential reading. For an understanding of the Chinese context, Roderick MacFarquhar's several volumes on the Cultural Revolution cannot be improved upon.

Rapprochement begins with Richard Moorsteen and Morton Abramowitz, *Remaking China Policy* (1971). The authors were the architects of the successful "one China but not now" formula. Henry Kissinger tells the story the way he wants it remembered in *White House Years* (1979) and *Years of Upheaval* (1982). William Burr, ed., *The Kissinger Transcripts* (1999) offers ample evidence for a different interpretation, such as might be found in James Mann's *About Face* (1999), which begins with Nixon and then dissects all who followed, including William Jefferson Clinton. Nancy Bernkopf Tucker's "Taiwan Expendable: Nixon and Kissinger Go to China," *Journal of American History*, 92 (2005) should destroy what was left of Kissinger's credibility on the issue. Another enormously important discussion of rapprochement can be found in Harry Harding's *Fragile Relationship* (1992). Harding, this generation's leading analyst of Chinese-American relations, writes of the 1980s as well as the 1970s. See also Robert Ross, *Negotiating Cooperation* (1995), covering much the same ground. John Garver offers an interesting interpretation of Chinese motivation in *China's Decision for Rapprochement with the United States, 1968–1971* (1982). Among the many valuable works already out on the 1970s, Samuel S. Kim's *China, the United Nations, and World Order* (1978) should have relieved Rusk's concerns. I found Kenneth G. Lieberthal's monograph *Sino-Soviet Conflict in the 1970s* (1978) extraordinarily helpful.

The normalization story can be followed in Cyrus Vance's memoir, *Hard Choices* (1983). Closer to the events was his bete noir, Zbigniew Brzezinski, who tells it as it really was in *Power and Principle* (1983). See William C. Kirby, et al., eds., *Normalization of U.S.-China Relations* (2005) for contrasting Chinese and American scholarly analyses of the normalization process and its aftermath. Brzezinski's chief adviser on policy toward China, Michel Oksenberg, reflects on policy as scholar and participant in "A Decade of Sino-American Relations," *Foreign Affairs, 61* (1982), but Harding, Mann, and Ross offer different perspectives. In addition to these last three authors, American policy in the 1980s is described by George Shultz in his memoir *Turmoil and Triumph* (1993). Superb insights into Chinese thinking can be found in everything written by the late A. Doak Barnett, but his *The Making of Foreign Policy in China* (1985) is especially useful for this period. David Shambaugh's *Beautiful Imperialist* (1991) gives us a rare look at how China's specialists on the United States function. Shambaugh and Thomas W. Robinson have edited an excellent collection of essays on *Chinese Foreign Policy* (1994) in which they are joined by more than a dozen of the world's finest analysts. The nature and development of Chinese-American cultural and educational exchanges and the growing euphoria about them are evident in Joyce Kallgren and Denis Fred Simon, eds., *Educational Exchanges* (1987). Paul A. Cohen's "The Post-Mao Reforms in Historical Perspective," *Journal of Asian Studies, 47* (1988) is thoughtful and provocative, an article on the 1980s that will never be dated.

An understanding of Taiwan's evolution into a functioning democracy starts with Ralph N. Clough's *Island China* (1978), which carries the story up to the normalization of relations between Beijing and Washington. Jay Taylor's, *The Generalissimo's Son,*" is a monumental portrait of Chiang Ching-kuo, the man who led Taiwan to democracy. Nancy Bernkopf Tucker's prizewinning *Taiwan, Hong Kong, and the United States, 1945–1992* is the standard work on the subject. See also Tien Hung-mao, *The Great Transition* (1989) and Robert G. Sutter and William Johnson, eds., *Taiwan in World Affairs* (1994). Tensions in the Taiwan Strait and cross-Strait relations, including the American role generally, have received intensive coverage from Richard C. Bush, *At Cross Purposes* (2004) and Alan D. Romberg, *Rein in at the Brink of the Precipice* (2003) and in Nancy Bernkopf Tucker, ed., *Dangerous Strait* (2005) and Tucker's magnum opus, *Straight Talk* (2009).

Bush administration views of the Tiananmen massacre and the American response can be found first in James A. Baker III's memoir, *The Politics of Diplomacy* (1995), and subsequently in George Bush and Brent Scowcroft, *A World Transformed* (1998)—in which there is no mention of the sale of F-16s to Taiwan or of China as an issue in the 1992 campaign. Mann's *About Face* provides important correctives. See also the oral histories of James Lilley and Winston Lord in the Association for Diplomatic Studies Oral History Project at Georgetown University and in Tucker's *China Confidential* (2000). The American reaction to the Tiananmen massacre is analyzed thoughtfully by Richard Madsen in *China and the American Dream* (1995).

Warren Christopher's memoir, *In the Stream of History* (1998), details the problems he faced as Clinton's first secretary of state. Tucker's *China Confidential* has substantial material from the interviews with Lord, who served as Clinton's first assistant secretary of state for East Asia and the Pacific. Robert L. Suettinger analyzes policy from 1989 to 2000 from the perspective of the China specialist on the National Security Council in *Beyond Tiananmen* (2003). David M. Lampton provides a scholar's view of the same period in *Same Bed, Different Dreams* (2001). Jim Mann has talked to everyone who knows anything, and his book has considerable information on the Clinton years. Robert Sutter's study of interest groups and policy, *U.S. Policy Toward China* (1998), describes the competing efforts of business groups and human rights organizations—and the successful lobbying effort by the Taipei government in 1995. Nancy Bernkopf Tucker's essay, "Clinton's Muddled China Policy," *Current History*, 97 (1998), epitomizes the view of most leading specialists on Chinese-American relations.

There is a vast literature on the rise of Chinese power in the twenty-first century. Among the best studies are Avery Goldstein's *Rising to the Challenge* (2005), a superb analysis of China's grand strategy, Alastair Iain Johnston and Robert Ross, eds., *New Directions in the Study of China's Foreign Policy* (2006), David Shambaugh, ed., *Power Shift* (2005), and Robert G. Sutter, *China's Rise in Asia* (2005). And every student of contemporary Chinese-American relations must read James Mann's *China Fantasy* (2007), the literary equivalent of a dose of smelling salts.

Two other works that have helped me are less easily grouped: William L. Neumann's "Ambiguity and Ambivalence in Ideas About National Security in Asia," in Alex DeConde, ed., *Isolation and Security* (1957) and Harold Isaacs's *Scratches on Our Minds* (1958). Neumann raised questions that intrigued me. I hope I have answered a few of them. Isaacs played on my weakness for studying attitudes—in this instance American attitudes toward Chinese and Indians. My own efforts along the same lines can be found in "American Perceptions of China," in Michel Oksenberg and Robert Oxnam, eds., *Dragon and Eagle* (1978), "Mutual Images in U.S.-China Relations," Occasional Paper no. 32 of the Asia Program of the Woodrow Wilson International Center for Scholars (1988), and, with Nancy Bernkopf Tucker, "America in Asian Eyes," *American Historical Review*, 111, no. 4 (2006).

Index

Academia Sinica, 152

Acheson, Dean: Chiang and, 190; on Chiang's regime, 177; China, attitude toward, 179–180; Communist expansion, attitude toward, 187; Formosa, policy on, 183–184; North Korean aggression, response to, 186; and PRC, recognition of, 185–186; U.S. aid to China, announcement of, 171; U.S. China policy and, 182, 193–194

Adams, Brooks, 43, 61

Adams, John Quincy, 29

Afghanistan, 229

AIG, 263

Alaskan purchase, 32

Allen, Horace, 38

Allen, Richard, 226

America First, 135

American Asiatic Association, 41, 42, 43, 44, 55

American China Development Company, 65

American Institute on Taiwan, 223

America's Coming War with China (Carpenter), 275–276

Amnesty International, 244, 277, 282

Anglo-Japanese alliance, 56–57, 62, 94

anti-Americanism: after NATO bombing of China's embassy in Belgrade, 261; 266; China's anti-American boycotts, 63–64, 65, 66; in Chinese Communist Party, 179, 184–185; in Kuomintang, 125; Mao's, 171–172, 194, 198–199

anti-imperialism, Soviet emphasis on, 149

anti-secession law, 273

appeasement, of Japan over aggression in China, 119–120, 123, 124, 128, 137–138

Armitage, Richard, 267, 272

arms race, 94, 95, 236–237

arms sales: by China, 233, 247; by Russia to China, 250; by U.S. to China, 171, 176, 229; by U.S. to Japan, 132–133, 134, 136, 146; by U.S. to Taiwan, 225, 226–228, 249–251, 268, 279, 285, 288

Armstrong, James, 21–22
art (Chinese), American interest in, 89,
    90–91
ASEAN (Association of Southeast Asian
    Nations), 265, 287
Asia, U.S. involvement in, 202. *See also*
    East Asia
Asia Watch, 244
"The Awakening of China" (Roosevelt), 67
Axis Alliance, 135–136

Baker, James, 246, 248
balance of power: at end of WWII,
    164–165; in Manchuria, 60–61,
    68–69; Roosevelt on China's place
    in, 67–68
bandit-suppression campaigns, 112
barbarian experts, 6–7, 28, 31
barbarians, China's attitude toward, 3–4,
    7, 8, 17
Beijing Olympics, 268, 281, 284–285
Belgrade, bombing of China's embassy in,
    261
Bevin, Ernest, 180
Blair, Dennis, 281
Boeing, 244, 263, 269
Bonin Island, 37
Borah, William, 121
Borodin, Michael, 100, 107
Boston Museum of Fine Arts, 90
bourgeois liberalization, 235, 240
Bowles, Chester, 208, 209, 210
Boxer uprising, 48, 50–54
boycotts, 63–64, 65, 66, 92, 93
Bradley, Omar, 189
Brezhnev Doctrine, 215
Bridges, Styles, 185
Brown, Ron, 252
Bryan, William Jennings, 78, 83, 84
Brzezinski, Zbigniew, 222, 225
Buchanan, James, 22, 24
Buchanan, Patrick, 249
Buck, Pearl, 143
Bundy, McGeorge, 209
Bundy, William P., 213
Burlingame, Anson, 30, 32
Burlingame Treaty, 32, 34

Burma, 269, 280, 284
Bush, George H. W., and Bush
    administration: arms sales to Taiwan
    and, 250–251; China, knowledge of,
    232; China-U.S. relationship, vision of,
    232–233; China's internal affairs, lack
    of intervention in, 236; China's MFN
    status and, 243–244, 246–248, 249;
    Deng's support for, 229; Hainan Island
    incident and, 267; Iraq's Kuwait
    invasion, response to, 246; president,
    election as, 231; during Reagan
    administration, 226, 227, 228;
    self-delusion over China relations, 241,
    242; Tiananmen Square massacre,
    response to, 239–242
Bush, George W., and Bush
    administration: Chen Shui-bian,
    unhappiness with, 278–279; China,
    schizophrenic relationship with, 278;
    China, trip to, 269, 274; China policy,
    initial, 266–267; Hu Jintao, meeting
    with, 271, 276; Iraq, invasion of, 270;
    policies, results of, 289; proclamation
    on PRC's trade status, 269
business community (U.S.), U.S. China
    policy, influence over, 253
businessmen (China), class
    status of, 4
Byrnes, James F., 167

C. C. Clique, 143
Cairo Conference (1943), 144
California, 33, 62
Cambodia, 217, 223–224, 245
Camranh Bay, 136
Canton, 4, 20–22
Canton Commune, 109
Carpenter, Ted Galen, 275–276
Carter, Jimmy, and administration of,
    221–225
Cass, Lewis, 22
Castle, William, 113
Central Intelligence Agency (CIA),
    202, 233
Chang Chih-tung, 36, 52, 57, 65
Chang Hsueh-liang, 111, 129

Chang Tso-lin, 105, 110

Changchun, 170

Ch'en Chiung-ming, 99

Chen Shui-bian: Bush and, 271–272; China, baiting of, 269–270, 275–276; China's distrust of, 273; election as president, 266; U.S. unhappiness with, 278–279

Chen Yi, 204, 213

Chenbao Island incident, 216

Cheney, Richard, 277, 278

Chennault, Claire, 142

Ch'i-ying, 1–2, 11, 12–14, 17, 23

Chiang Ching-kuo, 223

Chiang Kai-shek: arrest, 129; Communists, concern over, 150; Communists, efforts against, 107, 115, 152, 170–171; Communists, rapprochement with, 129–130; Communists, renewed tensions with, 139; Eisenhower administration, hopes for, 203; Formosa, flight to, 178; Japan, refusal to fight, 142, 143, 191; Japanese aggression, fears of, 137; Kalgan, duplicity over, 172; Korean War and, 186–190; Mao, talks with, 164, 165; Moscow, trip to, 100; Nanking murders and, 107–108; personal power, interest in, 125; resignation as president, 117; retirement of, 109; rivals, defeat of, 112; Roosevelt and, 144–145; Stalin and, 161–162; Stilwell and, 139, 142; Treaty of Friendship, response to, 163; U.S., attitude toward, 128; U.S.-Japan war, support for, 122; U.S. support for, 138–139, 160, 166–168, 174, 176–177, 182; waning political strength of, 155. See also Kuomintang; Nationalist government

Chiang Kai-shek, Madam, 138, 163

Chiao t'ung University, 91

China: as cultural entity, 9; diplomatic missions to Western powers, 31–32; finances of, 84, 111–112, 126–127; foreign countries, balance of power plays with, 21, 28, 57, 58, 68, 71–72; foreign incursions in, 20–22, 24–25,

55–58 (See also Manchuria); foreign powers' cooperation in, 30–31; growing openness of, 1980s, 234–235; human rights and (See human rights, China's violation of); maps of, 16, 45, 104, 201; modernization of, 35–37, 76, 80–81, 93, 105; as Republic of China, 77, 79; sovereignty of, U.S. attitudes toward, 43–44, 46–48, 52–53, 59, 96, 105, 111; superiority, sense of, 2, 4, 13, 17; weakness of, U.S. exploitation of, 196. See also Chinese Communist Party; extraterritoriality; Mao Tse-tung; Nationalist government; People's Republic of China; spheres of influence; Taiwan; trade; treaty ports; treaty system

China Consortium, 126

China Daily (newspaper), 272, 278

China National Offshore Oil Company, 274

China White Paper, 182

China's Destiny (Chiang), 146

Chinatowns, 33–34

Chinchow–Aigun railroad, 72, 73

Chinese Communist Party: anti-Americanism of, 179, 184–185; Changsa, attack on, 149; Chiang and, 112, 139; end of WWII and, 163–165; establishment of, 94–95, 99; information, control over, 287–288; Japan, declaration of war on, 129; Japan, fight against, 143; Korean War, intervention in, 189–191; Manchuria, actions in, 165, 169–170; Marxist-Leninism, commitment to, 152; misinformation about, 153–154; at Moscow Congress, 98; Nelson Johnson's characterization of, 150–151; popularity of, 143, 154–155; power monopoly, international environment and, 290; Soviet Union, relationship with, 157, 164; Tiananmen Square massacre and, 239–240; U.S., attitude toward, 102, 156–157, 179; U.S., hope for aid from, 160; U.S.'s attitude to Japan's Manchurian conquest, response to, 117;

Chinese Communist Party (*continued*)
U.S.'s attitude toward, 148–149;
U.S.'s understanding of, 151–153, 192;
workers' rights and, 286. *See also*
Kuomintang–Chinese Communist
Party relations

Chinese Eastern Railroad, 98–99, 113, 158

chinoiserie, desire for, 2

Chou En-lai (Zhou Enlai): Mao's
succession and, 220–221; Marshall
and, 169; Nixon administration and,
215, 216, 217–218; Stuart and, 181;
U.S. attitude toward, 143; U.S.-Chiang
relationship, response to, 203; U.S.,
hope for aid from, 160, 178–179;
U.S., negotiations with, 204–205

Christian schools and colleges (in China),
89–90, 91–92

Christopher, Warren, 252–253

Chu Teh, 112, 115

Ch'un, Prince, 71, 72

Churchill, Winston, 137

CIA (Central Intelligence Agency),
202, 233

circular note on Boxer uprising (Hay), 51–52

civil war (China, 1913), 79–80

civil war (China, post-WWII), 170–174.
See also Kuomintang–Chinese
Communist Party relations

Cleveland administration, 38–39, 40

Cline, Ray, 226

Clinton, Bill, and Clinton administration:
1992 campaign of, 249; China,
working relationship with, 259;
China's MFN status and, 251–253;
comprehensive engagement policy of,
257; election of, 251; Jiang, summit
with, 258–259, 264; sex scandal and,
260–261; trip to China by, 259–260

Clinton, Hillary, 286

clipper ships, 14

Clubb, O. Edmund, 161, 190

coaling stations, 55

cold war, end of, 236–237

collective security, 124, 131, 132–135, 137

Comintern: Canton, orders for uprising
in, 109; Congress of the Toilers of the

Far East, 98; emissary to Canton from,
100; foreign aggression, call for united
front against, 129; Northern
Expedition, support for, 107

Commission on Human Rights (UN),
260, 270

Committee for Non-Participation in
Japanese Aggression, 131, 133

Committee of 100, 282

Committee to Defend America by Aiding
the Allies (White Committee), 135

Communism: U.S. fear of, 198–199;
in Vietnam, 211. *See also* Chinese
Communist Party; Comintern

comprehensive engagement policy, 257

Comprehensive Nuclear Test Ban
Treaty, 265

concessions: after Sino-Japanese
War, 39; China's weakness and, 9–10;
railroad development and, 65–66

Conger, E. H., 51

Congress (U.S.): Chiang and, 175–176, 177,
180; China treaties, actions ignoring,
34; on China's currency revaluation,
274; China's human rights record,
report on, 283; China's MFN status
and, 247–248; Democratic control of,
after 2006 elections, 278; Manchurian
crisis and, 119; on recognition for PRC,
225; Silver Purchase Act and, 126;
Taiwan's lobbying of, 255; Tiananmen
Square massacre, response to, 240,
241, 242–244; WWII, actions during,
133, 139

Congress of the Toilers of the Far East, 98

Consortium: Hu-kuang Railroad loan and,
76; U.S. admittance to, 74; Wilson
and, 78; Yüan Shih-k'ai and, 77

containment without isolation policy, 211

Coolidge, Calvin, and administration of,
149

Cuba, 41, 59

Cuban missile crisis, 209

Cultural Revolution, 213, 215

currency reform (China), 127–128

Cushing, Caleb, 2, 12–13

Czechoslovakia, 215

Dairen (port city), 158, 162

Dalai Lama, 248, 282, 283–284

Darfur, 264, 269, 277, 281

Davies, John Paton, 157, 190

Davis, Norman, 131, 132

de Gaulle, Charles, 213

Defense Department (U.S.), *2007 Report on Chinese Power*, 282

defensive perimeter (U.S.), 184

Democracy Wall (Beijing), 234

Democratic Progressive Party (Taiwan), 254, 266

Democrats (U.S.), 278, 286

Denby, Charles, 40

Deng Xiaoping (Teng Hsiao-p'ing): Carter administration and, 222; China's role in global economy and, 263–264; Clinton and, 252; humane rule by, 234; student protests and, 238; Tiananmen Square massacre and, 239, 240–241, 245; U.S.-Taiwan relations and, 221–222, 225–229; U.S., tour of, 223; Zhou and, 220

Department of Defense (U.S.), *2007 Report on Chinese Power*, 282

Department of State (U.S.): China, attitude toward, 124; China specialists, abuse of, after Korean War, 190; on China's human rights efforts, 268, 274; China's MFN status, actions on, 252–253; on China's National government, 125; Chinese Communists, confusion over, 151–152, 155; Chinese Communists, interest in, 148; Chinese Communists, possible accommodations with, 181; on Chinese Communists–Soviet Union relationship, 157; human rights report (2007), 283; on Japan, conflict with, 126; Kim and, 277; Korean War and, 188; Lee and, 255; McCarthyism and, 199; neutrality law, revision of, 133; on silver-purchasing program, 126–127; Taiwan, meetings with, 269–270; on Treaty of Commerce and Navigation, 134; Wei's arrest, reaction to, 234

Department of the Treasury (U.S.), 127, 136

Detzer, Dorothy, 117, 130

Dewey, George, 41

Dewey, John, 93

Dewey, Thomas E., 176–177

Division of Far Eastern Affairs (U.S.), 125–126

Dobrynin, Anatoly, 209

Dole, Robert, 258

dollar diplomacy, 70–76, 85

drug enforcement, 271

Drumright, Everett, 155

Dulles, John Foster, 199, 203, 204–206

earthquakes, 284

East Asia: balance of power, at end of WWII, 164–165; China as stabilizing force in, 155–156; U.S., importance to, 286–287; U.S. involvement in, incidental nature of, 198. *See also* China; Japan; Korea; North Korea; South Korea

education system (China), 89–90, 91–92, 191, 229

Eichelberger, Clark, 135

Eisenhower, Dwight, and administration of, 173, 199, 203–206

elites, contact between American and Chinese, 89

Empress of China (sailing ship), 2

engagement: Americans' attitude toward, 262; comprehensive engagement policy, 257; praise for U.S. policy of, 281–282

entertainment industry, pirating and, 253

entrepreneurs, American, in China, 36

Europe: U.S. focus on, 135, 175, 197–198; U.S., relationship to, 202. *See also* France; Germany; Great Britain

Ever Victorious Army, 25

Everett, Edward, 12

extraterritoriality: early Chinese attitude toward, 9; end of, negotiations on, 113; National government's actions on, 111; rights to, U.S. surrender of, 138; U.S. position on, 15, 97, 101, 102, 103; by U.S., in treaty ports, 14; Washington Conference and, 95. *See also* China, sovereignty; Manchuria; Shantung; treaty ports

F-16 fighters, sale of, to Taiwan, 250–251
Falun Gong, 268
Fang Lizhi, 235, 236, 239, 242, 244, 245
Far Eastern Agreement (from Yalta Conference), 158–159
Farrow, Mia, 277
Fenollosa, Ernest, 90
Ferguson, John C., 91
Fingar, Thomas, 279
Five-Power Treaty, 95
Fleisher, Wilfred, 124
Fogg Museum, 91
force, ideals and, 122
Ford, Gerald, 220
foreign devils. See barbarians
foreign exchange reserves, 264
Foreign Military Sales Program, 229
Formosa. See Taiwan
Forrestal, James V., 166
fortress Europe, 202
four modernizations, 224
Four Policemen, 155–156
Four-Power Treaty, 95
France: Canton, incursions in, 21; China, incursions in, 24–25; in Indochina, U.S. aid to, 202; Knox plan, response to, 73; Sino-Japanese War, response to, 39; treaty revisions, demands for, 22
Freer, Charles L., 90–91
Freer Gallery of Art, 91

G-7 meeting, 244–245
Galbraith, John Kenneth, 210
Gang of Four, 220–221, 234
Gates, Robert, 282
Gauss, Clarence, 142, 154, 155
General Dynamics, 250
General Order No. 1, 164
Gephardt, Richard, 253
Gere, Richard, 277
Germany, 39, 68, 69, 73, 135
Goddess of Democracy and Freedom, 238
Gorbachev, Mikhail, 230, 236–237
Gordon, Charles ("Chinese"), 25

Great Britain: China, incursions in, 24–25; consular officials of, 14; equality with China, desire for, 8; force, use of, 20–21; Japan, alliance with, 56–57, 81; Knox plan, response to, 73; most-favored-nation status, 9; Opium War and, 6, 10–11; Taiping Rebellion, response to, 18–19; Twenty-One Demands, response to, 83; U.S., cooperation with, 19–21; U.S. support for, 134–135; at Washington Conference, 96–97
Great Depression, 116
The Great Peace and Development Debate, 265–266
Great Proletarian Cultural Revolution, 213
Greene, Roger, 134–135
Grew, Joseph, 130, 160
Griswold, A. Whitney, 286
Gulf War, 245–247
gunboat diplomacy, 64, 103
Guomindang. See Kuomintang

Haig, Alexander, 226, 227
Hainan Island incident, 267
Harding administration, 94
Harriman, Averell, 162, 163
Harriman, E. H., 72
Hart, Robert, 31
Harte, Bret, 33
Hay, John: on America's China interests, limits of, 59; Boxer uprising and, 51–53, 54–55; China policy and, 42–44; Open Door notes, 44, 46–48, 59; Russia's Manchurian interests and, 56–58; as sustainer of illusion of U.S. role in China, 196
Hayes, Rutherford, 34
higher education, U.S.-Chinese ties, 229
Hill, Carla, 281
Hill, Christopher, 281
Hilsman, Roger, 210–211
Hippisley, Alfred, 44, 48, 52
Hirohito, Emperor, 236
Hitler, Adolph, 133, 135, 145

Ho Chi Minh, 186, 202, 211

Holbrooke, Richard, 221

Holdridge, John, 228

Hong Kong, 9, 206, 287

Hoover, Herbert, and administration of, 116, 117, 119–123, 183

Hoover-Stimson Doctrine, 120

Hopkins, Harry, 142

Hornbeck, Stanley K.: China's complaints, response to, 128; on Manchuria, Japan's domination of, 116, 119; on silver-purchasing program, 127; on Sino-Japanese dispute, 124; Tripartite Pact, response to, 135

House Foreign Affairs Committee (U.S.), 171

Howard, Roy, 153

Hsi-liang, 72

Hsüan-tsung, 11

Hu Han-min, 106, 109

Hu Jintao, 269, 271, 276, 277

Hu-Kuang railroad, 76

Hu Yaobang, 234, 235, 237

Hua Guofeng, 221

Huang Hua, 181, 222, 227

Hughes, Charles Evans, 94, 97

Hughes Electronics, 259

Hull, Cordell, 125, 127, 130, 133–134, 152

human rights, China's violation of: Beijing Olympics and, 284–285; Clinton's criticisms of, 258, 260; concerns over, 277; impact of, 253–254; lack of resolution of, 282–283; State Department report on, 268; subordination to U.S. national security concerns, 233–234; U.S. Congress's response to, 243

Human Rights Watch, 277, 282

Hung Hsiu-ch'üan, 17

Hurley, Patrick, 117, 144, 159–160, 161–162, 166, 192

Hussein, Saddam, 245–246

Huston, J. C., 101, 149

i-i-chih-i policy, 7

I-li-pu, 11

Ickes, Harold, 137

immigrants, Chinese in U.S., 32–35, 47, 62, 64, 139

immigration, 33, 66

Imperial Maritime Customs Service, 19–20, 44

imperialism: foreign territories near China and, 45; Roosevelt's defense of, 56; of U.S. in Philippines, 41–42. See also extraterritoriality; treaty ports; treaty system

India, 209, 265

Indochina, 202, 208

industrialization, of U.S., 39–40

intellectual property rights, 247, 248, 253, 274, 276

international business community, China's importance to, 263

international trade. See trade

investments: foreign, in China, 80–81; by U.S. in China, 42, 71–72, 75, 84, 118, 230

Iran, 233, 264, 269, 275, 280

Iraq, 245–246, 270

Ishii Kikujiro, 85–86

Israel, 255

jackal diplomacy, 27

Jackson, Andrew, 5

Jackson-Vanik Amendment to Trade Act of 1974, 224–225

Japan: appeasement of, over aggression in China, 119–120, 123, 124, 128, 137–138; China, control over, 92; China, investments in, 80–81; China's relationship with, 265; Chinese Communists, antagonism toward, 153; embargo against, calls for, 137; foreign powers' cooperation in, 31; Great Britain, alliance with, 56–57, 81; Korea, relationship with, 37, 38; Manchuria, power in, 73–74, 113; Manchurian crisis and, 56–57, 58, 68–70; militarism in, 110; Nationalist movement, attitude toward, 108; naval building program of, 94; potential Chinese civil war, involvement in, 166; power of, Roosevelt's response to, 60–61, 62;

Japan (*continued*)
  Seward's attitude toward, 29;
  Sino-Japanese War and, 38–39;
  Tripartite Pact, signing of, 135;
  Twenty-One Demands and, 81–87; U.S.
  cooperation with, 74–75, 273; on U.S.
  recognition of Republic of China, 79;
  Washington Conference and, 95–97;
  West, response to, 37
Jiang Qing, 215
Jiang Zemin: Bush (George W.) and, 268,
  269; Clinton, summit with, 256,
  258–259, 264; September 11 terrorist
  attacks and, 269; U.S., policy of
  cooperation with, 266, 267; U.S.
  response to Tiananmen and, 242
Joffe, Adolf, 99
Johnson, Louis, 186
Johnson, Lyndon B., and administration
  of, 210–211, 211–213
Johnson, Nelson T.: as advisor to
  MacMurray, 105; Chiang's return,
  response to, 109; China, reports on,
  122; China's complaints, response
  to, 128; Chinese Communists, views
  on, 150–151, 152, 153, 154; on Manchuria,
  113, 119; National government in China,
  attitude toward, 113; on Sino-Japanese
  dispute, 124
Joint Chiefs of Staff (U.S.), 166–167,
  183–184

Kadeer, Rebiya, 283
K'ang Yu-wei, 50, 76
Karakhan manifesto, 98–99
Kearny, Lawrence, 10–11
Kellogg, Frank, 102, 103, 105, 107, 108, 110
Kellogg-Briand Pact (Kellogg Peace Pact),
  113, 116, 118
Kennan, George, 162, 173, 183, 188
Kennedy, John F., and administration of,
  206–207, 207–208, 210
Khrushchev, Nikita, 205, 207
Kiaochow, 81
Kim Jong Il, 277, 281
Kissinger, Henry, 218, 220, 242, 283
Kitty Hawk, U.S.S., 279

Knowland, William, 183, 185
Knox, Philander, 70, 72–74, 75, 87
Korea, 37–38. *See also* North Korea;
  South Korea
Korean War, 186–191, 194, 199–200
Kosovars, 261
Kowloon, 25
kowtow, 3
Krugman, Paul, 289
Kung, H. H., 112, 122, 127, 128, 133
Kung, Prince, 25–26, 31–32, 36
Kuomintang (Guomindang):
  anti-American tendencies, 125;
  establishment of, 77; factionalism in,
  106–107, 115; Formosa, control of, 183;
  at Moscow Congress, 98; Northern
  Expedition of, 102, 107, 110, 149;
  reactionary actions of, 143; Taiwan,
  economic reforms in, 200; U.S.
  support for, 160, 171, 190; Yüan and,
  80. *See also* Nationalist government;
  Taiwan
Kuomintang–Chinese Communist Party
  relations: cease-fire by, 169–170; civil
  war and, 170–174; coalition against
  Japan, 99–100, 106; Communist
  military successes, 177–178; mutual
  antagonism, 139, 143–144, 156;
  post-WWII, 168–170; potential
  hostilities, 139, 143–144
Kuril Islands, 158
Kuwait, 245–246
Kwantung army, 113, 115, 121

Lake, Anthony, 251, 256, 257
Lamont, Thomas, 124–125
land reform, 112, 143, 151
Lansing, Robert, 81, 85–86, 87, 99
Lattimore, Owen, 153, 154
League Council, 117
League of Nations, 87, 88, 94, 112, 121–122
Lee Teng-hui, 254, 255, 257
lend-lease, 136, 139
Lenovo, 274
Leopold, Richard W., 41
Li Hung-chang, 25, 36–37, 52, 57
Li Peng, 235, 238, 245, 248, 253

Libby, Frederick, 130
Libya, 233
Lilley, James, 250
Lin Biao, 215, 216
Lincoln, Abraham, 29
Lodge, Henry Cabot, 43, 87
Long March, 152
Loral Corporation, 259
Lord, Winston, 236, 251

Ma Soo, 97
Ma Ying-Cheou, 279
Macao, 1
MacArthur, Douglas: Chiang and, 203;
    Formosa, attitude toward, 183, 186;
    Formosa, independent actions on, 187;
    Korean War and, 188, 189–190
MacMurray, J. V. A.: Chiang's return,
    response to, 109; China's tariff
    autonomy and, 97, 110; May 30th
    Movement, response to, 103; Nanking
    incident, response to, 108; National
    government in China, response to, 111;
    on Sino-Japanese dispute, 124; U.S.
    China policy, control of, 101–102
Magruder, John, 139
Mahan, Alfred, 43, 61
Maine, U.S.S., 41
Manchu dynasty, 6, 43, 48, 76
Manchuko, 121
Manchuria: balance of power in, 60–61,
    68–69; Chinese Communists in,
    165–166; Japan's conquest of, 114–115;
    Japan's conquest of, U.S. response to,
    116–128; Japan's power in, 73–74, 113;
    National government's efforts to
    reclaim, 110, 111, 113–114; railroads in,
    72–73; Russian incursion in, 55–57;
    Soviet policy in, 192
manufacturing, in China, 247
Mao Tse-tung (Zedong): Chiang,
    talks with, 164, 165; Japanese
    aggression, fears of, 137; National
    government, actions against, 112, 115;
    new tactics, end of WWII, 168; Nixon
    and, 217, 218–219; People's Republic
    of China, establishment of, 178;

Soviet Union, ties to, 181; Stalin and,
    161, 186; Stuart, meeting with, 181;
    U.S.-Chiang relationship, response to,
    203; U.S., criticisms of, 93, 171–172, 177,
    194, 198–199; U.S., hope for aid from,
    160–161, 178–179
maps: of China under warlords, 104; of
    imperialist territories near China, 45;
    of Pacific war, 140–141; of Taiwan
    and China, 201; of treaty ports,
    16, 45
Marcos, Ferdinand, 237
Marcy, William, 22
Marshall, George C.: airpower, opposition
    to use of, 142; Chinese civil war and,
    170–171, 172–173; economic aid to China
    and, 169; on Korean War, 189; as
    Truman's representative to China, 166,
    167–168, 193; U.S. China policy and,
    175–176, 193–194
Marshall, Humphrey, 18
Marshall Plan, 174–175
Martin, W. A. P., 26, 31
May Fourth Movement, 87, 93
May 30th Movement, 101–102
McCarthy, Joseph, and McCarthyism,
    190–191, 199, 202, 208
McKinley, William, and administration of:
    American missionaries and new China
    policy and, 50; Boxer uprising and,
    51–54; Denby and, 40; inaction on
    China policy, 43; Open Door notes and,
    46–48; Philippines, policy on, 41–42;
    territorial acquisitions in China,
    possibility of, 54–55; on trade with
    China, 42
McLane, Robert, 19
Meese, Edwin, 226
Metropolitan Museum of Art, 91
Mexico, 79
MFN status. *See* most-favored-nation
    (MFN) status
middle class (China), 291
Middle East, 173–174, 233
Midway Island, 32
military cooperation (U.S.-China),
    277, 282

missionaries: Asia, focus on, 195; in
    Canton, 5; Chiang, support for, 132;
    China, assistance to, 81; French, 25;
    importance of, 13; murder of, 66;
    opening of China to, 26; reactions
    against, 48–51; schools and colleges
    in China, 89–90, 91–92
Mitchell, George, 253
Molotov, V. M., 157
Mondale, Walter F., 229
Mongolian People's Republic, 158
moral diplomacy, 119–120
Morgan, J. P., 65, 66, 91
Morgenthau, Henry, 127, 136, 137
Morse, Edward, 90
Moscow Congress, 98
most-favored-nation (MFN) status: of
    China, 32–33; in China-U.S. agreement
    (1928), 110; of China's exports to U.S.,
    243–244, 246–248, 249, 251–253; early
    treaties and, 9–11; Manchurian treaty
    ports and, 57; treaty review and, 19;
    U.S. foreign policy and, 30. See also
    trade, U.S.-China
Mr. Science and Mr. Democracy, 235
Mu-chang-a, 17
Mugabe, Robert, 269, 280
Mukden, Manchuria, 114, 115
Museum of Fine Arts (Boston), 90

names, Romanization table for,
    xxi–xxii
Nanking, attacks on foreigners in, 107–108
Nanking University, 91
National Council for Prevention
    of War, 130
National Economic Council, 253
National People's Congress (NPC), 273
National Security Council (U.S.), 180
National Unification Council, 275
nationalism: in China, 62–63, 66–67, 101;
    Seward's, 29. See also Chinese
    Communist Party; Kuomintang
Nationalist government (China): Chinese
    Communists, relationship to, 153–154;
    Communists' call for unity with,
    against Japan, 129; decline and collapse

of, 155, 177–178; factionalism in,
    108–109; Japan, conflict with, 110;
    Nanking incident and, 107–108,
    109–110; problems facing, 111–112;
    southern base for, 106; Soviet support
    for, 159; Treaty of Friendship, response
    to, 163; U.S. Department of State on,
    125. See also Chiang Kai-shek;
    Kuomintang; Sun Yat-sen
NATO, 174–175, 261, 266
naval race, Japan-U.S., 94
Negroponte, John, 279
neutrality law, 131, 133
New Fourth Army (China), 139
New York Times, 227
Nimitz, U.S.S., 256
Nine-Power Treaty, 87, 96, 121, 133
Nitze, Paul, 188
Nixon, Richard, and administration of, 215,
    217–218, 218–219, 242
nonrecognition policy, 119–120, 121
North Korea: China's leverage with, 281;
    invasion of South Korea, 186; nuclear
    weapons development, 252, 265, 276,
    277; six-power talks on, 271
Northern Expedition (Kuomintang), 102,
    107, 110, 149
NPC (National People's Congress),
    273
nuclear weapons, 204, 212, 259

Obama, Barack, 285
oil, access to, 264, 275
Oksenberg, Michel, 221
Old China Hands, 53
Olney, Richard, 50
Olympic Committee, 268
one China, but not now policy, 218
one China, one Taiwan policy, 211, 256
one-China policy, 249, 258, 260, 272
Open Door notes (Hay), 44, 46–48, 59
Open Door policy, 11, 71, 73, 84, 163
opium trade, 5–6, 23
Opium War, 6, 10–11
Oriental exclusion policy (U.S.),
    33–35, 139
Outer-Mongolia, 158

pacifism, in U.S., 131
Pai Chung-hsi, 153
Pakistan, 233
Palmer's Raids, 148
Panic of 1893, 40
Paris Peace Conference, 86, 92
Parker, Peter, 11, 13, 15, 17, 21, 22
Patterson, Robert P., 166
Paulson, Henry, 277
peace movement (U.S.), 116, 117, 130;
    Chinese Revolution (1920s) and, 105;
    Mukden Incident and, 116–120,
    122–123; Sino-Japanese war (1937–1945)
    and, 130–133; Washington Conference
    and, 94
Pearl Harbor, bombing of, 138
Peiyang Army, 76
Pelosi, Nancy, 242, 243, 253
People's Liberation Army (PLA):
    modernization of, U.S. fears about,
    276–277; strength of, 290; Taiwan and,
    256, 279; Tiananmen Square massacre,
    238–239; U.S. accommodation with,
    acceptance of, 266; U.S., hostility
    toward, 179
People's Republic of China (PRC):
    Beijing Olympics, 268, 281, 284–285;
    Chen, displeasure at, 272; currency
    revaluation, 274, 275; as enemy of U.S.,
    190, 191; establishment of, 178; four
    modernizations of, 224; global
    economy, role in, 263–264; Iraq's
    Kuwait invasion, response to, 245–246;
    Johnson administration, response to,
    214; multilateral activities of, 265;
    as outside world order, 212; political
    reform, lack of, 291; Resist America,
    Aid Korea Movement, 191; rising power
    of, relative to U.S., 288–290; Soviet
    Union and, 207, 216, 237; succession
    crisis, after Mao, 220–221; Taiwan
    problem and, 203–206; U.S. arms
    sales to Taiwan and, 226–228; U.S.
    as enemy of, 199; U.S. as Soviet
    counterbalance, 224; U.S. engagement
    with, 262; U.S. recognition of, 184–186,
    223–224; U.S.-Taiwan rapprochement,

response to, 255–256; values gap with
    U.S., 257; Vietnam War and, 212–213.
    See also Mao Tse-tung; Taiwan; trade,
    U.S.-China
Perry, Matthew, 15, 27, 37
pet food, toxins in, 280
Philippines, 41, 59, 265
Phillips, William, 124
Pierce, Franklin, 18, 22
Pillsbury, Michael, 226
Pittman, Key, 126, 127, 133
PLA. See People's Liberation Army
Pol Pot, 224
Political Consultative Conference,
    168–169, 170
Port Arthur, 158, 162
Potsdam Conference, 162–163
Powell, Colin, 268, 272
PRC. See People's Republic of China
preemptive strikes, doctrine of, 275
product safety, 280

Qian Qichen, 246, 248, 268, 272
Quadrennial Defense Review (Pentagon),
    274–275
quarantine speech (Roosevelt), 131–132
Quemoy and Matsu, 202

racism, in U.S., 33, 63
Radio Free Asia, 260
railroads: China's desire for control of,
    65–66; Chinese Eastern Railroad,
    98–99, 113, 158; foreign financing of,
    71–73, 76; in Manchuria, 69, 113,
    158, 162
Reagan, Ronald, and administration of:
    China, rapprochement with, 229–230;
    China, travel to, 229; Ford, challenge
    to, 220; Gorbachev and, 236; Taiwan,
    resumption of relations with, 225–229;
    technology exports to China, restrictions
    on, 233
Realpolitik, 234
recessions, 126, 289
Red Scare, 148
Reed, William, 22
regionalism, 80

Reinsch, Paul: on China's view of U.S., 86; on loans to China, 84–85; Shantung problem and, 82–83; Sun Yat-sen, attitude toward, 99; on unrest in China, 92, 93

Renmin Ribao (newspaper), 227, 230

Report on Chinese Power (2007, Dept. of Defense), 282

Republic of China, 77, 79, 199, 203–204. *See also* Taiwan (Formosa)

Republicans (U.S.), 175, 182, 183

Resist America, Aid Korea Movement, 191

Rice, Condoleezza, 271, 272, 273, 281

Ridgway, Matthew, 190

Roberts, Edmund, 5

Roberts, Issachar, 18

Robertson, Walter, 203

Rockhill, William: Asian balance of power and, 52; breakup of China, views on, 43–44; China's anti-American boycott, response to, 64; on Japan's actions in China, 39; Open Door notes and, 48; railroad concession, actions on, 66; U.S. as China's protector, belief in, 196

Rogers, Will, 117

Romanization of Chinese names, xxi–xxii

Roosevelt, Franklin D., and administration of: air attacks, approval of, 142; Chiang, relationship with, 144–145; Chiang regime, support for, 192; China, indifference to, 145–146; China policy, summary of, 147; Chinese hostility toward, 134; disagreements, method of resolving, 127; Four Policemen and, 155–156; Hurley, support for, 160; Japan, policy toward, 123–125, 133–134; neutrality law and, 131, 133; quarantine speech, 131–132; at Yalta Conference, 146–147, 157–158

Roosevelt, Theodore, and administration of: China, indifference to, 61, 62; on China, progress of, 291–292; China's anti-American boycott, response to, 63–64; China's modernization, response to, 67–68; China's nationalism, response to, 66–67; Freer and, 91; influences on, 43; Japan's power,

response to, 60–61, 62, 87; Manchurian crisis and, 68, 69; materialism, attitude toward, 40; as president, 55; railroad concession, actions on, 66; Russia's Manchurian interests and, 56, 57–58; Taft's China policy, response to, 73; on U.S. immigration policy, 66; on Wu T'ing-fang, 67

Root, Elihu, 52, 67, 68–69, 71, 96

Root-Takahira agreement, 70

Rumsfeld, Donald, 271, 274, 277

Rusk, Dean: central beliefs, 212; Chiang, opposition to supporting, 209; on China, 194, 207–208, 213; on Laos, 210; North Korean aggression, response to, 186; on Vietnam, 211

Russia: China's strategic cooperative partnership with, 265; Knox plan, response to, 73; Manchuria, incursion in, 55–58; Sino-Japanese War, response to, 39; treaty revisions, demands for, 22. *See also* Soviet Union

Russo-Japanese War, 58, 60

Ryukyu Islands, 37

sailors, behavior of, 15

Sakhalin, 158

SALT agreement, 221–222

Samsah Bay, 55

Sanya Initiative, 282

Saudia Arabia, 233

Schurman, Jacob Gould, 95–96, 99, 100, 101

Scowcroft, Brent, 236, 240–241, 242

SEATO (Southeast Asia Treaty Organization), 203

security dilemma, 265

self-determination, 38

self-strengthening movement, 37

September 11, 2001 terrorist attacks, 269

Serbia, 261, 266

Service, John Stewart, 190

Seventh Fleet (U.S.), 186, 187, 200, 202, 217

Seward, William, 29, 32–33

Shanghai, 14, 107, 120

Shanghai Communique (1972), 219, 225, 250, 272

Shanghai Five, 265

Shantung, 81–87, 92–93, 97

Shattuck, John, 253

Shijie Jingji Dabao (weekly newspaper), 230

Shultz, George, 229

Sian Incident (1936), 129, 153

Silkworm missiles, 233

Silver Purchase Act, 126–127

Sino-Japanese Wars, 38–39, 115–137

six-party talks (on North Korea), 277

six-power consortium, 74–79, 80–81

Snow, Edgar, 129, 153, 217

sojourners, 33–34

Soong, T. V.: Chiang, warnings about, 172; on Communist threat, 115; financial reforms by, 112; government, establishment of, 109; Stalin, negotiations with, 162–163; Treaty of Friendship, response to, 163

South China Sea, 265

South Korea, 186–187, 188, 245

South Manchuria Railroad, 114, 158

Southeast Asia Collective Defense Treaty, 199

Southeast Asia Treaty Organization (SEATO), 203

Soviet Union: arms reductions by, 236 237; Chiang, support for, 129; China, aid for, 136; China, border clashes with, 216; China, exclusion from, 110–111; China, rapprochement with, 237; China, rift with, 207; China's use of U.S. as counterbalance to, 224; Chinese Communist Party and, 99–100, 157; Chinese nationalists and, 98; Czechoslovakia, invasion of, 215; Karakhan manifesto, 98–99; Korean War, interest in, 189; Manchuria and, 165, 168; Moscow Congress, 98; Sun Yat-sen and, 99–100; U.S. concerns about, 149, 192. *See also* Comintern; Russia

Spanish-American War, 41

spheres of influence, 39, 44, 46, 95, 96

spiritual pollution, 240

Stalin, Joseph, 157–158, 161–162, 162–163, 186

State Department (U.S.). *See* Department of State

Stevenson, Adlai, 208

Stilwell, Joseph, 139, 142, 144–145

Stimson, Henry: attacks on Yangtze River Patrol, response to, 150; Japan oil embargo, support for, 137; Japan's aggression, response to, 116, 117, 120–123; moral diplomacy, belief in, 119–120; Roosevelt and, 123; Sino-Soviet conflict, response to, 113; Soviet Union, concern over, 163

Straight, Willard, 69, 70, 72

strategic ambiguity (on Taiwan), 273

Strategic Economic Dialogues, 280

Stuart, John Leighton, 172, 177, 180–181

student movements, 92–93, 235–236, 237–240

Sudan, 264, 277, 281

summit meetings, 258

Sun Ch'uan-fang, 105, 107

Sun Yat-sen: Chinese reunification, plans for, 94–95; death of, 101; as provisional president, 77; as revolutionary movement leader, 76; Russians, negotiations with, 99–100; U.S. response to, 100; Washington Conference and, 95; Yüan Shih-k'ai and, 80

Sung Chiao-jen, 77, 79

Syria, 233

Szechuan, unrest in, 76

Ta Kung Pao (newspaper, Hong Kong), 229

Ta Kung Pao (newspaper, Shanghai), 122, 130

Taft, Robert, 183

Taft, William H., and administration of, 69, 70–76, 87–88, 196

Tai Li, 143

Taiping Rebellion, 17–19, 25, 36

Taiwan (Formosa): anti-secession law and, 273; Bush's rebuke to, 271; Carter administration and, 223, 224, 225; Chen's election, 266; GATT, admission to, 247, 248, 249; Japanese pressure on, 37; mainland China, contact with, 231; map of, 201; Nixon's policy on, 219; one China, but not now policy, 218; one China, one Taiwan policy, 211; one-China policy and, 249, 258, 260, 272, 275; Parker's plan for, 15; PRC's intimidation of, 256–257; as source of U.S.-China friction, 204, 272–276, 287, 288; Truman administration and, 183–184, 186–187; two-China policy and, 203–206, 207; U.S. aid to, 200, 204; U.S., importance to, 200

Taiwan Relations Act, 225, 226, 227, 249, 250, 272, 288

Taiwan Strait, 217, 256, 264, 273, 279

Takahira Kogoro, 68

Taku forts, 21, 23

T'ang Shao-yi, 67, 69, 71, 77

Tao Kuang Emperor (Hsuan-tsung), 11–12, 17

tariffs: China's autonomy on, U.S. actions on, 102, 110; China's desire for autonomy on, 95, 96, 97; Open Door notes on, 44; Treaty of Nanking and, 9

Tatnall, Josiah, 24, 30

tea, American colonists' use of, 2

Temple of Kun Yam, 1–2

Teng Hsiao-p'ing. See Deng Xiaoping

Terranova case, 4

territorial integrity. See China, sovereignty

textile trade, 229, 274

theater missile defense (TMD) program, 288

Tiananmen Square massacre, 237–242, 251–260, 282

Tibet: Bush and, 248; China's repression of, 250, 252, 254, 268, 277, 283–284; demands for cultural integrity of, 244

TMD (theater missile defense) program, 288

trade: human rights and, 244; international, China's place in, 263–264; international, U.S. place in, 40; Sino-American treaty on, 224–225; Taiwan-mainland China, 231; U.S., Euro-centrism of, 195; U.S. exports, statistics on, 197; U.S.-Japan, statistics on, 136. See also tariffs

trade, U.S.-China: under Clinton, 263; clipper ships and, 14; during eighteenth century, 2–3; global recession and, 289; growth in, 254; imbalance in, 233, 247, 249, 254, 274; McKinley and, 42; during Reagan administration, 229, 230; reduction in, early twentieth century, 61–62; statistics on, 42, 75, 118, 136; Taft administration and, 70–71; varying agreements on, 280. See also most-favored-nation (MFN) status

Trade Act of 1974, Jackson-Vanik Amendment to, 224–225

trans-Manchurian railroad, 72–73

Treasury Department (U.S.), 127, 136

treaties: commercial, early attitudes toward, 5; first Sino-American, 2; unequal, 27, 95, 102–103, 106, 107, 146; U.S. demands for revisions to, 20–22; U.S. desire for, 11–13; U.S.-Taiwan mutual defense treaty, 203–204

Treaties of Tientsin, 23–24

Treaty of Commerce and Navigation, 134

Treaty of Friendship, 163, 164

Treaty of Nanking, 7, 8–10

Treaty of Versailles, 87, 94

Treaty of Wang-hsia, 13–14

treaty ports: Manchurian, 57, 58; map of, 16, 45; resentment against, 62; Tientsin as, 25; under Treaties of Tientsin, 23; U.S. demands for, 57

treaty system: Anglo-American cooperation, 19–21; China's attitude toward U.S. under, 14, 21, 27–28; China's desire for end of, 95; China's subjugation under, 23; Great Britain and, 8–10; most-favored-nation status under, 9–11; Open Door policy and, 11; Taiping Rebellion and, 17–19, 25;

Treaties of Tientsin and, 23–24; Treaty of Nanking and, 7–10; Treaty of Wang-hsia and, 13–14; treaty revisions, demands for, 19–22; U.S. and, 10–15, 17; U.S. China policy during, 26–27; U.S. support for end of, 109. *See also* treaties

treaty tariff, 9

tribute system, 2, 3–4, 8

Tripartite Pact, 135, 137, 181

Trotsky, Leon, 107

Truman, Harry, and administration of: anti-Communist policies, 199; China, aid program for, 177; China policy, at end of WWII, 166–168; China policy, problems of, 174–176, 179–182; China White Paper, 182; China's civil war, failure to prevent, 173–174; Communist expansion, attitude toward, 187; Formosa, defense of, 186; Formosa, statement on, 184; Hurley policy, continuation of, 161; Korean War and, 186–191, 194; Republican criticisms of, 175; Soviet Union and, 192–193

Tseng, Kuo-fan, 25–26, 36

Tsungli Yamen, 31

Turner, Frederick Jackson, 40

Twenty-One Demands, 81–87

two-China policy, 203–206, 207, 256

Tyler, John, 11

Tz'u-hsi, 31, 37, 50–51, 55

Uighers, China's repression of, 269, 277, 283

unequal treaties, 27, 95, 102–103, 106, 146

united front, 129–130

United Nations: China as great power and, 146; China's seat in, 188, 191, 199, 208–209, 218; Commission on Human Rights, 260, 270; Covenant on Civil and Political Rights, 259; Korean War and, 188

United States: anti-Communist feelings in, 174–175; Asian influences on, 287; Chiang, changing attitudes toward, 216; China, early indifference to, 14–15, 17; China's boycott of, 63–64, 65, 66; China's modernization, belief in, 39; China's suppression of student dissent, response to, 235; consular service of, 14–15; declining power of, relative to China, 288–290; election campaign, 1992, 249–250; election campaign, 2000, 260–261; elections, 2006, 278; elections, 2008, 277, 284, 285; embassy in China, staff disagreement with Hurley, 159–160; Euro-centrism of, 135, 175, 197–198; external affairs, growing concern with, 195; Great Britain, cooperation with, 19–21; industrialization of, 39–40; internal focus of, 93–94; international activism of, 47; isolation of, 202; moral leadership, loss of, 289; politics in, China as issue in, 94; Seventh Fleet, 186, 187, 200, 202, 217; Southern states' secession, 29; special role in China, pretense of, 196–197. *See also* Congress; Department of State; trade, U.S.-China; treaties; treaty system; and *names of individual Presidents*

Universal Declaration of Human Rights, 233, 254

UNOCOL, 274

UNRRA, 172

U.S.-China Business Council, 275

U.S.S. Kitty Hawk, 279

U.S.S. Maine, 41

U.S.S. Nimitz, 256

Vance, Cyrus, 221, 225

Vandenberg, Arthur, 175

Vietnam, 265

Vietnam War, 211–213, 284

Vincent, John Carter, 163, 190

violence: anti-Chinese, in U.S., 33, 34; anti-Japanese, in China, 92–93; of May 30th Movement, U.S. response to, 103, 105. *See also* human rights, China's violation of

Wainright, Admiral, 124

Walker, Richard L., 226

Wallace, Henry, 144

Wan Lee, 33
Wang Ching-wei, 106–107, 109
Wang Dan, 259, 260, 283
war materiel. *See* arms sales
Ward, Angus, 185
Ward, John, 24
warlords, 104, 105
Warner, Langdon, 91
Washington Conference (1921–1922),
    94–98
Watergate crisis, 219–220
weapons, nuclear, 204, 212, 259.
    See also arms sales
Webster, Daniel, 11–12
Wedemeyer, Albert, 160, 165, 176
Wei Jingsheng, 234, 253, 259, 283
Welles, Sumner, 137
Wen Jiabao, 271
Wen-tsung, 17, 24
West: rise in power, 6; Wen-tsung's
    attitudes toward, 17. *See also* Great
    Britain; United States
westernization process (China), 31
Whampoa Military Academy, 100
Wherry, Kenneth, 185, 197
White Committee (Committee to Defend
    America by Aiding the Allies), 135
White Terror, 109
Williams, E. T., 82–83
Wilson, Huntington, 69, 70, 79
Wilson, Woodrow, and administration of:
    China policy of, 77–81, 88, 196; defeat
    of, 94; investments in China, policy
    on, 84; at Paris Peace Conference, 92;

Shantung problem, response to,
    83, 86–87; Sun Yat-sen, attitude
    toward, 99
Wolfowitz, Paul, 270
women (Chinese), education of, 90
Women's International League for Peace
    and Freedom, 117, 130
Woodcock, Leonard, 222, 223, 226
World Disarmament Conference, 116
World Health Assembly, 272
World Trade Organization (WTO),
    268, 269
World War I, 81, 84–85, 86–87
World War II, 138, 140–141, 164–165
WTO (World Trade Organization),
    268, 269
Wu P'ei-fu, 105, 107
Wu T'ing-fang, 47, 57, 63, 66–67, 77
Wuchang, military revolt in, 76

xenophobia (Chinese), 30

Yalta Conference, 146–147, 157–159,
    192
Yangtze River Patrol, 150
Yeh Ming-ch'en, 20, 21, 22
young-China movement, 92
Yüan Shih-k'ai, 57, 71, 76–77, 79, 80
Yugoslavia, 261

Zhao Ziyang, 227, 234, 238, 240
Zhou Enlai. *See* Chou En-lai
Zhu Rongji, 261
Zoellick, Robert, 274, 275